𝔖𝔱𝔞𝔫𝔡𝔞𝔯𝔡 𝔏𝔦𝔟𝔯𝔞𝔯𝔶 𝔈𝔡𝔦𝔱𝔦𝔬𝔫

AMERICAN STATESMEN

IN FORTY VOLUMES
VOLUME XXXII

THE RE–UNITED NATION — GROWTH
AND PROSPERITY
ULYSSES S. GRANT

American Statesmen

STANDARD LIBRARY EDITION

Birthplace of Ulysses S. Grant

HOUGHTON MIFFLIN COMPANY

The Riverside Press
CAMBRIDGE · MASSACHUSETTS
PRINTED IN THE U. S. A.

EDITOR'S INTRODUCTION

THE sixth and last group of biographies in this series has to do with "The Reunited Nation: Growth and Prosperity." The statesmen selected as the representative men of this period are Ulysses S. Grant, John Sherman, James G. Blaine, Thomas B. Reed, John Hay, and William McKinley.

We are prone to depreciate the men of the present, to underestimate the importance of recent events, and to look to the distant past for our heroes and our transcendent issues. This is natural but unfortunate. The world is infinitely larger now than at the time of Columbus, and the forces with which a statesman of our day has to deal are far more powerful and complex than those of Washington's day. The men who precipitated the American Revolution were the leaders of perhaps a million people. They were shrewd and farseeing, and they transformed their minority of radicals into a majority of moderates, and they laid the foundations of a new nation in the world.

But the greater leaders of to-day, while it is not theirs to build a new nation, speak for one hundred millions of people, and the social forces with which they contend, or which they represent, are measured by the billion, if we may take money as a standard. We are prone to think of the remarkable development of the country during the decade when Henry Clay was possibly the greatest American leader as something unprecedented. But since the close of the Civil War a tenfold greater development has taken place. When Lincoln laid down his life as a martyr to the cause of nationalism, the American population numbered somewhat more than 35,000,-000. It now approaches 100,000,000. In 1865 the wealth of the country, which amounted to some twenty billions, was mortgaged and burdened with interest charges which only the optimist would view with any degree of confidence. The nation owed about three billions, or nearly one sixth of its taxable wealth. The Northern States, counties, and cities were similarly in debt; in the South there was sheer exhaustion, little but land and hungry people. In 1910 the wealth of the United States was more than $100,000,000,000; and while the States and cities still "carry" their burden of debt, the Federal Government scarcely owes anything when one counts its realizable assets. The annual output of the country is now greater than the total wealth of 1865.

It has been a marvelous half-century, and its leaders, its statesmen, are not less worthy of study than were those of the half-century which preceded the war. The issues have been more complex, the stakes, aside from the question of national existence, infinitely greater than those for which Jackson and John Quincy Adams contended.

The old issue of prime importance was whether we were a nation, and the three sections, East, South, and West, each strove to place the halo of nationalism on its brow, and to control the Federal law-making. The war broke the intensity of this sectional rivalry, yet the arms of Lee were not grounded at Appomattox before the East, with its enormous industrial interests at stake, sought to compel the West to endorse a policy of protection against all foreign competition which was regarded by Western statesmen as hardly less wicked than slavery itself. On the other hand, the West, always bearing the burden of mortgaged farms and homes, undertook to "scale" the national debt in a way that would have deprived the Eastern capitalist, great and small, of all the personal profits of the war.

The social conscience is only in our day recovering from the debaucheries which followed the Civil War. And the conflict of interests, true and imaginary, the contending forces in the national life, lawful or unlawful, made the task of statesmen difficult indeed. The times were chaotic beyond comparison.

Into this sea of troubles President Grant was thrust.
A friend of the South, he yet did not know how to
stay the hand of rapacity and bitter race hatred; an
enemy of corruption, he could not keep the skirts
of his own household clean. General Grant, the hero
of Appomattox, will ever be a figure of commanding interest; President Grant was in a more difficult
situation, and his life at this period compels attention if not approval. Mr. Coolidge's biography sets
before us clearly the issues and complexities of the
presidential term of 1869–77. Perhaps its chief interest and value lie in its illuminating chapters on a
troubled epoch.

What has been said in the foregoing paragraphs
is of no value unless it shows how difficult must have
been the rôle of the statesmen who tried to unravel
the tangled skein of national policies, social and economic, during the years from 1868 to 1896. And
among these leaders none attracts more sympathetic
attention than James G. Blaine, the "perpetual"
New England candidate for the presidency. As a
protectionist, a champion of the cause of sound
money, an advocate also of a closer union of all
American states, Blaine rises to the level of statesman on more than one occcasion. But the tragedy
of his career consists in his repeated failures. The
most popular man of his time, he was defeated by

his party in nominating conventions at the times when he could have been elected and placed at the head of the ticket when defeat at the polls was his portion. He reminds the reader of Henry Clay, whose career was filled with similar disappointments.

Of John Sherman the story is different. A Western man, interested in the cheap money programme of the farmers, he nevertheless championed the cause of those who would pay in gold the last penny of the war debt. In this he probably lost many followers in his own section, and perhaps the presidency, but he paved the way for national solvency in 1878 and made himself the undisputed champion of a sound national finance. As such we think of him to-day. He yielded later to the pressure of the silver interests and became the author of the so-called Silver Purchase Law. His name was also given to the marvelous legislation of 1893 for the suppression of monopoly, the famous Sherman Anti-Trust Act. Still it is the financier who found a way out of the sectional impasse of 1868 to 1878 whom the biographer and historian of this series portrays.

Grant, Blaine, and Sherman were contemporaries; they dealt with problems, legacies, I was about to say, of the Civil War epoch. All came from the Ohio River country, and all championed in final analysis the interests of the East, of industry and large business men. It was the masterful manufacturer, banker, or railway magnate to whom they listened, not the farmer whose wheat was sold every year in a falling market, nor the Southerner whose cotton was declining in value to the point where it was hardly worth cultivating. Such masterful men were the products of the war and the Eastern interests which saved the Union, and none could gainsay them.

"Speaker Reed," as one says till this day, was not quite of this group. The interest in his biography is twofold: the interest in a picturesque personality not unlike that of John Randolph, a very able and honest man, and the interest in one who mastered and domineered the national House of Representatives as no other leader had done since Henry Clay made that body a party weapon of great efficiency and a club to compel weak presidents to do his will.

What of the biographies of McKinley and Hay, the men who guided the American nation after 1896? They too were citizens of Ohio and champions of the East, but of an enlarged East with boundaries which included the business centers of the West, Chicago, St. Louis, Kansas City, Omaha, and Minneapolis. It was a great constituency on which rested the power that nerved President McKinley's arm and enabled John Hay to make the most masterful strokes of American diplomacy since the days of

John Quincy Adams or perhaps one should say James K. Polk.

In Thayer's *Hay* we see the quiet man of letters turned statesman, diplomat, at the suggestion of McKinley. It was a happy chance which set him at the head of the State Department when American "business," when a compact and fairly well-grown United States made up its mind to speak in international councils. Without an army, and with a navy inferior to those of most other great countries, the United States received attention unprecedented. At Hay's suggestion England yielded her fifty-year-old rights in Panama and the German Kaiser reversed his course in Venezuela. It was American counsel that saved China at the end of the Boxer movement and which delayed Japanese domination of the trade of the East after the Treaty of Portsmouth.

McKinley was the figure about which the growing and consolidating social forces of Grant's time were later ranged. A study of McKinley is therefore a study of America, — of the America which Lincoln and the North saved and made rich by the Civil War. The future historian of the later years of the nineteenth century must pronounce them marvelous, and the biography of McKinley points the way to the larger field of study, the social structure of American life in our time, with its multitudinous interests, its Crœsus-like riches, and its almost child-like fear of change.

"From Grant to McKinley" suggests many issues, many interesting characters which appear in minor rôles in these volumes, many defeats and some trag-edies hardly less important than earlier stories of success and victory so dear to the American mind. Unlike the volumes of the former series, the biog-raphies in the final group portray the life of a fairly homogeneous section of the United States, the sec-tion in which all the leaders treated were born, and which, in a sense, was during those years the country itself. These biographies also bring out strikingly the history of the Greenback Party, the Granger Movement, the struggle of the West and South against the trusts, and finally the great campaign of 1896. These issues will surely loom larger as time passes, and the men who dealt with them must be regarded as among the great men of the country. Other leaders and other problems are treated in this series and in the history of recent times only as they are associated with the dominant group of lead-ers or with these overshadowing interests.

WILLIAM E. DODD.

AN ACKNOWLEDGMENT

In writing this book it has of course been necessary to consult many others, reference to which could not be made in the run of narrative without impeding its flow.

On the military side of Grant's career: The *Personal Memoirs; Battles and Leaders of the Civil War;* Nicolay and Hay's *Lincoln;* Richardson's *Personal History of U. S. Grant;* Badeau's *Military History;* the books of Generals Sherman, Sheridan, Schofield, McClellan, and James H. Wilson; Dana's *Recollections of the Civil War;* Horace Porter's *Campaigning with Grant;* John Fiske's *The Mississippi Valley in the Civil War; Recollections of A. H. Stephens;* Grant's letters to his family, to Washburne, and to Badeau; the letters of the Sherman brothers — Tecumseh and John; Gamaliel Bradford's delightful series of Union and Confederate Portraits; Owen Wister's brilliantly brief and tantalizing sketch.

On the civil side a multitude of writers have contributed material or incident. No one can hope to deal with any phase of the period of the Civil War and Reconstruction without resorting frequently to

Rhodes's *History of the United States*, a monument of research and an exhaustless well of information. That one may be compelled at times to differ with his conclusions does not lessen the obligation due.

Among other books which have proved of service are: Blaine's *Twenty Years in Congress; The Autobiography* of George F. Hoar; the *Reminiscences* of John Sherman and of Carl Schurz; *The Diary of Gideon Welles;* Hugh McCulloch's *Men and Measures of Half a Century;* Merriam's *Life and Times of Samuel Bowles;* the lives of Stanton, Conkling, Morton, Chandler, and Trumbull; Badeau's *Grant in Peace;* the lives of Sumner, Chase, Stevens, Charles Francis Adams, Seward, Sherman, and Hay in the American Statesmen Series; Henry Adams's *Historical Essays;* John Bigelow's *Retrospections of an Active Life;* McPherson's *History of Reconstruction;* DeWitt's *Impeachment and Trial of Andrew Johnson;* John Russell Young's *Around the World with General Grant;* Haworth's *Disputed Election of 1876;* Joseph Bucklin Bishop's *Presidential Nominations and Elections;* Stanwood's *History of the Presidency;* James L. Post's little volume of *Reminiscences of Personal Friends;* the *Letters of Charles Eliot Norton;* the correspondence of John Lothrop Motley; Oliver Wendell Holmes's sketch of Motley's life; Senator Lodge's *Early Memories;* Charles Francis Adams's *The Treaty*

CONTENTS

xix

ILLUSTRATIONS

ULYSSES S. GRANT

CHAPTER I
THE MAN

No man who ever gained enduring fame was more the sport of chance than Grant. No character in history has achieved supreme success in war or the supreme reward of politics who owed less to his own ambition or design. A still and simple citizen, accustomed mostly to the ways of unkempt Western towns, ungifted with imagination, indifferent to the general stir of things, and barely equal to the task of furnishing his family such modest comforts as the neighbors had, he was untouched even by evanescent liking for a military life up to the moment when he flashed across the vision of the world — the greatest captain of his time. And when with war in retrospect he would have been content to live in quiet contemplation of his strange career, unskilled in politics, innocent of the arts of government, he was compelled by force of circumstance for eight eventful years to occupy the highest civil place his countrymen could give. He was the child of splendid opportunities which came to him unsought, for which he never seemed to care, and which he met with calm assurance of his own capacity.

He rode upon the turmoil which had tossed him to its top serenely confident in his ability to guide gigantic forces thrust into his hands. He saw his country reunited, well advanced upon a clearly marked and broadening road; then willingly went back to private life, rich only in the opulence of fame, unspoiled, unfretted by regrets, and undisturbed by dreams. When he was made Lieutenant-General and wrote to Sherman, acknowledging that soldier's aid in his advancement, Sherman with equal magnanimity replied: "I believe you are as brave, patriotic, and just as the great prototype Washington, as unselfish, kind-hearted, and honest as a man should be; but the chief characteristic is the simple faith in success you have always manifested which I can liken to nothing else than the faith a Christian has in a Saviour." So he seemed to one who saw him near at hand in war; thus looking back we all can now perceive his childlike trust in time of peace.

That this shy, silent man, after a humdrum life till middle age, should have beheld the span of his remaining years studded with triumphs and with tragedies presents a riddle to the student of his time. His mind was not attuned to notions of retreat, of indirection, or diplomacy. He thought straightforward and was free from artifice — rare qualities which served him well in war and in most great executive emergencies, but were not fitted to the sinuous ways of peace, the strategy of politics, the mysteries of finance, the subtle schemes of courtiers and dishonest satellites; and so it came about that both as President and as private citizen the record of his truly great accomplishments is soiled with pages which we would tear out if we could. Yet we should hate to lose the last heroic chapter, even though its sordid prelude is indispensable to the complete disclosure of unstained nobility of soul.

I. EARLY INFLUENCES

Straggling along the northern bank of the Ohio, a hundred years ago, there was a broken line of settlements which served as landings for the lazy river craft. One of them, twenty-five miles southeast of Cincinnati, perched on a river bend, was called Point Pleasant. Most of its dozen families had drifted in there from the South. A few other settlers were scattered within a radius of twenty miles. Here in a two-room cottage, near the river front, Grant was born on April 27, 1822.

His father was Jesse Root Grant, a recent comer from the northeast corner of the State, who was running a small tannery for another settler. His mother, Hannah Simpson Grant, was the daughter of a thrifty farmer lately arrived in the county from Pennsylvania, a few miles out of Philadelphia. His name was chosen by lot at a family gathering on the Simpson farm six weeks after he was born. It is said a maiden aunt drew from a hat a slip bearing the name "Ulysses," the choice of Grandmother Simpson who had been reading Fénelon's "Telemachus" and liked the character of whom it was written: "His wisdom is, as it were, a seal upon his lips, which is never broken but for an important purpose." "Hiram" was added to please some one else, and he was "Hiram Ulysses" till he went to West Point, when the Congressman who sent him there rechristened him "Ulysses Simpson Grant" through a mistake in making out the papers. That is his name in history. The neighbors called him "Useless" as a boy; his nickname at West Point was "Uncle Sam" or "Sam." His soldiers spoke of him as "Unconditional Surrender."

When Ulysses was a little over a year old, his father, having laid aside eleven hundred dollars, determined to set up in business for himself, and moved to Georgetown in the neighboring county, a backwoods settlement, twenty miles east and ten miles inland from the river. Though smaller even than Point Pleasant, it had advantages from a young tanner's viewpoint: it was a county seat, likely to grow; it was in the midst of an oak forest accessible to bark. Its dozen houses — some of frame, a few of brick — were cheerless, primitive, and crude — a downstairs room in which the family lived and ate, a garret where they slept, a lean-to kitchen in the rear. Jesse Grant built him one of brick, to which he added now and then as family and fortune grew, till it was bigger and somewhat better than the rest, though it would be black-listed by the health authorities in any self-respecting town to-day. Here the boy lived until he went to school.

Life had few comforts and no graces for the Grants. The furniture was rough and scanty, the walls were bare, the reading limited to a few sermons, hymn-books, and Weems's "Washington," unless they borrowed from the neighbors; the mother did her own housework like the other women in the village, cooking at an open fireplace with pots and crane; the children did the chores. The only thing resembling music was the wail of hymns in the tiny Methodist meeting-house, or the squeak of a fiddle in the primitive tavern where travelers dropped in off and on and the men of the village took their toddy, almost their only indoor sport. Throughout his life Ulysses Grant could never tell one note from another. "Old

Hundred" and the "Fisher's Hornpipe" were all the same to him.

And yet this ragged little place had its distinctions aside from having been the boyhood home of Grant. When the Civil War broke out it had a population of a thousand, largely of Southern tendencies. In some of the churches Grant himself has said that membership depended more upon hostility to the war and liberation of the slaves than upon belief in the authenticity of the Bible. There was no time during the Civil War when the majority would not have voted for Jefferson Davis for President instead of Lincoln, if they had had the chance. "Yet this far-off Western village," he writes, "with a population, including old and young, male and female, of about one thousand, — about enough for the organization of a single regiment, if all had been men capable of bearing arms, — furnished the Union army four general officers and one colonel, West Point graduates, and nine generals and field officers of volunteers."

Jesse Grant stood well, but had his idiosyncrasies and was not over-popular. He was thrifty, industrious, and independent, held emphatic opinions on politics and other questions, not altogether palatable to his neighbors, and was not tactful in the time and manner of expounding them. A Northern radical among Southern sympathizers he did not bother to adjust himself to his surroundings. He was a good debater, according to his son; read every book that he could borrow and remembered everything he read — almost his only education. He was muscular, six feet in height, and morally courageous, but credulous, ingenuous, garrulous, and disputatious. He was a rhymester, and some of his verses printed in the local weekly have been preserved, but he could write and speak tersely and forcefully. The tavern loafers with whom he did not fraternize laughed at his carriage and his gold-bowed spectacles, the first in the settlement, and were amused because of his transparent pride in young Ulysses, whom they called dull because he was not "smart" and "talky" like the other village boys.

Jesse had pride of ancestry and was at pains to trace his family to its New England source. He found that Matthew Grant in 1630 came from England to Dorchester in Massachusetts, and shortly moved to Windsor in Connecticut, where his descendants lived till his own father's day; that his grandfather had a commission in the English army and was killed in the French-and-Indian War. His father, Captain Noah Grant, was at the battle of Bunker Hill and served in the Continental Army through the Revolutionary War; after which he migrated first to Westmoreland County, Pennsylvania, and then to Deerfield, Ohio. Jesse had a half-brother, Peter, who went to Maysville, Kentucky, and grew rich. Noah, who was not forehanded, subsequently went to live with Peter, placing some of his other children in homes near Deerfield. Jesse worked for his "keep" with Judge Tod, the father of Governor Tod, and by a curious chance after learning his trade he worked for the father of John Brown of Ossawatomie, and lived in the house where John Brown himself was also living as a boy. Soon after he set up in business as a tanner chills and fever drove him to Point Pleasant, not far from Maysville, a seeming misfortune which he turned to good account; for with all his oddities he was resourceful in emergencies — a trait which he transmitted to his son.

From his mother Ulysses inherited the gift of reticence and self-restraint. Some said he got his sense from her. He never saw her shed a tear; she seldom laughed; she never tried to guide him save by her own sweet, silent influence. Deeply religious herself, she did not undertake to make him so against his will.

Even in his hour of fame she rarely spoke about her son or talked of his achievements except to say that she was thankful he had done so well. When the boy left home for his first long absence at West Point, she made him ready and said good-bye without a quiver of the lip. Thenceforth she saw him only at rare intervals. When he was President she never came to Washington, which swarmed with less considerate relatives, but stayed at home working as usual about the house. It is written that she prayed for him constantly up to the day she died. "I have no recollection of ever having been punished at home either by scolding or by the rod," writes Grant; he never heard a harsh word from either father or mother, or knew either to do an unjust act; from West Point and from Mexico he wrote them letters full of gossip and affection. He was a natural, human sort of boy.

II. BOYHOOD

A knack with horses was Grant's most noticeable boyish asset — a trick of use to him in later years. He had a way of sticking to a job till it was done, though he might have to figure out odd means by which to do it — a trait which stood him in good stead through life. The numerous anecdotes about his boyhood, current after he had won his fame, mostly illustrate one of these qualities, or both. Every one in the village who was at all well off worked with his hands; the better off, the harder. "It was only the very poor," Grant says, "who were exempt." He was a mere child when he began. His father had a farm as well as a tannery, with fifty acres of woods, a mile from the village, and before he was eight years old

Ulysses was hauling all the wood used in the house and the shops. He could not load it on the wagon, or unload it, but he could drive.

At eleven he was strong enough to hold a plough. "From this age till I was seventeen," he says, "I did all the work done with horses, such as breaking up the land, furrowing, ploughing corn and potatoes, bringing in the crops when harvested, hauling all the wood, besides tending two or three horses, a cow or two, and sawing wood for the stoves." For recreation there were fishing and swimming in the summer, — he was an expert swimmer and diver, — skating and sleighing in the winter. Nothing extraordinary about all this. The other boys in the village were fond of hunting. Grant never hunted in his life, or used firearms for amusement. The thought of killing was abhorrent to him. He loved horses — earned money by driving out into the country passengers arriving in Georgetown by stage; at nine had a horse of his own. At ten he used to drive a span of horses alone to Cincinnati, forty miles, and bring home a load of passengers. He could do stunts at riding, could teach horses to pace, could break them to harness. "If I can mount a horse I can ride him," he used to say. He could handle horses easily because he loved them. All his life he kept away from races. He thought them cruel.

When he was eleven his father, handy at making money in all sorts of ways, took a contract for building the county jail, a job which called for hauling a great many logs; he bought a horse called Dave for Ulysses, and set him to hauling. The woods were two miles from the site of the jail, the logs a foot square and fourteen feet long. Eleven men did the hewing and loaded the logs; the boy drove. One cloudy day the hewers were not in the woods, and Ulysses was left alone, but by his own ingenuity the boy did the job of several strong men. A fallen maple lay slanting with its top caught in another tree. Using this as an inclined plane the boy hitched Dave to the logs, hauled them up on the trunk till they nearly balanced, and then backing the wagon up to it hitched Dave to them again and snaked them forward upon the axles one at a time.

He was the best traveled boy in the village. At Flat Rock, Kentucky, on one of his trips he traded one of his horses for a saddle horse which caught his fancy. Here is his own illuminating story: "I was seventy miles from home with a carriage to take back and Mr. Payne said he did not know that his horse had ever had a collar on. I asked to have him hitched to a farm wagon, and we would soon see whether he would work. It was soon evident that the horse had never worn harness before; but he showed no viciousness and I expressed a confidence that I could manage him. A trade was at once struck, I receiving ten dollars difference." The next day with a Georgetown neighbor whose brother had swapped the horse he started home. The horses were frightened and ran away twice. "The road we were on struck the turnpike within half a mile of the point where the second runaway commenced, and there was an embankment twenty or more feet deep on the opposite side of the pike. I got the horses stopped on the very brink of the precipice. My new horse was terribly frightened and trembled like an aspen; but he was not half so badly frightened as my companion, Mr. Payne, who deserted me after this last experience and took passage on a freight wagon for Maysville. Every time I attempted to start my new horse would commence to kick. I was in quite a dilemma for a time. Once in Maysville, I could borrow a horse from an uncle who lived there; but I was more than a day's travel from that point. Finally I took out my bandanna . . . and with this blindfolded my horse. In this way I reached Maysville safely the next day."

He earned his first money by taking a load of rags to Cincinnati, and selling it for fifteen dollars. He was less than twelve years old and the business venture was his own device. "My best training," he con-

fided to Thomas Kilby Smith, at Vicksburg, "was
before I went to West Point."

There is another story made much of by biogra-
phers given to drawing lessons, as showing the boy's
guilelessness. It is about a colt which he was sent to
buy. His father had offered twenty dollars, but the
owner, Ralston, wanted twenty-five. "My father
. . . said twenty dollars was all the horse was worth,
and told me to offer that price. If it was not accepted,
I was to offer twenty-two and a half, and if that would
not bring him to give the twenty-five. I at once
mounted a horse and went for the colt. When I got
to Mr. Ralston's house I said to him: 'Papa says I
may offer you twenty dollars for the colt, but if you
won't take that I am to offer twenty-two and a half,
and if you won't take that to give you twenty-five!'
It would not take a Connecticut man to guess the
price finally agreed upon."

The story got out among the other boys, and it was
a long time before he heard the last of it; but Grant
was only eight years old. If we must have an incident disclosing Grant's guileless trust in others'
honesty, we can find one more pertinent of a later
date. There is a letter bearing date of October 24,
1859, when, writing to his younger brother Simpson
from St. Louis, he says: —

"I have been postponing writing to you hoping to

make a return for your horse — but as yet I have received nothing for him. About two weeks ago a man spoke to me for him and said that he would try him the next day, and if he suited give me $100 for him. I have not seen the man since; but one week ago last Saturday he went to the stable and got the horse, saddle, and bridle, since which I have seen neither man nor horse. From this I presume he must like him. The man I understand lives in Florisant, about twelve miles from the city. . . .

"P.S. The man that has your horse is the owner of a row of six three-story brick houses in this city and the probabilities are that he intends to give me an order on his agent for the money on the first of the month when the rents are paid. At all events, I imagine the horse is perfectly safe."

CHAPTER II

THE TRAINING OF A SOLDIER

I. WEST POINT

GRANT'S early schooling, the best the village gave, and then two terms in private schools, at Maysville and at Ripley, was limited to the "three R's." He never saw an algebra till after his appointment to West Point, and as he studied no more than he could help, his scholarship left much to be desired. The love of learning which lured him from the tannery was probably as much his father's passion as his own. The knowledge which he found of greatest use in after years he garnered in the University of Common Sense. The ingenuity he showed in solving boyish problems was classified as genius when later put to harder tests.

He says that as a boy he did not like to work, "but I did as much of it while young as grown men can be hired to do in these days and attended school at the same time"; yet, when he was not stirred to swift decision in emergencies, he was of sluggish habit all his days. "As I grow older I become more indolent, my besetting sin through life," he wrote, in 1873, when he was President, to Adam Badeau. But in necessity he was a thunderbolt. This mingling of torpidity and force throws light upon the seeming inconsistencies of his career. Other men with contradictory traits have been conspicuous in history, but the career of none of them exhibits greater contrasts.

Most of the villagers thought him backward when they thought of him at all, but they were rather fond of him in spite of his slow ways. He was pure-minded and clean of speech. He never swore; "a good steady boy with no bad habits"; "awkward and countrified"; "quiet and slow"; "a great hand to ask questions"; "said little himself, but he could answer questions if you gave him time"; "always carried a stick; whittled most of the time, but never made anything"; "stumpy, freckle-faced, big-headed"; "steadfast, manly"; "quiet gray-blue eyes, strong straight nose, straight brown hair and bulky build"; "not pugnacious"; "a lover of the woods"; "modest, unassuming, determined, self-reliant, decisive." These are some of the phrases those who knew him as a boy have given us. And then this suggestive line from one of them: "A favorite with the smaller boys of the village who had learned to look up to him as a sort of protector."

He loathed the tannery, shrank from the thought of taking up his father's trade, and on a fateful day, when home from Ripley for the holidays, he was condemned to help out in the beam room with its reeking hides, he told his father as he trudged along toward the repulsive task that he would work at it if necessary till he was twenty-one, but not a minute longer — that he had rather be a farmer or a down-the-river trader or get an education. Then Jesse Grant bethought him of West Point.

Five boys had already gone there from the county to get a start in life at government expense. The last of them, his nearest neighbor's son, had just been dropped for failure in examination, but was too proud to come back to the village, so that no one knew of his discomfiture except the Grants. Why not Ulysses for the vacancy? The Congressman, Thomas L. Hamer, belonged in Georgetown, and had once been Jesse's closest friend, but they had quarreled months before and were not then on speaking terms. He was a Democrat and Jesse was a Whig. So Jesse wrote to Thomas Morris, Senator from Ohio, but Morris turned the letter over to the Congressman, who, welcoming the chance to make up with his former friend, agreed to the appointment out of hand. This was the winter of 1838–39. When Jesse read the letter from Morris telling him that his request had been handed on to Hamer, writes Grant in his "Memoirs," "he said to me, 'Ulysses, I believe you are going to receive the appointment.' 'What appointment?' I inquired. 'To West Point; I have applied for it.' 'But I won't go,' I said. He said he thought I would, *and I thought so too if he did.* I really had no objection to going to West Point, except that I had a very exalted idea of the requirements necessary to get through. I did not believe I possessed them and could not bear the idea of failing."

Thus with reluctance Grant entered on the training for his great career. He says himself that he was led to fall in with his father's plan chiefly by his desire to travel. "I had been east to Wheeling, Virginia, and north to the Western Reserve in Ohio, west to Louisville and south to Bourbon County, Kentucky, besides having driven or ridden pretty much over the whole country within fifty miles of home. Going to West Point would give me the opportunity of visiting the two great cities of the continent, Philadelphia and New York. This was enough. When these places were visited I would have been glad to have had a steamboat or railroad collision or any other accident happen, by which I might have received a temporary injury sufficient to make me ineligible for a time to enter the Academy. Nothing of the kind occurred and I had to face the music. . . . A military life had no charms for me, and I had not the faintest idea of staying in the army even if I should be graduated, which I did not expect."

There was no thrill for him in the call of bugles or
the roll of drums. A bill had been introduced in Congress abolishing the Academy. He watched its progress impatiently, hoping it would pass, and when in
time he became reconciled to the curriculum his idea
was to get through the course, secure a detail for a few
years as assistant professor of mathematics at the
Academy, and afterward obtain a permanent position as professor in some respectable college, — "but
circumstances always did shape my course different
from my plans." At the same time there are occa-
sional flashes of another mood, as when he writes
his cousin: "I do love the place. It seems as though I
could live here always if my friends would only come
too." From his undemonstrative mother the boy had
drawn a vein of sentiment.

He took little interest in his studies; rarely went
over a lesson a second time during his cadetship; for
lack of something better got books from the library;
read Bulwer, Cooper, Marryat, Scott, Irving, and
Lever. Mathematics came "almost by intuition,"
he used to say, but other branches, especially French,
were hard and his standing was low. "In fact if the
class had been turned the other end foremost, I
should have been near head. I never succeeded in
getting squarely at either end of my class in any
one study during the four years. I came near it in

French, artillery, infantry and cavalry tactics, and conduct." He was good at draughtsmanship and did a few crude paintings which still survive.

A ten weeks' furlough at the end of two years he enjoyed beyond any other period of his life. "My father had sold out his business in Georgetown — where my youth had been spent, and to which my day-dreams carried me back as my future home if I should ever be able to retire on a competency. He had moved to Bethel, only twelve miles away, in the adjoining county of Clermont, and had bought a young horse that had never been in harness for my special use under the saddle during my furlough. Most of my time was spent among my old school-mates — these ten weeks were shorter than one week at West Point." A wholesome picture.

II. CADET GRANT

Among the highly pedigreed young Southerners trained in the graces of society and looking on a soldier's calling as fit for scions of a landed aristocracy, the slouchy little Grant must have seemed out of picture — hopelessly middle-class and common. But unobtrusively — perhaps without quite knowing it himself — he was absorbing knowledge of the traits of many whom in after years he met in active service either as friends or foes.

In the Academy while he was a cadet were several who won distinction on one side or the other in the Civil War: among them Sherman, Thomas, Longstreet, Hardee, McClellan, Ewell, Buell, Rosecrans, and Buckner. In his own class were Franklin, Quinby, Gardner, Hamilton, and Rufus Ingalls, who was his room-mate for a time; that splendid soldier, Charles F. Smith, was commandant of cadets. From some of these we get a few swift pencilings. Sherman, three years his senior, tells of seeing "'U. S. Grant' on the bulletin board where the names of all newcomers were posted. One said, 'United States Grant'; another, 'Uncle Sam Grant'; a third shouted, 'Sam Grant.' The name stuck to him and by it he was henceforth known by the cadets at the Academy."

"A lad without guile," says Viele; "I never heard him utter a profane or vulgar word." "A perfect sense of honor," says Longstreet. "The most scrupulous regard for truth," says Hardee. "Had a way of solving problems out of rule by the application of good hard sense," says Ingalls. Others say, "A clear thinker and a steady worker"; "Little enthusiasm in anything"; "Not a prominent man in the corps, but respected by all"; "A very much liked sort of youth"; "No bad habits whatever"; "No facility in conversation with the ladies, a total absence of elegance"; "Could n't dance, never attended parties or entered

a private house"; "He never held his word light, he
never said an untruthful word even in jest."

A single splash of color to relieve the gray monotony.
He was the most daring horseman in the Academy.
"Grant's jump on York" is still conspicuous in the
annals of West Point, when, in the presence of Winfield Scott and the official board of visitors, his horse
leaped a bar held high above the head of a soldier who
rested it against the wall. There is a tinge of the
dramatic in the story of another exploit told by
General James B. Fry, at the time a candidate
for admission to the Academy: "When the regular
service was completed, the class, still mounted, was
formed in a line through the center of the hall. The
riding-master placed the leaping-bar higher than a
man's head and called out, 'Cadet Grant!' A clean-
faced, slender, blue-eyed young fellow, weighing one
hundred and twenty pounds, dashed from the ranks
on a powerfully built chestnut sorrel horse and gal-
loped down the opposite side of the hall. As he
turned at the farther end and came into the stretch
across which the bar was placed, the horse increased
his pace, and measuring his strides for the great leap
before him, bounded into the air and cleared the bar,
carrying his rider as if man and beast had been
welded together. The spectators were speechless.
'Very well done, sir!' growled old Hirshberger, the

riding-master, and the class was dismissed and disappeared; but Cadet Grant remained a living image in my memory."

And there is the tale of his beating at the hands of a larger cadet, his going into training, and his final victory in a fourth encounter after a second and third defeat.

As for predictions of his future greatness, we need not give them special weight. Such casual prophecies are remembered only after one has made them good. But it may well be true that Hardee said, while both were still in the Academy, that "if a great emergency arises in this country during our lifetime Sam Grant will be the man to meet it"; that one of his teachers said, "the smartest man in the class is little Grant!" and that in the first days of the Civil War, Ewell, then a Southern officer, remarked: "There is one West Pointer whom I hope the Northern people will not find out. I mean Sam Grant. . . . I should fear him more than any of their officers I have yet heard of. He is not a man of genius, but he is clear-headed, quick and daring."

Grant has told how he was dazzled by Winfield Scott, who in his first year's encampment came to review the cadets. "With his commanding figure, his quite colossal size and showy uniform, I thought him the finest specimen of manhood my eyes had ever beheld. I believe I did have a presentiment for a moment that some day I should occupy his place on review — although I had no intention then of remaining in the army. My experience in the horse trade ten years before and the ridicule it caused me were too fresh in mind to communicate this presentiment even to my most intimate chum." He regarded General Scott and Captain C. F. Smith as "the two men most to be envied in the nation."

Grant graduated from West Point in 1843, number 21 in a roll of 89. He would have gone into the Dragoons, as the Cavalry was called then, but there was no room for him in the single regiment, and he was given his second choice, the Fourth Infantry. Before entering service he was furloughed at Bethel for three months, and while there the officers of the militia asked him to drill the troops at general muster. He was sickly at the time, a victim of the malady known as "Tyler's Grip." One who saw his exhibition says that "he looked very young, very slender, and very pale"; that his voice "was clear and calm, cutting across the parade ground with great precision — rather high in pitch but trained."

Grant has told of two trifling incidents during this furlough which gave him a distaste for military uniforms from which he never recovered. Setting out bravely for Cincinnati in his regimentals he was

followed by a boy who called out, "Soldier, will you
work? No, sirree! I'll sell my shirt first"; and back
in Bethel again he was mortified to find the drunken
stable-man at the tavern parading the streets and
doing the stable chores in bare feet with a pair of sky-
blue nankeen pantaloons, "just the color of my uniform trousers, with a strip of white cotton sheeting
sewed down the outside seams in imitation of mine."

III. MEXICO

Grant wore his uniform eleven years. When he
left West Point the regular army had 7500 men —
not enough troops to go around among the officers
who were graduated at the Academy. He was assigned
to his regiment as a "supernumerary" with the rank
and pay of a second lieutenant, and was ordered to Jefferson Barracks, near St. Louis, then "Far West."

He was anxious to quit the service, and as a step
toward getting a professorship in some little college
he wrote to West Point asking for a detail to the Academy as an assistant in mathematics. But before that
could be brought about, Mexico began to boil, and
in May, 1844, after nine months of garrison life, he
was ordered south with his regiment. He had lost his
heart meantime to Julia, the sister of his classmate
Fred Dent, whose father, "Colonel" Dent, had a
large plantation, "White Haven," about five miles

from the Barracks, with negroes enough for comfort.

There was his usual persistence in the manner of his wooing. He was on leave of absence when his regiment was ordered south, and when he got back to St. Louis the rest were gone. Before following them, he saddled a horse and set out for White Haven. On the road he had to cross a creek which ordinarily ran nearly dry, but on account of recent heavy rains was now overflowing with a rapid current. "I looked at it for a moment to consider what to do. One of my superstitions had always been, when I started to go anywhere or to do anything, not to turn back or stop until the thing intended was accomplished. I have frequently started to go to places where I had never been, and to which I did not know the way, depending upon making inquiries on the road; and if I got past the place without knowing it, instead of turning back I would go on until a road was found turning in the right direction, take that, and come in by the other side. So I struck into the stream, and in an instant the horse was swimming, and I being carried down by the current. I headed the horse toward the other bank and soon reached it, wet through, and without other clothes on that side of the stream." He kept on, borrowed a dry suit from his future brother-in-law, and thus caparisoned declared his love.

A year later he went back to St. Louis, and although the Colonel thought his daughter ought to look higher than "the small lieutenant with the large epaulets," he won a reluctant consent to an engagement. They did not marry till August 22, 1848, six months after the war with Mexico had come to an end.

Before war was actually declared, Grant's regiment lay in camp for over a year at Fort Salubrity, in the pine woods near Natchitoches, between the Red River and the Sabine, then for two months in barracks at New Orleans, then by boat to Corpus Christi, at the mouth of the Nueces River in Texas, where the "army of occupation," three thousand men, was assembling under the command of Zachary Taylor.

All this time the movement ostensibly had been to prevent filibustering, though there was no question among the troops that its real purpose was the menacing of Mexico and the annexation of Texas. "For myself," says Grant, "I was bitterly opposed to the measure, and to this day regard the war which resulted as one of the most unjust ever waged by a stronger against a weaker nation. It was an instance of a republic following the bad example of European monarchies, in not considering justice in their desire to acquire additional territory. . . . The occupation, separation, and annexation were, from the inception of the movement to its final consummation, a conspiracy to acquire territory out of which slave States might be formed for the American Union. Even if annexation itself could be justified, the manner in which the subsequent war was forced upon Mexico cannot. . . . The Southern rebellion was largely the outgrowth of the Mexican War. Nations like individuals are punished for their transgressions."

But Grant was a soldier and took his orders. His Mexican service did him credit, though it did not give him fame. He went into the battle of Palo Alto a second lieutenant in May, 1846, and entered the City of Mexico, sixteen months later, with the same rank, — "after having been in all the battles possible for one man, and in a regiment that lost more officers during the war than it ever had present at any one engagement." But he was mentioned in reports and was brevetted first lieutenant and then captain for gallant conduct. General Worth made his "acknowledgments to Lieutenant Grant for distinguished services"; at Chapultepec, Major Francis Lee reported that "Lieutenant Grant behaved with distinguished gallantry on the 13th and 14th"; Colonel Garland says: "I must not omit to call attention to Lieutenant Grant, who acquitted himself most nobly upon several occasions under my observation."

He was early made regimental quartermaster, but

this could not keep him out of action. At Monterey, he mounted a horse, left camp, rode to the front, and joined the charge — the only mounted man and thus a special target. When ammunition was low and there was a call for a volunteer to take out a message asking for new supplies, he swung himself over a saddle, and, with one foot holding to the cantle and one hand clutching the horse's mane, dashed down the empty street, within the range of fire from every side, leaped a four-foot wall and delivered his appeal.

At Chapultepec he found a belfry which commanded an important position, dragged a mountain howitzer to the top of it with the help of a few men, and dropped shots upon the enemy to their great confusion.

At Molino del Rey, says Longstreet, "You could not keep Grant out of battle. The duties of quartermaster could not shut him out of his command. . . . Grant was everywhere on the field. He was always cool, swift, and unhurried in battle . . . unconscious apparently, as though it were a hail storm instead of a storm of bullets. . . . I heard his colonel say: 'There goes a man of fire.'"

"You want to know what my feelings were on the field of battle," he wrote home; "I don't know that I felt any peculiar sensation. War seems much less terrible to persons engaged in it than to people who read of battles." To an officer who asked him years later whether he ever felt fear on the battlefield he replied, "I never had time."

Yet he was an eminently practical and efficient quartermaster. At Tacubaya and at Monterey he rented bakeries and ran them for the benefit of the regiment. "In two months I made more money for the regimental fund than my pay amounted to during the entire war." From his experience, then, as quartermaster, with freedom to range in time of battle, he got ideas about feeding and clothing an army which stood him in good stead throughout the Civil War; and he learned other lessons in Mexico. He saw Scott cut loose from his supplies and live on the country; he saw Taylor cool and unhurried under fire, commanding his troops, without a uniform save for a private's blouse, and learned from him simplicity in army regulation; he learned that he could keep his head while under fire; and he became familiar with the points of strength and weakness of officers against whom he was to be pitted in the Civil War. Lee, Longstreet, Buckner, Jackson, Pemberton, and the two Johnstons, Southerners, most of them of higher rank, never thought that in plain little Grant they were disclosing their true military quality to a coming conqueror.

CHAPTER III

AD INTERIM

I. WASTED YEARS

PEACE with Mexico brought lethargy to Grant. After his mild experience with the world as a cadet and then in garrison and camp, he had had his fling with war and had come through with merit, though no great prestige. But he was now condemned to the monotony of a subaltern's life in frontier posts, with nothing to look forward to but years of drudgery, unless he had the luck to strike a tour of duty which would open up the way to resignation and agreeable employment in civil life — like the professorship in mathematics to which he had aspired. But there was nothing of the kind in sight. As quartermaster he was stationed first at Sackett's Harbor, on Lake Ontario, for a cheerless winter, because another officer with greater pull at Washington had grabbed Detroit, the regimental headquarters which was supposed to have attractions in a social way, although a frontier post. Then for two years, Scott having righted this injustice, Grant had Detroit, to which he was entitled by position, but as he had no social instincts, being dumb with women, awkward and shy with men,

he got no pleasure from its tinsel gayeties. Few people
knew that he was there. Another gloomy winter at
Sackett's Harbor, and then in 1852 orders to gold-
crazed California with his regiment. There was a
baby boy, born two years earlier at White Haven, and
a second on the way. He left his little family at
Bethel and started on the tiresome journey to the
coast.

On this trip he had a chance to show resourceful-
ness in an emergency, his only worthy opportunity
between Chapultepec and '61. Transportation across
the Isthmus had broken down by reason of the rush,
and it was unexpectedly put up to Grant as quartermaster, by such ingenious methods as he could devise,
to get his expedition of eight hundred people to the
other side. There he found cholera and a far heavier
burden — all the details of caring for the sick, the
burial of a hundred dead, the countless grewsome and
mournful offices of such a plague. "Grant seemed to
be a man of iron . . . seldom sleeping and then only
two or three hours at a time . . . he was like a min-
istering angel to us all," writes one who knew him
there. It is a striking thing that Grant in later years
spoke oftener of his experience at Panama than of his
battles in the Civil War.

His service on the coast was at Vancouver, on the
Columbia, and at Humboldt, two hundred miles

from San Francisco, where in due time he gained his captaincy. It was a dismal life. He abhorred hunting, fishing bored him — the only recreations of his fellow officers; there were few books to read; he pined for wife and babies, one of whom he had not seen. He showed a letter once to an old sergeant on which his wife had traced the outline of his baby's hand, and as he put the letter back without a word his eyes were wet — a likely incident; for all his life his deepest sentiment was for his home.

Like many another officer thus circumstanced, he drank more than he should and in his case a little was too much. It did not cloud his judgment or impede his speech, but it impaired his power of locomotion and he was physically helpless while his mind was clear. Those who knew him testify to this so uniformly that it must be true; and while not of supreme importance it cannot be ignored. It helps explain the obstacles he had to overcome at the beginning of the war and the peculiar influence which Rawlins had so long as Rawlins lived. Without it we should miss an angle of his character which throws a dart of color for our better understanding of the man. We should not have had Lincoln's pat comment after Shiloh: "I can't spare this man. He fights." Or his whimsical remark that if he knew Grant's brand of whiskey he would send a barrel to his other generals.

Just why Grant quit the army has been a question in dispute. The reason which he gives in his own story, that he saw no chance of supporting wife and children on his pay and so concluded to resign, is no doubt strictly true. It is in harmony with what we know was his intention when he left West Point. There was nothing in the service, especially in time of peace, for which he cared, and when he left it no one could foresee the conflict close at hand. But there were circumstances not entirely pleasant which conspired to fix the date of his decision upon a step which had been long in mind. He would, of course, have liked to turn his military training to account in some profession better suited to his taste, but in his exile to the coast that prospect disappeared, and two or three unlucky business ventures taught him that he could not supplement his meager earnings in that way. His monthly pay as a lieutenant was thirty dollars, and besides he had for rations eighty cents a day and for a servant, sixty-five, with wood for fuel, a single room and kitchen — an income all told of seventy-three dollars and fifty cents a month. His monthly pay and allowance as captain during his last month of service was ninety-two dollars and fifty cents, and with the slowness of promotion that was all he could have expected for years — a dismal prospect for a man whose wife and babies were by the speediest route eight thousand miles away. As he was near his captaincy he, of course, had pride in taking on the higher rank, but after that the sooner civil life for him the better. Thus it stood with him in April, 1854, when, having been intoxicated while paying off his men, he was reproved by his commanding officer, Major R. C. Buchanan, noted throughout the service as a martinet, who told him that if he did not resign charges would be preferred. Grant resigned. He did not have to, and officers who served with him have said that he would not have been sentenced to dismissal if he had stood trial. But he was tired of barracks life; he had just become a captain. He was anxious to get East where he could be with those who loved him and were dependent upon him, and without reflecting that the incident might later prove embarrassing, he wrote a letter resigning his new commission the same day he accepted it, to take effect July 31, 1854. By doing this he left his record clear of a court martial, but he could not guess that he would ever wear a uniform again or be of consequence enough to stir to life old service scandal and stimulate its sting. To Jefferson Davis, as Secretary of War, it fell to accept Grant's resignation. Jesse Grant was thriftily disturbed when he got word of it from the War Department. There is on file there his letter to Davis of June 1, protesting: "I never wished him to leave the servis. I think after spending so much time to qualify himself for the army, and spending so many years in the servis he will be poorly qualified for the pursuits of private life. . . . Would it then be asking too much for him to have such leave that he may come home and make arrangements for taking his family with him to his post? . . . I will remark that he has not seen his family for over two years, and has a son nearly two years old he has never seen. I suppose in his great anxiety to see his family he has been ordered to quit the servis."

In spite of his dislike for garrison routine there was nothing in his California life to cause especially unpleasant recollections. Otherwise he never could have written: "I left the Pacific coast very much attached to it, and with full expectation of making it my future home. That expectation and that hope remained uppermost in mind until the Lieutenant-Generalcy bill was introduced into Congress in the winter of 1863-64. The passage of that bill and my promotion blasted my last hope of ever becoming a citizen of the farther west."

II. A STRUGGLE FOR A LIVING

"When you hear from me next," he told his comrades as he said good-bye, "I'll be a farmer in Missouri." That was his hope. But he was in worse

straits than he had thought. Money owing him in
San Francisco did not materialize. A good-natured
quartermaster clerk cashed a draft and found him
transportation to New York. He landed strapped.
A creditor at Sackett's Harbor failed him. If his
classmate Buckner, who was recruiting officer, had
not guaranteed his board at a New York hotel, he
would have slept outdoors until his father sent him
money to get home. There was no great joy in
Bethel over his return. His younger brothers were
doing fairly well in leather, but with all his West
Point training he had not made good. Jesse, who had
been so proud of him, could hardly think of him without a shade of shame. He went on to his wife and
babies at White Haven and settled on an unbroken
tract of eighty acres which Colonel Dent had turned
over to his wife for a wedding present six years before. He cleared it, built him a log cabin out of trees
he felled and hewed himself, and with grim humor
called the new estate "Hard Scrabble." He worked
hard for a living, peddled grain and cordwood in St.
Louis for ready money, grubbed stumps, bought
hogs at sales, and did the things a farmer must. He
was more thrifty than his neighbors and showed more
ingenuity. While they were burning wood for fuel
he sold his at good prices to the coal mines near by
for use as timber props, and used for fuel the less ex-

pensive coal. Chills and fever hit him. He gave up farming, swapped his place for a little frame house in St. Louis, and tried his hand at real estate, combining with a cousin of his wife named Boggs who had desk-room in a lawyer's office. Money was slow after the panic of 1857. He was too soft-hearted to collect rents from hard-pressed tenants. There was not business enough for two. He applied to the County Commissioners for appointment as County Engineer, the salary of which was nineteen hundred dollars; but they gave it to another applicant. There were five commissioners, two of whom were Democrats and three Free-Soilers, and the selection was made on party lines. His father-in-law was a slaveholder, strongly Southern in his sympathies, and Grant had no particular political affiliations. "You may judge from the result of the action of the County Commissioners," he wrote his father on September 23, 1859, "that I am strongly identified with the Democratic party. Such is not the case. I never voted an out-and-out Democratic ticket in my life. I voted for Buchanan for President to defeat Frémont, but not because he was my first choice. In all other elections I have universally selected the candidates that, in my estimation, were the best fitted for the different offices, and it never happens that such men are all arrayed on one side." [1]

[1] *Letters of Ulysses S. Grant,* p. 20.

He had a place as clerk in the Custom-House for a month, but the collector died and he was hard put to it. "I do not want to fly from one thing to another, nor would I," he wrote his father; "but I am compelled to make a living from the start, for which I am willing to give all my time and all my energy." His father had prospered. He was worth $100,000, it is said, a sizable fortune for that day. He had established his tannery in Covington, Kentucky, where he now lived and he had also bought a wholesale leather business in Galena, Illinois, which was in charge of Simpson and Orvil, his two younger sons. Ulysses, much against his will, acknowledging at last his failure in farming and real estate, turned to Jesse for advice and help. Jesse referred him to Simpson, and Simpson sent him to the Galena store, "to stay until something better should turn up." The house bought leather and sold shoe findings, saddlery, fancy linings, and morocco. Ulysses served as clerk because he was good at figures; the other brothers did the bargaining for which he was not fit. He was allowed eight hundred dollars salary, and drew seven hundred more to settle obligations in St. Louis, a sum which he paid back afterwards. He had a comfortable little house, attended the Methodist church, wore an old blue army coat which he had bought on the Pacific Coast, traveled to Iowa and Wisconsin once to buy hides, and was becoming gradually settled to his environment, although few people knew him even by sight. "In my new employment I have become pretty conversant," he wrote a friend in December, 1860, "and am much pleased with it. I hope to be a partner pretty soon, and am sanguine that a competency at least can be made out of the business."

And then came Sumter and the call for troops.

CHAPTER IV

THE AWAKENING

How, when the North sprang to Lincoln's call, the men of Galena found among themselves the unassuming captain with his shabby army coat, singled him out because he had seen service, putting him in the chair at their war meeting, offering him the captaincy of their company which he declined, asking him to form and drill them and see that they were suitably equipped, and how when they marched to the station through flags and cheers, he stood in the crowd and watched them pass, trailing along with his old carpetbag, following them to Springfield, to be of service if he might, has been recited many times. But this is not all the story. For months Grant's mind had been in process of slow fermentation. All through the pregnant winter filled with secession talk, he was observing the approach to war. "It is hard to realize," he wrote in December, "that a State or States should commit so suicidal an act as to secede from the Union, though from all reports I have no doubt but five of them will do it. And then, with the present granny of an executive, some foolish policy will doubtless be pursued which will give the seceding States the support and sympathy of the Southern States that don't go out."

To Rowley, who said in February, "There's a great deal of bluster about these Southerners, but I don't think there's much fight in them," he replied earnestly, "You are mistaken, . . . if they ever get at it they will make a strong fight. . . . Each side underestimates the other and overestimates itself." Seven days after Sumter he was writing to his Democratic, slaveholding father-in-law: "Now is the time, particularly in the border slave States, for men to prove their love of country. I know it is hard for men to apparently work with the Republican party, but now all party distinctions should be lost sight of and every true patriot be for maintaining the integrity of the glorious old Stars and Stripes, the Constitution and the Union. No impartial man can conceal from himself the fact that in all these troubles the South have been the aggressors and the Administration has stood purely on the defensive, more on the defensive than she would have dared to have done but for her consciousness of strength and the certainty of right prevailing in the end. . . . In all this I can but see the doom of slavery. The North do not want, nor will they want, to interfere with the institution. But they will refuse for all time to give it protection unless the South shall return soon to their allegiance."

To his abolition father, two days later, his words were dutiful, as befitting filial and financial dependence, but clear: " We are now in the midst of trying times when every one must be for or against his country, and show his colors too by his every act. Having been educated for such an emergency, at the expense of the Government, I feel that it has upon me superior claims, such claims as no ordinary motives of self-interest can surmount. I do not wish to act hastily or inadvisably in the matter, and as there are more than enough to respond to the first call of the President, I have not yet offered myself. I have promised, and am giving all the assistance I can in organizing the company whose services have been accepted from this place. I have promised further to go with them to the State Capital, and if I can be of service to the Governor in organizing his state troops to do so. What I ask now is your approval of the course I am taking or your advice in the matter. . . . There are but two parties now, traitors and patriots, and I want hereafter to be ranked with the latter, and, I trust, the stronger party."

To his sister: "The conduct of eastern Virginia has been so abominable through the whole contest that there would be a great deal of disappointment here if matters should be settled before she is thoroughly punished. This is my feeling and I believe it universal. Great allowance should be made for South Carolinians; for the last generation have been educated from their infancy to look upon their government as oppressive and tyrannical and only to be endured till such time as they might have sufficient strength to strike it down. Virginia and other border States have no such excuse, and are therefore traitors at heart as well as in act."

CHAPTER V
CALLED TO THE COLORS

GRANT understood the sober side of war, and so at Springfield in the brood of patriots chirping for recognition he did not push his way. He was not eager for spectacular distinction after the way of politicians hunting for a rostrum to address the pyramids, confusing oratory with a genius for command. He was indifferent to gold lace and epaulettes — just a plain soldier who had not done well in civil life and thought he saw a chance to work again at the one trade he knew. The city was a scene of cheap confusion. Richard Yates, the governor, eager and keen of wit in politics, was struggling blindly in a flood of strange emergencies. Every man of consequence in Illinois was pressing for commissions for himself or for his friends. Companies of volunteers were pouring in, undrilled, unskilled, ununiformed, unarmed, hardly a musket to a dozen men; regiments of raw-boned boys and awkward squads, officered by village Cromwells and country-store Turennes, — among them soldiers to the core like Logan, — soon to comprise the nucleus of the hardiest veteran army the world had ever seen.

Of all of the companies one of the best came from

Galena, hastily drilled and uniformed by Quarter-master-Captain Grant, who now, neglected in the crowd and having done his duty by his local volunteers, was on the point of leaving Springfield, when Yates, perceiving that his military training might be utilized, found him a corner in a dingy closet, which served the adjutant-general as an office, and let him spend his time in filling blanks for orders — the sort of thing a boy might do after once having caught the trick.

"My old army experience I found indeed of great service," Grant wrote after twenty years. "I was no clerk, nor had I any capacity to become one. . . . But I had been quartermaster, commissary, and adjutant in the field. The army forms were familiar to me and I could direct how they should be made out!" So he stuck to his simple task, — looked up old muskets in the arsenal, made reports, answered questions about regulations, showed such familiarity with military things that he was made drill-master at outlying camps, and was so quietly effective that Yates made him "mustering officer and aide," calling him "colonel" and paying him three dollars a day. It is a singularity of Grant's career that he never asked for an appointment or promotion which he obtained and that he never shirked a job no matter whether mean or great which came his way.

So numerous and eager were volunteers that the Legislature provided for additional regiments. It was some of these that Grant was set to muster in, and when that should be done, he wrote his father three weeks after Lincoln's call, "I presume my services may end. I might have obtained the colonelcy of a regiment possibly, but I was perfectly sickened at the political wire-pulling for all these commissions, and would not engage in it. I shall be in no ways backward in offering my services when and where they are required, but I feel that I have done more now than I could do serving as a captain under a green colonel, and if this thing continues they will want more men at a later day. I can go back to Galena and drill the three or four companies there and render them efficient for any future call. My own opinion is that this war will be but of short duration."

A few days in St. Louis, while mustering in a slowly gathering regiment, just as Francis P. Blair and Nathaniel Lyon were cleaning up Camp Jackson which the secession Governor Claiborne Jackson had established on the outskirts with a view to seizing the city and the Federal arsenal. He saw the rebel flag hauled down from the secession headquarters, and he recites how, when a spruce young fellow in a street car turned to him to say, "Things have come to a pretty pass when a free people can't choose their own flag; where I came from, if a man dares to say a word in favor of the Union we hang him to the first tree we come to," he replied, "After all, we are not as intolerant in St. Louis as we might be; I have not seen a single rebel hung yet nor heard of one; there are plenty of them who ought to be, however."

His work at mustering in was quickly over. Brigadier-General John Pope, a native of the State stationed at Springfield as Federal mustering officer, whom he had known at West Point and in Mexico, offered to get him recommended for appointment to the Federal service; but Grant, who was a carpet-bagger and had no influential friends to push him, would have none of it. "I declined to receive endorsement for permission to fight for my country."

So back to Galena for a week, where he was filled with restlessness. "During the six days I have been at home," he writes, "I have felt all the time as if a duty were being neglected that was paramount to any other duty I ever owed. I have every reason to be well satisfied with myself for the services already rendered, but to stop now would not do."

During this visit he wrote the Adjutant-General of the Army tendering his services and offering the only suggestion he ever made about his rank: "Having served for fifteen years in the regular army, including four years at West Point, and feeling it the duty of every one who has been educated at the government expense to offer their services for the support of the Government, I have the honor, very respectfully, to tender my services until the close of the war in such capacity as may be offered. I would say, in view of my present age and length of service, I feel myself competent to command a regiment if the President, in his judgment, should see fit to entrust one to me. Since the first call of the President, I have been serving on the staff of the Governor of this State, rendering such aid as I could in the organization of our state militia, and am still engaged in that capacity. A letter addressed to me at Springfield, Illinois, will reach me." No letter ever came. The application was buried among department papers and the Adjutant-General never saw it till long after the war was over.

But other avenues of service opened to the diffident soldier, who later wrote: "I had felt some hesitation in suggesting rank as high as the colonelcy of a regiment, feeling somewhat doubtful whether I would be equal to the position. But I had seen nearly every colonel who had been mustered in from the State of Illinois, and some from Indiana, and felt that if they could command a regiment properly and with credit, I could also."

Yates would have recommended his appointment

as a brigadier, but he declined; said he did n't want rank till he had earned it. "What kind of a man is this Captain Grant?" Yates asked a bookkeeper from the Galena store; "though anxious to serve he seems reluctant to take any high position. . . . What does he want?" "The way to deal with him," was the reply, "is to ask him no questions, but simply order him to duty. He will obey promptly." Whereupon Yates wired Grant, then visiting his father at Covington: "You are this day appointed Colonel of the Twenty-first Illinois Volunteers and requested to take command at once." His commission was dated June 16, 1861.

CHAPTER VI

IN COMMAND

GRANT had been set, a month before, to muster in the regiment now put under his command, a raw and ragged lot of country boys, camped near Mattoon, their former colonel, chosen by themselves by reason of his warlike aspect, a former Costa Rican filibuster with a propensity for bowie knives and whiskey, and a way of making daily harangues to his helpless men, dragging his sentries sometimes from their posts for nightly orgies. When it came to serving under him in war, the officers objected, and remembering the quietly effective soldier who had taught them how to drill they asked the Governor to give them Grant. That was how Grant came by his first regiment.

The new commander had no uniform, although he bought one later with three hundred dollars which he borrowed from a friend. His rusty clothes and stooping shoulders contrasted queerly with the military strut of some of the militia colonels. He tells how, when he went to take command, Logan and Mc-Clernand, two Democratic Congressmen, both later to be generals of volunteers, went with him to inspire

Richard Yates
governor

the backward regiment with military fervor; and he relates how Logan's speech aroused his men to such a pitch that "they would have volunteered to remain 'n the army as long as an enemy of the country con- :inued to bear arms against it." But he neglects to say that after the first burst of oratory, when Mc- Clernand presented him as the new colonel, and the men, looking for another thrill, called out, "Grant! Grant!" he simply said, "Go to your quarters," in the clear, carrying, inevitable voice which years be- fore had caught the ears of loiterers on the Bethel Green and which would soon have its incisive way on more tumultuous fields. Nor does he tell how his new regiment, for the first time catching the inflection of control, went to their quarters silently, under the unaccustomed spell.

He drilled and disciplined them for a month. Or- dered to the Missouri line, where secession was still struggling for the border State, he marched his men across the country, so as to teach them how, instead of waiting for a train.

His six weeks in Missouri gave him no chance for much of anything, but to his father he confides that his services with the regiment have been "highly satisfactory to me. I took it in a very disorganized, demoralized, and insubordinate condi- tion and have worked it up to a reputation equal to the best, and, I believe, with the good-will of all the officers and all the men. Hearing that I was likely to be promoted, the officers with great unanimity have requested to be attached to my command. This I don't want you to read to others, for I very much dislike speaking of myself," — a disagreeable restraint for Jesse, whose paternal pride was just beginning to revive.

An incident illuminating in the naïveté with which he tells it: At Mexico, Missouri, where he encamped for several weeks, he had his earliest opportunity to exercise his regiment in battalion drill. "I had never looked at a copy of tactics from the time of my graduation . . . had not been at a battalion drill since 1846. The arms had been changed and Hardee's tactics had been adopted. I got a copy of tactics and studied one lesson, intending to confine the exercise of the first day to the commands I thus learned. I do not believe that the officers of the regiment ever discovered that I had never studied the tactics that I used," — an instance, slight it may be, of the saving common sense which served him all his life for genius. "I never maneuver," he said to Meade before the battle of the Wilderness. "My only points of doubt were as to your knowledge of sound strategy and of books of science and history," Sherman wrote him in a memorable letter, "but I confess your common sense seems to have supplied all this." And after he had gained his fame he said to a young officer, who would have talked to him of Jomini, that he had never paid much attention to that authority on military strategy. "The art of war is simple enough. Find out where your enemy is. Get at him as soon as you can. Strike at him as hard as you can, and keep moving on."

In his meager library there were no books on war, and he never seemed to care about the strategy of the great generals of history. To him the Civil War with every campaign in it was a problem by itself. His only purpose was to wrest success out of conditions placed before him, with such weapons as were nearest to his hand. The game of war had no attraction for him. "You ask if I should not like to go in the regular army," he writes his father, just after being made a colonel. "I should not. I want to bring my children up to useful employment and in the army the chance is poor."

Another story helps to explain a trait which was of service to him through his life. The first serious task to which his regiment was put was to disperse a band of troops under a guerrilla officer who had become a terror in that part of the State. "As we approached the brow of the hill from which it was expected we could see Harris's camp and possibly

find his men ready formed to meet us, my heart kept
getting higher and higher until it felt to me as though
it was in my throat. I would have given anything
then to have been back in Illinois, but I had not the
moral courage to halt and consider what to do; I kept
right on. When we reached a point from which the
valley was in full view I halted. The place where
Harris had been encamped a few days before was
still there, and the marks of a recent encampment
were plainly visible, but the troops were gone. My
heart resumed its place. It occurred to me at once
that Harris had been as much afraid of me as I had
been of him. This was a view of the question I had
never taken before, but it was one I never forgot
afterwards. From that event until the close of the
war I never experienced trepidation upon confronting an enemy, though I always felt more or less
anxiety. I never forgot that he had as much reason to fear my forces as I had his. The lesson was valuable."

It was his first experience in independent and responsible command — and so, according to his own
interpretation, he was dubious of the result. Like
Grant's other lessons, this was one which he had to
learn only once. He never was concerned about the
opposition; considered only what he had to do himself. "When I go into battle," Sherman said years

later, "I am always worrying about what the enemy is going to do. Grant never gives a damn!" [1]

[1] General James H. Wilson says that just before the march to the sea, Sherman said to him: "Wilson, I am a damned sight smarter man than Grant; I know a great deal more about war, military history, strategy, and grand tactics than he does; I know more about organization, supply, and administration, and about everything else than he does; but I'll tell you where he beats me, and where he beats the world. He don't care a damn for what the enemy does out of his sight, but it scares me like hell!" (*Under the Old Flag*, vol. ii, p. 17.)

CHAPTER VII

BRIGADIER–GENERAL

JOHN C. FRÉMONT, the "Pathfinder," major-general by reason of a reputation picturesquely gained, a dashing figure, futile in command, yet idolized beyond all other Northern men at the beginning of the war, was at the head of the Department of the West including Illinois, Kentucky, Kansas, and Missouri, with quarters at St. Louis, — which held the key to the strategical control of the Confederacy, — the waters joining there within a radius of a hundred miles to form the great flow of the Mississippi, the sole effective channels for transportation of supplies and troops. McClellan was at Cincinnati. Scott was general-in-chief at Washington and under him the regulars, McDowell, Meigs, and Rosecrans. Grant under Frémont, who had a scant conception of the strategical importance of his own command, was ordered from one place to another in Missouri, knocking his regiment into shape, doing police duty at Ironton, Jefferson City, and Mexico, establishing order here and there; for Claiborne Jackson's State was desultory fighting ground by reason of the close division of the population between the sympathizers with the North

and South. Without formality and by consent, because he was the only educated soldier in the lot of
recently created colonels, he found himself commander of an improvised brigade, and then one day
in early August, 1861, his chaplain showed him a
news paragraph that Lincoln had appointed him a
brigadier. "It must be some of Washburne's work,"
he said.

Elihu B. Washburne, a "down East" Yankee,
transplanted early to the West, had been the Congressman from the Galena District since 1852, one of
the very earliest Free-Soilers or Republicans to get
office, so that when his party gained control, with
Lincoln at the head, he was a factor to be reckoned
with. Shrewd, forceful, rangy, a fair type of the un-
cultured politician of his time, serving the public
many years in Congress and as Minister to France,
he is known chiefly now because Grant was his unknown neighbor at Galena when Lincoln called for
troops. He saw Grant handle the Galena company,
talked with him about the war and found him full of
sense, gave him a note to Yates and kept an eye on
him when he became a colonel. His unsought friendship was the nearest thing to "influence" Grant ever
had, and Grant was right in guessing that the appointment was "some of Washburne's work."

When Congress met in August and Lincoln had to

send in names of officers for the new army, he gave his own State four brigadiers and asked the delegation in Washington to meet and designate the men. Grant named by Washburne topped the list, receiving every vote. The others named were Hurlbut, Prentiss, and McClernand in the order given; none of whom had a West Point training. Lincoln sent in these names on August 7, together with thirty-three other brigadiers, among whom Grant was number seventeen. Ranking him were Hunter, Heintzelman, Keyes, Fitz-John Porter, Franklin, Sherman, Stone, Buell, Lyon, Pope, Kearny, and Hooker. The major-generals were Scott, McClellan, Frémont, McDowell, and Halleck, regulars, with Dix, Banks, and Butler, volunteers.

Thus at the outset of the war Grant was brigadier, unsponsored it is true, and guiltless of prestige, but placed without his own design with a detached command at the one key by touching which the forces could be set in motion to surround and crush the armies of the South.

Others saw the military value of commanding rivers near the junction of the Ohio and the Mississippi as a first step toward controlling the Mississippi to its mouth. Grant was the only one to see the absolute necessity of doing it at once with just the implements in hand. To him must go the credit of achieving what the rest only dreamed. He translated into terms of conquest the cry which sounded through the armies of the West: "The Rebels have closed the Mississippi; we must cut our way to the Gulf with our swords!"

CHAPTER VIII
PADUCAH, BELMONT

GENERAL LEONIDAS POLK, the fighting Bishop, commanded the Confederate forces thereabout. Working in harmony with a comprehensive military plan evolved by the trained soldiers of the South, something then lacking in the North, he had set out to gain Kentucky, a border State still split in sympathy between secession and the Union. His eye was fixed on Cairo, at the southern tip of Illinois, where the Ohio joins the Mississippi, a vantage-point of contact with three border States, and with that end in view he seized Columbus, twenty miles below, on the east bank of the Mississippi just above the boundary line between Kentucky and Tennessee. On that very day, September 4, as soon as he could do a task at which Frémont had set him in Missouri, Grant pitched his tent at Cairo.

When he learned that Polk was sending troops to seize Paducah, forty-five miles up the Ohio at the mouth of the Tennessee, — to hold which meant the locking of those rivers as the Mississippi was already locked, — Grant wired Frémont that he would start that night for Paducah if he received no orders to

the contrary, manned his boats, and hearing nothing
from headquarters was on his way, seizing the town at
daybreak of September 6, anticipating by a few hours
Polk's troops which Paducah had hoped to welcome.
To reassure the frightened citizens he issued a short
proclamation: —

I have come among you, not as an enemy, but as your
friend and fellow citizen, not to injure or annoy you, but to
respect the rights and to defend and enforce the rights of all
loyal citizens. An enemy, in rebellion against a common
government, has taken possession of and planted its guns
upon the soil of Kentucky and fired upon your flag.
Hickman and Columbus are in his hands. He is moving
upon your city. I am here to defend you against this enemy
and to assert and maintain the authority and sovereignty
of your government and mine. I have nothing to do with
opinions. I shall deal only with armed rebellion and its
aiders and abettors. You can pursue your usual avocations
without fear or hindrance. The strong arm of the government is here to protect its friends, and to punish only its
enemies. Whenever it is manifest that you are able to
defend yourselves, to maintain the authority of your government, and protect the rights of all its loyal citizens, I
shall withdraw the forces under my command from your
city.

He left troops at Paducah under General Charles
F. Smith, his old commander at West Point and notified the Kentucky Legislature, then playing with
"neutrality" at the state capital. The Legislature
promptly adopted resolutions favorable to the Union
and the State was saved; on his return to Cairo he

found Frémont's authority to take Paducah "if he felt strong enough," a reprimand for corresponding with the Legislature, and a warning against doing it again.

He could have seized Columbus then and wanted to, but Frémont kept him for two months at Cairo, and by November Polk was so intrenched that he was strong enough to hold his own against a siege and to assist the rebel forces in Missouri stirring trouble under Generals Earl Van Dorn and Sterling Price. Besides, by Frémont's order Grant had sent three thousand men under Dick Oglesby to chase guerrillas in Missouri and Oglesby must be protected in the rear.

It was to keep Polk engaged at home that Grant sailed down the river, on November 7, with three thousand men to reconnoiter at a little camp of shanties just opposite Columbus bearing the pretentious name of Belmont, where Polk had put twenty-five hundred men who, resting under the protection of his batteries, were ready for quick expeditions. Instead of simply reconnoitering, Grant, sensing what Polk had in mind, landed with his troops, dispersed the enemy, and seized the camp — his first real fighting for the war. He would have demanded the surrender of the beaten forces and withdrawn, his task completed, had not his green troops, their heads turned by what seemed a striking victory, become a jubilant mob, ransacking the camp for souvenirs, reddening the day with speeches, cheers, and songs, and uncontrollable till Grant, with genius born of common sense, set matches to the tents, the flames from which invited fire from the Columbus batteries and reinforcements from the fort, giving the enemy a chance to rally. His men, surrounded and attacked, were ready now for orders, but they would have surrendered had not Grant, saying grimly that they had cut their way in and could cut their way out, forced them fighting to the boats, he with a private's blouse, his horse shot under him, embarking last of all and nearly left behind.

McClernand, soldier politician, who was there with Grant, issued a vainglorious address to his command on his return to Cairo. But Grant said nothing save to his father, to whom he wrote next day: "Taking into account the object of the expedition the victory was most complete. It has given me a confidence in the officers and men of this command that will enable me to lead them in any future engagement without fear of the result." The newspapers of Illinois were filled with tales of how McClernand saved the day. Grant let him have his little glory with the folks at home and would not enter on a controversy. It was a local rivalry at best, for neither general was known outside the State, and news of Belmont did not excite the East.

The country's gloomy face was turned toward the Potomac and the James, waiting for victories to wipe out Bull Run, while McClellan at the head of his great army was wearing out its patience marching up and down. Belmont with its loss of life was criticized for years as an unnecessary fight. It was not intended for a battle, but a demonstration. If Belmont had not been fought, said Grant years later, "Colonel Oglesby would probably have been captured or destroyed with his three thousand men. Then I should have been culpable indeed."

Besides, we should have missed an episode unique and picturesque, illustrating the peculiar temper of the time.

CHAPTER IX

DONELSON

THIRTEEN more weeks of waiting, not altogether wasted because the time was used in drilling troops at Cairo and teaching officers the ways of war.

There were few regulars in Grant's command. The South had scattered its West Point graduates throughout its service, so that the volunteers had the advantage of instruction by trained officers. The educated soldiers of the North had kept their old commands and rank until the war had lasted many months, and while there was one whole "regular brigade" in the Army of the Potomac, in which every officer, from general to second lieutenant, had been educated in his profession, there were elsewhere entire divisions serving under commanders who had had no military training. Grant, face to face with such conditions, suggested while at Cairo that, except for the staff corps, the regular army should be disbanded and the officers detailed to lead and drill the volunteers, a condition brought about through natural process as the war progressed.

Grant was not alone in trouble with Frémont. Lincoln was having difficulty too. The more Fré-

mont displayed his pompous incapacity, the harder
for his chief to handle him, and he was bright enough
to play spectacularly upon the anti-slavery sentiment, which looked upon him as the champion of the
negro's cause, while those above him would subordinate it if thereby the Union might be saved. On
August 30 came the final test of patience. In that
morning's paper Lincoln was amazed to read a proclamation issued by Frémont confiscating the property
of all persons in Missouri who had taken active part
with the enemies of the United States, and declaring
free their slaves, — a proclamation hailed with joy
throughout the North, but with dismay by the Administration, which knew that Kentucky and the
other border States would not hold to the Union if
they thought their slaves were to be free.

To Lincoln Frémont's proclamation meant defiance and a usurpation of legislative power, but
patiently he asked Frémont to modify it; at Frémont's request issued himself the modifying order,
and brought down on his head the North's denunciation with threatenings of impeachment. Some would
have made Frémont dictator. "How many times,"
wrote James Russell Lowell, "are we to save Kentucky and lose our self-respect?" Such was the spirit
Lincoln faced in the first months of war. In view of
the part politics so largely played in the conduct

of the war, only incorrigible ineptitude could have elicited the order issued two days after Belmont, putting Halleck in Frémont's place.

To Grant the substitution was of little benefit. Halleck, an educated West Point soldier, of great learning, a master of the technique of war, — "Old Brains" they called him, — had been for years a San Francisco lawyer, having seen service in Mexico. He had just been made a major-general of volunteers, and great things were expected of him. He was a pundit, not a fighter; his big head stuffed with strategy, but not alive with wit. He had no aptitude for such emergencies as now confronted him in an unusual kind of war. He never learned what Gibbon had in mind when he declared a century before that "the great battles won by the lessons of tactics may be enumerated by the epic poems composed from the inspirations of rhetoric." To Halleck, Grant, with his plain, practical ideas, was a specimen unclassified, and besides, there was a lurking memory of the way Grant quit the service on the coast.

Grant, left to vegetate at Cairo, weary of inaction, at last sought Halleck out. He had a scheme for opening a roadway through the South and pushing back the first line of defense, which Smith, his old West Point preceptor, had approved, to his great satisfaction, and he thought it merited consideration higher up. But having grudgingly been granted leave to visit Halleck, he met scant courtesy. "I was received with so little cordiality that I perhaps stated the object of my visit with less clearness than I might have done, and I had not uttered many sentences before I was cut short as if my plan was preposterous. I returned to Cairo very much crestfallen."

The "preposterous" plan was this: Albert Sidney Johnston, in chief command west of the Alleghanies, had established the outward defensive line of the Confederacy in southern Kentucky stretching from Columbus on the Mississippi to the Cumberland Gap in eastern Tennessee. Along this line strongholds had been set up at Fort Henry and Fort Donelson commanding respectively the Tennessee and Cumberland just where those rivers, coming toward each other in the State of Tennessee, begin running parallel through Kentucky to the Ohio. The two forts were only twelve miles apart. Other outposts were at Bowling Green, ninety miles northeast of Donelson, and at Mill Springs, a hundred miles still farther east, guarding the approach to the Cumberland Mountains. Buckner was Confederate commander at Bowling Green, Zollicoffer at Mill Springs. Thomas watching Mill Springs commanded the Union left, Buell at Louisville watching Bowling Green, the Union center; Grant was in command at Cairo on

the Union right; while Polk was at Columbus and
Gideon J. Pillow at Donelson — Pillow, whom Grant
had known in Mexico, of whom, while still a han-
ger-on at Springfield, he had written with contempt
that, as "he would find it necessary to receive a
wound on the first discharge of firearms, he would
not be a formidable enemy."

The weak point of the Confederate line was the district including Donelson and Henry, where those two
forts alone held back the Federal navy from running
up the Cumberland and Tennessee as far as Nashville and Savannah and beyond. General Charles
F. Smith, at Paducah, under Grant, commanded the
little district at the mouth of these two rivers, and
Grant's plan after conference with him and Foote,
commander of our queer little fleet, was to sail up the
river, seize Fort Henry, and so indent the South's line
of defense — forcing the Union front southward to
Alabama. Sherman and Buell had thought of this,
and spoke of it to Halleck: McClellan, in command at
Washington, believed in it on paper, but with his
passion for delay thought eastern Tennessee should
first be occupied.

"There has been much discussion as to who originated the movement up the Tennessee River," writes
Colonel William Preston Johnston, in his biography
of his father. "Grant *made* it, and it made Grant."

And Grant himself wrote Washburne, within a month of the event: "I see the credit of attacking the enemy by the way of the Tennessee and Cumberland is variously attributed. It is little to talk about it being the great wisdom of any general that first brought forth this line of attack. Our gunboats were running up the Tennessee and Cumberland Rivers all fall and winter watching the progress of the rebels on these waters. General Halleck no doubt thought of this route long ago, and I am sure I did." But Halleck thought he needed sixty thousand men to carry out whatever dilatory scheme he had in mind, three times as many as there were with Grant, and if an army big enough for Halleck had been handy, he would rather not have picked Grant for the job.

Thomas, in middle January, 1862, took Mill Springs, a rare little victory which gave the North new heart, quite out of keeping with its real significance, and Grant grew more impatient to try out his plan. He wired to Halleck, Foote coöperating, that "if permitted" he could take and hold Fort Henry; and on the 1st of February he was given leave to move. He started the next day, and on the morning of the 6th the fort surrendered, guns abandoned, garrison in full retreat to Donelson. "Fort Henry is ours," he wired to Halleck; "the gunboats silenced the batteries before the investment was completed." Then, without orders or permission, for Halleck, thinking Grant would stay at Henry and intrench it, had never mentioned Donelson to him, he set out for the Cumberland at once, wiring Halleck, "I shall take and destroy Fort Donelson on the 8th and return to Fort Henry." His fifteen thousand men that day, he felt, could do more service than three times the number a month hence against a strengthened garrison.

John B. Floyd, Buchanan's traitorous War Secretary, who the preceding winter had depleted Northern arsenals to strengthen Southern forts, had just been sent by Johnston to command at Donelson; Pillow was under him; Grant knew both, and he was not afraid. It was a cruel week in February, warm by day, then overnight quick snow and sleet, with mercury not far from zero; the Union forces without shelter and inadequately clothed. But Grant with his inferior force invested Donelson, the garrison apparently asleep till on the 15th Floyd and Pillow led out their men. There was a desperate battle, the Union forces beaten back till Grant, who on a gunboat had been counseling with Foote, rode on the field. His men, discouraged, told him the enemy had come out with haversacks and knapsacks as evidence that they were prepared to fight for several days. But he was imperturbable. Examining a haversack he found it filled with three days' rations; supplies for flight. He realized at once that the despairing garrison, in order to avoid surrender, were cutting their way out. "They have no idea of staying here to fight us," he said; "whichever side attacks first now will win." Convinced of this, he turned his troops against the fort, Smith, Wallace, and Mc-Clernand fighting splendidly.

Smith with his men swept up the ridge and seized the rifle-pits; the Southerners were driven back into the fort where that night was enacted a curious, discreditable scene. Pillow and Floyd, with Buckner, who was there with reinforcements, decided at a council that their force must be surrendered. Floyd, under indictment at Washington for embezzling public funds, was obsessed with the belief that if the Yankees captured him, he would be hanged for treason, and the vain Pillow likewise thought the Yankees eager for his head. They begged Buckner, one of the bravest soldiers of the South, to take command, and under cover of the night fled down the Cumberland to Nashville, leaving Buckner to receive the enemy as best he could.

So Buckner sent his flag of truce asking for terms and for an armistice, and Grant sent back the message which electrified the North, "No terms except an unconditional and immediate surrender can be accepted. I propose to move immediately upon your works"; bringing the prompt response, "The distribution of the forces under my command, incident to an unexpected change of commanders, compel me, notwithstanding the brilliant success of the Confederate arms yesterday, to accept the ungenerous and unchivalrous terms which you propose."

Grant saw Buckner now for the first time since Buckner had helped him in New York when penniless, eight years before. "He said to me that if he had been in command I would not have got up to Donelson as easily as I did. I told him that if he had been in command I should not have tried in the way I did." Grant does not relate an incident, which comes with better grace from Buckner's lips: "He left the officers of his own army and followed me with that modest manner peculiar to himself into the shadow, and there tendered me his purse. . . . In the modesty of his nature he was afraid the light would witness that act of generosity, and sought to hide it from the world."

There is a passage in the "Memoirs" which from every aspect does human nature credit: "General Sherman had been sent to Smithland, at the mouth of the Cumberland River, to forward reinforcements and supplies to me. At that time he was my senior in rank, and there was no authority of law to assign a junior to command a senior of the same grade. But

W. T. Sherman

every boat that came up with supplies or reinforcements brought a note of encouragement from Sherman, asking me to call upon him for any assistance he could render and saying that if he could be of service at the front I might send for him and he would waive rank."

More men fought at Donelson than ever before on American soil save at Bull Run. It was the first substantial victory for the Union forces after nine months of procrastination and defeat. Grant, who had been unknown the week before outside the jurisdiction of his own department, was by a flash on February 17, 1862, the military idol of the day. In " Unconditional Surrender " his countrymen at last had found a rallying cry. Yet they had faint conception of what had really been achieved by Grant in opening the Cumberland and the Tennessee.

CHAPTER X

UNDER A CLOUD

WITH Donelson and Henry under Grant's control, the whole line from the Appalachians to the Mississippi crumbled like a shell. The indentation carried the Union forces into Nashville, which Johnston, having already abandoned Bowling Green, could no longer hold. Polk had to quit Columbus, and retired to Island No. 10, a hundred miles below. Mill Springs was gone. The Confederacy was pressed back to its second line, reaching easterly from Memphis through Corinth and Chattanooga, and northeasterly through Knoxville along the Cumberland Mountains to Virginia. The Northern people saw one outpost fall and then another, till it seemed to them like wizardry, and in the quick reaction they looked for speedy and complete success. But they took poor account of Vicksburg and the military problems it involved, and they knew little about service jealousies.

All the world was praising Grant but Halleck, who was for praising everybody else. Three days after Donelson he wired to Stanton: "Smith, by his coolness and bravery at Fort Donelson, when the battle was against us, turned the tide and carried the enemy's outworks. Make him a major-general. You can't get a better one. Honor him for this victory, and the whole country will applaud." Nothing was said of Grant. He wired congratulations to Foote for his work with the fleet and to Hunter, who had simply sent from Kansas prompt reinforcements — but not a word to Grant. Later, when he caught the temper of the North, he wired: "Make Buell, Grant, and Pope major-generals of volunteers." He wired McClellan on the 26th: "I must have command of the armies in the West. Hesitation and delay are losing us the golden opportunity. . . . Answer quick." Neither Buell nor Pope, good soldiers, had seen fighting then, and Halleck never did.

It was a plain discrimination, and Lincoln, appreciating the proprieties, sent in Grant's name alone, as major-general of volunteers dating from February 16. There should be no mistake about the cause of his promotion. Five weeks later came McClernand, Smith, and Wallace, with Buell and Pope; and still later, Thomas, who would have had the earlier recognition he deserved had it not been for Stanton's unaccountable distrust. Grant had now fought his way unfriended to a rank well toward the top.

Now comes a painful episode in Grant's career; Halleck seemed incapable of letting him alone. While still in front of Donelson he had been assigned to the command of the new military district of West Tennessee, with "Limits not defined." It was uncertain where his jurisdiction overlapped with Buell's; and on the 28th of February, after wiring Halleck that, without orders to the contrary, he should go at once to Nashville, Grant went there to consult with Buell at the place which was to be a center of activity. The next day he returned to Donelson, and on March 3 got orders to move his whole command back to Fort Henry with a view to an expedition up the Tennessee to capture Corinth, the most important outpost in the South's new defensive line, protecting Memphis and Vicksburg upon which Grant for weeks had had his eye.

The next day to his amazement Halleck wired: "You will place Major-General C. F. Smith in command of the expedition and remain yourself at Fort Henry. Why do you not obey my orders to report strength and position of your command?" He had not disobeyed any order, had reported daily the condition of his command, had reported every position occupied, and so wired Halleck; but on the 6th came this reply: "Your neglect of repeated orders to report the strength of your command has created great dissatisfaction and seriously interfered with military plans. Your going to Nashville without authority, and when your presence with your troops was of the utmost importance, was a matter of very serious complaint at Washington, so much so that I was advised to arrest you on your return."

"I did all I could to get you returns of the strength of my command," Grant, mystified, wired back. "Every move I made was reported daily to your chief of staff, who must have failed to keep you properly posted. I have done my very best to obey orders and to carry out the interests of the service. If my course is not satisfactory remove me at once. I do not wish in any way to impede the success of our arms. . . . My going to Nashville was strictly intended for the good of the service, and not to gratify any desire of my own. Believing sincerely that I must have enemies between you and myself who are trying to impair my usefulness, I respectfully ask to be relieved from further duty in the department."

Then followed daily messages between the two; Grant urging that he be relieved, Halleck retreating slowly from his stand; and finally, when ordered by the President summarily to send a full report to Washington, retracting grudgingly, restoring Grant to his command. "As he acted from a praiseworthy although mistaken zeal for the public service in going to Nashville and leaving his command," he wired the Adjutant-General on March 13, "I respectfully recommend that no further notice be taken of it."

In his dispatches to Grant, Halleck had let the responsibility for the misadventure rest with McClellan, and Grant accordingly was duly grateful to Halleck for having set him right. After the war the truth came out through McClellan's revelation of Halleck's original complaint.[1]

"I have had no communication with General Grant for more than a week," he had wired McClellan on March 2. "He left his command without my authority and went to Nashville. His army seems to be as much demoralized by the victory of Fort Donelson as was that of the Potomac by the defeat of Bull Run. It is hard to censure a successful general immediately after a victory, but I think he richly deserves it. I can get no returns, no reports, no information of any kind from him. Satisfied with his victory he sits down and enjoys it without regard to the future. I am worn out and tired with this neglect and inefficiency. C. F. Smith is almost the only officer equal to the emergency."

To this McClellan replied: "The success of our cause demands that proceedings such as Grant's should be at once checked. Generals must observe discipline as well as private soldiers. Do not hesitate to arrest him at once if the good of the service requires it, and place C. F. Smith in command. You

[1] *McClellan's Own Story*, p. 216.

are at liberty to regard this as a positive order if it will smooth your way." In replying to which Halleck intimated, perhaps, the real secret of his dislike: "A rumor has just reached me that since the taking of Fort Donelson Grant has resumed his former bad habits. If so it will account for his repeated neglect of my oft-repeated orders. I do not deem it advisable to arrest him at present, but have placed General Smith in command of the expedition up the Tennessee. I think Smith will restore order and discipline."

Grant subsequently learned that some of his reports to Halleck had been held up at Cairo, but this mishap would not excuse his summary execution without a chance to enter a defense.

There is a nice adjustment of justice with delicacy of feeling in this comment in his "Memoirs": "General Halleck unquestionably deemed General C. F. Smith a much fitter officer for the command of all the forces in the military district than I was, and, to render him available for such command, desired his promotion to antedate mine and those of the other division commanders. It is probable that the general opinion was that Smith's long services in the army and distinguished deeds rendered him the most proper person for such command. Indeed, I was rather inclined to this opinion myself at that time, and would have served as faithfully under Smith as he had done under me. But this did not justify the dispatches which General Halleck sent to Washington or his subsequent concealment of them from me when pretending to explain the action of my superiors."

In disgrace at Fort Henry, Grant had congratulated Smith on turning over the command and wrote him, "Anything you may require, send back transports for and if within my power you shall have it." There could be no jealousy between Grant and Smith. Grant's feeling for his old commander was almost one of awe, and when Smith first had come under his command he found it hard to give him orders. It was for the elder in service, now lower in rank, to relieve Grant's embarrassment. "I am now a subordinate," he delicately said; "I know a soldier's duty. I hope you will feel no awkwardness about our new relations." Smith died in a few weeks from hardships at Fort Donelson. He was too ill to serve at Shiloh. Sherman said once that if "Smith had been spared us Grant would never have been heard of"; he subsequently took it back, but with this early estimate Grant would then have agreed.

CHAPTER XI

SHILOH

"My opinion was and still is that immediately after the fall of Fort Donelson the way was opened to the National forces all over the Southwest without much resistance. If one general who would have taken the responsibility had been in command of all the troops west of the Alleghanies, he could have marched to Chattanooga, Corinth, Memphis, and Vicksburg with the troops we then had; and as volunteering was going on rapidly over the North there would soon have been force enough at all those centers to operate offensively against any body of the enemy that might be found near them. . . . Providence ruled differently. Time was given the enemy to collect armies and fortify his new positions." Thus Grant has placed himself on record, and thus it might have happened with Grant himself or Charles F. Smith in sole command, but not with Halleck.

Having smashed the South's defensive line at Donelson, the armies of the West turned next to Corinth, a little town in northern Mississippi of strategical importance because two railroads came together there which, thus connecting, brought Memphis on

the Mississippi and Mobile on the Gulf in touch
with Charleston and the South Atlantic States.
So long as the Confederates had Corinth, they had
the base for a campaign to keep the lower Mississippi under their control and hold the Northern
forces back. Beauregard, summoned from Virginia
with the prestige of success, was there already and
other generals were on the way — all to be under the
command of Albert Sidney Johnston, still in good
favor with the Cabinet at Richmond in spite of the
catastrophe at Donelson and his enforced retreat.
When men from Tennessee asked for another general,
Davis had replied: "If Sidney Johnston is not a general, the Confederacy has none to give you." Center-
ing at Corinth were nearly fifty thousand men.

Halleck had formed ambitious plans. Commanding all the armies in the West he was to lead in
person the armies of the Tennessee and the Ohio, with
Grant and Buell serving under him. He would have
chosen Charles F. Smith instead of Grant if Washington had let him, but Smith was laid up at Savannah on the Tennessee, sick with the injury received at Donelson of which he shortly died.

The move on Corinth was to be assault by Halleck's armies; but events precipitated battle on a
field where Grant and Halleck had not planned to
fight. Smith, while Grant was undergoing punish-

ment at Halleck's hands, had chosen as a rendezvous for the Union armies a bluff at Pittsburg Landing, twenty miles northeast of Corinth on the west bank of the Tennessee, preferring that place to Savannah, on the eastern bank and nine miles farther north, as Halleck had designed. Grant picked the Landing also on the theory that, as the plan was to attack and crush the enemy, the west side of the river was the place from which to strike. It would never do to let the Southern troops possess the bluff. He would wait there for Buell, when their united forces could advance on Corinth. His troops were at the Landing, but he continued temporary quarters for himself at Savannah where Buell was expected hourly to arrive.

But Beauregard and Johnston, instead of waiting for attack at Corinth where they were intrenched, moved down the river to the western bank in order to catch Grant before Buell could arrive; and on a muddy, foggy Sunday morning, April 6, 1862, Johnston's army of forty thousand, under cover of the forest and the night having come up to the Union lines, brought on one of the deadliest battles of the war. McClernand, Sherman, Hurlbut, Prentiss, and William Wallace, who was temporarily commanding Smith's division, were encamped around Pittsburg Landing. Others were close at hand, — Lew Wallace at Crump's Landing, five miles below; Nelson, one of Buell's generals, who had arrived the day before, camped near Savannah on the eastern bank; thirty thousand men in all potentially at Grant's disposal, while Buell with as many more was on the way. McClernand and Lew Wallace were major-generals, the rest brigadiers.

Grant, for two days on crutches from a fall, was at Savannah looking for Buell whom he expected there that day; at breakfast he heard the firing at the front and started on a boat at once for Pittsburg Landing where he found the battle on. The Union camp was not intrenched. The Western armies had not learned the habit then; while Grant, convinced like all the rest, that Johnston would make his stand at Corinth, thought his raw troops would be less advantageously employed in digging than in drill and discipline. The Southern troops poured in over an exposed line about three miles from Pittsburg near a log-cabin meeting-house called Shiloh, where Sherman was encamped; and here the battle raged ferociously, giving a name to the day's engagement.

Sherman's men, experiencing their first battle, thrown into confusion and losing their identity as a division, mixed themselves with McClernand's troops; and two divisions, scrambled into one, took orders indiscriminately from the two commanders, so desperate was the fight defying all the rules of war. Thus the battle went in all parts of the field, and thus Grant found it when he reached the scene.

In the wild combat he was imperturbable as he had been at Donelson. "I can recall only two persons," writes Horace Porter, "who throughout a rattling fire of musketry always sat in their saddles without moving a muscle or winking an eye: one was a bugler and the other was General Grant." He rode from place to place wherever bullets flew and gave commands, as was his way, in a low, vibrant, penetrating voice, alert but undemonstrative; there was no mad rushing back and forth, no stirring calls to action; he might be beaten, but he could not be perturbed. The odds throughout were with the South. Lew Wallace, with seven thousand men, mistook his road and did not reach the field until late afternoon when the exhausted armies were welcoming the night. Prentiss was captured with his improvised brigade after a day of desperate fighting at the "Hornet's Nest." Nelson did not cross the river. Just who was blameworthy for these mishaps has been the theme of controversy ever since.

As night approached, the Confederates had the best of it. They held the ground where Sherman's troops had slept the night before. The Union army,

mercilessly battered, had been forced toward the
river, beneath the bank of which thousands of panic-
stricken stragglers chased to the rear were swarming.

There have been few great battles with so little
planning. Grant in command could not coördinate
his forces or direct them from a given vantage-point.
He must be where he could best be of service, now
with Sherman, now with McClernand, now with
Prentiss in the "Hornet's Nest," reorganizing, re-
adjusting, realigning, ceaselessly encouraging first
one brigade and then another, inspiring them with
his indomitable will.

The enemy were superior in numbers and not inferior in ability to fight. If in the middle of the afternoon the knightly Johnston had not fallen while
rallying his men, no one can guess what might have
happened. The South has said that his death turned
the tide of battle; Jefferson Davis wrote years later
that "the fortunes of a country hung by the single
thread of the life that was yielded on the field of
Shiloh." The world will never know.

When Beauregard at sunset issued his order to suspend the fight till morning, Braxton Bragg, who was
for risking everything upon a grand attack that night,
declared to the staff officer who brought the message,
that if it had not already reached the other generals
he would not obey it, and added dismally, "The

battle is lost." But Beauregard always held that he was right, which is to-day the general view.

Bragg would have fought ahead upon the theory that when opposing forces seemingly have spent their strength, the one which gathers first its lagging energies for a renewed assault is almost sure to win. That was the theory of which Grant gave a striking demonstration the next morning, and on which he turned the day at Donelson, which was a fundamental feature of his strategy; but it must presuppose that in power of endurance the enemy does not excel, and that was not the case at Shiloh.

With fewer men the Federal brigades had obstinately disputed every foot of ground since morning, though taken where they had not thought to meet the enemy in formidable force, and that too without adequate formation. Lew Wallace had just reached the battered right with his seven thousand unscathed veterans. Nelson was on the opposite bank and Buell's army was already landing from the transports, while Beauregard had no reserves in sight. He had been held back two hours at the "Hornet's Nest" by Prentiss and William Wallace, and after Wallace had been killed and Prentiss captured, with two thousand men, he had been impeded by having to send captives to the rear. When night fell the time had passed when he could hope to seize the Union line by assault and cut off Grant's communication with approaching reinforcements. Bragg was right when he declared the battle lost, but he was doubtless wrong in thinking a final charge could save it.

Grant, so constituted that he could not know when he was beaten, had never doubted ultimate success, and when the armies bivouacked for the night, sleeping on their arms because the rebels had their tents, he had already planned to knit his line of battle and with fresh troops drive back the enemy.

To Buell, who had reached Pittsburg Landing hours in advance of his men that Sunday afternoon, and saw the stragglers huddled by the thousand on the bank, defeat seemed imminent. "What preparations have you made for retreat?" he asked Grant. "I have n't despaired of whipping them yet," said Grant. "Of course! But if you should be whipped, how will you get your men across the river? These transports will not take more than ten thousand troops." "If I have to retreat, ten thousand will be as many as I shall need transports for."

Brutal indifference to human life it seemed; and when the news of Union losses came, — twelve thousand men, wounded or killed, — the Northern press began to call him "Butcher Grant." But that night with his aching leg he could not bear the sights and sounds in the shelter of the shanty where he tried to sleep and where they had brought the wounded, but went out in the mud and driving rain to get what sleep he could, propped up against a tree. He has said of the one bull-fight he ever witnessed, "the sight to me was sickening." He could not bear the sight of blood or that of other men in pain, and he has written that one reason why, after the second day at Shiloh, he did not pursue the beaten enemy, was that he had not the heart to demand more work of his own jaded men; which may be set with Sherman's whimsical reply when John Fiske asked him why the rebels were not chased: "I assure you, my dear fellow, we had had quite enough of their society for two whole days, and were only too glad to be rid of them on any terms"; [1] and Buell's bitter comment: "I make no attempt to excuse myself or blame others when I say that General Grant's troops, the lowest individual among them not more than the commander himself, appear to have thought the object of the battle was sufficiently accomplished when they were reinstated in their camps; and that in some way that idea obstructed the organization of my line until a further advance that day became impracticable."

Certain it is the Southern forces were badly thrashed that second day. Beauregard must have realized that they would lose before the battle was

[1] *The Mississippi Valley in the Civil War*, p. 99.

renewed because he must have known that his depleted lines could not contend on equal terms against
Grant's army reinforced by Wallace, with Buell's
fresh divisions hourly pouring in. By four o'clock the
remnant of his shattered force was in retreat toward
Corinth. He had lost in missing, dead, and wounded
over twelve thousand troops. The Union loss was
equal, besides the capture of Prentiss and his force,
but Grant and Buell had more men to spare.

"I saw an open field in our possession on the second
day," writes Grant, "over which the Confederates
had made repeated charges the day before, so covered
with dead that it would have been possible to walk
across the clearing, in any direction, stepping on dead
bodies, without a foot touching the ground. . . . On
one part . . . bushes had grown up, some to the
height of eight or ten feet. There was not one of
these left standing unpierced by bullets."

In the grewsome light of evidence like this of
gallant and grim encounter, there is a Gascon touch
in what Beauregard wrote to Grant from Corinth,
when asking leave to bury his dead: "At the close of
the conflict yesterday, my forces being exhausted by
the extraordinary length of time during which they
were engaged with yours . . . I felt it my duty to
withdraw my troops from the immediate scene of
conflict."

And now came Halleck ponderously from his arm-chair in St. Louis, to assume direct command four days after the battle had been won. He found awaiting him an army of one hundred thousand men, Pope, by the capture of Island No. 10, having opened the Mississippi down to Memphis and joined his army to those of Grant and Buell. With this great army, after prodigiously elaborate preparation, Halleck crept stealthily toward Corinth, where Beauregard was lingering with fifty thousand, covered the distance in a month, intrenching daily, keeping his army busy with axes, picks, and shovels, holding back his generals eager for a fight, and finally closed in triumphantly, only to find an empty town, which Beauregard had never meant to hold and had quit long before, leaving wooden guns frowning over useless earthworks to deceive the Federal commander. Beauregard knew, like almost everybody else, that Corinth had been captured when his assault at Shiloh failed.

"After all," Halleck admitted finally to Grant, "you fought at Pittsburg Landing the battle of Corinth!"

CHAPTER XII

HUMILIATION

WHILE his superior was crawling through his evolutions, Grant underwent a cruel test of loyalty and patience. After Shiloh a storm of hot denunciation broke upon him. He could have been in hardly worse repute had he betrayed his country. If he were really guilty of a lapse he paid a bitter price.

The first reports of Shiloh to reach the North were those of hostile critics, inspired in part by envious rivals. Buell's men were quick to say that only their arrival saved Grant's army and that the triumph of the second day belonged to them. McClernand, ready with his pen, wrote home, as after Donelson and Belmont, claiming the glory of the day. The Sunday skulkers on the river-bank thought everybody else had also run away, and told this tale wherever they could hold a listener among the gullible and sympathetic visitors to camp. The Northern press defiled itself with slander: Grant was drunk before the battle and while it was on, loafing behind and letting others fight; Prentiss and his men had been caught sleeping in their tents and bayoneted in their beds; thousands of Northern volunteers had been slaughtered wantonly.

Fed by such tales the Western States, whose troops had suffered most, were glad when Halleck came, remodeling the army, now reinforced to more than one hundred thousand men, into three great divisions, one under Buell, one under Thomas, one under Pope — Grant looking on as "second in command" with no one subject to his order except his personal staff. Thus it was while Halleck crept toward Corinth, and then, "Why not press on to Vicksburg before it can be strengthened?" he suggested, bringing from Halleck the rebuke, "When your advice is needed it will be asked." For Halleck thought the aim of war was to get places, and Corinth was a place; while Grant was taught at Shiloh that the South could not be conquered until its armies were destroyed and its resources gone, and to seize Vicksburg promptly would give the Union army the Mississippi, cut off the Southern sources of supply from the Southwest and Mexico, and hasten the contraction and compression of the rebel forces to receive the final crushing blow. Vicksburg once captured, Corinth would again become a railroad junction — nothing more.

And so with each strategic point; to Grant its only value was as a resting-place from which to spring upon the next. To hold it longer wasted men who could be put to stouter service somewhere else. But

Halleck clung to Corinth, letting Vicksburg wait until the Southern armies gathered strength for its defense; so that what might have been accomplished in a month by swift advances called after Shiloh for a year's campaign with grueling encounters over a broad field, while Corinth itself, which fell to Halleck unresisted in early May, was held by Rosecrans the next October only after one of the historic battles of the war. "I think the enemy will continue his retreat, which is all I desire," was Halleck's message while Beauregard was trekking south. Hence no precautions against the prospect of the enemy's recovery and return.

So Grant lay rusting in his tent while Halleck dawdled and the critics bawled; not sulky or resentful, but chafing inwardly and sick at heart that a great opportunity should pass which he thought he knew how to seize. Orders were sent his troops without his knowledge. Reports of his subordinates at Shiloh were forwarded to Washington without passing through his hands. On the strength of his unselfish praise Halleck asked higher rank for Sherman, but did not mention Grant by name.

"The President desires to know," wired Stanton, "whether any neglect or misconduct of General Grant or any other officer contributed to the sad casualties that befell our forces on Sunday "; to which

Halleck significantly replied: "The casualties were due in part to the bad conduct of officers utterly unfit for their places. . . . I prefer to express no opinion in regard to the conduct of individuals till I receive reports of commanders of divisions" — evasive save by insinuation.

Grant asked to be relieved from duty altogether and have his command defined. "You have precisely the position to which your rank entitles you . . ." replied Halleck. "For the last three months I have done everything in my power to ward off the attacks which were made upon you." Sherman heard from Halleck that Grant had leave to go away — Sherman who had no fame till Shiloh, except the tale that he was crazy because at the beginning of the war the press had quoted him as saying that to occupy Kentucky would take two hundred thousand men, and who had just begun to love and prize the silent soldier whose traits were in such contrast to his own. He rode straightway to Grant's headquarters and asked why he was going. "Sherman, you know," said Grant, "You know that I am in the way here. I have stood it as long as I can." Where was he going? "To St. Louis." Had he any business there? "Not a bit." Then Sherman argued, his own case in mind, that if he went, the war would go right on and he would be left out; while if he stayed, some accident might bring him back to favor and his true place.[1]

Grant stayed, but found it irksome. The flunkeys at headquarters still ignored him; the attacks at home persisted; Congress debated him. John Sherman in the Senate almost alone dared come to his defense, drawing upon himself the angry protest of Harlan, of Iowa, against this "attempt to bolster up Grant's reputation." "The Iowa troops," said Harlan, "have no confidence in his capacity and fitness for the high position he now holds. They regard him as the author of the useless slaughter of many hundreds of their brave comrades. . . . There is nothing in his antecedents to justify a further trial of his military skill. . . . At Belmont he committed an egregious and unpardonable military blunder. . . . At Fort Donelson the right wing . . . under his immediate command was defeated and driven back. . . . The battle was restored by General Smith. . . . On the battlefield of Shiloh his army was completely surprised . . . and nothing but the stubborn bravery of the men fighting by regiments and brigades saved the army from utter destruction. The battle was afterwards restored and conducted by General Buell and other generals. . . . With such a record, those who continue General Grant in an active command will in

[1] *Memoirs of W. T. Sherman*, vol. I, p. 283.

my opinion carry on their skirts the blood of thousands of their slaughtered countrymen."

The riot of detraction stirred the War Department and the White House. It was then that Lincoln met the plea of powerful delegations that Grant should be relieved from duty, with the not-to-be-forgotten answer, "I can't spare this man — he fights!"

After two months Halleck restored Grant to a separate command, and Grant betook himself to Memphis, lately fallen into Union hands with the capitulation of Island No. 10 and Corinth. There, having fixed his headquarters, he remained, still rusticated, but no longer stung by daily slights in front of Halleck's armies, till there came one of the fantastic shifts which were so frequent in the first months of the war.

Things were in sad odor in Virginia — McClellan forced back to the James by Lee had shattered Lincoln's faith, and Lincoln, casting around in his perplexity for military competence, called Halleck from the West to Washington, ordering on July 11 that he "be assigned to command the whole land forces of the United States as General-in-Chief," for Halleck was in nominal command of all the armies of the West, by whom the only Union victories had been won.

"In leaving this department," he wired to Stanton,

"shall I relinquish the command to next in rank, or will the President designate who is to be the commander?" Stanton wired to turn the army over to the next in rank — and Halleck ordered Grant to come to Corinth.

"Shall I bring my staff?" Grant asked. "You can do as you please," was the response. "Corinth will be your headquarters."

There he set up his camp with fifty thousand men to hold the district between Corinth and Cairo, Halleck's big army having been broken up; and, through the summer, under orders, he lay still. He would have been forgotten, so fickle is fame gained in war, had it not been for the dispute concerning Shiloh which had spasmodic life with politicians and the press of the Middle Western States. He suffered keenly, but in silence, except with Sherman, who had won his confidence and who was in command at Memphis; with Washburne, to whom as his one friend in Washington he felt some explanation due; and with his father, sputtering with parental indignation, writing and talking in his defense among his old friends near his boyhood home.

"I would scorn being my own defender against such attacks," he wrote to Washburne in early May, "except through the record which has been kept of all my official acts. . . . To say that I have not been distressed at these attacks would be false; for I have a father, mother, wife, and children who read them and are distressed by them, and I necessarily share with them in it. Then, too, all subject to my orders read these charges, and it is calculated to weaken their confidence in me, and weaken my ability to render efficient service in our present cause. . . . I cannot be driven from rendering the best service within my ability to suppress the present rebellion. . . . Notoriety has no charms for me. . . . Looking back at the past I cannot see for the life of me any important point that could be corrected."

To his father he writes in August: "I do not expect nor want the support of the Cincinnati press on my side. Their course has been so remarkable from the beginning that should I be endorsed by them I should fear that the public would mistrust my patriotism. I am sure that I have but one desire in this war and that is to put down the rebellion. I have no hobby of my own with regard to the negro either to effect his freedom or to continue his bondage. . . . I do not believe even in the discussion of the propriety of laws and official orders by the army. One enemy at a time is enough and when he is subdued, it will be time enough to settle personal differences."

Just before Corinth, in September, he writes his father one of the few letters in which there is a sign of petulance. "I . . . have never had any other feeling either here or elsewhere but that of success. I would write you many particulars, but you are so imprudent that I dare not trust you with them; and while on this subject let me say a word. I have not an enemy in the world who has done me so much injury as you in your efforts in my defense. I require no defenders and for my sake let me alone. I have heard this from various sources, and persons who have returned to this army and did not know that I had parents living near Cincinnati have said that they found the best feeling existing toward me in every place except there. You are constantly denouncing other general officers, and the inference with people naturally is that you get your impressions from me. Do nothing to correct what you have already done, but for the future keep quiet on this subject."

Almost brutal in the directness of the rebuke, such words could have been forced from Grant only by deep feeling long suppressed. And yet how tame compared with Sherman's fire, who wrote home with his wounded hand: "It is outrageous for the cowardly newspapers thus to defame men whose lives are exposed." For Sherman's anger burned and blazed against the "little whip-snappers who represent the press, but are in fact spies in our camps," warning that "death awaits them whenever I have the power" — Sherman of whom Charles Eliot Norton said to Curtis, "How his wrath swells and grows . . . he writes as well as he fights."

CHAPTER XIII

THE MISSISSIPPI CAMPAIGN

HEADED toward Vicksburg in command, at last Grant
had the chance he had been looking for, though handi-
capped by the dispersion of a splendid army and by
the dilatory tactics which gave the enemy an opportunity to fortify and man the place. His strategy in
following a line of conquest which paralleled the
Mississippi, compelling the evacuation of the hostile
river strongholds one by one, had cleared the water
highway for the fleet of Union gunboats all the way
down from Cairo. Paducah, Henry, Donelson, and
Shiloh, in giving the Union armies the Tennessee as
far south as Nashville and beyond to Corinth, had
also transferred to their control Columbus, Memphis,
Fort Pillow, and Island No. 10; for though Island
No. 10 was seized by Pope while Shiloh was in fight,
it would have dropped into his hands without resistance if he had waited a few days.

Farragut had seized New Orleans three weeks after Shiloh and Butler was earning his sobriquet of
"Beast" as military governor of the town. Farragut's boats could ply the river as far north as fortified Port Hudson, while those of Davis could convey
supplies to feed the Federal armies as far south as

Vicksburg. Thus these two strongholds still in rebel hands were of the utmost value to the Southern cause. Not only did they cut in two the Union navy, but they controlled the gateway to the granary of the South, in Arkansas, Texas, and Louisiana, rich enough in soil to feed the Southern armies and rich enough in men to reinforce them with one hundred thousand fresh recruits. The Red River, running through Texas and Louisiana, emptied into the Mississippi below Vicksburg and above Port Hudson. To close its mouth against the contributions of the territory which it drained and to open up the Mississippi from Cairo to the Gulf was a high stake to play for, and Grant was not the only general who had it in his eye, although no other set such store upon the need of speed in forcing the assault.

Now that he was on the road to the achievement, he chafed with waiting. The enemy had been greatly reinforced while Halleck loitered and were now trying to regain part of the ground which they had lost. Iuka and Corinth were saved by Ord and Rosecrans only after fierce attack by Sterling Price and Earl Van Dorn. Vicksburg, which had been lightly manned and thinly fortified in April, had been growing stouter every day till it was now well-nigh impregnable. Nature had guarded it on the north by swamps, bayous, and shallow lakes through which invading armies could not hope to force their way; on the west by a steep bluff two hundred feet in height, from which its batteries could rain a plunging fire upon the rash fleet which should undertake assault and up to which no ship could hope to train its guns; on the south by the promontories of Port Hudson and Grand Gulf, by this time manned and fortified till they were strongholds in themselves. The sole approach was from the west and there the strengthened Southern armies intervened, Van Dorn for his defeat at Corinth, for which he was not really culpable, having given place to Pemberton, a Pennsylvanian by birth, trained at West Point, a rebel out of friendship for the Confederate President, who gave him rank above his seniors and responsible command unjustified by service or by the event.

Grant's first plan was to parallel the river without approaching it, just as from Paducah to Pittsburg Landing, compelling Vicksburg's fall, as he had forced the fall of all the other strongholds between Vicksburg and Cairo by seizing points of vantage along the Tennessee. He would abandon Corinth as no longer necessary, now that its railroad connections were in his hands and press hard on the rebel forces which protected Vicksburg.

Having in mind the moss-grown axiom of war that a great army in a hostile country should have a base

to which it could fall back in case of need, he fixed
Columbus as his base and deserting Corinth marched
his force along the Mississippi Central Railroad from
Grand Junction to Grenada, while Sherman with
Memphis for a base moved down the Mississippi on
transports to effect a landing at the bluffs just north
of Vicksburg and thus coöperate with Grant, who
hoped to keep the enemy engaged while Sherman
captured Vicksburg by assault. When he set out,
both he and Sherman, with whom he talked it out at
Oxford, would have chosen rather to move in full
force on Jackson, the Mississippi capital, using
Memphis as a base, but the Mississippi Central
Railroad, which ran from Memphis to Jackson, had
been torn up between Memphis and Grenada, and to
wait for its repair would eat up time, already grown
too dear. Even as it was the time was wasted.
Grant kept getting mystic messages from Washington
whose meaning did not dawn on him till after the
event. Forrest with his cavalry left Bragg in front of
Rosecrans at Murfreesboro, and darting through the
State of Tennessee cut Grant's communication with
Columbus by spoiling sixty miles of railroad and
leveling the telegraph, so that Grant, completely
isolated and unable even to tell Sherman of his
plight, had to work slowly back living off the country during the eighty miles' retreat, since Holly

Springs, where stores had been accumulated for an emergency, was at that moment surrendered to Van Dorn, who in a quick dash from the rear had found a coward in command. Grant, after three weeks' isolation, again in touch with Memphis on January 8, learned that Sherman ten days before had been beaten back in his assault upon the bluffs near Vicksburg, and that McClernand was in command of the Mississippi River expedition, supplanting Sherman on the strength of Lincoln's order.

It was now midwinter and nothing had been gained since spring except experience, though Grant's offensive had at least diverted Forrest's cavalry from Bragg, likewise ten thousand men whom Bragg sent to help Pemberton, thus weakening his own force and doubtless giving Rosecrans the victory in the close-fought battle of Stone River, January 1, which opened up the way for Missionary Ridge and Chattanooga, the possession of Knoxville and Atlanta, and Sherman's march through Georgia.

CHAPTER XIV

McCLERNAND

McCLERNAND's plottings and ambitions, his rivalry and jealousy of Grant, comprise a curious chapter of the time — one of the episodes of Grant's career which seem to indicate a hovering Providence. Nothing but unfaltering faith and an unswerving loyalty could have enabled him to meet unquestioning the obstacles he faced, especially those set before him early in the war before his fame was fixed. The brigadiers from Illinois whom Lincoln named with him at the beginning had been tangled in his fortunes ever since. Though he outranked them by coming earliest on the list, they held themselves as his superiors. Why not? Newly arrived, he had been selling leather in Galena only four months ago, while they had long been men of much repute. At that stage of the war a regiment was like a militant town meeting. To stand high in politics marked one as fitted for command. When Prentiss in Missouri found himself subordinate to Grant, he quit in anger, flashing hotly, "I will not serve under a drunkard!" — but came back later, fought under Grant at Donelson and Shiloh, and gallantly on many other fields. Hurlbut marred a creditable record with

wearisome complaints. McClernand represented
Lincoln's town in Congress — a Douglas Democrat.
It was important at the outbreak of the war that he
and Logan should stand by the Union cause, and
Lincoln, always politic, courted their favor. Had it
not been for his self-seeking vanity McClernand
might have left a record to compare with Logan's,
but his ambition overleaped itself. Scheming for
praise at home, he claimed such glory as there was at
Belmont, Donelson, and Shiloh, filling the local press
with tributes to his valor, poisoning the mails with
scandal about Grant, presuming on a neighbor's
privilege to make reports direct to Lincoln, intriguing
for a separate command, and now, when Vicksburg
was in sight, running to Washington with a pre-
sumptuous plan for self-aggrandizement. He was to
organize an independent expedition to clear the
Mississippi to New Orleans, picking up Vicksburg on
the way, and for this purpose Lincoln ordered him to
raise the necessary troops in Indiana, Iowa, and
Illinois. In patriotic fervor of appeal McClernand
could not be excelled. He swiftly garnered forty
thousand volunteers, and by the time Grant started
south with Sherman was prepared to enter on a con-
quering career. "I have a greater general now than
either Grant or Sherman," Lincoln said to Admiral
Porter; but in issuing his order to McClernand he

cautiously refrained from giving him the free hand
which McClernand sought, providing that "when a
sufficient force not required by the operations of
General Grant's command shall be raised, an expedition may be organized under General McClernand's
command against Vicksburg and to clear the Mississippi River and open navigation to New Orleans."
It was this order which lay behind the disconcerting
messages Grant had from Halleck. McClernand
thought it gave him equal place with Grant. His
error did not dawn upon him till, after superseding
Sherman, having gained a foothold in Arkansas, and
encouraged thus to undertake the wanton task of
leading thirty thousand men to clear the State of
rebel troops, he was called back summarily by Grant,
aghast at the proposal to divert so great a segment of
his army from the immediate work in hand. Grant
wired to Halleck that McClernand had "gone on a
wild-goose chase"; McClernand, sullenly obedient,
wrote confidentially to Lincoln, "My success here is
gall and wormwood to the clique of West Pointers
who have been persecuting me for months"; Sherman, who six months before had steadied Grant, now,
wounded to the quick, wrote to his brother John:
"Mr. Lincoln intended to insult me and the military
profession by putting McClernand over me, and I
would have quietly folded up my things and gone to

St. Louis only I know in times like these all must submit to insult and infamy if necessary." Of the three generals, Grant was the one to hold his poise.

Embarrassing as was the controversy with McClernand, its ultimate result was to make Grant in person assume the task of taking Vicksburg instead of leaving it to Sherman, who otherwise would have been chosen for the work and who would not have followed without specific orders the plans Grant had in mind; but unless he changed his nature it was inevitable that McClernand should be relieved from a command which brought him into conflict with his superior. So long as he remained with Grant he was profanely insubordinate, lingered behind when ordered to advance; arranged spectacular reviews when fighting was at hand, cumbered himself with wagons when told to leave them in the rear, continued firing when instructed to harbor ammunition, swore at Wilson, who brought him directions from Grant, " I 'll be God damned if I will do it — I am tired of being dictated to."

Finally he issued a vainglorious order to his corps congratulating them for gallantry in an assault on Vicksburg which did not succeed and taking other corps to task for failure to coöperate. He sent this on to Illinois for publication without submitting it to Grant, and for this gross breach of discipline, resented

angrily by Sherman and McPherson and their men,
Grant sent him home to Springfield, relieving him
summarily from his command. From Springfield
three months later he sent to Washington a virulent letter requesting a court of inquiry. "How far
General Grant is indebted to the forbearance of
officers under his command for his retention in the
public service so long," he wrote, " I will not undertake to state unless he should challenge it. None
know better than himself how much he is indebted
to their forbearance. Neither will I undertake to
show that he is indebted to the good conduct of
officers and men of his command at different times
for the series of successes that have gained him applause, rather than to his merit as a commander,
unless he should challenge it too." When this attack
reached Washington, it was too late to do Grant any
harm. The President would not consent to an inquiry, taking the ground that it "would necessarily
withdraw from the field many officers whose presence
with their commander is absolutely indispensable to
the service and whose absence might cause irrepar-
able injury to the success of active operations now
in active progress."

"McClernand played himself out," Sherman
wrote home the day after Vicksburg fell, "and there is
not an officer or soldier here but rejoices he is gone

away. With an intense selfishness and love of notoriety he could not let his mind get beyond the limits of his vision, and therefore all was brilliant about him and dark and suspicious beyond. My style is the reverse. I am somewhat blind to what occurs near me, but have a clear perception of things and events remote. Grant possesses the happy medium, and it is for this reason I admire him. I have a much quicker perception of things than he, but he balances the present and remote so evenly that results follow in natural course."

CHAPTER XV

VICKSBURG

SHERMAN's rebuff near Vicksburg revived the storm of criticism and stirred the Northern press to new attacks on Grant, as well as on other Union generals East and West. The story in Virginia had been one of procrastination and defeat and now the gleam of hope in Mississippi seemed to have vanished too. McClernand's advocates were vocal. But there was nothing in it now for Grant except to feel his way. He could not force his troops through the net of creeks and bayous swollen with winter's freshets, but transferring his army to the west bank of the river he encamped at Milliken's Bend and utilized the time till spring in testing schemes to get boats and supplies around the Vicksburg batteries to help the army later operate below; cutting canals to change the river's winding course; breaking levees, uniting lakes, hunting for channels; and all the time attending to the disagreeable details of army management. Dishonest and disloyal traders from the North infested his department, drawn by the lure of cotton speculation, and at last in desperation he ordered the expulsion of "Jews as a class" — a drastic step which raised a storm of protest in Congress and the press till Lincoln countermanded it — Lincoln, who knew Grant's feeling toward the traders in necessities of war, his old friend Leonard Swett, of Springfield, having once been ordered out of Cairo on pain of being shot because he tried to force on Grant a questionable deal in hay. When Swett sought Lincoln at the White House with his protest, Lincoln said, "Well, Swett, if I were in your place, I should keep out of Ulysses Simpson's bailiwick, for to the best of my knowledge and belief Grant will keep his promise if he catches you in Cairo."

Amid distractions such as these Grant worked out his daring plans for seizing Vicksburg. He was on trial at Washington. Discontent was spreading through the North, discouraged by the months of dreary waiting. It was a dark hour for the Union cause. Stanton, hard pressed on every side, was moved in his impatience to do a foolish thing. He thought to bribe his generals into action and sent a letter to Grant, Rosecrans, and Hooker promising to make the victor of the first important battle a major-general in the regular army. Rosecrans, commanding the Army of the Cumberland in Tennessee, wrote a petulant reply. Hooker promptly led the Army of the Potomac to humiliating defeat at Chancellorsville. Grant ignored the letter; he did not let it hasten him or influence his course.

When all was ready on the night of April 16, 1863, Porter bravely ran the blazing Vicksburg batteries with a portion of his fleet, following with others later, safely performing almost without a scar a feat which Sherman and most of Grant's other generals thought too perilous to undertake. The army, having marched down the western bank by a circuitous route, was camped at Carthage in Louisiana ready to be ferried across the Mississippi, and on the 30th of April it landed on the eastern side at Bruinsburg, south of Vicksburg.

There began the wonderful campaign which ended two months later in Pemberton's capitulation of the rebel stronghold. "When this landing was effected," Grant says, "I felt a degree of relief scarcely ever equaled since. Vicksburg was not yet taken it is true, nor were its defenders demoralized by any of our previous moves. I was now in the enemy's country with a vast river and the stronghold of Vicksburg between me and my base of supplies. But I was on dry ground on the same side of the river with the enemy. All the campaigns, labor, hardships, and exposures from the month of December previous to this time that had been made and endured, were for the accomplishment of this one object."

How in a flash he seized Port Gibson and then, without a word to Halleck, and in the face of Sherman's doubts, with only three days' rations, cutting loose from base, struck out for Vicksburg, feeding his army off the country as he rushed them on from fight to fight; how Halleck, too late learning what was on, ordered him back to help Banks at Port Hudson; how he caught Joe Johnston at Jackson, separating Johnston's Army from Pemberton's, and seized the Mississippi capital and railroad center, cutting off Vicksburg from this dépôt of supplies; how in eighteen days he marched two hundred miles, won five pitched battles, took eight thousand prisoners and eighty cannon, scattered a hostile army larger than his own fighting on its chosen ground, and had the rebel army penned in Vicksburg, is a story whose mere recital emblazons the chronicles of war. "This is a campaign," cried Sherman as he rode out with Grant on May 18, and looked down on the bluffs where he had been repulsed so signally five months before. "Until this moment I never thought your movement a success. But this is a success, even if we never take the town."

There came one set-back. On May 22, hearing that Johnston was gathering an army to raise the siege, he ventured an assault, and after a reverse, misled by an appeal for aid from McClernand, who fancied he alone was carrying the forts, ordered a second assault, resulting in a bad repulse. He then renewed the siege, his army strengthened by recruits to seventy thousand men, and on the morning of July 4, swift on the heels of Gettysburg, he entered Vicksburg, Pemberton surlily surrendering thirty-one thousand men and one hundred and seventy-two pieces of artillery. "Grant ..." Dana wired to Stanton, "was received by Pemberton with ... marked impertinence. ... He bore it like a philosopher."

After all was over Grant handed back to Sherman the letter Sherman wrote advising him against his daring plan. He says the subject was not mentioned subsequently by either till the end of the war, and that "Sherman gave the same energy to make the campaign a success that he would or could have done if it had been ordered by himself."

"The campaign of Vicksburg," Sherman later wrote, "in its conception and execution, belonged exclusively to General Grant, not only in the great whole, but in the thousands of its details. I still retain many of his letters and notes, all in his own handwriting, prescribing the routes of march for divisions and detachments, specifying even the amount of food and tools to be carried along. Many persons gave his adjutant-general, Rawlins, the credit for these things, but they were in error; for no commanding general of any army ever gave more of his personal attention to details, or wrote so many of his own orders, reports, and letters, as General Grant." [1]

Even if Grant's career had ended then, his fame was safe, for subsequent defeat could not have spoiled the perfect record of his high achievement. No matter what had gone before or what might happen after Vicksburg, he now had confidence in his own destiny. He felt that he would be the one to bring the war to a successful end. Vicksburg had been before his eye ever since Paducah, and it had come at last to him among a great array of Union generals who had at the beginning more prestige, without intrigue for self-advancement on his part, and in the face of personal rebuffs which would have dismayed a man of ordinary mould.

"Every one has his superstitions," he wrote years later, referring to his silence under criticism. "One of mine is that in positions of great responsibility every one should do his duty to the best of his ability when assigned by competent authority, without application or the use of influence to change his position.

"While at Cairo I had watched with very great interest the operations of the Army of the Potomac, looking upon that as the main field of the war. I had no idea myself of ever having any large command,

[1] *Memoirs of W. T. Sherman*, vol. i, p. 362.

nor did I suppose that I was equal to one; but I said
I would give anything if I were commanding a
brigade of cavalry in the Army of the Potomac and
believed that I could do some good. Captain Hillyer
suggested that I make application to be transferred
there to command the cavalry. I then told him that
I would cut my right arm off first."

He had now conquered Halleck's prejudice as he
had justified the trust of Lincoln. "In boldness of
plan, rapidity of execution, and brilliancy of results,"
wrote Halleck handsomely, "these operations will
compare most favorably with those of Napoleon
about Ulm." Sherman wrote years later that the
campaign would rank with the best of the young
Napoleon in Italy in 1796, and that the "position at
Vicksburg was more difficult than that at Sebasto-
pol," which he had seen.

"I would not have risked the passing of the batteries at Vicksburg and trusting to the long route by
Grand Gulf and Jackson to reach what we both knew
were the key-points to Vicksburg," Sherman acknowledged when the siege was over. "But I would
have aimed to reach the same points from Grenada.
But both aimed at the same points, and though both
of us knew little of the actual ground, it is wonderful
how well they have realized our military calculations.
As we sat at Oxford last November we saw in the

future what we now realize, and like the architect who sees developed the beautiful vision of his brain, we feel an intense satisfaction at the realization of our military plans. I thank God no President was near to thwart our plans and that the short-sighted public could not drive us from our object till the plan was fully realized."

Yet Sherman always thought that if Grant had kept on from Oxford after the capture of his supplies at Holly Springs, he would have saved the six months used in reaching Bruinsburg and have achieved the same result. Grant might have done this had his troops then had the seasoning he gave them later.

The chapter cannot properly be closed save with the letter Lincoln wrote to Grant at Vicksburg within a week after it had fallen: —

"I do not remember that you and I ever met personally. I write this now as a grateful acknowledgment for the almost inestimable service you have done the country. I wish to say a word further. When you first reached the vicinity of Vicksburg, I thought you should do what you finally did — march the troops across the neck, run the batteries with the transports, and thus go below; and I never had any faith, except a general hope that you knew better than I, that the Yazoo Pass expedition and the like could succeed. When you got below and took Port Gibson, Grand

Gulf, and vicinity, I thought you should go down the river and join General Banks, and when you turned northward, east of the Big Black, I feared it was a mistake. I now wish to make the personal acknowledgment that you were right and I was wrong."

Lincoln at once named Grant a major-general in the regular army. He had not needed Stanton's bribe.

CHAPTER XVI

RAWLINS AND DANA

"THE simple fact is that the great character which has passed into history under the name of Grant was compounded of both Grant and Rawlins in nearly equal parts. While one has become a national hero whose fame will never die, the other unnecessarily effaced himself and is now scarcely known beyond the acquaintance of his surviving comrades or the limits of the community from which both took up arms for the cause of the Union." Thus a distinguished soldier, who was on Grant's staff and intimate with both men, has written.[1] It has even been asserted that Rawlins spoke with Grant's lips and looked out of Grant's eyes so closely did they intertwine. Hyperbole like this will not be credited by those who read the record, yet it is no great stretch to say that Rawlins was Grant's conscience, though he did not compare with him in the peculiar qualities which were responsible for Grant's success.

It was Grant's great good fortune that, in the casual thought he gave his staff when he became a brigadier, he should have hit on Rawlins, a crude, young lawyer who had worked his way up from the

[1] General James H. Wilson, *Life of Charles A. Dana*, p. 241.

Jno. A. Rawlins

charcoal pit, whom Grant had hardly seen until the
first war meeting in Galena, and who had caught his
fancy there in an impassioned plea for volunteers.
With one or two exceptions the early members of his
staff, chosen for old times' sake or to please his family,
were found to be incumbrances and were perforce
discarded as he shouldered heavier burdens, to be
replaced by men like Wilson, Porter, Comstock,
Badeau, Leet, and Babcock, each of whom had some
peculiar merit. Rawlins and Bowers were with him
till they died. But indispensable as Rawlins came to
be, there is no evidence that he contributed to
Grant's supreme achievement except by giving him
unselfishly the service of an unfailing adjutant and
devoted friend. He had scant learning and no military training but what he gained in camp with Grant.
He was robustly honest, grim of face and crudely
mannered, outspoken and explosive with profanity,
at heart a Puritan. He protected Grant in countless
ways from those who would impose on his simplicity,
made others show Grant deference which Grant
would not exact himself, and watched him constantly to save him from mistakes. Perhaps his
greatest service was in keeping him from drink, for
he appreciated more than Grant the handle envious
rivals made of any lapse, and that while Grant might
drink no more than others, he could not afford to

drink as much, by very reason of the stories which were widely spread and of the damage they might do the Union cause. Of course there is no question of Grant's habit, and that at times he favored it too much, but envious tongues gave it far greater emphasis than it deserved. If Grant had not been as successful as he was, his habits would have cut no figure. Who cares if other Union generals abstained or not? Yet those who did were in a small minority. With some it is about their only claim to fame. Lincoln, responding about this time to an appeal from Sons of Temperance, quizzically remarked that "in a hard struggle I do not know but what it is some consolation to be aware that there is some intemperance on the other side too."

Charles A. Dana, who had been sent by Stanton to spy out the Western armies and learn the truth of the conflicting tales about their generals, Grant in particular, and give him independent information, wrote him of Rawlins after Vicksburg: "Lieutenant-Colonel Rawlins never loses a moment and never gives himself any indulgence except swearing and scolding. . . . A townsman of Grant's, and has a great influence over him, especially because he watches him day and night, and whenever he commits the folly of tasting liquor hastens to remind him that at the beginning of the war he gave him

(Rawlins) his word of honor not to touch a drop as long as it lasted. Grant thinks Rawlins a first-rate adjutant, but I think this is a mistake. He is too slow, and can't write the English language correctly without a great deal of careful consideration. Indeed illiterateness is a general characteristic of Grant's staff and in fact of Grant's generals and regimental officers of all ranks."

Over thirty years later, with the full history of the war in retrospect, he gave his judgment that Rawlins was one of the most valuable men in the army. "He had a very able mind, clear, strong, and not subject to hysterics. He bossed everything at Grant's headquarters. He had very little respect for persons, and a rough style of conversation. I have heard him curse at Grant, when, according to his judgment, the general was doing something that he thought he had better not do. But he was entirely devoted to his duty, with the clearest judgment, and perfectly fearless. Without him Grant would not have been the same man. Rawlins was essentially a good man, though he was one of the most profane men I ever knew; there was no guile in him — he was as upright and as genuine a character as I ever came across."[1]

Dana himself, though a civilian, was a factor in the fixing of Grant's reputation. Stanton and Lincoln

[1] *Recollections of the Civil War*, p. 62.

owed to him their knowledge of the Vicksburg venture as the campaign progressed, for Grant was chary of his correspondence, sent only brief dispatches, neglected expositions of his plans, moved silently and swiftly to his ends, ignoring the malicious work of slanderous tongues. It needed Dana's quick intelligence, keen eye, and vivid pen to dissipate the fogs which clouded Washington. It was due in large degree to his reports that Lincoln clung to Grant while, pending Vicksburg, politicians pressed him to make a change, demanding Grant's removal almost up to the very day the town capitulated. "I rather like the man," said Lincoln; "I think we will try him a little longer."

It was Dana who set Stanton right about McClernand, and kept him straight; told him the manner of man he had in Grant, described the obstacles which must be overcome, and gave him thumb-nail sketches of the generals in the West.

Grant trusted Dana, who lived at headquarters throughout the siege of Vicksburg, to keep Stanton posted, and turned his own attention to more pressing things. Dana, with Rawlins and Wilson of the staff. were with Grant constantly, and in his confidence so far as that was true of any one, for Grant, who never held a council of war, harbored his thoughts and husbanded his intimacies: "I heard what men had to say — the stream of talk at headquarters — but I made up my own mind and from my written orders my staff got their first knowledge of what was to be done. No living man knew of plans until they were matured and decided."[1] "Grant was an uncommon fellow," Dana writes; "the most modest, the most disinterested, and the most honest man I ever knew, with a temper that nothing could disturb, and a judgment that was judicial in its comprehensiveness and wisdom. Not a great man, except morally; not an original or brilliant man; but sincere, thoughtful, deep, and gifted with courage that never faltered; when the time came to risk all, he went in like a simple-hearted, unaffected, unpretending hero, whom no ill omens could deject, and no triumph unduly exalt. A social, friendly man, too, fond of a pleasant joke and also ready with one; but liking above all a long chat of an evening, and ready to sit up with you all night talking in the cold breeze in front of his tent. Not a man of sentimentality, not demonstrative in friendship, but always holding to his friends, and just even to the enemies he hated."[2]

Dana after Vicksburg suggested Grant as the commander of the Armies of the West.

[1] Young, vol. II, p. 306.
[2] *Recollections of the Civil War*, p. 61.

CHAPTER XVII

CHATTANOOGA AND MISSIONARY RIDGE

GRANT would have lost no time in clearing up the Mississippi problem if Washington had given him his head. He could have captured Mobile easily with his exultant army, and operating from that base, have thrown troops against Bragg's rear, diverting him from southern Tennessee where he confronted Rosecrans. But Washington had other plans, and again, as after Corinth, dispersed Grant's army, sending troops to Schofield in Missouri, to Banks in Louisiana, and to Burnside in East Tennessee. Lincoln would have invaded Texas to threaten Maximilian in Mexico, and he was set upon relieving the loyal mountaineers of East Tennessee. The scattering of Grant's army and his forced idleness gave Joe Johnston an opportunity to recruit his forces and to gather up the men whom Grant, with a mistaken generosity, had let march out of Vicksburg on parole, thus strengthening the army which, on the 19th and 20th of September, came near crushing Rosecrans at Chickamauga Creek, compelling his retreat to Chattanooga with McCook and Crittenden, while Thomas with his corps stood alone unshakable for hours against great odds, thus saving a complete catastrophe and gaining for himself the name he carried ever after — "the Rock of Chickamauga."

The Army of the Cumberland might have been spared this blow had its commander, obedient to Grant's suggestion and Halleck's order, moved against Bragg while Vicksburg was in siege and Johnston occupied in trying to aid Pemberton, but Rosecrans objected then because he said it was a military maxim "not to fight two decisive battles at the same time." If true, Grant thought this maxim was not applicable: "It would be bad to be defeated in two decisive battles fought the same day, but it would not be bad to win them" — a flash which throws light on the difference between the two. Rosecrans was a trained and scholarly commander, ingratiating, vacillating, fearful to give offense, loved by his men, grieving incessantly that his hazy aims were balked by those above him. Grant thought him insincere and Jesuitical, while he thought Grant a fool for luck.

During this time there was much talk about Grant's coming East to take command, as other Western generals had been brought East before. McClellan, Pope, Burnside, and Hooker had been found wanting one by one; and now Meade, victorious at Gettysburg, had lost the confidence of Lincoln by letting Lee cross the Potomac without another fight. But

Grant discouraged these suggestions. "They have there able officers who have been brought up with that army and to import a commander to place over them certainly could produce no good. While I would not positively disobey an order, I would have objected most vehemently to taking that command or any other except the one I have — I can do more with this army than it would be possible for me to do with any other, without time to make the same acquaintance with others that I have with this. . . . I believe I know the exact capacity of every general in my command."

But a far greater opportunity was at hand. In the rout at Chickamauga, before he knew that Thomas had stood firm, Dana, watching the day for Stanton, had wired him, "My dispatch to-day is of deplorable importance; Chickamauga is as fatal a name in our history as Bull Run." There was dismay in Washington, which was not relieved by later tidings of the plight in which defeat and indecision had left the Army of the Cumberland — Rosecrans was cooped up in Chattanooga strongly intrenched, but cut off from supplies by Bragg, whose eager army held the hills above the town. He might hold out till reinforced by Sherman and Hooker, who were on the way, but food and fuel were getting scarce, his horses starving, and winter coming on. His idle army was demoralized and he seemed dazed. In spite of the respect his men had for him, he must be relieved of his command in order to escape a worse catastrophe.

Stanton would have supplanted him with Thomas, but Thomas, who six months before stood loyally by Buell when offered Buell's place, now stood as loyally by Buell's successor. He said he would not take that command, though he would welcome any other. He would do nothing to countenance suspicion of intrigue against his commander's interest.

Then Stanton, acting quickly, created a brand-new division comprising everything between the Alleghanies and the Mississippi except Banks at New Orleans; chose Grant for command, ordered Grant to Louisville, hurried West himself, and on the train to Louisville told Grant, whom he had never seen before, the plan he had in mind. Word came to Louisville from Dana that Rosecrans was thinking of retreat — a disastrous thing which would have left the rebels in complete control of one of the three great strongholds of the war, whereupon Grant, responding instantly to Stanton's frantic urging, assumed immediate command of the Divison of the Mississippi, and simultaneously wired Thomas assigning him to head the Army of the Cumberland and telling him he must "hold Chattanooga at all hazards." Thomas replied by telegraph, "We will hold the town till we starve."

That night Grant went to the theater, to the great distress of Rawlins, who looked upon it as a time for penitence and prayer. At daybreak he was on his way by rail and swollen roads to Chattanooga, where he arrived October 23, "wet, dirty, and well," as Dana wired to Stanton, but still on crutches and suffering agony with his crushed leg.

Those present at Grant's meeting with Thomas at headquarters, soon after his arrival, agree that Thomas treated him with curious lack of courtesy, forgetful that he was his guest as well as his commanding general. Just why has never been explained, but it is certain that throughout the war there was reserve between the two; for neither ever learned truly to comprehend the other, and with Thomas there was a marked absence of the cordial feeling which was so strikingly in evidence with Sheridan and Sherman. While no one ever saw in Thomas a trace of envious rivalry with Grant, his coolness was transmuted into hot controversy by his partisans in the great Army of the Cumberland.

A swift change came with Grant's arrival. That night, says Horace Porter, who saw him then for the first time, after sitting absolutely silent for a while listening attentively to what the others said and following on the map the disposition of the troops, he straightened in his chair and began firing questions at his new subordinates, pertinent, incisive, comprehensive, showing that he had in mind not only the prompt lifting of the embargo on supplies, — "opening up the cracker line," he called it, — but a speedy move against the enemy. He was as always eager to push on. Then turning to a table he wrote dispatches for an hour — the first to Halleck: "Have just arrived; I will write to-morrow. Please approve order placing Sherman in command of Department of the Tennessee, with headquarters in the field." The next day, with Thomas and "Baldy" Smith, he viewed the Union lines, and ordered Smith to set at once upon the work of opening communication with supplies.

That night again he wrote dispatches with his own hand, as was his way. "His work was performed swiftly and uninterruptedly, but without any marked display of nervous energy," writes Porter. "His thoughts flowed as freely from his mind as the ink from his pen; he was never at a loss for an expression, and seldom interlined a word or made a material correction. He sat with his head bent low over the table, and when he had occasion . . . he would glide rapidly across the room without straightening himself and return to his seat with his body still bent over at about the same angle at which he had been sitting. . . . Looking over the dispatches I found that he was ordering up Sherman's entire force from Corinth to within supporting distance, and was informing Halleck of the dispositions decided upon for the opening of a line of supplies and assuring him that everything possible would be done for the relief of Burnside in East Tennessee . . . the taking of vigorous and comprehensive steps in every direction throughout his new and extensive command. . . . I cannot dwell too forcibly on the deep impression made . . . by the exhibition . . . of his singular mental powers and his rare military qualities. . . . Hardly any one was prepared to find one who had the grasp, the promptness of decision, and the general administrative capacity which he displayed at the very start as commander of an extensive military division in which many complicated problems were presented for immediate solution."[1]

When Grant appeared in Chattanooga the town was in almost as desperate a case as Vicksburg just before its fall. Bragg, with superior forces encamped on Lookout Mountain and Missionary Ridge only three miles away, could calmly contemplate the starving enemy below. Burnside, with twenty-five thousand men in siege at Knoxville one hundred miles

[1] *Campaigning with Grant,* p. 7.

to the northeast, was also in sore straits and calling vainly for relief. Within five days, as the result of swift and daring moves by "Baldy" Smith and others which Grant hastened, the "cracker line" was open; there was no further danger of starvation, surrender, or retreat, and Grant and Thomas were in position to hold the town all winter or till reinforcements should arrive. Shortly Sherman was there from Mississippi and Hooker from the East.

And now there broke for Grant the most resplendent day of his career. He had no thought of holding Chattanooga with hostile guns surveying him complacently from neighboring heights. He would wait only till the forces he had summoned should arrive. Then he would leap out at the enemy. As early as October 28 he wired to Halleck: "The question of supplies may now be regarded as settled. If the rebels give us one week more I think all danger of losing territory now held by us will have passed away, and preparations may commence for offensive operations." Sherman, having led his army three hundred miles through a rough, hostile country, rode into Chattanooga on November 15, and one week later, on November 23, Grant began the three days' fight of Chattanooga, the most completely planned of all his battles, a feat unmarred in its perfection and as a spectacle unequaled in the history of war.

The secrecy and skill of the preliminary strategy, the military panorama, with its sublime scenic setting unrolled before the eyes of Grant and Thomas, posted on Orchard Knob, watching their armies in glittering pageant march to undimmed success, the glimpse of Hooker and his men fighting "above the clouds" on Lookout Mountain, the marvelous charge of Sheridan and Wood with nearly twenty thousand bayonets up to the very top of Missionary Ridge, mowing the enemy like wheat, the panic-stricken flight of Bragg's astonished troops, the frantic joy and tumult of the victorious Union army as Grant rode down the lines, blend in a battle picture with no parallel.

The three days' engagement is known as "Chattanooga," the third day's fight as "Missionary Ridge," in memory of the culminating glory of a deed which has been called "one of the greatest miracles in military history." Dana, who stood with Grant and Thomas witnessing the charge, wrote the next day: "No man who climbs the ascent by any of the roads that wind above its front can believe that eighteen thousand men were moved up its broken and crumbling base unless it was his fortune to witness the deed; it seems as awful as a visible interposition of God. Neither Grant nor Thomas intended it. Their orders were to carry the rifle-pits along the base of the ridge and capture their occupants; but when this was accomplished, the unaccountable spirit of the troops bore them bodily up those implacable steeps, over the bristling rifle-pits on the crest and the thirty cannon enfilading every gully. The order to storm appears to have been given simultaneously by Generals Sheridan and Wood, because the men were not to be held back.''

It was the only battle of the war in which its four great figures, Grant, Thomas, Sherman, and Sheridan, were engaged together. Knoxville was saved at Chattanooga as Corinth was fought at Shiloh, Burnside was liberated from his pen, and East Tennessee was cleared. On December 8 Lincoln sent Grant this telegram: "Understanding that your lodgment at Chattanooga and Knoxville is now secure, I wish to tender you, and all under your command, my more than thanks, my profoundest gratitude, for the skill, courage, and perseverance with which you and they, over so great difficulties, have effected that important object. God bless you all!"

Grant, starting with Paducah, had moved resistlessly, slowly at first, but gathering momentum as he advanced, pressing the rebel forces steadily toward Richmond. A sense of the inevitable was beginning to pervade the North, and to be felt abroad. "Thank Heaven! the 'coming man,' for whom we have so long been waiting, seems really to have come," wrote Motley from Vienna. ". . . Ulysses Grant is *at least* equal to any general now living in any part of the world, and by far the first that our war has produced on either side."[1] A German writer spoke of Chattanooga as "an action which both for scientific combination and bravery of execution is equal to any battle of modern times from the days of Frederick the Great downwards."

It happened that the country heard of Missionary Ridge on the last Thursday in November — Thanksgiving Day — just as it heard of Vicksburg on July 4. It was the week after the Address at Gettysburg. Within a fortnight a bill was introduced in Congress reviving the grade of Lieutenant-General, a title which Washington had borne. Before the winter ended, the bill had passed by great majorities and Lincoln had given Grant the rank — making him General-in-Chief of all the armies of the United States.

[1] *The Correspondence of John Lothrop Motley*, vol. II, p. 146.

CHAPTER XVIII

LIEUTENANT–GENERAL

IT was Washburne, his earliest influential friend, and at times almost his sole defender, who first proposed that Grant be made Lieutenant-General, hardly waiting for Congress to assemble before he introduced the bill. When Grant learned what was doing he wrote at once from Chattanooga: —

"I feel under many obligations to you for the interest you have taken in my welfare. But recollect that I have been highly honored already by the Government, and do not ask or feel that I deserve anything more in the shape of honors or promotions. A success over the enemy is what I crave above everything else, and desire to hold such an influence over those under my command as to enable me to use them to the best advantage to secure this end." [1]

Lincoln was worried, lest at last "the man on horseback" might have come, who with an army at his call would seize the reins of power; for at that time Grant was the people's hero while Lincoln was in rather poor repute by reason of the scanty harvest of his other generals, and an election was at hand momentous in its possibilities. But Lincoln was not

[1] *Letters to a Friend*, p. 32.

kept long in suspense. "I am not a candidate for any office," Grant wrote his father. "All I want is to be left alone to fight this war out." To a friend who wrote him that he had it in his power to be the next President he replied: "This is the last thing in the world I desire. I would regard such a consummation as highly unfortunate for myself if not for the country. Through Providence I have attained to more than I ever hoped, and, with the position I now hold in the regular army, if allowed to retain it, will be more than satisfied."[1] When he went to St. Louis from Nashville, where he made his headquarters that winter, he stayed with his old humble friends, Mr. and Mrs. Boggs, and took them in a street-car to the theater.

Lincoln, who longed for reëlection, not only on his own account, but because he felt that any change just then would mean disaster to the Union cause, heard these things gladly. They dissipated his unrest.

Grant would have followed Missionary Ridge by throwing his army from Chattanooga to Mobile, thus clearing Georgia of the rebel troops, cutting the South again as he had cut it at the Mississippi, seizing a port through which supplies reached the Confederacy, and tightening the pressure upon Lee. But Washington did not approve, and consequently he

[1] Richardson, *Personal History*, p. 374.

remained at Nashville through the winter getting his army ready for a spring campaign, just where he did not know until after he was named Lieutenant-General and went to Washington for his commission. It was then that he determined to take command in person of the armies in Virginia and dispose his other armies so as best to conquer Lee. But before he left for Washington he did a gracious and great-hearted thing. He wrote to Sherman a letter which will live as long as he and Sherman are remembered: —

"Whilst I have been eminently successful in this war, in at least gaining the confidence of the public, no one feels more than I how much of this success is due to the energy, skill, and the harmonious putting forth of that energy and skill, of those whom it has been my good fortune to have occupying subordinate positions under me. There are many officers to whom these remarks are applicable to a greater or less degree, proportionate to their ability as soldiers; but what I want is to express my thanks to you and McPherson as the men to whom, above all others, I feel indebted for whatever I have had of success. How far your advice and assistance have been of help to me, you know; how far your execution of whatever has been given to you to do entitles you to the reward I am receiving, you can not know as well as I."

Nor will men forget Sherman's fine reply: —

" You do McPherson and myself too much honor. At Belmont you manifested your traits, neither of us being near. At Donelson, also, you illustrated your whole character. I was not near, and McPherson in too subordinate a capacity to influence you. . . . I believe you are as brave, patriotic, and just as the great prototype, Washington; as unselfish, kind-hearted, and honest as a man should be; but the chief characteristic is the simple faith in success you have always manifested, which I can liken to nothing else than the faith the Christian has in the Saviour. This faith gave you victory at Shiloh and Vicksburg. Also, when you have completed your best preparations, you go into battle without hesitation, as at Chattanooga, — no doubts, no reserve, — and I tell you, it was this that made us act with confidence. I knew wherever I was, that you thought of me; and if I got in a tight place you would come — if alive. My only points of doubt were in your knowledge of grand strategy, and of books of science and history; but I confess your common sense seems to have supplied all these."

"Don't stay in Washington," cried Sherman. "Come West; take to yourself the whole Mississippi Valley. Let us make it dead sure. . . . Here lies the seat of coming empire; and from the West, when our task is done, we will make short work of Charleston and Richmond, and the impoverished coast of the Atlantic."

But Sherman could not have his way. Grant would have stayed with his old army which he had organized and knew; but he was quick to see in Washington that he must take himself the task of facing Lee, with self-taught strategists near by ready to trip his feet in their entangling schemes.

His coming to the Capital, which he had never seen, was commonplace — almost too typical of his plain habit — unostentatious and unknown. Waiting his turn to register at the hotel, the clerk, who sized him up for what he seemed, assigned him to a top-floor room and gasped with incredulity when he saw him write, "U. S. Grant and son — Galena, Illinois." He went with Cameron to the White House unannounced, found Lincoln holding a reception and would have run away if Seward had not taken him in tow. When he was handed his commission the next day by Lincoln and read the few words he had written in response to Lincoln's little speech, he was hardly audible and fumbled with his paper like a boy, but it was noticed that he had not taken Lincoln's diplomatic hint to mollify the feelings of the Eastern troops by saying something to ingratiate himself with the new armies placed in his command.

Pictures have come down to us of his appearance at this time which have peculiar interest in the glimpse they give of his impress upon contemporaries of quite different types. Richard Henry Dana, a Boston scholar of the Brahmin class, happened upon him in the Willard lobby, and thus wrote: "A short, round-shouldered man, in a very tarnished major-general's uniform came up. . . . He had no gait, no station, no manner, rough, light-brown whiskers, a blue eye, and rather a scrubby look withal. A crowd formed around him; men looked, stared at him, as if they were taking his likeness, and two generals were introduced. Still, I could not get his name. It was not Hooker. Who could it be? . . . I inquired of the bookkeeper. 'That is General Grant.' I joined the starers. I saw that the ordinary, scrubby-looking man, with a slightly seedy look, as if he was out of office and on half-pay and nothing to do but hang around the entry of Willard's, cigar in mouth, had a clear blue eye, and a look of resolution, as if he could not be trifled with, and an entire indifference to the crowd about him. Straight nose, too. Still, to see him talking and smoking in the lower entry of Willard's, in that crowd, in such times, — the generalissimo of our armies, on whom the destiny of the empire seemed to hang! . . . He gets over the ground queerly. He does not march, nor quite walk, but pitches along as if the next step would bring him on his nose. But his face looks firm and hard, and his eye is clear and resolute, and he is certainly natural, and clear of all appearance of self-consciousness."[1]

Beside this we can set the portraiture of Horace Porter and Adam Badeau, who had lately joined Grant's staff: Porter describes him as slightly stooped, five feet, eight inches in height, weighing only a hundred and thirty-five pounds, modest and gentle in his manner; face not perfectly symmetrical, the left eye a little lower than the right; his brow, high, broad, and rather square creased with horizontal wrinkles which helped to emphasize the somewhat careworn look, though not an index to his nature which was always buoyant. "His voice was exceedingly musical and one of the clearest in sound and most distinct in utterance that I have ever heard. It had a singular power of penetration, and sentences spoken by him in an ordinary tone in camp could be heard at a distance which was surprising." His gait in walking was decidedly unmilitary; he never carried his body erect; never kept step to the airs played by the bands; was often slow in his movements, "but when roused to activity quick in every motion and worked with marvelous rapidity."[2]

Badeau tells of his clear but not penetrating eye, his

[1] Rhodes, vol. IV, p. 438.   [2] *Campaigning with Grant*, p. 13.

heavy jaw, his sharply cut mouth, "which had a singular power of expressing sweetness and strength combined, and which at times became set with a rigidity like that of fate itself." The habitual expression of his face was so quiet as to be almost incomprehensible; his manner plain, placid, almost meek; "in great moments disclosed to those who knew him well immense but still suppressed intensity." In utterance he was slow and sometimes embarrassed, but the well-chosen words never left the slightest doubt of what he meant to say. "The whole man was a marvel of simplicity, a powerful nature, veiled in the plainest possible exterior. He discussed the most ordinary themes with apparent interest, and turned from them in the same quiet tones, and without a shade of difference in his manner, to decisions that involved the fate of armies, his own fame or the life of the republic. . . ." But unexpectedly and in the most casual way he would utter the clearest ideas in the tersest form; "announcing judgments made apparently at the moment, which he never reversed — enunciating opinions or declaring plans of the most important character in the plainest words and commonest manner, as if great things and small were to him of equal moment, or as if it cost him no more to command armies than to direct a farm, to capture cities than to drive a horse. In battle, however, the sphinx awoke . . . the utterance was prompt, the ideas were rapid, the judgment was decisive, the words were those of command. The whole man became intense as it were with a white heat."[1]

Here we catch a composite portrait of the new chief of the Union forces in command of more than half a million men, who, setting out upon the campaign which he meant should crush the rebel armies and bring an end to war, bore with him to the front these parting words from Lincoln: —

"I wish to express in this way my entire satisfaction with what you have done up to this time, so far as I understand it. The particulars of your plans I neither know nor seek to know. You are vigilant and self-reliant; and, pleased with this, I wish not to obtrude any constraints or restraints upon you. While I am very anxious that any great disaster or capture of our men in great numbers shall be avoided, I know these points are less likely to escape your attention than they would be mine. If there is anything wanting which is within my power to give, do not fail to let me know. And now, with a brave army and a just cause, may God sustain you."

"It shall be my earnest endeavor that you and the country shall not be disappointed," was Grant's reply. ". . . Should my success be less than I desire

[1] *Military History of Ulysses S. Grant*, vol. II, p. 20.

or expect, the least I can say is, the fault is not with you."

Lincoln had already told Grant in their first interview that all he wanted or had ever wanted was "one who would take the responsibility and act, and call on him for all the assistance needed"; and Grant had said that he would do the best he could with what he had at hand and would not annoy him or the War Department more than could be helped.

It was like Grant that through the war he did not once complain to Lincoln or appeal to Washington, even when Halleck hazed him after Donelson and Shiloh; and Lincoln, who wrote often quaintly to his other generals, regarded with complacency one whom he could let alone. McClellan, Buell, Hooker had notes of admonition in which reproof was deftly clothed in homely phrase; but Grant had none. Lincoln told Buell he did not understand "why we cannot march as the enemy marches, live as he lives, and fight as he fights, unless we admit the inferiority of our troops and of our generals."[1] He tarnished Hooker's joy in being placed at the head of the Army of the Potomac with a memorable letter chiding him for thwarting Burnside and telling him he thought it best "for you to know there are some things in regard to which I am not quite satisfied with you."[2]

[1] Lincoln's *Comptete Works*, vol. II, p. 248.   [2] *Ibid.*, p. 306.

When McClellan wired that his horses were sore-tongued and fatigued, Lincoln wired back, "Will you pardon me for asking what the horses of your army have done since Antietam that fatigues anything?" [1].

These are mild samples of rebukes which Lincoln penned. One cannot see him writing thus to Grant.

[1] Lincoln's *Complete Works*, vol. II, p. 250.

CHAPTER XIX

THE CLINCH WITH LEE

REBELLION was in flower when Grant was put in chief command. In spite of his successes in the West and those gained by the gallant little navy, ten Southern States were in revolt — nine million people inhabiting eight hundred thousand miles — an empire in extent and population, rich in resources and the world's respect. Europe still looked to see the South prevail; the South still thought itself impregnable. After three years of war she seemed no nearer conquest than at first except to those who saw in true perspective just what had been done west of the Alleghanies and along the coast.

The Northern forces held the Mississippi strongly garrisoned from St. Louis to its mouth. The territory west of this below the Arkansas was still in rebel hands except New Orleans, a few other points in southern Louisiana, and a small post in Texas near the mouth of the Rio Grande. The Western armies having cleared the border States of Tennessee, Kentucky, and Missouri, except for irresponsible guerrilla bands, held all the railroad lines from Memphis as far east as Chattanooga and then the Tennessee and Holsten Rivers to the Alleghanies. Western

Virginia had been transformed into a loyal State. The Northern forces occupied a narrow segment of eastern Virginia, fringing its northern border to the Rapidan. With garrisons at Norfolk and at Fort Monroe, they held the entrance to the James; and there were federal footholds at other points along the coast. The motley wooden navy had maintained a fairly good blockade — good enough to throttle cotton exports from the South and starve the mills and laborers of Lancashire.

The South, though worn by war, was full of spunk. Her people, trusting to their press, looked upon Grant's achievements in the West as, at the worst, sporadic Northern victories; while in the East, which to their thinking was the real seat of the war, they could see nothing but unmarred success. They had Manassas, Fredericksburg, Chancellorsville to brag about, — unquestioned triumphs, — while in their eyes Gettysburg and Antietam were merely incidental to protecting Richmond and preventing the invasion of the South; Gettysburg was a rebuff, not a significant defeat; Antietam (Sharpsburg, as they termed it) was a draw; because Meade and McClellan were content to let the Army of the Potomac rest upon its victories, without annihilating Lee or chasing him back home, the South called both engagements indecisive; it still thought Lee invincible.

Against this unity of spirit in the South were set a Northern public honeycombed with rebel sympathy, a commerce cankered with disloyalty, a party organized against the conduct of the government and Lincoln's handling of the war, a propaganda of distrust spread by disgruntled politicians and censorious writers disclosing ugly phases of an irresponsible press-fed democracy. Grant had no holiday in sight when he came East.

He at once put Sherman at the head of the Division of the Mississippi, and on the 17th of March announced that his own headquarters would be in the field and for the present with the Army of the Potomac, then under Meade's command. Meade nobly offered to give up the place which he had held since Gettysburg, nine months before, thinking that Grant might want a friend like Sherman near at hand, and said that for himself wherever ordered he would do his best, that in the work before them the feeling or wishes of no one person should interfere with picking the right men. Grant did not demand the sacrifice. "This incident," he says, "gave me even a more favorable opinion of Meade than did his great victory at Gettysburg the July before. It is men who wait to be selected, and not those who seek, from whom we may always expect the most efficient service."

So Meade stayed where he was; but it was not a

happy case no matter how hard each might try to
have it so. Meade, who for months had held an independent and responsible command, looking ahead to
crown the work begun at Gettysburg by crushing
Lee, was now thrown into the shade of one he scarcely
knew and in such close proximity that, however
tactfully the thing was handled, nothing could hide
from his subordinates the ever-present fact that he
was a subordinate himself. As for Grant, he found
himself in daily contact with a proud army to which
he was a stranger, whose officers and men through
years of trial in camp and field were grown attached
to their own generals. Grant's orders couched in
general terms, trickling through Meade, must lose
significance, and sometimes, acting of necessity in
haste, he had to issue them direct, greatly to Meade's
chagrin. Except that both were single-minded, there
were few points of likeness between these two.
"Sedgwick and Meade," said Grant, "were men so
finely formed that if ordered to resign their generals'
commissions and take service as corporals, they would
have fallen into the ranks without a murmur." So,
too, would Grant, and so would Thomas, but it is
hard to think of many more; Sherman would have
fallen in, but with profanity. Meade was of delicate grain and sensitive, high-spirited, confiding disappointments only to his wife. "You may look now

for the Army of the Potomac putting laurels on the brow of another," he writes her; and at the end, when Sheridan, not he, was made Lieutenant-General by Grant, "we must find consolation in the consciousness . . . that it is the cruelest and meanest act of injustice." [1] But from the public Meade, while in service, hid his hurt, and Grant has testified that Meade would take another's plan, even when he did not approve it, and carry it out as zealously as if it were his own. Yet Meade shrank from the responsibility of supreme command; in full authority he would hesitate. After Gettysburg, when Lincoln wrote that if Meade would attack Lee "on a field no more than equal for us, the honor will be his if he succeeds and the blame may be mine if he fails," Meade replied as it is unthinkable that Grant would have responded in like case: "It has been my intention to attack the enemy, if I can find him on a field no more than equal for us, and I have only delayed doing so from the difficulty of ascertaining his exact position, and the fear that in endeavoring to do so my communications might be jeopardized." [2]

And Meade had other traits which throw needed light upon the history of the last year of war. His violent temper stirred the dislike of his subordinates

---

[1] *Life and Letters of George Gordon Meade*, vol. II, p. 300.
[2] *Union Portraits*, p. 76.

and in a measure their distrust. Dana writes that no man, no matter what his business or his service, approached him without insult, in one way or another, and his own staff officers did not dare speak to him unless first spoken to. In action on the field and under nervous strain, especially when things went wrong, he was irascible up to the very edge of madness.

It has been said that for the North the war began with Gettysburg and Vicksburg. Till then the time had been spent in training generals and armies and picking the right man to lead. Campaigns had been haphazard, a summer's fighting and a winter's rest, a victory or defeat and then withdrawal to recuperate. There had been no comprehensive military plan, no fixed and certain aim. Grant said the Army of the Potomac had never been fought through to a finish, and with the constant meddling from Washington, induced sometimes by politics, he might have said the same of other armies, even of his own except near Vicksburg and at Chattanooga; but he steadily had this in mind: that there could be no stable peace until the military power of the rebellion was entirely broken. In his report of the last year's operations he presents the military problem which he faced when he assumed command: —

"From an early period in the rebellion," he says,

"I had been impressed with the idea that active and continuous operations of all the troops that could be brought into the field, regardless of season and weather, were necessary to a speedy termination of the war. The resources of the enemy, and his numerical strength, were far inferior to ours; but, as an offset to this, we had a vast territory, with a population hostile to the Government, to garrison, and long lines of river and railroad communications to protect, to enable us to supply the operating armies.

"The armies in the East and West acted independently, and without concert, like a balky team, — no two ever pulling together, — enabling the enemy to use to great advantage his interior lines of communication for transporting troops from East to West, reinforcing the army most vigorously pressed, and to furlough large numbers, during seasons of inactivity on our part, to go to their homes and do the work of providing for the support of their armies. It was a question whether our numerical strength and resources were not more than balanced by these disadvantages and the enemy's superior position."

He determined, "first, to use the greatest number of troops practicable against the armed force of the enemy, preventing him from using the same force at different seasons against first one and then another of our armies, and the possibility of repose for refitting and producing necessary supplies for carrying on resistance; second, to hammer continuously against the armed force of the enemy and his resources, until, by mere attrition, if in no other way, there should be nothing left to him but an equal submission with the loyal sections of our common country to the Constitution and laws of the land."

The task Grant set himself was to destroy Lee's army. That done rebellion must disintegrate. With Lee eliminated the Confederacy would crumble of itself; there could be no formidable fighting elsewhere — only guerrilla raids. To capture Richmond was important because it was Lee's base. To occupy the Southern Capital had sentimental value, but in Grant's plan it was subordinate — not the main purpose of his strategy. "On to Richmond!" had been the Northern cry till Grant's arrival. After he came the aim was to get Lee. "Lee's army will be your objective point," he ordered Meade. "Wherever Lee goes, you will go also." When once Lee should capitulate, Richmond must also fall. With Lee at large his tent was the real heart of the Confederacy.

Butler at Fort Monroe commanded, with the Army of the James, Richmond's main artery from the sea. Grant gave him a spectacular detail — to seize the Southern Capital and cut off Lee's supplies. Opposed

to him was Beauregard. A small force of 12,000 men
were strung along the banks of the Potomac protecting Washington, guarding against a possible invasion
of the North. Sigel was in command; opposed to him
was Breckinridge. Sherman in command of Grant's
old armies, with Thomas, Schofield, Hooker, Howard,
and Slocum under him, was at Chattanooga ready to
lead them against Johnston, who at Dalton, just
across the Georgia line, had an army of 100,000
guarding the railway center at Atlanta one hundred
miles below. Banks held New Orleans, commanding
the Department of the Gulf. The remaining Union
forces were scattered among many garrisons.

Grant's purpose, in a word, was to crush Lee and
Johnston and smother the Confederacy, which involved the capture of Richmond and Atlanta and
shutting off the few remaining breathing-places on the
coast through which the South could touch the sea —
Mobile, Savannah, Charleston, and Wilmington, protected by Fort Fisher. To Sherman he gave orders
"to move against Johnston's army, to break it up
and to get into the interior of the enemy's country as
far as you can, inflicting all the damage you can
against their war resources." Banks was to seize
Mobile; but Banks was busy on expeditions in
Arkansas and Louisiana inspired from Washington,
and missed his opportunity. Grant's first idea for

Sherman was to slice Georgia from Atlanta after whipping Johnston's army, and join Banks at Mobile, but this was subsequently changed by force of circumstance and Sherman's genius, and Sherman mowed his swath through to Savannah and then north through both Carolinas, whence he could press Lee upwards from the south while Grant pressed down upon the other side. "I do not propose," Grant wrote him, "to lay down for you a plan of campaign, but simply lay down the work it is desirable to have done and leave you free to execute it in your own way."

For the first time since Sumter the keys controlling all the Northern armies were in a single hand, and when everything was ready for the word, Grant touched them all at once. From Culpeper, where he had pitched his tent, the signal flashed for every general to move on the 4th of May; Meade against Lee, Sherman against Johnston, Butler toward Richmond, Sigel along the Shenandoah. From that time till the end, Grant kept his finger on the pulse of all his armies. While he was hammering away at Lee and Richmond, he was sending daily orders also to every captain under his command. No other general since war was known had, while himself in action on the field, handled the maneuvers of so many armies scattered over so broad a territory and centered toward a common aim. Lee was responsible only for his own command. Davis in Richmond, a West Point graduate who had seen service in the war with Mexico, dispósed the other Southern armies in the field.

Now came a cruel test of fiber, such as few other men were ever called upon to face. With seasoned armies at his call, ample in size and skillfully disposed, Grant had prepared for every physical contingency — supplies, equipment, all the necessities for active service, a commonplace of war in which he was himself adept and for which he now had at his side his own superior in Quartermaster-General Rufus Ingalls; he had unusual knowledge of the field of operations gained from a study of the late campaigns, together with his Indian instinct for topography, a sixth sense of his which some called genius; for all agree that at a glance he used to master a strange map or catch the guiding military features of a chartless and bewildering country. But with all his foresight he had not quite foreseen the quality of Lee. It was Lee's vigilance which upset his first attempt to hammer down the Southern forces by assault.

Moving his army quickly across the Rapidan on the morning of the 4th of May, Grant had thought to clear the tragic tangle of the Wilderness with its sad memories of Chancellorsville, before he fell upon the enemy, but Lee, who had once fought with Hooker on that very ground successfully against great odds, took the chance of meeting Grant's superior forces on a field where he had already demonstrated that victory did not necessarily attend the heaviest battalions.

The two days' battle of the Wilderness with its ghastly toll which Lee precipitated on the 5th of May brought home to Grant the horror of the path in which his feet were set. There were hours in which defeat was hovering close; disaster had never pressed him quite so hard; and with it comes a human touch which we would not forego.

Rawlins and Bowers both say that when the first news reached him from the right indicating complete repulse and officer after officer rode up with new details, Grant, realizing that he faced the crisis of his life, still gave his orders calmly and coherently without a sign of undue tension; but when all proper measures had been taken and there was nothing else to do but wait, he "went into his tent and throwing himself face downward on his cot gave way to the greatest emotion," without uttering a word. He was stirred to the very depths of his soul. Not till it was plain that the enemy was not pressing his advantage did he entirely recover his composure.[1]

[1] *Under the Old Flag*, vol. i, p. 390.

Now we come to a revealing and dramatic episode in Grant's career. Lee with his hard-fought forces for the third time lay near the Rapidan facing a hostile army on its Southern side. He had twice seen the Army of the Potomac, once under Pope, once under Hooker, pushed back across the stream, when they had thought to march toward Richmond, but now he saw an enemy which had failed to break his lines crouched for another spring. Grant in the opening encounter of his Virginia campaign, disastrous though it may have seemed, had forced his army forward and had held his advance. His loss was nearly 18,000 men, but Lee, considering his inferior strength, had suffered more. The next night Grant was headed south toward Richmond. It is told that, as he rode in silence in the dusk along his shattered ranks, his worn and wounded soldiers saw which way his face was turned and rose up from the ground with cheers. His mute assurance of immediate advance, after their long acquaintance with procrastination and retreat, inspired them with a trust in their new chief which could not afterwards be shaken. As for Grant it was a disclosure of his soul. This reticent, shy, tender-hearted citizen, who shrank from giving others pain and sickened at the sight of blood, had without faltering kept his feet upon the road which led through slaughter. He felt that in no other way could the

Confederacy be quickly overthrown; it was the way of mercy in the end.

"I shall take no backward steps," Grant wrote to Halleck. For thirty days he hammered at the enemy, rained heavy blows upon Lee's head; hurled his men frequently against Lee's weakening lines, engaged in daily skirmishes, defied the rules and precedents of war by frontal charges on the enemy intrenched, costing both armies dearly in the toll of wounds and death. There had been nothing like it in the world before. Lee was forced backwards step by step on Richmond, returning blow for blow, the two contending armies leaving a trail of carnage from the Wilderness through Spotsylvania Court-House, with its five days' fighting and its "bloody angle" at the salient, the crossing of the North Anna River to Cold Harbor, where, with the spires of Richmond almost in sight, the final stand was made, and where Grant was repulsed with heavy loss after a frontal charge which he admitted later that he ought never to have ordered, but which blazes like a beacon disclosing the unflinching courage of the Northern volunteer, just as Pickett's hopeless charge ordered by Lee at Gettysburg still enshrines Southern gallantry. Porter has told how, on the night before the charge, while walking among the troops he saw the soldiers pinning slips upon their blouses, on which each had written his name and home so that his body the next night might not lie unidentified.

"I propose to fight it out on this line if it takes all summer," Grant had written Halleck from Spotsylvania, but at Cold Harbor his gallant army had their fill. After the Wilderness, Lee had not once accepted battle in the open, but had sought intrenched positions to withstand attack. It was a new and strange experience for him. This master in the artistry of war now found his match in one less skilled in tactics but stronger in offense and in tenacity. No matter how he played his tempered sword, no matter how he turned and stepped with faultless strategy, there stood Grant facing him like a decree of Fate.

At last both Lee and Grant viewing their haggard armies were content to change the character of the campaign. After Cold Harbor they never fought each other face to face. Grant had not been able, as he had hoped, to crush Lee north of Richmond, but that was only one link of his plan. The second was to throw his army to the south side of the James, seize Petersburg, which controlled the approach to the Confederate Capital twenty miles below, besiege Lee in Richmond or follow him south if he should retreat. Therefore, on the 5th of June, while the dead and wounded at Cold Harbor still lay on the ground, he wrote Halleck that he should throw his army across the James as soon as possible, cut off all sources of supply, and press the enemy from the other side. Swiftly and silently he marched around Lee's flank for fifty miles, to the southeast, eluding him completely, and on the 15th of June, while Lee was guessing where the enemy might be, Grant wired to Washington that the Army of the Potomac would cross the James on pontoon bridges the next day, and that he would have Petersburg secured if possible before Lee got there in much force. Lincoln wired back: "I begin to see it; you will succeed. God bless you all."

CHAPTER XX

FROM COLD HARBOR TO PETERSBURG

FROM the Wilderness to Cold Harbor, Grant had hammered Lee for seventy miles and had lost over 40,000 men, of whom 10,000 had been killed. In each engagement his losses had been fairly matched by Lee's, except at Cold Harbor; and the net benefit had been with Grant. The Army of the Potomac had been sadly shattered, but Lee's army had been shattered too, and Lee had fewer men to spare. Yet it had cost Grant some repute in Washington. While Spotsylvania was in fight, Lincoln told a crowd of serenaders, "I know that General Grant has not been jostled in his purposes, that he has made all his points, and to-day he is on the line as he purposed when he moved his armies." "He has the grip of a bull-dog," he told Frank Carpenter the painter; "when he once gets his teeth in nothing can shake him off"; and two weeks later he endorsed Grant's declaration that "everything looks exceedingly favorable for us." It was after Cold Harbor that he wrote: "I begin to see it; you will succeed." But others had less confidence than Lincoln. "All under God depends on Grant," wrote Chase. "So far he has achieved very little and that little has cost beyond computation." Grimes, of Iowa, wrote: "He has lost a vast number of men and is compelled to abandon his attempt to capture Richmond on the north side, and cross the James River. The question is asked significantly, why did he not take his army south of the James River at once and thus save seventy-five thousand men?"

Grimes had not fully fathomed the significance of Grant's campaign; and those who criticized him, because McClellan had maneuvered nearer Richmond without much fighting and without much loss, failed to remember that McClellan's aim was to invest the rebel Capital, while Grant primarily was after Lee, not Richmond; that McClellan had abandoned all he gained, while Grant held his advance, and that McClellan, having neared his goal with little damage to the enemy, fell back, while Grant, contesting every hard-fought step, had chopped deep into Lee's defense. If Grant had gone toward Richmond first by sailing up the James, he would have found Lee fixed in the Confederate Capital in the best possible position to withstand a siege against far greater numbers, while rebel troops would have been free to roam the State and threaten Washington. There would have been many months of siege and fighting. The easier-seeming way would have been harder in the end.[1]

Had it not been for blunders by the Army of the James, Grant, when he crossed the river, would have found Butler's troops in Petersburg to welcome him, thus sparing him ten months of siege, and Lee with Richmond might have fallen speedily, for Petersburg, twenty miles to the southeast, a railroad center on the Appomattox, was the real key to Richmond. When in the first week of May, Butler had been sent up the James, the plan was that he should take Petersburg and batter at the gates of the Confederate Capital, while Grant kept Lee engaged, or else by threatening it divert Lee from Grant's front; but Butler, ignoring

[1] I remember asking the General why he had not invested Richmond, as he had invested Vicksburg and starved out Lee. "Such a movement," said the General, "would have involved moving my army from the Rapidan to Lynchburg. I considered the plan with great care before I made the Wilderness move. I thought of massing the Army of the Potomac in movable columns, giving the men twelve days' rations, and throwing myself between Lee and his communications. If I had made this movement successfully — if I had been as fortunate as I was when I threw my army between Pemberton and Joe Johnston — the war would have been over a year sooner. I am not sure that it was not the best thing to have done; it certainly was the plan I should have preferred. If I had failed, however, it would have been very serious for the country and I did not dare take the risk. . . . If it had been six months later, when I had the army in hand, and knew what a splendid army it was, and what officers and men were capable of doing, and I could have had Sherman and Sheridan to assist in the movement, I would not have hesitated for a moment." (Young, vol. II, p. 307.)

Petersburg, tried to seize Drewry's Bluff, under the very eyes of Richmond, and beaten back with heavy loss, withdrew into the curious pocket of the James known as Bermuda Hundred, where he was "bottled up" safe from attack, but worthless as a part of Grant's command.

He could now have taken Petersburg with ease and held it pending Grant's arrival, for the place was guarded by a feeble garrison; but he assigned the task to "Baldy" Smith, lately transferred to his command, who after an assault on June 15, carrying the outside works, withdrew without pursuing his advantage for reasons never adequately explained, and when the next day he was ready for a second trial, Beauregard had filled the town with rebel troops.

When Grant approached the town he found it strongly garrisoned. The place, which should have welcomed him had Butler's army done their part, repulsed three days' assault; he lost 10,000 men. His army were disheartened because they did not enter on the 15th as they had hoped. After Cold Harbor and the crossing of the James, they had thought to have a respite from fighting against odds; but here they found themselves at once in the old desperate game. Lee, having learned at last where Grant had reappeared, had brought his army up to Petersburg,

and on June 18 Grant gave directions that there
should be no more assaults.

From that day till the spring of 1865, Meade's
army lay in front of Petersburg holding the town in
siege, sending out expeditions, recuperating broken
regiments, hardening raw recruits, many of them
bounty-lured, keeping Lee occupied. Grant set up
his tent at City Point, the junction of the Appomattox and the James.

The next two months were gloomy in the North.
They have been called the darkest of the war. Election was near at hand. Lincoln had been renominated
on June 6, with Andrew Johnson for his mate; Frémont had been named by a little group of radical
Republicans who thought that Lincoln was too slow;
it was known that McClellan would be nominated
by the Democrats. It seemed as if the Union armies
everywhere were held in check, while early in July
Lee had sent Early flying through Maryland raiding the country up to the very edge of Washington
and throwing the Capital into a panic, Grant un-
suspicious of the move till he began to get inquiries
from Stanton, followed by frantic calls for help.

While Grant was fighting through to Petersburg,
Sherman in the West was forcing Johnston back
upon Atlanta, dislodging him from one intrenched
position and another, while he conducted a retreat as

masterly as Lee's before Grant, and Davis having foolishly put Hood in Johnston's place because of failure to arrest the enemy's advance, Sherman, after pounding Hood and crippling him in the last week of July, remained in check before Atlanta for a month.

Lincoln, at the request of Congress, fixed a day of humiliation and prayer, but pending that he justified his faith by works in issuing on July 18 a call for 500,000 volunteers, 200,000 more than Grant himself at the same time was asking for, and on the 17th of August, as if in response to Northern clamor that Grant be superseded by McClellan, he was wiring Grant, who had expressed unwillingness to break his hold: "Neither am I willing. Hold on with a bull-dog grip and chew and choke as much as possible."

It was on August 23 that Lincoln penned and signed the memorandum which he had each member of his Cabinet endorse unread and which remained unopened till November 11: —

"This morning, as for some days past, it seems exceedingly probable that this Administration will not be reëlected. Then it will be my duty to so coöperate with the President-elect as to save the Union between the election and the inauguration; as he will have secured his election on such ground that he cannot possibly save it afterwards."

During these gloomy days Grant had his own annoyances. His major-generals were at loggerheads. Meade was unpopular; had scolded Warren; had rebuked Wilson because a Richmond newspaper charged his men with stealing negroes, horses, silver plate, and clothing on a raid. There was talk of superseding Meade. But the most vexatious quarrel was in the Army of the James. Smith was forever quarreling with Gillmore and Butler fussed with both. Gillmore was soon eliminated, but Smith and Butler squabbled all their lives. Smith, a West Point soldier with a brilliant record, an engineer of proved ability, perhaps too much addicted to maneuvers, irascible, fault-finding, and opinionated, had made a fatal slip at Petersburg. Butler, a blustering, contentious politician in a uniform, bitterly hostile to the West Point regulars, teeming with ingenious schemes, and reveling in Gargantuan blunders, unbridled in ambition and audacity, a stench in controversy, the Thersites of the war, when in command of troops was a grotesque and tragical mistake. Since neither Smith nor Butler had been broken to the harness, they could not pull together. One of them had to go, and Grant chose Butler for the sacrifice. Then overnight, after a call by Butler at Grant's quarters, the order was reversed. Butler was retained and Smith relieved from duty: just why has been in controversy ever since.

Smith wrote for Lincoln's eye a letter charging that Butler, having seen Grant in his cups, had blackmailed him, and this interpretation has found a place in history; but Grant had weathered charges of that kind before without a whimper when he had fewer friends; he had no need to fear them now. We cannot credit the result to such a threat by Butler, unless we shall assume, as some have thought, so slimy is the trail of this old quarrel, that there could be no infamy which he would not embrace, and even then we cannot think that Grant, as happened later, should become his friend and write about him kindly in his book; for Grant was not mean-spirited. Smith's punishment can be accounted for on other grounds. His temper sentenced him to exile if Butler was to stay; and besides, he had whipped Grant over Meade's shoulders by tactlessly abusing Meade to Grant for the disaster at Cold Harbor, for which he must have known that Grant was himself to blame.

It is far more likely that Butler's neck was saved by Lincoln, who, with his reëlection in the balance, feared to let loose upon the voters of the north a Douglas Democrat with a war record, a grievance, and a poisoned tongue. Later Butler was ordered to New York to guard against election riots, and subsequently, after his fiasco at Fort Fisher, he was sent home to Lowell "for the good of the service," Grant

writing Stanton on January 4, 1865, "In my absence General Butler necessarily commands, and
there is a lack of confidence felt in his military ability,
making him an unsafe commander for a large army.
His administration of the affairs of his department
is also objectionable."

EVEN as Lincoln penned his gloomy memorandum of August 23, the skies were clearing. Farragut's operations at Mobile, which had been going on for weeks, were already crowned with victory, though the news had not come North. On September 2, while the Democrats in their convention at Chicago were resolving that the war had been a failure, Sherman was entering Atlanta, whence he had driven Hood the day before, leading into the rebel stronghold with hardly any loss the army he led out of Chattanooga four months before, thus tearing out of the Confederacy its chief manufacturing center and dépôt of supplies. On September 3, Lincoln, by proclamation, summoned the people of the North to offer thanks to God for Union triumphs at Atlanta and Mobile.

Up to the time that Grant came East, the cavalry had been held in some contempt by the commanders of the Army of the Potomac, available for picket duty and for little else. "Who ever saw a dead cavalryman?" was a Service jest. But Grant drafted Sheridan to transform Meade's cavalry into a fighting force, and Sheridan, unknown east of the Alleghanies except for the assault on Missionary Ridge, had startled Meade by telling him that the mounted men should be concentrated to fight the rebel horse instead of doing routine guard and picket duty for the infantry. When Meade asked who would protect the transportation trains, cover the front of moving infantry columns, and secure their flanks from intrusion, he had another shock from the pugnacious little Irishman, — he was only thirty-three, stood five feet five, and weighed one hundred and fifteen pounds, — who said that with 10,000 mounted men he could make it so lively for the rebel cavalry that the flanks and rear of the Army of the Potomac would require little or no defense, and that moving columns of infantry should take care of themselves. He hoped to defeat the enemy in a general engagement and move where he pleased, breaking Lee's communications and destroying his resources.

Meade later had a peppery interview with Sheridan, in which the young man told him he could whip J. E. B. Stuart, the Confederate cavalry leader, if Meade would only let him try. When Meade reported it to Grant, Grant's only comment was, "Did he say so? Then let him go out and do it!" Whereupon Sheridan went out, and on the 11th of May, at Yellow Tavern, within six miles of Richmond, whipped Stuart's forces and killed Stuart himself, inflicting on the Confederate mounted troops the worst defeat that had befallen them. Then Sheridan made an independent raid, broke up the railroads that connected Lee with Richmond, and frightened the Confederate Capital, penetrating its outer fortifications, though that was not his aim.

Early, returning from his raid on Maryland, controlled at Winchester the fertile Valley of the Shenandoah, to which the rebel army looked for food that fall, and Grant picked Sheridan to operate against him, though Stanton had objected to putting Sheridan in command of the department because he was too young. "I see you played around the difficulty," Lincoln said to Grant, "by picking Sheridan to command the boys in the field." "I want Sheridan put in command of all the troops in the field with instructions to put himself south of the enemy and follow him to the death," Grant wired to Stanton. "Wherever the enemy goes, let our troops go, also"; and Lincoln, seeing the dispatch, wrote back: "This, I think, is exactly right as to how our forces should move; but please look over the dispatches you may have received from here ever since you made that order, and discover if you can that there is any idea in the head of any one here of 'putting our army south of the enemy' or of 'following him to the death' in any direction. I repeat to you, it will neither be done nor attempted, unless you watch it every day and hour and force it."

Grant knew Sheridan better than Washington. He instructed him, on August 5, that in pushing up the Shenandoah Valley it was desirable that nothing should be left to invite the enemy to return. "Take all provisions, forage, and stock wanted for the use of your command. Such as cannot be consumed, destroy." Then in September, having put Sheridan in charge of a new division, and having visited him to find out how he lay, he gave the order to "Go in," and Sheridan "went in" at once at Winchester, flashing Grant that he had "sent Early's army whirling up the Valley." Just a month later came Cedar Creek and Sheridan's ride, transforming panic-stricken flight into resplendent victory. The little cavalry leader in one summer had dashed into history as one of the great figures of the war and had revolutionized the theory of cavalry service for all wars to come.

"As a soldier, as a commander of troops, as a man capable of doing all that is possible with any number of men," Grant said years later, "there is no man living greater than Sheridan. He belongs to the very first rank of soldiers, not only of our country, but of the world. I rank Sheridan with Napoleon and Frederick and the great commanders of history. No

P.H. Sheridan

man ever had such a faculty of finding out things as
Sheridan, of knowing all about the enemy. He was
always the best informed man of his command as to
the enemy. Then he had the magnificent quality of
swaying men which I wish I had — a rare quality in
a general."

Sherman had no sooner lighted in Atlanta than he
began to think of longer flights. Grant had suggested
slicing Georgia to the Gulf, but Sherman had a vision
of marching to the sea. "If you can whip Lee," he
wrote Grant, "and I can march to the Atlantic, I
think Uncle Abe will give us a twenty days' leave of
absence to see the young folks." Hood was getting
active; Sherman had sent Thomas to Nashville to
protect Tennessee. He would leave Tennessee to
Thomas, destroy Atlanta, and move to Charleston
or Savannah. "I can make the march and make
Georgia howl," he wrote. He thought Hood would be
forced to follow him, but at any rate, "I would be on
the offensive; instead of guessing at what he means to
do, he would have to guess at my plans." Lincoln
and Stanton were solicitous; "a misstep by General
Sherman might be fatal to his army." But Grant,
though dubious at first, approved the plan. Thomas
objected, and Sherman argued with him. He knew
he must succeed, for if he failed, "this march would
be adjudged the wild adventure of a crazy fool." He

would demonstrate the vulnerability of the South and make its people feel that war and individual ruin were synonymous. Hood crossed the river into Tennessee, and Grant thought Hood should be destroyed before the march began, but Sherman thought it was a scheme to lure him out of Georgia, and Grant said, "Go as you propose." Sherman had perfect faith that Thomas could handle Hood, and having sent him Schofield's corps for an emergency, destroyed Atlanta with its factories and supplies, cut loose November 12 from all communication with the North, and for a month was swallowed up in Georgia with 60,000 men.

Hood, forced to choose between following Sherman or invading Tennessee, began to move toward Nashville with over 40,000 men. At Franklin, on his way toward Nashville, he found Schofield with his corps of 30,000; made a desperate assault, and was repulsed with frightful loss. He followed Schofield on to Nashville and sat down before the city, his army now reduced to 26,000, while Thomas held the town with nearly twice Hood's force. Thomas had told Sherman to have no fear about Hood. "If he does not follow you I will then thoroughly organize my troops, and I believe I shall have men enough to ruin him unless he gets out of the way very rapidly." He now took time to organize, waiting for Wilson and his

cavalry to get equipments; and thus put Grant and
Lincoln to a hard test of patience. With his numerical
supremacy they could not understand why he delayed attacking Hood. "This looks like McClellan
and Rosecrans strategy, to do nothing and let the
rebels raid the country," wired Stanton to Grant.
"The President wishes you to consider the matter."

Grant had never valued Thomas at his real worth,
and he knew that in Hood's place he would himself
set out at once on an invasion of the North, eluding
Thomas and crossing the Ohio. Were Hood to do
this, it would be a heavy blow. All would be criticized for letting Sherman disappear; it might be
necessary to divert troops from Virginia, which perhaps would mean a loss of months in getting Lee.
And Grant was later justified in his belief, when
Hood himself wrote that he then had dreams of
conquest, defeating Thomas, seizing Nashville for a
base, raiding Kentucky, threatening Cincinnati, and
marching a victorious army through the gaps of the
Cumberland Mountains to join Lee, whip Grant and
Sherman in succession, and sweep down on Washington with the combined armed forces of the Confederacy.[1] Fate had now delivered Hood into the
hands of Thomas and Thomas seemed to toy with
Fate. Grant sent dispatches on December 2 urging

[1] *Battles and Leaders of the Civil War*, vol. IV, p. 427.

him to take the offensive. Thomas replied that in two or three days he would probably be ready. Four days passed and Grant dispatched a peremptory order: "Attack Hood at once and wait no longer for a remount of your cavalry. There is great danger of delay resulting in a campaign back to the Ohio River." Thomas answered that he would obey, though "I believe it will be hazardous with the small force now at my service."

Nothing happened. Then Grant lost his patience; for once seemingly cast aside his usual restraint and poise. "If Thomas has not struck yet," he wired to Halleck on December 8, "he ought to be ordered to hand over his command to Schofield. There is no better man to repel an attack than Thomas; but I fear he is too cautious to ever take the initiative." The next day he directed Halleck to relieve Thomas and put Schofield in command. Thomas, hiding his grief, replied with dignity: "I regret that General Grant should feel dissatisfaction at my delay in attacking the enemy. I feel conscious that I have done everything in my power to prepare and that the troops could not have been gotten ready before this, and that if he should order me to be relieved I shall submit without a murmur. A terrible storm of freezing rain has come on since daylight which will render an attack impossible until it breaks." Grant sus-

pended the order, but after two days' further
waiting, with eager interchange of telegrams, he
ordered Logan to Nashville to replace Thomas in
command of the Army of the Cumberland. In his
anxiety he started West himself, but on his way
at Washington, on December 15, got word that
Thomas had attacked, and then that Hood was
routed with Thomas in pursuit. The battle of Nashville, on December 15 and 16, was the most complete
victory won by the Union forces during the rebellion,
a perfect battle in the eyes of experts in the science of
war. Hood's army was so badly beaten that when
after the pursuit he left its wreckage on the south
side of the Tennessee, it hardly numbered 15,000
men, and was soon disintegrated save for a few who
turned up afterwards with Johnston's little force in
North Carolina. Grant did not quarrel with success.
He asked that Thomas be made a Major-General
in the regular army, overwhelmed him with congratulations, wrote in his report that the defeat of
Hood was so complete that it would be accepted
as a vindication of the successful general's judgment.

On the 10th of December, thirty days after he cut
loose from his communications at Atlanta, Sherman
could see Savannah. His march of three hundred
and sixty miles through hostile territory had been a
holiday, and on the 21st he occupied the town and

offered it to Lincoln as a Christmas present for the North. Half of the task Grant set himself when he came East was now accomplished. Organized rebellion west of the Alleghanies had been crushed. The whole Southwest was open to the Union troops whenever they saw fit to occupy it.

Sherman for the moment far outdazzled Grant in popular esteem. The fine audacity of his accomplishment had caught the fancy of the world. Lincoln congratulated him: "The undertaking being a success the honor is all yours; for I believe none of us went further than to acquiesce." Some would have made him a Lieutenant-General and put him over Grant, who to appearances had loafed at City Point, while his subordinates were winning victories. "I would rather have you in command than anybody else," Sherman wrote Grant, "for you are fair, honest, and have at heart the same purpose that should actuate all. I should emphatically decline any commission calculated to bring us into rivalry"; and Grant replied: "No one would be more pleased at your advancement than I, and if you should be placed in my position and I put subordinate, it would not change our relations in the least. I would make the same exertions to support you that you have ever done to support me, and I would do all in my power to make our cause win."

CHAPTER XXII

PEACE

GRANT, for the moment partly in eclipse, bided his time. Events were shaping the success of his grand strategy, which he now knew the end would justify. His lines were tightening on the Confederacy. Sherman was on his way north from Savannah, cutting a path of devastation across the Carolinas; marching four hundred miles through winter sleet and icy floods, quagmires and swamps and rutty roads, a bitter contrast to the Georgia frolic. Fort Fisher, after many trials, was seized at last by Terry brilliantly in early January, and Wilmington, which it protected, the sole remaining port of the Confederacy, fell into Union hands as had already happened with every other rebel stronghold south or west of Richmond. Lee's army could no longer live upon the crops of the Southwest or tap its former granary in the Valley of the Shenandoah. The time was near at hand when the compressed Confederacy, upon which Grant was closing in, must either choke or starve unless Lee's ragged and emaciated troops slipped through the Union lines to the Southwest. No recruits were coming, and there could be no hope for a successful fight against the Union army, which now, almost encircling Petersburg and Richmond after months of siege, was hardening the latest levies into veterans. While Lee had lost his sources of supply, Grant had at call the teeming farms and factories of the North. Davis had reached the limit of his credit, while Lincoln still had full financial reservoirs to drain.

Yet Davis could not bring himself to think his cause was lost; he was for goading his exhausted armies to fight on, and if compelled to flee, he would transfer the Richmond archives to a roving capital, and keep rebellion bristling in the Alleghany wilds. His patriotic selfishness would not have stopped at any sacrifice by his devoted men.

City Point, with Grant's log-cabin headquarters, was a secondary Union Capital. Lincoln came there with Seward and other members of the Cabinet; members of Congress drifted in to look things over; there was an unbroken line of Northern visitors. At the end of January the "Peace Commission," Stephens, Campbell, and Hunter, came from Richmond on their futile errand, and Grant, who was a soldier not vested with authority in such affairs, asked Lincoln to come down with Seward to hear their tale.

Stephens, who then for the first time saw Grant,

has said that he was never more surprised in any man. "He was plainly attired, sitting in a log cabin busily writing on a small table by a kerosene lamp. There was nothing in his appearance or surroundings which indicated his official rank. There were neither guards nor aides about him. Upon Colonel Babcock rapping at his door the response, 'Come in,' was given by himself"; and he soliloquizes: "In manners he is simple, natural, and unaffected; in utterance frank and explicit; in thought, perception and action, quick; in purpose fixed, decided, and resolute." [1]

The commissioners met Lincoln and Seward on Lincoln's boat in Hampton Roads. The peace they had in mind did not contemplate the dissolution of the Confederacy, which was of course the one condition Lincoln could consider; but they learned from him that the Thirteenth Amendment abolishing slavery had just been passed by Congress, that the restoration of the Union was the first requirement in any peace, and that the way for this to be assured by them was "by disbanding their armies, and permitting the National authorities to resume their functions."

The conference had its value in revealing Lincoln's mind. "Stephens," he said, "if I were in Georgia and entertained the sentiments I do, . . . I would go

[1] *Recollections of Alexander H. Stephens,* pp. 79, 80; 401–02.

home and get the Governor of the State to call the
Legislature together and get them to recall all the
state troops from the war; elect senators and members to Congress, and ratify the constitutional amendment prospectively so as to take effect — say in five
years. Such a ratification would be valid in my opinion. . . . Slavery is doomed. It cannot last long in any
event, and the best course, it seems to me, for you
public men to pursue would be to adopt such a policy
as will avoid as far as possible the evils of immediate
emancipation." He said he should be in favor individually of the Government paying a fair indemnity
to the owners. He knew some who were in favor of an
appropriation as high as four hundred million dollars
for this purpose. This was on February 3, and two
days later, at Washington, Lincoln laid before his
Cabinet a message which he proposed to send to
Congress, recommending a joint resolution empowering the President to pay to sixteen Southern and
border States four hundred million dollars in six per
cent government bonds as compensation for their
slaves, the distribution to be dependent "on the
ceasing of all resistance to the National authority
by the first of April next." The members of the Cabinet were all opposed, and Lincoln seemed surprised.
"How long will the war last?" he asked; and when
no one answered, he said: "A hundred days. We are

spending now in carrying on the war three millions a day which will amount to all this money besides all the lives"; and with a deep sigh he added, "but you are all opposed to me and I will not send the message."

In the last week of March, Sherman reached Goldsboro, in North Carolina, and found Schofield waiting for him there, while Johnston with a remnant of his old army hung about Raleigh, fifty miles away.

Grant, waiting for the spring campaign which he had planned to end the business, indulged his troops in desultory fighting mostly by Sheridan and Wilson, who with their mounted horse were cutting Lee's communications, raiding his outposts, smiting stray regiments now and then, ruffling the rebel Capital's defense. At last the time approached for operations all along the line, and Lee, foreseeing this, thought to anticipate it by breaking through the Union lines at Petersburg, and by forced marches, eluding Grant, join Johnston in the Carolinas for a final stand. It was a desperate chance, dramatically taken, resulting in repulse.

On the 29th of March, Grant bade farewell to City Point, Lincoln's "God bless you" lingering in his ears. It is written that as his wife stood in his cabin door saying good-bye, he held her tight and kissed her many times with tenderness unusual, even for him. From that time to the end he mingled with his army at the front, taking the same exposure as his men.

It fell to Sheridan to strike the last swift blow, when on the 1st of April at Five Forks his forces stormed the intrenched enemy, slashing their way through raking fire, charging with drawn sabers and fixed bayonets, the little General himself leading his men, waving his battle-flag, praying, swearing, flashing from one point to another, till Merritt in a final dash carried the earthworks with a wild hurrah. Few battles like it ever have been waged, and none has since been fought on this side of the Atlantic with which we can compare its brilliant daring strategy. "It seems to me," said Porter, "that you have exposed yourself to-day in a manner hardly justifiable on the part of a commander of such an important movement"; and Sheridan replied, "I have never in my life taken a command into battle and had the slightest desire to come out alive unless I won."

As soon as he was told what Sheridan had done, Grant ordered an assault on Petersburg, and on the morning of the 2d it was made, without great loss to Lee, who knew, of course, that after Five Forks he could not hope to hold the place. That night, in cover of the darkness, Lee's men filed out of Peters-

burg, and shortly after daybreak Grant rode in. Then
Lincoln came and seized Grant's hand and thanked
him. "I had a sort of sneaking idea all along that
you intended to do something like this," Lincoln
said; "but I thought some time ago that you would
so maneuver as to have Sherman come up and be near
enough to coöperate with you." And Grant, revealing a fine tactfulness, replied: "I had a feeling that it
would be better to let Lee's old antagonists give his
army the final blow and finish up the job. The Western armies have been very successful in their campaigns, and it is due to the Eastern armies to let them
vanquish their old enemy single-handed."

That same day Davis fled from Richmond and
Ewell's troops absconded, letting the Union forces in.
To Richmond Lincoln went from Petersburg; but
not Grant, who was too busy keeping an eye on Lee,
with Ord and Meade and Sheridan dogging Lee's
trail. Lee, with his poor, starved army, was trying to
reach Johnston, and at last, near Jetersville, Sheridan
found him still militant, though in a sorry way. But
Meade, who had the old idea of occupying Richmond,
forgetful of Grant's first instructions, had disposed
his troops with that in view, leaving a space between
the Union lines through which Lee might escape.
Sheridan alarmed, and having no authority to
change Meade's plan, sent Grant a secret message

telling him the tale and adding, "I wish you were here yourself."

Grant was immediately on his way to Sheridan and learned at Farmsville of fighting still going on with some of Lee's divisions. Word came in that Ewell had said the rebel cause was lost, and on April 7, at 5 P.M., Grant, thinking further bloodshed wicked, now that fighting was in vain, wrote to Lee asking the surrender of his army. There was need of diplomacy. Lee, not admitting that his case was hopeless, asked the terms which would be offered on condition of surrender, and Grant replied with delicacy: "Peace being my great desire, there is but one condition I would insist upon, namely, that the men and officers surrendered shall be disqualified for taking up arms against the Government of the United States until properly exchanged. I will meet you or will designate officers to meet any officers you may name for the same purpose, at any point agreeable to you, for the purpose of arranging definitely the terms upon which the surrender of the Army of Northern Virginia will be received." Lee held back. He tried to think the time had not yet come for abdication of his cause. "I cannot, therefore, meet you with a view to surrender the Army of Northern Virginia, but as far as your proposal may affect the Confederate States forces under my command and tend to the restora-

tion of peace, I shall be pleased to meet you at 10
A.M. to-morrow on the old stage-road to Richmond,
between the picket lines of the two armies."

Grant, who was suffering excruciating pain, sleep-
less, pacing up and down his room, his splitting head
held in his hands, was at first cast down by this reply,
but wrote the next day in response: "As I have no
authority to treat on the subject of peace, the meeting proposed for 10 A.M. to-day could lead to no good.
I will state, however, General, that I am equally anxious for peace with yourself and the whole North
entertains the same feeling. The terms upon which
peace can be had are well understood. By the South
laying down their arms they will hasten that most
desirable event, save thousands of human lives, and
hundreds of millions of property not yet destroyed."
Before Lee got this letter, Lee had held a council of
his officers, who were insistent on a new assault in
hope of breaking through the Union lines, and Gordon, leading the assault by Lee's direction, suffered
a repulse. This misadventure, and the temper of
Grant's note, magnanimous, yet placing upon Lee
the sole responsibility for any further loss of life,
resulted in a quick compliance. "I now request an
interview, in accordance with the offer contained in
your letter of yesterday," he wrote; and when Grant
read the note, the pain from which he had been suf-

fering disappeared. "I will push forward to the front for the purpose of meeting you," he replied; then riding on with members of his staff, joined on the road by Sheridan and Ord, he came at noon to Appomattox Court-House, near which the Union and Confederate forces lay on their arms, and entered the brick dwelling with its tawdry furnishings where Lee and his great hour awaited him.

The story has been written many times, but no American can weary of its telling. Lee, dressed immaculately in a uniform of gray which emphasized his faultless bearing and his noble form; Grant, as he has been pictured heretofore, clad in a private's blouse, soiled with much riding, on which were sewn the shoulder straps to let his soldiers know his rank; Lee carrying a handsome sword, but Grant with none.

"What General Lee's feelings were, I do not know," writes Grant. "They were entirely concealed from my observation; but my own feelings, which had been quite jubilant on the receipt of his letter, were sad and depressed. I felt like anything rather than rejoicing at the downfall of a foe who had fought so long and valiantly and had suffered so much for a cause, though that cause was I believe one of the worst for which a people ever fought and one for which there was the least excuse."

Grant talked awhile of ordinary things, ignoring

the momentous theme that brought them there, and
gently leaving that for Lee to introduce, — about old
army times, service in Mexico, where he was a subaltern and Lee Scott's chief of staff, — till Lee, reminding him that they had business in hand, said he had
asked the interview to learn the terms that it was
proposed to give his army. Grant told him, and they
fell again in talk till Lee suggested that the terms be
written out. Then, turning to a table, Grant wrote
as he was wont to write, swiftly and clearly without
erasure, not knowing when he took his pen what the
first word would be, but knowing what was in his
mind and wishing to express it unmistakably. "As
I wrote on," he says, "the thought occurred to me
that the officers had their own private horses and
effects which were important to them, but of no
value to us; also that it would be an unnecessary
humiliation to call upon them to deliver their side
arms." When Lee read over that part of the terms,
"he remarked with some feeling, I thought, that this
would have a happy effect upon his army." [1]

[1] *General R. E. Lee,*
    Commanding Confederate States Armies.
General:
    In accordance with the substance of my letter to you of the 8th
inst., I propose to receive the surrender of the Army of Northern
Virginia on the following terms, to wit:
    Rolls of all the officers and men to be made in duplicate, one
copy to be given to an officer designated by me, the other to be

Then Lee spoke about his mounted men, most of whom owned their horses, and asked if he should understand that these should be retained. This had not been in the terms as written out, but Grant said that he hoped and thought that there would be no further battles in the war. "I took it that most of the men in the ranks were small farmers. The whole country had been so raided by the two armies that it was doubtful whether they would be able to put in a crop to carry themselves and their families through the next winter without the aid of the horses they were then riding." So he said that any man who claimed to own a horse or a mule might take it home. Lee remarked again that this would have a happy effect, and straightway wrote out his acceptance of Grant's terms. Then there was a final touch. As Lee was going, he spoke again about his men, told Grant

retained by such officer or officers as you may designate. The officers to give their individual paroles not to take up arms against the Government of the United States until properly exchanged, and each company or regimental commander sign a like parole for the men of their commands.

The arms, artillery and public property to be packed and stocked and turned over to the officer appointed by me to receive them. This will not embrace the side arms of the officers nor their private horses or baggage. This done, each officer and man will be allowed to return to their homes, not to be disturbed by the United States authorities so long as they observe their parole and the laws in force where they may reside.

Very respectfully,
U. S. Grant,
Lieutenant-General.

that they were badly off for food; that for some days they had been living only on parched corn; he would have to ask for rations; and Grant told him to send his commissary and quartermaster to Appomattox Station, where his men could get all the food they needed from the trains which Sheridan had stopped.

Then Lee went out, and as he passed, the aides, who had been waiting on the steps, arose respectfully. He did not seem to notice them, but looking over the green valley toward his surrendered army he smote his hands abstractedly until his orderly led up his horse. He took the bridle. Grant walked by and touched his hat, and Lee, returning the salute in silence, rode back to his own lines.

That afternoon Grant telegraphed to Stanton in three lines informing him of Lee's surrender.[1] When his men learned what had been done, they began a salute in honor of the victory; but Grant, hearing the first volley, ordered them to stop. He would not add to the distress of a defeated foe. Thus he had stopped the cheers at Donelson and Vicksburg.

[1] HEADQUARTERS, APPOMATTOX COURT-HOUSE VIRGINIA,
April 9, 1865, 4.30 P.M.
Hon. E. M. Stanton, Secretary of War,
Washington.
General Lee surrendered the Army of Northern Virginia this afternoon on terms proposed by myself. The accompanying additional correspondence will show the conditions fully.
U. S. GRANT,
Lieutenant-General.

The next morning he rode out beyond the Union lines toward Lee's headquarters, and Lee, perceiving who it was, rode out to meet him. They talked again, this time about the need for peace. Lee hoped that there would be no further sacrifice of life, but could not say; the South was a big country and time might pass before the war could be entirely ended; he could not foretell. Then Grant told him that his influence was greater than that of any other man in the Confederacy and said that if he should now advise surrendering all the armies, no doubt his counsel would be followed with alacrity. But Lee said that he could not do that without consulting Davis, and Grant knew that there would be no use in urging him to do what he did not think was right. So Lee went back again among his men, and shortly home to lay aside his uniform. Davis was even then in flight toward Texas, hoping to keep rebellion there alive; but he was caught in Georgia on the way.

Grant went to Washington at once. They would make much of him, but he would not be lionized. He talked with Lincoln, but declined an invitation to Ford's Theater, hurrying on to Burlington, New Jersey, where his children were at school. At Philadelphia he heard of Lincoln's murder and came back to be a tower of strength in the grief-stricken city.

In Washington, a few days later, he received from

Sherman the news of Johnston's surrender, and learned the impossible terms which Sherman had innocently given, terms which invaded the province of politics and reconstruction, and which inflamed the North when Stanton made them public. Stanton's announcement conveying the information that Sherman had been disciplined, and carrying a sinister suggestion that the hero of the march through Georgia was implicated in a scheme to let Confederate officials get away with plunder from the Richmond banks, for a time made Sherman a target for the people's wrath. Grant was sent to Raleigh to cancel Sherman's terms and order the resumption of hostilities. Instead of superseding Sherman and humiliating him before a beaten enemy, he tactfully allowed him on his own initiative to reverse his course and to exact surrender on the terms Grant gave to Lee according to instructions from the powers in Washington, then stole away from Raleigh without letting any one but Sherman know that he was there.

Thus the war ended, a gentle spirit pervading the spent armies North and South, due in chief measure to the generosity of Grant, who shortly after received his army's salutations in the solemn pageant of the Grand Review crowned with the glory of his country's gratitude.

CHAPTER XXIII

A GENERAL WITHOUT HIS ARMY

AT the crest of his renown Grant found himself in Washington encumbered with high military rank, but shorn of power. The day he came from Appomattox he put himself to work curtailing the expense of war by canceling the orders for superfluous munitions and supplies. He set out also to disband the armies, so that in a little while he, who yesterday had headed half a million men, commanded a small force of regulars, in numbers hardly more imposing than Scott had handled just before the war. Congress in 1866 revived for him the grade of General, but did not couple with it new battalions or brigades. There was not much for him to do except to trim the ragged edges of rebellion by clearing up the stragglers in the South who were reluctant about laying down their arms. He was a stranger to the Capital, and had a limited acquaintance with public men.

He had brought with him several members of his staff; but there were hardly half a dozen men in Congress whom he knew except by name, and in the Cabinet, Stanton and Seward were the only two with whom he had been closely brought in touch.

Seward, he distrusted because of his diplomacy and indirection.

Stanton he disliked instinctively, and his dislike was aggravated by the Sherman episode. Stanton, a zealot, deeply versed in Bible lore, was an unamalgamated mixture of strangely contradictory traits, domineering, superstitious, cowardly, intolerant, sympathetic, devoid of loyalty to his co-workers, though passionately loyal to the Union cause, consistent only in his fervid love of country and of power and in undeviating lack of tact. With Stanton, formally, Grant had to keep on friendly terms, and so with Johnson, who was really weak and vacillating, though outwardly pugnacious, and who, when entering on his new and onerous responsibilities, could think of nothing more appropriate to say than to extol his own past record, concluding with the words: "The duties have been mine, the consequences God's."

Grant had now to deal in strange surroundings with politicians whom he did not know, coping with questions altogether new. The kindly feeling of the South, stirred by his chivalry toward Lee, was strengthened by his stand against the threat of Johnson to try Lee for treason in defiance of the promise of his parole. A super-serviceable judge at Norfolk had the grand jury find indictments against some of the paroled Confederates, and when Lee heard that he, too, would be indicted, he wrote to Grant reminding him of the protection he understood was granted him and applying for amnesty and pardon. Grant needed no reminder. He promptly forwarded to Johnson, through the Secretary of War, the request for amnesty, earnestly recommending that it be granted, and sent Lee's letter to the Secretary with this endorsement: —

"In my opinion the officers and men paroled at Appomattox Court-House and since, upon the same terms given Lee, cannot be tried for treason, so long as they observe the terms of their parole. This is my understanding. Good faith as well as true policy dictates that we should observe the conditions of that convention. . . . The action of Judge Underwood in Norfolk has already had an injurious effect, and I would ask that he be ordered to quash all indictments found against paroled prisoners of war and to desist from the further prosecution of them."

Grant was not content with written words. He hurried to the White House, where for once he found his tongue in controversy. "A general commanding troops," he said, "has certain responsibilities and duties and power which are supreme. . . . I have made certain terms with Lee, the best and only terms. If I had told him and his army that their

liberty would be invaded, that they would be open
to arrest, trial, and execution for treason, Lee would
have never surrendered, and we should have lost
many lives in destroying them. . . . I will resign the
command of the army rather than execute any order
directing me to arrest Lee or any of his commanders
so long as they obey the laws."

That was a contingency which Johnson dared not
face. He could not hope to put his influence to the
test against the all-pervading popularity of Grant.
The indictments were withdrawn, though Johnson
still denied to Lee his amnesty.[1]

In Texas Kirby Smith was slow in his surrender,
and Grant rushed Sheridan to force his hand, much
to the discontent of Sheridan, who greatly longed to
lead his troopers in the Grand Review. But Grant
had more in mind than Kirby Smith's chastisement.
Grant had always looked on Maximilian's venture as

[1] In November, 1865, Grant gave to Longstreet, who from West
Point days had been his friend, a letter to the President recommending Longstreet's pardon. Armed with this letter, Longstreet
sought Johnson. "The President was nervous, ill at ease, and
somewhat resentful . . . and at length closed the interview by
saying, 'There are three men this Union will never forgive — they
have given it too much trouble. They are Jefferson Davis, Robert
E. Lee, and James Longstreet.' General Longstreet said, 'Those
who are forgiven much, love much, Mr. President.' Johnson
answered, 'You have high authority for that statement, General,
but you cannot have amnesty.' " (*Lee and Longstreet at High Tide*,
p. 106.)

closely intertwined with the rebellion, since it had been encouraged by the heads of the Confederacy and instigated by the European powers when Lincoln's hands were tied and Washington could not effectively protest. He held the French invasion to be an act of war on the United States, and thought that we should treat it so whenever we were free to strike. He often spoke of it to Lincoln while at City Point, and urged that when the war was over troops should be thrown across the border to drive the French invaders out.

He thought then that it would have a noble influence at home if soldiers of the North and South, recently fighting one another, could unite in war against a common foe, and while he had no definite response from Lincoln, he inferred that Lincoln sympathized with him in this. Grant always held Napoleon III in detestation and would have taken keen delight in his discomfiture. He looked upon him as the special foe of the United States and liberty.

Though Lincoln's hands were tied, Johnson's were now free; and Sheridan was an ideal instrument, impatient to be used. In middle June Grant wrote to Johnson proposing "open resistance to the establishment of Maximilian's government in Mexico." If such a government should be established, he could "see nothing before us but a long, expensive, and bloody war. . . . Every act of the empire of Maxi-

milian has been hostile to the United States. . . .
What I would propose would be a solemn protest
against the establishment of a monarchical government in Mexico by the aid of foreign bayonets. . . .
How all this could be done without bringing on an
armed conflict, others who have studied such matters
could tell better than I."

But Johnson was not greatly interested. He had
fish of his own to fry at home and found it easy to let
Mexico alone, especially as Seward, who was always
at his ear, was altogether hostile to the use of force,
hoping to get everything we needed through the
means of diplomatic notes.

To Sheridan's disgust his cavalry could only chafe
on this side of the Rio Grande, while Grant recorded
an experience in rank without authority — not his
last, for the unlovely days of Reconstruction were
at hand.

CHAPTER XXIV

RECONSTRUCTION

THERE is no period of our history more mortifying to our national pride than that just following the Civil War, no time when in the hour of need exalted statesmanship was more nearly in eclipse. We can now only guess what would have been the course of Reconstruction if Lincoln had not died; though we know broadly what he had in view to heal the wounds of war. The charity which permeates the scriptural phrases of the second inaugural is a precious heritage, and is in keeping with constructive plans which he proposed for the regeneration of the South, as well as with his words at Hampton Roads. What he did in Louisiana while the war was on gives us an inkling of what he would have tried to do in other States after the war was over; but the strong opposition to his Louisiana policy in Congress must be accepted as foreshadowing the hostile attitude of radical Republicans if he had sought to carry through a policy like that in time of peace.

He would, no doubt, have found the people with him, for a time, and would have had an influence commensurate with his fame upon Republicans who against Johnson went almost to the limit of fanaticism. The ultimate result would surely have been better, but at a cost to Lincoln's name. If he had tilted with an intolerant Congress in a time of peace, no matter what the outcome, we almost certainly should have a different Lincoln in our legends than we have to-day.

Lincoln outlined a Reconstruction policy in his message of December, 1863, in accordance with which State Governments were set up in Louisiana and Arkansas by order of the military commander of the department acting under the President's direction. This did not meet the views of Congress. In 1864 a bill was passed providing for appointment of provisional governors in the Confederate States for purposes of civil administration until State Governments should be recognized. No State Governments were to be formed until after the suppression of military resistance to the United States and until the people had "sufficiently returned to their obedience to the Constitution and laws." The bill provided that the President should not proclaim a State Government as reëstablished without the assent of Congress. It emancipated all slaves.

The President did not sign the bill, and after adjournment he gave his reasons in a special proclamation; he was not ready to set aside the free State

Constitutions and Governments recently adopted in Louisiana and Arkansas and to declare a constitutional competency in Congress to abolish slavery in States.

Lincoln would have treated each case by itself. He would have let the loyal citizens of a State under the protection of the military governor organize a State Government and adopt a constitution. This was done in Louisiana early in 1864. The constitution adopted there abolished slavery forever, and while restricting suffrage to white males, empowered the Legislature to confer the suffrage on colored men according to the principles laid down by Lincoln, that in the reconstructed States the right of suffrage should be given to "very intelligent" colored people and to those who had "fought gallantly in the ranks."

The question came up in the Senate in February, 1865, on a joint resolution recognizing this Government as the legitimate Government of Louisiana. The resolution had the support of all the Republicans in the Senate except five radicals led by Sumner, and it would have been adopted had it not been for Sumner, who, declaring, "I shall regard its passage as a national calamity," prevented a vote before the close of Congress on the 4th of March by dilatory motions.

Thaddeus Stevens would have none of Lincoln's

plan; after the war the South must be treated like any other conquered territory.

Sumner held that the President should not do the work of Reconstruction by military order, but that Congress should do it by law. He wanted Congress to impose indiscriminate negro suffrage on the States which had seceded as a condition precedent to their restoration. Lincoln believed that the State through moral pressure should be induced to give the suffrage to those "colored people who were qualified for it."

It is a striking fact that Lincoln's very last public utterance was on this subject. Speaking on Tuesday evening, April 11, three days before his assassination, to a crowd gathered at the White House, he commented on the constitutional question as to whether the seceded States were still in the Union or out of it, a question which during the next three years occupied a share of executive and legislative attention far out of proportion to its real importance.

"As it appears to me, that question has not been nor yet is a practically material one and that any discussion of it while it thus remains practically immaterial could have no effect other than the mischievous one of dividing our friends. As yet, whatever it may hereafter become, that question is bad as a basis of a controversy, and good for nothing at all — a mere pernicious abstraction. We all agree that the seceded States, so-called, are out of their proper practical relation with the Union and that the sole object of the Government, civil and military, in regard to those States is to again get them into that proper practical relation. I believe that it is not only possible, but in fact easier, to do this without deciding or even considering whether these States have ever been out of the Union, than with it. Finding themselves safely at home, it would be utterly immaterial whether they had ever been abroad."

In the light of history, these words seem reasonable; yet Sumner, writing of them to his friend, Dr. Lieber, said: "The President's speech and other things augur confusion and uncertainty in the future, with hot controversy. Alas! Alas!" And strange as it may seem to us to-day, Sumner was not alone even in that hour of triumph and good-will.

A few hours later and Lincoln was dead. Andrew Johnson in a tragic flash was President of the United States. It was the sport of Fate that to one so totally unlike the gentle, wise, and patient Lincoln should have been assigned the task which he laid down, yet while the nation was still plunged in grief there were not lacking honest-minded men who thought they saw the guiding hand of Providence in what was done.

George W. Julian, of Indiana, a leading member of the House, tells how on the very day of Lincoln's death he spent most of the afternoon in a political caucus held for the purpose of considering the necessity for a new Cabinet and a line of policy less conciliatory than that of Mr. Lincoln, "and while everybody was shocked at his murder, the feeling was nearly universal that the accession of Johnson to the Presidency would prove a Godsend to the country. As for Mr. Lincoln's known policy of tenderness to the rebels which now so jarred upon the feelings of the hour, his well-known views on the subject of Reconstruction were as distasteful as possible to radical Republicans."

The next day, Wade, Chandler, Julian, and other radical Republicans called on the new President. Wade exclaimed: "Johnson, we have faith in you. By the gods, there will be no trouble now in running the Government." Johnson thanked him and replied in words which came often to his lips: "I hold that robbery is a crime; rape is a crime; *treason* is a crime; and *crime* must be punished. Treason must be made infamous and must be punished, and traitors must be impoverished."

Yet, shortly, Johnson was vehemently agitating policies which went much farther toward the rehabilitation of the old leaders in the seceded States than those which Lincoln had gently urged, and the very radicals who had hailed him as a savior were damning him for treason to the cause. A few months later, John Hay, revisiting Washington after a brief tour of duty abroad, recalls that the first words of his old friend, Harry Wise, were, "Everything is changed; you'll find us all Copperheads." While U. H. Painter, war correspondent, Lincoln's and Stanton's confidant and friend, declared, "You will find the home of virtue has become the haunt of vice." [1]

In an atmosphere like this, stifling with intrigue and passion, with an ignorant, stubborn, and loquacious President, a Cabinet jealous and divided among themselves, a Congress groping in the dark, the honest-minded, trustful, straight-thinking Grant, after forty years of obscurity and four years of life in camp, received his first lesson in politics.

Johnson believed with Lincoln in the indestructibility of the States, but his methods were radically different. On May 29, 1865, hardly a month from the time he assumed office, he issued his proclamation of amnesty and pardon to all who would take an oath to observe all laws and proclamations made during the war with reference to the emancipation of slaves, excluding from its provisions, however,

[1] *Life of John Hay*, vol. i, p. 251.

fourteen specified classes. Among the classes specified were not only most of the men who had held
civil or military offices of any distinction, but also
all whose taxable property was estimated at over
twenty thousand dollars. Thus, with or without intention, he would eliminate from the new order of the
South most members of that intellectual, landed, and
pedigreed aristocracy against which he had set his
face throughout his political career. He would help
create a new governing class, to be chosen chiefly
from the poor-white population, who hated the
negro with a peculiar hatred arising from conditions prior to the war, when of these two classes socially submerged, the slaves, by very virtue of their
slavery, came in more sympathetic contact with the
aristocracy and held the freemen in contempt.

Johnson, obstinate, narrow, suspicious, and disputatious, a poor white with a poor white's prejudices,
a Southerner with a Southerner's illogical adherence
to a strictly logical interpretation of the Constitution, a Democrat and partisan by instinct and training, was temperamentally incapable of coöperation
with Northern Republicans like Sumner, Chandler,
Stevens, and Butler, radical to the last degree and
indisposed themselves to coöperation except on lines
which they themselves laid down. Prior to his accession to the Presidency he had hardly been north of

Mason and Dixon's line. His contact with Northern men and Northern sentiment was confined to his experience in Washington and with such Federal officers as he had dealings with while military governor of Tennessee. He was unfamiliar with large cities, had no first-hand knowledge of industrial communities, and was profoundly ignorant of the manifold activities upon which the prosperity of the North has always rested. The North in turn knew almost nothing good of him, except that he had been stoutly for the Union, while others in the South, of wider culture and under great moral obligations to the Union, had been either willfully or weakly disloyal. Fresh with all was the humiliating spectacle of his installation into office as Vice-President with his pitiful, rambling, maudlin speech, just a few days before he was called so unexpectedly to succeed to greater power than had been entrusted to any other American except Lincoln.

A wiser man would have been humble and prayerful under such a load, striving with all his might so to conduct himself as to win support from the strong men in Congress upon whom he must depend; but Johnson, driven by a perverse fate, set out to force them to his own way of thinking without even trying o discover whether there might not be a common ground upon which all could stand while struggling with a gigantic problem. True, he might not have got along with Sumner and Stevens in any circumstances. Neither might Lincoln if he had lived. But Lincoln would at least have tried.

The one man whom Johnson went out of the way to make his friend was Grant. With Lincoln dead, he recognized in Grant, not only the strongest personal force in the North, but the man in the North for whom since Appomattox the conquered Southerners had the highest esteem, and Johnson was shrewd enough to see the advantage of having Grant on his side. Lacking real knowledge of Northern sentiment, he looked to Grant as its embodiment. He sought Grant out. He sent him almost daily notes. He formed a habit of dropping in casually at Grant's house or office; he made it a point to attend Mrs. Grant's receptions. He sought every opportunity to have Grant by his side in public.

There was a degree of shrewdness in this course, which was in marked contrast with Stanton's tactlessness. Ever since Grant's arrival in Washington, Stanton had taken obvious delight in asserting his authority, sending for Grant to come to his own office on all sorts of occasions and in all sorts of weather, though Grant was thus frequently compelled to cross the broad and muddy expanse of Pennsylvania Avenue and climb painfully up the War

Department stairs; for those were the days before asphalt pavements, telephones, and electric elevators, and the headquarters of the Army was in a building widely separated from the office of the Secretary of War.

Grant, throughout the early months of the Administration, conducted himself with great good sense, accepting the President's attentions without comment and without committing himself to any line of policy. In fact, the general course of the Administration, from the time of the proclamation of amnesty of May 29, up to the time when Congress met on December 5, had much to commend it.

While holding that the question of suffrage was a matter for the States themselves to determine, Johnson was favorable to a qualified suffrage for the negro, although at that time the negro had the right to vote in only six Northern States — Maine, New Hampshire, Vermont, Massachusetts, Rhode Island, and New York; and New York required a property qualification for the negro voter which was not necessary for the white. In light of all conditions Johnson showed breadth of view as well as cunning when he wrote in a telegram to Governor Sharkey, of Mississippi, on August 15, 1865, with reference to the work of the Constitutional Convention: —

" If you could extend the elective franchise to all

persons of color who own real estate valued at not less than two hundred and fifty dollars and pay taxes thereon, you would completely disarm the adversary and set an example the other States will follow. This you can do with perfect safety, and you thus place the Southern States in reference to free persons of color upon the same basis with the free States. I hope and trust your convention will do this."

If Johnson had been blessed with Lincoln's tact or could have used the prestige of his name, who can say that he might not have brought Congress into line with some such programme, thus obviating the tragedy of immediate universal negro suffrage? But it was inevitable that Congress should have a hand in the work of Reconstruction, especially with Sumner the leader of the Senate and Stevens the leader of the House, two strong, persistent idealists and radicals, determined upon universal suffrage for the recently emancipated slaves. "Refer the whole question of Reconstruction to Congress where it belongs," Sumner cried in August. "What right has the President to reorganize States?" — a perfectly logical and defensible position, but significant in contrast to Sumner's earlier willingness in April to have Reconstruction by executive decree so long as he supposed the franchise would be conferred upon the negro through this means. Sumner was less concerned about the encroachment of the Executive than about giving the negroes in the South the indiscriminate right to vote.

It was during this period of executive supremacy, with eight States reconstructed by executive decree and awaiting the action of Congress on the admission of their Senators and Representatives, that Grant was sent by Johnson on a mission to the Southern States in order that he might report to Congress the feeling among those lately in rebellion. Grant left Washington on November 29, 1865, and visited Raleigh, Charleston, Savannah, Augusta, and Atlanta. His trip was short, but everywhere he " said much and conversed freely with the citizens of those States, as well as with officers of the army who have been stationed among them."

" I am satisfied," he wrote in his official report under date of December 18, " that the mass of thinking men of the South accept the present situation of affairs in good faith.

" My observations lead me to the conclusion that the citizens of the Southern States are anxious to return to self-government within the Union as soon as possible; that while reconstructing they want and require protection from the Government; and that they are in earnest in wishing to do what is required by the Government, not humiliating to them as citizens, and that if such a course was pointed out they would pursue it in good faith. It is to be regretted that there cannot be a greater commingling at this time between the citizens of the two sections and particularly of those entrusted with the lawmaking power."

He did not meet any one, "either those holding places under the Government or citizens of the Southern States," who thought it practicable to withdraw the military from the South at present. "The white and black mutually require the protection of the General Government," and the reason he gives is that "four years of war, during which law was executed only at the point of the bayonet throughout the States in rebellion, have left the people possibly in a condition not to yield that ready obedience to civil authority the American people have generally been in the habit of yielding."

General James H. Wilson, then in command at Macon, Georgia, and once a member of Grant's staff, relates how on this trip Grant summoned him to Atlanta and how they sat up all night discussing the war and the problem of Reconstruction. In the conversation, while Grant "did not hesitate to discredit the judgment of Andrew Johnson nor to conceal his dislike of Stanton's arbitrary ways, he distrusted the senatorial group with which Stanton was associated, and declared that his own views were not only thoroughly conservative, but thoroughly kind as to the generals and politicians of the South."

The Southern people at this time looked for harsh treatment, especially in view of Johnson's repeated threats to make treason odious and to impoverish the traitors. They would not have been surprised if there had been an attempt to confiscate their property and distribute it among the emancipated slaves. Such a punishment they would have submitted to sullenly, and almost anything short of that they would have accepted as a disagreeable price for resuming their place in the Union.

If at this period men like Sumner, Stevens, and Wade had been willing to confer with Johnson, and had not been radically insistent upon securing for the negro rights and privileges which the negro was not qualified to exercise, Reconstruction might have resulted far differently, and we might have been spared the sorry spectacle of a bitter fight between Congress and the President with the unseemly impeachment proceedings. Fessenden and Henry Wilson, more generous and farseeing than Sumner, were inclined to think the President right in all questions except suffrage; and Wilson wrote: "We have a President who does not go as far as we do in the right direction; but we have him and cannot change him, and we had better stand by the Administration and bring it right."

Of the military commanders in the South, one of the most sagacious was General John M. Schofield, who years later became Lieutenant-General of the Army on the death of Sheridan. He had attributes of statesmanship, and might with great advantage have been consulted by the civilians who had to solve in Washington the grave problems of Reconstruction. With regard to the proposal of Chase, Sumner, and other radicals, that the negro should be given the immediate right to vote, a step which he contended rightly was unconstitutional — he wrote on May 10, 1865: —

". . . My second reason for objecting to the proposition is the absolute unfitness of the negroes as a class for any such responsibility. They can neither read nor write. They have no knowledge whatever of law or government. They do not even know the meaning of the freedom that has been given them, and are much astonished when they are informed that it does not mean that they are to live in idleness and be fed by the government. . . . I have yet to see a single one among the many Union men in North Carolina who would willingly submit for a moment to the immediate elevation of the negro to political equality with the white man. They are all, or nearly all, content with the abolition of slavery. Many of them are rejoiced that it is done. But to raise the negro in his present ignorant and degraded condition to be their political equals would be in their opinion to enslave them (the white citizens). If they did not rebel against it, it would only be because rebellion would be hopeless. A government so organized would in no sense be a popular government."

If Reconstruction could have been left to soldiers like Grant and Schofield, who had fought the South, knew its leaders, and held their respect, the result would have been infinitely better than that which came from the unseemly quarrels of civilian politicians.

If there was ever a time when a military government might have proved beneficent in the United States, this was that time. No soldier could have made a sorrier mess of Reconstruction than the political leaders who wrangled it into shape, and almost any one of the great Union generals could have been trusted to do a better job. Under a military government the country would have been spared the miserable squabbles in Washington, the bungling attempts of Johnson to force upon the country policies the good features of which he inadequately comprehended and the bad features of which were bound to raise impossible expectations among the Southern people, the persistence of the radicals in Congress in imposing indiscriminate negro suffrage upon resentful communities, the appointment of provisional civilian governors, the letting loose of a devastating swarm of carpet-baggers upon a proud and helpless people, the imposition of proscriptive qualifications which debarred the best men in the South from holding office, thus limiting those who exercised the suffrage to a choice of carpet-baggers and negroes for places of political and judicial responsibility.

But it is idle to conjecture what might have happened if Grant or Sherman or Thomas or Schofield had been in supreme control. With all their fame the military leaders of the Civil War were in positions of hopeless subordination, taking orders from civilians far less familiar than they with Southern necessities, in most cases wholly ignorant of the Southern temper, many of them actuated by vindictiveness or personal ambition, the best of them obsessed with the delusion that for the negro there could be no middle ground between the suffrage and slavery, that there could be no charm in liberty without a vote.

CHAPTER XXV

LESSONS IN POLITICAL INTRIGUE

GRANT would have been far better off if he had
kept away from Washington, but it was ordered
otherwise, and he who had commanded all the Union
armies in the field was at the beck and call of men
who could not lead a regiment. True, he was learning
something of the devious ways of politics in preparation for the baffling tasks before him; but what he
learned was at a heavy cost. " Do not stay in Washington," Sherman had written him in affectionate
warning when he was made Lieutenant-General.
"Halleck is better qualified than you to stand the
buffets of intrigue and policy. . . . For God's sake
and for your country's sake, come out of Washington!"

And four years later, in his letter to the President,
after Grant's wretched fray with Johnson, Sherman
returned to the same theme, this time not as a seer
of evil but as its chronicler: —

" I have been with General Grant in the midst of
death and slaughter, — when the howls of people
reached him after Shiloh; when messengers were
speeding to and from his army bearing slanders to

induce his removal before he took Vicksburg; in Chattanooga when the soldiers were stealing the corn of the starving mules to satisfy their own hunger; at Nashville when he was ordered to the 'forlorn hope' to command the Army of the Potomac so often defeated — and yet I never saw him more troubled than since he has been in Washington, and been compelled to read himself a ' sneak and deceiver' based on reports of four of the Cabinet, and apparently your knowledge."

The period between these letters had been packed with incident. Grant had come out of war triumphantly, and with the death of Lincoln found himself a giant plagued by pygmies, a figure looming higher in the estimation of the people than he himself quite realized, yet led about by an ill-bred, accidental President, and subject to humiliating treatment by a domineering Secretary, only to be entangled at the end in a dispute between these two which raised with partisans of each a question of his own veracity.

If at the close of war, when conditions were nearly ripe for a real welding of spirit North and South, Grant had been in supreme control, that work might have gone on to a complete fruition, for even Johnson, in spite of all his truculence and the instinctive prejudice against him, commanded for a time a measure of support. Johnson perversely managed

first to alienate the South by vehement denunciation of its leaders and then the North by equally
violent urging of his policies when sane persuasion
might have brought North and South together in
lasting unity of sentiment; Grant would have had
no animosities and would have had no policy except
the cultivation of good-will. But as General of the
Armies, subject always to authority and military discipline, he could not influence events and had to
watch them drift. His ideas on the negro problem
had been of slow growth. Before the war he had
not been an abolitionist nor even an anti-slavery
man, but he came to see that slavery must go.

Twenty years later in his book he wrote: "I do not
believe that the majority of the Northern people at
that time were in favor of negro suffrage. They supposed that it would naturally follow the freedom of
the negro, but that there would be a time of probation in which the ex-slaves could prepare themselves
for the privileges of citizenship before the full right
would be conferred; but Mr. Johnson, after a complete revolution of sentiment, seemed to regard the
South, not only as an oppressed people, but as the
people best entitled to consideration of any of our
citizens. This was more than the people who had
secured to us the perpetuation of the Union were
prepared for, and they became more radical in their
views."

And again: " But for the assassination of Mr. Lincoln, I believe the great majority of the Northern people, and the soldiers unanimously, would have been in favor of a speedy reconstruction on terms that would be the least humiliating to the people who had rebelled against their Government. They believed, I have no doubt, as I did, that besides being the mildest, it was also the wisest policy. The people who had been in rebellion must necessarily come back into the Union and be incorporated as an integral part of the nation. . . . They surely would not make good citizens if they felt they had a yoke around their necks."

Yet with feelings at the outset of consideration toward the South, with his instinctive chivalry, without natural sympathy for radical men or measures, he was driven by events, by the tactlessness of the President, by the perverseness of the time, into a position where he could align himself no otherwise than with the advocates of wholesale suffrage for the negro in the South, protected if need be by military force.

CHAPTER XXVI

JOHNSON'S BREAK WITH CONGRESS

JOHNSON's programme met with no organized resistance up to December, 1865, when the new Congress gathered after a nine months' vacation from the 4th of March. Indeed, the people of the North left to themselves seemed to approve it. Beginning in August, State after State in the South, acting in accordance with the Executive's decree, had held conventions which repealed or nullified the ordinance of secession, abolished slavery, and in most cases repudiated the debts incurred in war. Mississippi, South Carolina, Georgia, Alabama, North Carolina, fell into line, balking only at the President's proposal in some cases that the negro should be given qualified suffrage. The men who sat in constitutional conventions and in legislatures chosen under the new order were of high character, willing to accept conditions. The "erring sisters," chastened in spirit, were ready to come home. It looked as though a reunited country would stand behind the President. Republican and Democratic conventions in Northern States vied with one another in endorsing his policy and pledging their support. Pennsylvania, under the lead of Stevens, and Massachusetts, under that of Sumner, alone refused assent. Andrew and Morton, the best of the War Governors, urged coöperation with the President, expressing sympathy for the South and opposing unconditional suffrage for the blacks. Even Stanton, as late as May, 1866, expressed approval of Johnson's acts up to the time that Congress met. His quarrel was of gradual development. It was not until after Congress adjourned in July, 1866, that the open rupture came.

With the gathering of Congress, Stevens in the House and Sumner in the Senate set out to organize the opposition. Up to that time there were no differences which could not have been reconciled, and for nearly three months thereafter nothing happened which might not have been adjusted with fair concession on each side. Sumner and Stevens with their radical proposals could not have carried Congress with them if Johnson had been inclined to counsel with the majority, yielding here and there for harmony; for Sumner and Stevens wanted to go much farther and faster than the great body of Northern men were ready then to follow. And while these two detested Johnson, they wrangled with each other and in reality had slender bonds of sympathy. Stevens, though a partisan fanatic, was intensely practical. Sumner was a turgid visionary, a devotee, who in spite of his nobility of purpose could never quite adjust himself to facts.

If Johnson had been wise enough to play on individual traits, as Lincoln doubtless would have done, if he had not persisted in having things exactly his own way, he might have gained all his essentials and the story of his stormy term need never have been told. Reconstruction might have come about in such a manner as to leave lasting friendliness between the sections, with the Southern States restored to their old places in the Union and gradual enfranchisement of the negro as he became qualified to vote.

Few Northern people really thought the negroes should have suffrage right away. They looked for it in time, but with a hazy expectation. On the whole they were amenable to Johnson's plan of admitting the Senators from Southern States and leaving to the States themselves the suffrage question so long as former slaves received protection in their natural rights. In the election held that fall, Connecticut, Wisconsin, and Minnesota had declared specifically against giving the vote to colored persons and in a general way the elections were regarded as an endorsement of the Administration. The people were not concerned about the prerogatives of the Executive and Congress. They were interested in results and Johnson seemed to be doing fairly well. There had been no impressive number of abolitionists at the beginning of the war, and there was no overwhelming love for the negro at its close. The mass of the people understood that problem of the South better than Sumner or Garrison or Phillips. There were not many who would have been so ingenuous as Garrison on his visit to Charleston in April, 1865, when, overcome by the apparent gratitude of a crowd of twelve hundred emancipated plantation hands, he cried out: "Well, my friends, you are free at last. Let us give three cheers for Freedom"; and was astonished that there was no response. The freedmen did not know how to cheer. Like children they looked on emancipation as a Christmas present. Yet Sumner would have given them the vote at once. Early in December, after informing Gideon Welles in one of his delicious talks, that he had read everything on republican government from Plato to the last French pamphlet, he denounced the President's policy as the greatest and most criminal error ever committed by any government and solemnly asserted that a general officer from Georgia had informed him within a week that the negroes of that State were better qualified to establish and maintain a republican government than the whites.[1] So far credulity could go with a high-minded man.

[1] *Diary of Gideon Welles*, vol. III, pp. 176–81.

The Congress elected a year before, at the same time with Lincoln, had not been chosen with anything like this in view; but the majority were greatly interested in maintaining their prerogatives against executive encroachment and here they were on common ground with Stevens. At the beginning they refused seats to Senators and Representatives from States reorganized under Johnson's plan, thus giving Johnson his contention that Congress was not constituted properly since eleven States remained unrepresented.

The President's first message, written by George Bancroft, was temperate and admirable in tone, met with general approval among the people, and irritated only a few implacables in Congress. Three days before the Senate met, Sumner had talked for two hours and a half with Johnson at the White House, recording his opinion that the President "does not understand the case. Much that he said was painful from its prejudice, ignorance, and perversity," and discontinued all personal relations then and there. On the other hand, John Sherman was writing to his brother, "he seems kind and patient with all his terrible responsibilities." So much depends upon the angle of approach.

Lyman Trumbull, once a Democrat and never a radical Republican, chairman of the Senate Judi-

ciary Committee, reported after the holidays a bill to
enlarge the powers of the Freedmen's Bureau so as to
secure for the freedmen, among other things, civil
rights and "equal and exact justice before the law."
The bill passed House and Senate by a two-thirds
vote in each, but on February 19 the President vetoed
it. Congress had never yet in all its history passed
a really important bill over a veto, and did not do
so now; but on the next day, February 20, the House
adopted a concurrent resolution, reported by Stevens from the Committee on Reconstruction, that no
Senator or Representative from any Southern State
should be admitted to either body until Congress had
declared such State entitled to representation.

Up to this hour Johnson seemed to have the country with him. All the members of his Cabinet, including Stanton, acquiesced. And then his fatal failing,
intemperance in speech, worked his undoing. On
February 22 a crowd of his supporters who had been
meeting in a theater marched to the White House
and he went out to see them. Members of the Cabinet
urged him not to talk and he said he would follow their
advice; but his pet passion overcame him; there were
no bounds to his vituperative tongue. Goaded on by
the crowd he cried: —

"I look upon as being opposed to the fundamental
principles of this government and as now laboring to

destroy them: Thaddeus Stevens, of Pennsylvania, Charles Sumner and Wendell Phillips, of Massachusetts. . . . Are those who want to destroy our institutions and change the character of the government not satisfied with the blood that has been shed? Are they not satisfied with one martyr? . . . Have they not honor and courage enough to effect the removal of the presidential obstacle otherwise than through the hands of the assassin? I am not afraid of assassins!"

In ten minutes he had lowered himself beyond rehabilitation in the country's eyes and had given Congress an advantage that they could not have gained without his aid. From that moment his was a losing cause. Later, Congress passed a Civil Rights Bill. He vetoed it and Congress now established a precedent; it overrode his veto. In June the resolution upon which the Fourteenth Amendment is based was adopted, and in July a new Freedmen's Bureau Bill was passed, in spite of the President's objection. Congress had acquired the habit of defiance. Vetoes had become too cheap and frequent to challenge their respect.

Thus Congress carried through its plan for Reconstruction, moderate and sensible, as a whole, and Johnson saw himself discredited. It was not till June, 1866, that Stanton let the public know that he had opposed the veto of the Civil Rights Bill.

It is not easy now to put one's finger on a serious objection to Johnson's plan divorced from personal dislike of the Executive; but the fact that he had undertaken to reconstruct the Southern States without waiting for Congress to assemble, and had failed to insist upon the franchise for negroes as well as whites, had given his opponents needed ammunition; his own intemperate denunciation had done the rest.

By the same token, in the congressional plan, as crystallized in legislation during that session, one can distinguish little to which Johnson might not with self-respect have given his endorsement. On the whole it was as good a piece of work as could have been expected, opening a path through which the Southern States might have resumed their places in the Union without self-abasement. The Fourteenth Amendment did not impose negro suffrage upon any State, but left that question to the States concerned, subject only to curtailment of representation in proportion to the number of citizens to whom the franchise might be denied. The Freedmen's Bureau Bill and the Civil Rights Bill in the form then passed contained no onerous conditions. The States lately in rebellion were left to the control of their own local affairs.

If Johnson had then only shown a spirit of concession, the Southern question might have been set-

tled with the adjournment of that first session in
July, 1866. To his appeal the South would doubtless
have listened with respect; but so long as he kept up
the controversy and continued his assaults upon the
motives of all who took exception to his plan, they
would have been superhuman not to wait for terms
more satisfying to their pride. Their tardiness, encouraged by Johnson's folly, led to the deplorable
enactments later which held the seeds of years of
sectional strife.

Elections to a new Congress were to be held in the
autumn following adjournment of the first session,
and there was nothing to it for Johnson, with his passion for dispute, except to utilize the opportunity to
force the North to his own way of thinking. Late in
August he set out on the " swing around the circle,"
taking Grant, Farragut, and several members of the
Cabinet on his train.

Grant did not want to go. He had for months been
drifting farther and farther away from Johnson. But
he was indispensable to Johnson's purpose. In the
controversy between the President and Congress it
had been assumed both North and South that his
sympathies were with Johnson and when he now
left Washington in Johnson's company and appeared
day after day on the same platform with him, the
suspicion was strengthened: but this was all a part

of Johnson's cunning scheme, conceived by Seward, it is said.

Johnson left a vituperative trail in every city of importance between Washington and Chicago. At Cleveland he was manifestly in his cups. And he was hardly started on his trip before the country knew that he was lost. The most praiseworthy cause could not have weathered such a champion. The people were humiliated and ashamed. Grant seized the earliest opportunity to plead sickness, quit the party, and return to Washington. He had seen Johnson at his worst; and he could never hold him in respect again.

Already the relations between Johnson and Stanton were badly strained. Stanton was loath to carry out Johnson's orders interfering with the work of the district commanders in the South, and the President was soon hunting for some one who would be amenable.

Uprisings in the South seemed imminent. There had been riots in New Orleans two days after the adjournment of Congress, July 28, and Grant began to look for trouble. On October 12 he wrote confidentially to Sheridan, who had quit Texas and was in command at New Orleans: " I regret to say that since the unfortunate difference between the President and Congress, the former becomes more violent with the opposition he meets with, until now but few people who were loyal to the Government during the rebellion seem to have any influence with him. None have unless they join in a crusade against Congress and declare their acts, the principal ones, illegal; and indeed I much fear that we are fast approaching the time when he will want to declare the body itself unconstitutional and revolutionary. Commanders in Southern States will have to take care and see if a crisis does come that no armed headway can be made against the Union."

The result of the elections was cumulative in its irritating effect upon the discredited Johnson. Maine and Vermont in September, Pennsylvania, Ohio, Indiana, and Iowa in October, and all the other Northern States in November gave great majorities against the Administration. Only Maryland, Delaware, and Kentucky were Democratic. The Republicans had a larger majority in House and Senate than ever, amply more than the two thirds needed to override a veto of any Reconstruction measure they might see fit to pass.

Another man in Johnson's place would have accepted the result of the elections as determining the question of Reconstruction so far as his administration was concerned, for the Congress just chosen would not expire until his own term ended. Only colossal egotism or abounding ignorance could have prompted opposition to so overwhelming a majority, and only devotion to an all-absorbing moral issue could have excused it. But Johnson fatuously undertook to thwart the will of Congress, with sorry results both to himself and to the section he set out to serve.

The Southern leaders as a rule would reluctantly have taken the Fourteenth Amendment had it not been for Johnson's influence, but owing to his encouragement, every one of the eleven seceding States in the period between August, 1866, and February, 1867, refused to ratify. As a practical necessity, therefore, Congress was forced to adopt more drastic measures to bring the recalcitrants into line. It was intolerable that the Southern States, who before the war had enjoyed representation in Congress for only three fifths of the number of their slaves, should, as a result of insurrection and defeat, come back into the Union with representation based on the entire number of citizens, both white and black, while only the whites had the privilege of the vote, thus giving the whites of the South, in spite of the terrible loss in Northern lives and treasure during the rebellion a greater proportionate representation than ever in the House and the Electoral College. The Southern leaders would have seen this had they been let alone. But Johnson blocked the way.

CHAPTER XXVII

AT ODDS WITH JOHNSON

GRANT was entirely out of sympathy with Johnson by this time, though as a soldier under orders he did not publicly take issue with his official chief. His immediate superior, Stanton, by the fall of 1866, had gone over boldly to the radicals in Congress, with whom for months he had already been in secret correspondence, so that Grant was in a trying place. We have seen how he wrote to Sheridan, but outwardly he maintained a reticence so complete that only Johnson and some members of the Cabinet suspected how he really felt. In his testimony before the House Judiciary Committee on July 18, 1867, after the quarrel had progressed much farther, he thus explained himself: —

"I have always been attentive to my own duties, and tried not to interfere with other people's. I was always ready to originate matters pertaining to the Army, but I was never ready to originate matters pertaining to the civil government of the United States. When I was asked my opinion about what had been done I was willing to give it. I originated no plan and suggested no plan for civil government. I only gave my views on measures after they had been originated. I simply expressed an anxiety that something should be done to give some sort of control down there. There were no governments there when the war was over and I wanted to see some governments established and wanted to see it done quickly. I did not pretend to say how it should be done or in what form."

Riots were threatened in Baltimore at election time in November, 1866. It was a controversy between rival boards of police commissioners, one appointed by the Democratic Governor, Swann, the other claiming independent authority. Johnson wanted to send troops to help the Governor to uphold his own commissioners. He had with him all the Cabinet but Stanton. Grant protested earnestly, and when he found the President persisting, he wrote an official letter to the Secretary of War calling attention to the law which specified the only circumstances in which the military forces of the United States could be called out to interfere in state affairs. The troops were not sent and Grant, by his personal influence in two visits to Baltimore, persuaded the contending parties to leave their quarrel to the courts. If Johnson had prevailed, the Federal troops would have been used against the party which had been loyal to the Union and in behalf of former Confederates.

Grant thought he saw here a disloyal intent. Whatever its purpose, he saved an ugly situation.

Maximilian was still in Mexico. Napoleon, yielding to persistent pressure and convinced at last of the futility of his designs, had ordered the French troops withdrawn. He had good reason for this change of policy. Grant two years before had sent Schofield to Texas with secret orders to organize if necessary an army of American volunteers, for enrollment under the Liberal Government in Mexico, to drive out the invaders. He thought that Seward had befogged the issue and that if he had a partiality, it leaned toward imperial success. Grant was insistent on enforcing the Monroe Doctrine, and kept the Minister from France in Washington informed of how he felt. Napoleon knew that Grant would almost certainly in a few months be President, clothed with authority which now he lacked. At last Seward sent Schofield to Paris with instructions to "get your legs under Napoleon's mahogany and tell him he must get out of Mexico." So the French army quit, but Maximilian with quixotic chivalry remained. His fragile empire was already crumbling, and the republican government which we had recognized was coming to its own. There was no special reason why Grant or any other army officer should go to Mexico; yet in the middle of October, just as he had become annoyingly unsympathetic with Johnson's policies, a pretext was found to send him there.

Campbell, who had been appointed Minister a long while before and had dawdled the intervening time away, was due at last to enter on his service, and Johnson ordered Grant to accompany him "to give the Minister the benefit of his advice in carrying out the instructions of the Secretary of State." At the same time Sherman, who had been outspoken in favor of Administration policies, was ordered to Washington, the intention being to detail him to Grant's military duties.

To the amazement of Johnson and Seward, Grant refused to go. He had divined the purpose of the mission. Johnson renewed the order in a day or two. Grant again declined, this time in writing. A little later he was summoned to a Cabinet meeting. The Secretary of State read him detailed instructions for his mission as if nothing unusual had occurred. Grant was not disturbed. He told the President and the Cabinet that he did not intend to go. Turning to the Attorney-General, Johnson exclaimed: "Mr. Attorney-General, is there any reason why General Grant should not obey my orders? Is he in any way ineligible to this position?" "I can answer that question, Mr. President," said Grant, "without referring to the Attorney-General. I am an American citizen

and eligible to any office to which any American is
eligible. I am an officer of the Army and bound to
obey your military orders. But this is a civil office,
a purely diplomatic duty that you offer me, and I
cannot be compelled to undertake it." No one replied and Grant left the room.

Even after this the President persisted. Stanton
was told to ask Grant to proceed to Mexico; and
Grant had to write another letter declining to go.

When Sherman arrived in Washington, he reported
first to Grant, who told him what the President had
in mind. The rest of the story, as Sherman tells it in
his "Memoirs," sheds an interesting light upon the
characters of Grant and Johnson. The President's
plain misconstruction of Grant's attitude helps to
illuminate the controversy between the two over a
year later, when the issue of veracity became acute.

"General Grant," says Sherman, "denied the right
of the President to order him on a diplomatic mission
unattended by troops; said that he had thought the
matter over, would disobey the order and stand the
consequences. He manifested much feeling and said
it was a plot to get rid of him. I then went to President Johnson, . . . who said that General Grant was
about to go to Mexico on business of importance and
he wanted me at Washington to command the Army
in General Grant's absence. I then informed him that

General Grant would not go and he seemed amazed; said ... that Mr. Campbell had been accredited to Juarez ... and the fact that he was accompanied by so distinguished a soldier would emphasize the act of the United States. I simply reiterated that General Grant *would not go* and that he, Mr. Johnson, could not afford to quarrel with him at that time." Sherman suggested that if the real object were to put Campbell in official communication with Juarez, the bill could be filled better by Hancock or Sheridan, and that he himself could be sooner spared than Grant, who was engaged in the most delicate and difficult task of reorganizing the Army under the Act of July 28, 1866. "Certainly," answered the President; "if you will go, that will answer perfectly."

So Sherman went to Mexico with Campbell. As he sailed from New York Harbor on the Susquehanna, he turned to the captain and said: "My mission is already ended. By substituting myself I have prevented a serious quarrel between the Administration and Grant." As might have been expected, his journey, from which he returned three months later, was a waste of time.

When the Thirty-ninth Congress met for its second session on December 5, 1866, the Fourteenth Amendment had not yet been ratified. Congress had voted that no Senator or Representative should be ad-

mitted from either of the eleven States which had
been in insurrection until the right of such State to
representation had been agreed to by both Houses
of Congress. A bill proposed by Stevens, and reported from the Committee on Reconstruction in
the closing days of the session, providing for the re-
admission of the seceding States upon the acceptance by them of the Fourteenth amendment, had
not become a law.

Congress turned at once to Reconstruction measures. Stevens promptly introduced a bill providing for
valid governments in the States still unreconstructed,
on the basis of negro suffrage and white disfranchisement. He was goaded to vindictiveness by the contumacy of Southern Legislatures and Johnson's
stubbornness, while many who had been inclined to
moderation six months before were now ready to
take the verdict of the elections as justifying measures as radical as might be urged. The bill, which became known as the Reconstruction Act, brushed
aside the State Governments created through executive decree which had been in feeble operation for
many months, divided their territory into five military districts, each to be commanded by an army
officer of the rank at least of Brigadier-General, who
was to be designated by the General of the Army.
This bill, unpalatable to a numerous minority of his

own party, because it provided for indeterminate military rule, was whipped through the House by Stevens with a scourge of taunts which brought the tardy into line. While the bill was pending in the Senate, Grant quietly let it leak out that he would rather leave the designation of district commanders to the President than to the General of the Army — and in this form the bill became law over the President's veto on the 2d of March.

As finally enacted, the law provided that Senators and Representatives from a seceded State should be admitted to seats in Congress on the adoption of a constitution providing among other things for universal suffrage without discrimination as to color and the adoption of the Fourteenth Amendment. It was left to the military commander in each district to take the initiative in summoning a convention to pave the way for Reconstruction.

While the struggle between the President and Congress had been going on, Johnson had arbitrarily removed several thousand Republican office-holders and filled their places with his own sympathizers. To meet this, Congress, on March 2, passed over his veto the Tenure of Office Act, which took away from him the power, without the Senate's consent, to remove office-holders originally confirmed by the Senate. His disregard of this act in Stanton's case brought on the

series of events leading up to his impeachment; yet
it is a striking fact that Stanton himself, though not
then on cordial terms with Johnson, joined with
Seward in helping to frame the veto measure which
Johnson signed.

Thus the Thirty-ninth Congress, chosen six months
before the close of the war and meeting for the first
time nine months after Lincoln's death, placed on the
statutes over his successor's veto radical measures
for the reconstruction of the South which Lincoln
would not have stood for and which only a small
minority of its own membership would have favored
when it first assembled — measures which ushered
in a period of racial and sectional hate, of violence and
blood-letting, of extravagance, corruption, and national degeneracy for which our history presents no
parallel, not even in the stress of civil war. Grant,
though the first citizen of the Republic, already set
apart for the chief magistracy, had the habit of military subordination so firmly fixed and was so lacking
in political experience that he had little influence on
legislation. He had to watch the current drift, unconscious, for all that the records show, that he was
fated at his entrance upon the Presidency to find a
problem confronting him which the wisest and most
masterful of statesmen could hardly hope to solve.
He had no sympathy with Johnson, Stevens, or

Sumner in their quarrels. He owed them no gratitude for the hateful legacy bequeathed to him by their mistaken zeal.

The new Congress, which met on March 4 in accordance with a law enacted to curb Johnson's control, stirred Johnson's wrath still further by legislation stripping him of authority under the Reconstruction acts. Stanton approved this new legislation. There is evidence that he drafted its principal features. He was outspoken in Cabinet meetings against the President and his associates in the Administration. His breach with Johnson was complete. Congress adjourned, on July 20, to November 3. It was hardly out of the way before Johnson set out to get rid of Stanton and to displace Sheridan. Sheridan had really started the row by removing state and city officers concerned in the New Orleans riots a year earlier and Governor J. Madison Welles, "who," he wrote, was "a political trickster and a dishonest man . . . his conduct has been as sinuous as the mark left in the dust by the movement of a snake."

Before taking definite action Johnson told Grant what he had in mind. This was on August 1. Grant entered a strong protest which he embodied in a letter later in the same day: —

"I take the liberty of addressing you privately on the subject of the conversation we had this morning, feeling as I do the great danger to the welfare of the country should you carry out the designs then expressed.

"First, on the subject of the displacement of the Secretary of War. His removal cannot be effected against his will without the consent of the Senate. It is but a short time since the United States Senate was in session, and why not then have asked for his removal if it was desired? It certainly was the intention of the legislative branch of the Government to place Cabinet officers beyond the power of Executive removal, and it is pretty well understood that so far as Cabinet ministers are affected by the 'Tenure of Office Bill,' it was intended specially to protect the Secretary of War, whom the country felt great confidence in. The meaning of the law may be explained away by an astute lawyer, but common sense and the views of loyal people will give to it the effect intended by its framers.

"On the subject of the removal of the very able commander of the Fifth Military District, let me ask you to consider the effect it would have upon the public. He is universally and deservedly beloved by the people who sustained this Government through its trials, and feared by those who would still be enemies of the Government. . . .

"In conclusion allow me to say, as a friend, desiring

peace and quiet, the welfare of the whole country North and South, that it is in my opinion more than the loyal people of this country (I mean those who supported the Government during the great rebellion) will quietly submit to, to see the very men of all others whom they have expressed confidence in removed."

Whereupon the President, on August 5, sent Stanton this note: —

"*Sir:* — Public considerations of a high character constrain me to say that your resignation as Secretary of War will be accepted."

To which Stanton immediately replied: —

"I have the honor to say that public considerations of a high character, which alone have induced me to continue at the head of the Department, constrain me not to resign the office of Secretary of War before the next meeting of Congress."

CHAPTER XXVIII
ACTING SECRETARY OF WAR

THWARTED in his demand for Stanton's resignation, Johnson decided to suspend him and put Grant in his place. No one could say with certainty even then just where Grant stood on the disputed questions of the hour. It was a hard part to play, with passion raging everywhere, but he had thus far saved himself from taking sides. Ben Wade, one of the most bitter radicals in Congress, said he had often tried to find out whether Grant was for Congress or for Johnson or what he was for, but never could get anything out of him; "for as quick as he'd talk politics Grant would talk horse." Actually, however, we have seen that Grant was now convinced that the congressional policy, however regrettable in certain features, had become inevitable through Johnson's mistaken course. He believed primarily in strict obedience to the law.

On August 12, 1867, therefore, Johnson sent word to Stanton suspending him from the office of Secretary of War and directing him to turn the records of the office over to General Grant. Grant notified Stanton of his assignment, concluding a courteous note:—

"In notifying you of my acceptance, I cannot let

the opportunity pass without expressing to you my appreciation of the zeal, patriotism, firmness, and ability with which you have ever discharged the duties of Secretary of War."

Stanton responded with equal courtesy; but he enclosed with this communication the copy of a vivid letter which he had sent that same day to Johnson, denying the legality of his suspension and concluding: —

"But inasmuch as the General commanding the armies of the United States has been appointed *ad interim*, and has notified me that he has accepted the appointment, I have no alternative but to submit, under protest, to superior force."

Gideon Welles, the sturdy and vivacious chronicler of individual dislikes, gives in his "Diary" the memorandum of a conversation he had with Grant a few days later at the War Department, in which Grant clearly showed his sympathy with Congress, though not, it must be said, with cogent reasoning, as Welles transcribes his views. "On the whole," comments the controversial diarist, "I did not think so highly of General Grant after as before this conversation. He is a political ignoramus. . . . Obviously he has been tampered with and flattered by the Radicals, who are using him and his name for their selfish and partisan purposes."

It was a mistake for Grant to take Stanton's place. He served as Secretary from August, 1867, to January, 1868; and nothing was so eventful in his service as the manner of his leaving it, although he remedied abuses in administration, and rid the Government of unnecessary waste, in rotten contracts, growing out of war. The people did not understand his attitude. There was no reason why they should. His letter to the President protesting against the removal of Sheridan and Stanton was not published at the time. The North did not appreciate that he had kept the place from falling into the hands of one who might be more subservient to Johnson's whims. They were resentful and indignant at the sacrifice of Stanton and blamed Grant for what looked like acquiescence.

As Grant maintained his taciturnity, no one, outside the Cabinet and his personal staff, suspected the continual friction between the War Department and the White House. He attended Cabinet meetings as seldom as possible and avoided the discussion of political questions, leaving usually as soon as the routine business was ended. He tried to keep his civil and military characters distinct. It was an incongruous combination with a touch of Gilbert and Sullivan. As Acting Secretary at the War Department in the morning he would sign orders to himself as General of the Army and then trudge across the street to Army headquarters, where he would acknowledge their receipt and execute them.

The open break with Johnson came on Sheridan's removal. In that encounter Grant got the worst of it. In giving his order removing Sheridan and putting Thomas in his place, Johnson invited suggestions and Grant replied: —

" I am pleased to avail myself of your invitation to urge — earnestly urge, urge in the name of patriotic people — that this order should not be insisted upon. It is the will of the country that General Sheridan should not be removed from his present command. This is a republic where the will of the people is the law of the land. I beg that their voice may be heard."

This and more like it, so lacking in Grant's usual simplicity and restraint, Johnson punctured with the retort: —

"I am not aware that the question of retaining General Sheridan in command of the Fifth Military District has ever been submitted to the people themselves for determination. . . . General Sheridan has rendered himself exceedingly obnoxious by the manner in which he has exercised the powers conferred by Congress and still more so by the resort to authority not granted by law. . . . His removal, therefore, cannot be regarded as an effort to defeat the laws of Congress."

These letters were made public after Sheridan's removal. Johnson was praised in the South for his discomfiture of Grant and Grant was criticized in the North for the feebleness of his stand against Johnson. He might have drawn a lesson from the incident that he was less fit for controversy than command.

Johnson, on December 12, 1867, just three weeks after Congress met again after a long recess, sent a message telling all about Stanton's suspension, fortified with documents and containing interesting revelations in regard to Stanton's own attitude toward the Tenure of Office Act. For an example: —

"Every member of my Cabinet advised me that the proposed law was unconstitutional. All spoke without doubt or reservation, but Mr. Stanton's condemnation of the law was the most elaborate and emphatic. . . . I was so much struck with the full mastery of the question manifested by Mr. Stanton . . . that I requested him to prepare the veto upon this Tenure of Office Bill. This he declined on the ground of physical disability, . . . but stated his readiness to furnish what aid might be required in the preparation of materials for the paper."

Talk about impeachment rumbled in the air. During the preceding winter several resolutions had been presented in the House, had been considered by committees, and as late as February 15 had been disapproved.

Then in a week, committee and House reversed themselves. On February 22, 1868, just two years from the day Johnson made his ill-fated speech from the White House steps, the Reconstruction Committee unanimously reported a resolution of impeachment, and two days later the resolution was adopted by the House, 128 to 47, the negative votes all Democrats. What had happened to bring about so swift a change?

The Senate had duly considered Johnson's reasons for suspending Stanton and resolved that they were insufficient. This was late in the afternoon of January 13, the Senate having had the question under consideration since January 11. On the morning of the 14th, Grant went to the office of the Secretary of War, locked and bolted the door on the outside, turned the key over to the Adjutant-General, and at once sent a formal letter to the President, by the hand of General Comstock, saying that he had been notified of the action of the Senate and that by the terms of the law his own functions as Secretary of War ceased with the reception of the notice. Stanton was once more in possession.

With customary incivility almost his first act was

to send a messenger to Grant's office with word that he "wanted to see him." Had it not been before the days of electricity, he would no doubt have pressed a buzzer, as happened afterwards with other secretaries and other generals. Both Grant and Sherman four months before his removal had found Stanton's arrogance insufferable, and Grant at one time had concluded that either he or Stanton must resign.[1]

[1] "In 1866, 1867, and 1868, General Grant talked to me freely several times of his differences with Secretary Stanton. His most emphatic declaration on that subject, and of his own intended action in consequence, appears from the records to have been made after Stanton's return to the war office in January, 1868, when his conduct was even more offensive to Grant than it had been before Stanton's suspension in August, 1867, and when Grant and Sherman were trying to get Stanton out of the war office. At the time of General Grant's visit to Richmond, Virginia, as one of the Peabody Trustees, he said to me that the conduct of Mr. Stanton had become intolerable to him, and, after asking my opinion, declared in emphatic terms his intention to demand either the removal of Stanton or the acceptance of his own resignation. But the bitter personal controversy which immediately followed between Grant and Johnson, the second attempt to remove Stanton in February, 1868, and the consequent impeachment of the President, totally eclipsed the more distant and lesser controversy between Grant and Stanton, and doubtless prevented Grant from taking the action in respect to Stanton's removal which he informed me at Richmond he intended to take." (Schofield, *Forty-six Years in the Army*, pp. 412–13.)

CHAPTER XXIX

A QUESTION OF VERACITY — THE IMPEACHMENT PROCEEDINGS — ELECTION AS PRESIDENT

JOHNSON was furious. That day a bitter, far-reaching dispute began, involving the good faith and truthfulness of Grant and the veracity of Johnson. It severed all relations between the two. Johnson contended that the Tenure of Office Act was unconstitutional, and that in any event, by the manner of its phrasing, it did not apply to Stanton or any other of Lincoln's appointees. He wanted to test it in the courts, and he declared that Grant agreed to "return the office to my possession in time to enable me to appoint a successor before final action by the Senate upon Mr. Stanton's suspension, or would remain as its head awaiting a decision of the question by judicial proceedings."

Grant denied that he had made such an agreement. He admitted that some time after assuming the duties of Secretary, when the President asked his views as to the course which Stanton must pursue to gain possession of the office in case the Senate should not concur in his suspension, he had replied in substance that Stanton would have to appeal to the courts to reinstate him. "Finding that the President was desirous of keeping Mr. Stanton out of office, whether sustained in the suspension or not, I stated that I had not looked particularly into the Tenure of Office Bill, but that what I had stated was a general principle and if I should change my mind in this particular case I would inform him of the fact. Subsequently, on reading the Tenure of Office Bill closely, I found that I could not without violation of the law refuse to vacate the office of Secretary of War the moment Mr. Stanton was reinstated by the Senate,[1] even though the President should order me to retain it, which he never did. Taking this view of the subject and learning on Saturday, the 11th instant, that the Senate had taken up the subject of Mr. Stanton's suspension, after some conversation with Lieutenant-General Sherman and some members of my staff, in which I stated that the law left me no discretion as to my action should Mr. Stanton be reinstated, and that I intended to inform the President, I went to the President for the sole purpose of making this decision known and did so make it known. In doing this I

[1] Sec. 5 — That if any person shall, contrary to the provision of this Act, accept any appointment to or employment in any office, or shall hold or exercise any such office or employment, he shall be deemed, and is hereby declared to be, guilty of a high misdemeanor, and, upon trial and conviction thereof, he shall be punished therefor by a fine not exceeding ten thousand dollars or by imprisonment not exceeding five years, or both said punishments, in the discretion of the court.

fulfilled the promise made in our last preceding conversation on the subject."

The trouble was that Johnson did not know Grant. He could not comprehend finality of purpose in one who did not storm and bluster. Like many other stubborn men of narrow opportunities he overestimated his own power of persuasion. As Grant was leaving after announcing his decision, Johnson said he would expect to see him again. To Johnson this meant further argument with the probability of Grant's acceding to his views. To Grant it meant nothing of the sort. He had made up his mind. Johnson had misjudged Grant once before when he told Sherman Grant was going to Mexico after Grant had said he did not intend to go. He might have profited by that experience.

The 14th was Cabinet day. Johnson, in whose own hand Comstock had placed Grant's written notification and who had read it in Comstock's presence, ignoring the letter, sent word back by Comstock that he wanted to see Grant at the meeting. In his controversial letter to Johnson, dated January 28, 1868, Grant says: —

"At this meeting, after opening it as though I were a member of the Cabinet, when reminded of the notification already given him that I was no longer Secretary of War *ad interim*, the President gave a version of the conversations alluded to already. In this statement it was asserted that in both conversations I had agreed to hold on to the office of Secretary of War until displaced by the courts, or resign, so as to place the President where he would have been had I never accepted the office. After hearing the President through, I stated our conversations substantially as given in this letter. . . . I in no wise admitted the correctness of the President's statement, though, to soften the evident contradiction my statement gave, I said (alluding to our first conversation on the subject) the President might have understood me the way he said, namely, that I had promised to resign if I did not resist the reinstatement. I made no such promise."

Here the question of veracity arises. The next morning the "National Intelligencer," the Administration organ, had an editorial purporting to give an account of the meeting, leaving Grant in the position of having then admitted equivocation and a breach of faith. Grant called with Sherman at the White House to protest against it. At a meeting next day Johnson read the editorial to the members of the Cabinet and secured from each of them a confirmation of the "Intelligencer" report. Still later each gave the President a written statement confirming Johnson's recollection of the affair.

Gideon Welles, who had long included Grant in his accumulating collection of malevolents, thus describes the scene in his "Diary": —

"The President was calm and dignified, though manifestly disappointed and displeased. General Grant was humble, hesitating, and he evidently felt that his position was equivocal and not to his credit. There was, I think, an impression on the minds of all present (there certainly was on mine) that a consciousness that he had acted with duplicity — not been faithful and true to the man who had confided in and trusted him — oppressed General Grant. His manner, never very commanding, was almost abject, and he left the room with less respect, I apprehend, from those present than ever before. The President, though disturbed and not wholly able to conceal his chagrin from those familiar with him, used no hard expressions nor committed anything approaching incivility, yet Grant felt the few words put to him and the cold and surprised disdain of the President in all their force."

The correspondence between Grant and Johnson growing out of this dispute began with a request from Grant, on January 24, that the President give him in writing an order, given verbally five days earlier, to disregard Stanton's orders as Secretary of War. "I am compelled to ask these instructions in writing," he says in the letter of January 28 already quoted, "in consequence of the many and gross misrepresentations affecting my personal honor, circulated through the press for the past fortnight, purporting to come from the President, of conversations which occurred either with the President privately in his office or in Cabinet meeting. What is written admits of no misunderstanding."

So far as Grant was concerned the correspondence ended with his letter of February 3 in response to Johnson's letter of January 31. There is nothing in American history before or since to compare with this challenge of the President's veracity by the General of the Army.

Badeau says that Grant first wrote a reply much milder in tone, admitting the possibility that Johnson might have honestly misconstrued his position. But Rawlins, who unlike Grant saw the political bearing of the controversy, said: "This will not do; it is not enough"; and drafted a paragraph directly contradicting and defying the President. This may well be true; at any rate, the letter unequivocal and personal destroyed all possibility of further relations and made Grant at once the head of the Republican Party.

Grant in his letter said of Johnson's statement: —

"I find it but a reiteration, only somewhat more

in detail, of the 'many and gross misrepresentations' . . . which my statement of the facts set forth
in my letter of the 28th ultimo was intended to correct; and I here reassert the correctness of my statements in that letter; anything in yours in reply to it
to the contrary notwithstanding. I confess my sur-
prise that the Cabinet officers referred to should so
greatly misapprehend the facts in the matter of ad-
missions alleged to have been made by me. . . .

"From our conversations, and my written protest
of August 1, 1867, against the removal of Mr. Stanton, you must have known that my greatest objection to his removal or suspension was the fear that
some one would be appointed in his stead, who would,
by opposition to the laws relating to the restoration
of the Southern States to their proper relations to
the Government, embarrass the Army in the performance of duties especially imposed upon it by
these laws; and it was to prevent such an appointment that I accepted the office of Secretary of War
ad interim, and not for the purpose of enabling you
to get rid of Mr. Stanton by my withholding it from
him in opposition to law, or, not doing so myself,
surrendering it to one who would, as the statement
and assumptions in your communication plainly indicate was sought. . . . The course you would have it
understood I had agreed to pursue was in violation of

law, and without orders from you; while the course I did pursue and which I never doubted you fully understood, was in accordance with law, and not in disobedience to any orders of my superior.

"And now, Mr. President, when my honor as a soldier and integrity as a man have been so violently assailed, pardon me for saying that I can but regard this whole matter, from the beginning to the end, as an attempt to involve me in the resistance of law, for which you hesitated to assume the responsibility in orders, and thus to destroy my character before the country. I am in a measure confirmed in this conclusion by your recent orders directing me to disobey orders from the Secretary of War, — my superior and your subordinate, — without having countermanded his authority to issue the orders I am to disobey."

He concluded with the assurance "that nothing less than a vindication of my personal honor and character" could have induced this correspondence on his part.

From that day Grant refused to have any dealings whatever either with Johnson or with members of the Cabinet who, in confirming Johnson's version of their interview, gave the sanction of their names to his assault on Grant's veracity.

While Congress and the country were intent on his dispute with Grant, Johnson was nursing his determination to get rid of Stanton. He refused to recognize him as Secretary. He directed Grant to ignore Stanton's orders. He tried to get Sherman to take Stanton's place; but Sherman sturdily refused. Johnson's personal objection to Stanton was only one of the factors in his determination. He was obsessed with the idea of testing the Tenure of Office Act in the courts and thus gaining a tactical advantage over his enemies in Congress. On February 21 he ordered Lorenzo Thomas, the Adjutant-General, to take possession of the office of the Secretary of War, and gave him a letter which Thomas handed to Stanton removing Stanton. Stanton held on to the office and barred Thomas out. The defiance was on.

Then it was that Stevens presented his report, signed by all the Republican members of the Reconstruction Committee, impeaching Andrew Johnson of high crimes and misdemeanors in office. Two days later the House adopted the resolution, 126 to 47, every Republican present voting "aye." The trial in the Senate began almost immediately. Johnson escaped conviction by a single vote, and, strange to say, one of the earliest concessions on both sides was that, so far as Stanton's removal was concerned, he had acted entirely within the law. The charges on which the case against him was finally made were

Stevens's charges of general contumacy which the House had a few weeks earlier refused to regard as justifying impeachment.

The first vote of the Senate on the articles of impeachment was on May 16. Then a recess of Congress was taken to May 26, when the final vote was taken. During the recess the National Union Republican Convention assembled in Chicago, and on May 20 Grant was nominated for President by a unanimous vote, with Schuyler Colfax, Speaker of the House, for Vice-President. Grant had never voted but once in his life and then for Buchanan, "because I knew Frémont." If he had qualified in Illinois in 1860, he would have voted for Douglas. But his antecedents were Republican. That was the political faith of his father, and through his experience with Johnson he had developed a partisan bias which led him even to the point of hoping for Johnson's conviction on the articles of impeachment. There was no incongruity, therefore, in his becoming the Republican candidate, and it was lucky for the party that they could command the service of the outstanding figure of the time. The elections of the fall of 1867 had shown an alarming Democratic tendency. With any other candidate than Grant in 1868 the Republicans might have been hard pressed for success, assuming that the Democrats showed ordinary political sense in their selection of a candidate.

Grant received the notice of his nomination at Galena. His letter of acceptance was commendable for brevity and good taste. He undertook to discuss no issues, but gave assurances that he would try to carry out the purpose of the party which had named him, and, as an afterthought it is said, he appended to the letter the sentence, "Let us have peace," an appeal which went to the people's heart and proved to be the rallying cry of the campaign. But in spite of everything the result was by no means a foregone conclusion. Seymour and Blair, the Democratic candidates, carried New York, New Jersey, and Oregon among the Northern States. Pennsylvania, Ohio, and Indiana went Republican by unexpectedly close margins. Grant carried twenty-six States, it is true, with 214 electoral votes, and Seymour only eight States with 80 electoral votes, but the popular majority was much smaller than these figures would indicate. If it had not been for the negro vote in the South, which was still unsuppressed and which prevented that section from being solidly Democratic, as it afterwards became, Seymour would have been elected.

From the day of his election till he went back to Washington for his inauguration, Grant remained in intellectual seclusion. Although he spent much time in Washington, few men of standing in his party saw him, and with these few he was strangely reticent. As in the Army he had never held a council of war, so now he asked no one's advice about his Cabinet or his inaugural address. He made no suggestions to Republican leaders in Congress as to measures which he might like to see them enact pending his induction into office.

Stevens had died in the summer of 1868, and his mantle of leadership had been grabbed by the braggart Butler, who kept the House torn with dissension and noisy with turmoil in his determination to force through laws still further to harass the stricken South. In order to insure to Republican "carpet-baggers" and "scalawags" possession of the local offices in the unreconstructed States, a resolution was framed ordering the district commander to remove all civil officers who could not take the iron-clad oath and appoint in their places men who could subscribe to it, with a proviso that those whose disabilities had been removed by Congress might also be eligible to office. The resolution was passed unanimously in both houses without debate. At the time of its adoption it benefited only carpet-baggers and ex-Confederate "scalawags" who had become Republicans. To put beyond the reach of legislative recall the negro's right to vote, the Fifteenth Amendment of the Constitution was framed, providing that " The right of citizens of the United States to vote shall not be denied or abridged by the United States or by any State on account of race, color, or previous condition of servitude."

Thus Grant, in entering upon the Presidency, — the first strictly civil office he had ever held, — found himself confronted by political conditions in the South which might have staggered a statesman of lifelong experience and for which he was in no way responsible, while domestic questions affecting the nation's financial credit and foreign problems affecting its standing among the nations of the world pressed for consideration. Those who criticize the course of his Administration and condemn him for his choice of advisers might first point out what statesman of the day would have done better in his place and what advisers would have aided him to more beneficent results.

CHAPTER XXX

PRESIDENT OF THE UNITED STATES

WHEN Grant became President, it seemed for the moment as though a second "era of good feeling" were at hand. Democrats as well as Republicans looked on him as their chosen leader. There was only one unpleasant feature about his assumption of office. Grant refused to ride in the same carriage with Johnson from the White House to the Capitol on inauguration day. He could not forget that Johnson had called his truthfulness in question.

Grant's first inaugural was written entirely by himself; no one saw a draft of it until the day of its delivery. As the 4th of March approached without an intimation of what Grant had in mind, A. R. Corbin — a prospective brother-in-law who was gaining a livelihood on the fringe of Wall Street — handed the President a complete draft of an inaugural. But, without glancing at the contents, Grant handed the document to Badeau, telling him to lock it up in a desk, keep the key, and let no one look at it until after the 4th of March.

The inaugural was brief, — only twelve hundred words, — yet in spite of its brevity it contained sentences which stuck in the mind and some of which have since become embedded in our common speech: "The responsibilities of the position I feel, but accept them without fear. The office has come to me unsought; I commence its duties untrammeled." "All laws will be faithfully executed, whether they meet my approval or not. I shall on all subjects have a policy to recommend, but none to enforce against the will of the people. Laws are to govern all alike — those opposed as well as those who favor them. I know no method to repeal bad or obnoxious laws so effective as their stringent execution."

In spite of some criticism of certain seemingly self-sufficient passages, the inaugural took well; but when the new Cabinet was announced, Republican politicians gasped with dismay. Only two of the names had ever been guessed and some were not suspected by the nominees themselves until they appeared in the list. Elihu B. Washburne, of Illinois, was named Secretary of State; it had been assumed that Grant would recognize in some way the services of his earliest influential friend, but this particular distinction had not been foreseen. When it appeared in a few days that the appointment was intended as a personal compliment, and that Washburne was to hold the position just long enough to enjoy the title, the criticism was general. To one who complained that

the occupant of the position of Secretary of State
ought to be able to speak the French language correctly, the reply was made, "He ought at least to be
able to speak his own." But Washburne's creditable
record as Minister to France, during the Franco-
Prussian War and during the trying days of the Com-
mune, saved his reputation in the end.

A. T. Stewart was named Secretary of the Treasury. The Senate promptly confirmed his nomination, and until somebody recalled a long-buried law,
enacted early in the century, providing that this
particular office should not be filled by any man engaged in commerce, no one in Washington realized
that the great merchant and importer was ineligible
to the place. Grant, with sublime indifference to
technicalities, asked the Senate to repeal the law and
John Sherman, himself to be Secretary of the Treasury later, moved the repeal; but owing to Sumner's
opposition the motion was defeated. Grant was no
more to blame for making the nomination than the
Senate for confirming it. They might have been expected to be familiar with the law. Sumner in his
subsequent attacks on Grant denounced him for trying to upset a statute which "had stood unquestioned
until it had acquired the character of fundamental
law," yet Sumner himself must have been ignorant
of this "fundamental law" when he first aquiesced in

Stewart's confirmation. George S. Boutwell, a member of the House from Massachusetts, once a business man in a small way, Commissioner of Internal Revenue during the Civil War, was named in place of Stewart — an unexceptionable appointment.

E. Rockwood Hoar, of Massachusetts, was made Attorney-General; he was a learned lawyer of distinguished antecedents and high character, a member of the House, a friend of Sumner, a scholar of pungent wit and exalted ideals of public duty. He gained the ill-will of certain Republican Senators because of his austerity in rebuking their demands for the appointment of judges, district attorneys, and United States marshals in the South whom he believed to be unfit, and when Grant subsequently nominated him to fill a vacancy on the Supreme Bench caused by Stanton's death, these Senators, urged on by Butler who hated him, brought about the rejection of the nomination. Grant stood squarely with Hoar in his effort to preserve the quality of the Federal Bench. The story of his final withdrawal from the Cabinet is an interesting chapter in the history of the times.

General Schofield, whom Johnson had made Secretary of War after Stanton's retirement, was requested by Grant to retain his place for a while. A personal compliment this. Schofield was succeeded in a few weeks by Rawlins whom Grant needed always near his side. No one could fairly object to his selection. Adolph E. Borie was named for Secretary of the Navy. He was a wealthy and philanthropic Philadelphian whom no one outside Philadelphia had ever heard of. He was an invalid and had no thought of the Cabinet until he saw that he had been nominated. He resigned as soon as he could gracefully retire, and was succeeded by George M. Robeson, of New Jersey, then a young lawyer of striking ability, who was reputed at the time to have been recommended by Borie for the succession. The Secretary of the Interior was Jacob D. Cox, Governor of Ohio, who not only had a fine record as brigadier-general in the Civil War, especially at Franklin and Antietam, but who was a man of education and wide reading, a forceful and interesting writer and a Republican of conservative tendencies. When running for Governor of Ohio he had announced himself boldly as opposed to negro suffrage. The Postmaster-General was John A. J. Creswell, of Maryland, for a short time a member of the House and Senate, like some others in the Cabinet hardly known outside his own community.

For eight years Grant was President. His two administrations were marked by extraordinary achievement both in the domestic and in the foreign field. True, he was the target of abuse and criticism; no

President in the long list, with the possible exception of Johnson, has been more bitterly assailed, and he was vulnerable at many points. He was a soldier with a limited experience in dealing with men of affairs and only a superficial acquaintance with politics; with no great knowledge of history, or literature, and innocent of the science of government; yet William Tecumseh Sherman, in one of his flashes of political insight, came very near the mark when he wrote in the summer of 1868: "My own opinion is that, considering the state of the country, Grant will make the best President we can get. What we want in national politics is quiet, harmony, and stability, and these are more likely with Grant than any politician I know of."

Grant made serious mistakes; but almost without exception they were errors arising from childlike trust and unfortunate asssociations. They seldom affected adversely measures of broad public policy. When we recall the great accomplishments of his administrations, — the establishment of the principle of international arbitration through the Treaty of Washington and the adjudication of the Alabama claims by the Geneva Tribunal; the upholding of American dignity and the assertion of American rights in the matter of the Virginius and the handling of the Cuban complications; the rehabilitation of the national credit, and the maintenance of the national honor, the inauguration of a consistent and merciful policy toward the Indians; the recognition of the principle of civil service reform; and the restoration of a semblance of order in the South, — we are tempted to subordinate, though we cannot honestly ignore, the personal differences which marred the period of his service and the public scandal attaching to some of those who, in the shelter of his friendship and of offices bestowed upon them through his favor, betrayed his trust. It was a time of universal prodigality and extravagance, when speculation flourished and the nation's moral fiber had been coarsened by the excesses of war. It was not strange that the widespread taint invaded public place. It would have been more strange if it had not.

Grant's first choice for Secretary of State had been James F. Wilson, of Iowa. Wilson would have been a creditable selection, although foreign affairs were not directly in his line, for he was able, industrious, and high-minded. He first accepted the appointment, but at Grant's request consented that Washburne should hold the place a little while, so that Washburne might go to Paris with enhanced prestige. The understanding was that Washburne's tenure should be nominal, that he should not initiate a policy or make appointments, but he did both, and

them than they are likely to learn from him. . . . Grant has lost prestige enormously in the country."

"He [Grant] seems to have no comprehension of the nature of political forces," writes Bigelow three weeks later. "His Cabinet are merely staff officers, selected apparently out of motives of gratitude or for pecuniary favors received from them. His relatives and old friends were among the first provided for. . . . No President before was ever got in the family way so soon after inauguration. By his secretiveness in regard to his choice of a Cabinet and by his taking men unknown to his party or to any party, he wounded the pride of Congress incurably. . . ."

Carl Schurz tells in his "Reminiscences" an anecdote heard in the cloak-room of the Senate at this time. One of the best lawyers in the Senate heard a rumor that President Grant was about to remove a federal judge in one of the Territories, a lawyer of excellent ability and uncommon fitness for the bench. The Senator remonstrated and Grant admitted that as far as he knew there was no allegation of the unfitness of the judge; "but," he added, "the Governor of the Territory writes me that he cannot get along with that judge at all, and is very anxious to be rid of him; and I think the Governor is entitled to have control of his staff." So much for contemporary criticism!

CHAPTER XXXI

PERSONAL EQUATIONS

"I LIKE Grant," wrote James Russell Lowell after a visit to Washington in March, 1870, "and was struck with the pathos of his face; a puzzled pathos, as of a man with a problem before him of which he does not understand the terms."[1]

Grant had then been President a year — a year crowded with pressing problems, some of which were complicated, it is true, but all of which might almost be stated in terms of Grant himself, and Sumner, with Fish and Motley as ever-present factors. If in the early weeks of the Administration there had been at hand a disinterested friend endowed with the ability to handle men of widely differing tastes and antecedents, the personal misunderstanding between the President and the leader of the Senate might never have developed into a feud endangering the success of the Administration and embittering the lives of all concerned; for Grant and Sumner had common aspirations, although their methods of approach were so unlike. But no such friend appeared to put his finger on the point of sympathetic contact

[1] Letter to Leslie Stephen, March 25, 1870.

through which harmonious relations could have been maintained.

It might be thought that Fish, by virtue of his place and of his earlier relations with Sumner in the Senate, could at least have been of service as a go-between; but whatever may have been his inclination, he was not the man to undertake the task. Sumner, while glad to have him as a friend, had never looked upon him as an intellectual equal, and held him somewhat lightly as a figure in affairs. While Fish, at first regarding Sumner as his mentor, came slowly to resent the other's condescensions, and true to his Dutch ancestry, once having set his mind against his old associate, aligned himself immovably with his official chief, thus helping to accentuate the feud. Besides, he early came to formulate a sane, far-seeing diplomatic programme of his own.

Sumner had a low opinion of Grant's political sagacity. He never thought Grant should have been made President as a reward for military success, took no part in his nomination, and acquiesced reluctantly when he saw that it was bound to come. There was nothing strange in this. Sumner was not alone in questioning the wisdom of Grant's selection, and Grant was not the only President about whose fitness he had been in doubt. He never quite approved of Lincoln or understood him. "Mr. Lincoln was a constant puzzle to him," says Carl Schurz. "He frequently told me of profound and wise things Mr. Lincoln had said, and then again of other sayings which were unintelligible to him, and seemed to him inconsistent with a serious appreciation of the task before us. Being entirely devoid of the sense of humor himself, Mr. Sumner frequently — I might almost say always — failed to see the point of the quaint anecdotes or illustrations with which Mr. Lincoln was fond of elucidating his arguments, as with a flashlight. . . . Many a time I saw Sumner restlessly pacing up and down in his room and exclaiming with uplifted hands: 'I pray that the President may be right in delaying. But I am afraid, I am almost sure he is not. I trust his fidelity but I cannot understand him.'" [1]

As for Grant, he had no skill in handling men of Sumner's type, differing therein from Lincoln, who had a way of dropping in at Sumner's house to drink a cup of the inimitable tea, in brewing which the Massachusetts statesman took peculiar pride, and after sipping it like an old gossip purring the real object of his visit into Sumner's ear. Nor would Grant have done as Lincoln did after his second inauguration, when Sumner's hostility to the Louisiana policy threatened a fatal break. "Dear Mr. Sum-

[1] *The Reminiscences of Carl Schurz*, vol. II, pp. 312–14.

ner," Lincoln wrote, "unless you send me word to the contrary I shall this evening call with my carriage at your house to take you to the Inauguration Ball"; and at the Ball Lincoln walked in with Sumner arm in arm and kept him by his side.

Sumner thought in 1864 that Lincoln should give way to a more forceful candidate, just as in 1868 he thought a recognized Republican of ripe political experience would have been better qualified than Grant to meet the problems of the time. It may be he was right. The trouble would have been to find the man.

When Grant took office Sumner was the unchallenged chieftain of the Senate. He had been chairman of the Committee on Foreign Relations ever since Seward entered Lincoln's Cabinet, and, as Chase had also gone, no one was left to rival him in seniority or reputation. All things conspired to give him prominence and swell his own conception of his place in national affairs. He was well born and highly educated and had been trained almost from boyhood for a political career. He had read every serious book which had been written on the science of government, knew the best writings of all times and countries, and had stored in a capacious memory a prodigious mass of information about many things, with which he tiresomely embellished his speeches in the Senate and his daily talk. He was one of the few Americans of his day who had familiar correspondence with scholars, writers, and public men abroad. Politically invincible at home in Massachusetts, he was regarded elsewhere as a hero and the champion of liberty, for his fame as an uncompromising advocate of the rights of men ran back to the fermenting time of 1848.

Mr. Lodge in his " Early Memories" has given us a delightful portrait of Sumner. He speaks of his wide learning, of his power of devouring books with extraordinary rapidity, and the gift of remembering everything. "Sumner," he says, "was by nature a dreamer, a man of meditation, a man of books, and a lover of learning. By the circumstances of his time and by the hand of fate he was projected into a career of intense action and fierce struggle. There he played a great part, but his nature was not changed. He still remained at bottom a dreamer and a man of books. . . . A statesman in the largest sense, although not a legislator who drafted laws and attended to legislative details . . . he cared nothing for politics in the ordinary acceptation of the word. . . . He was a most imposing figure. Tall, large, not regularly handsome in features, but with a noble head and a fine intellectual face. No one could look upon him and fail to be struck and attracted by his looks and presence. To all this was added that rarest of gifts, a very fine voice, deep and rich with varied

tones and always a delight to the ear. . . . Coupled
with his deficiency in a sense of humor, and akin to it,
was a curious simplicity of nature. . . . He was anything but conceited, but he had vanity . . . in a
marked degree. . . . It was not the vanity which
offends, for it was too frank, too obvious, too innocent to give offense, but it made him an easy prey to
those who wished to profit by it. . . . No man had
better manners in daily life, manners at once kindly,
stately, and dignified, and he could do a courteous
action in a most graceful way."

Schurz said that in himself Sumner felt the whole
dignity of the Republic; in sporting language, "he
had a good eye for country, but no scent for a trail."

A marked contrast, this, to Grant, small in stature,
slouchy in dress and bearing, taciturn in public, without ostentation or vanity, meagerly read and hardly
educated beyond West Point necessities, careless of
refinements, unfamiliar with the graces of society,
his clothing reeking always with the stale odor of
tobacco, ill at ease with men of culture, yet simple
and direct in speech and in his manner of approaching other men.

"As different in their mental attributes as in their
physical appearance," says Charles Francis Adams.[1]
"While Mr. Sumner was, intellectually, morally, and

[1] *Before and after the Treaty of Washington*, p. 75.

physically, much the finer and more imposing human product, Grant had counterbalancing qualities which made him, in certain fields, the more formidable opponent. With immense will, he was taciturn; Sumner, on the contrary, in no way deficient in will, was a man of many words, a rhetorician. In action and among men Grant's self-control was perfect, amounting to complete apparent imperturbability. Unassuming, singularly devoid of self-consciousness, in presence of an emergency his blood never seemed to quicken, his face became only the more set, tenacity personified; whereas Sumner, when morally excited, the rush of his words, his deep, tremulous utterance, and the light in his eye, did not impart conviction or inspire respect. Doubts would suggest themselves to the unsympathetic, or only partially sympathetic, listener whether the man was of altogether balanced mind. . . . Quite unconsciously on his part he assumed an attitude of moral superiority and intellectual certainty, in no way compatible with a proper appreciation of the equality of others. In the mind of a man like Grant, these peculiarities excited obstinacy, anger, and contempt."

Charles Eliot Norton has preserved one of Grant's rare gleams of humor, when he replied to somebody who told him Sumner had no faith in the Bible: "Well: he did n't write it."

Motley was Sumner's personal friend; a member of the same literary and social group in Boston,[1] — a group embracing Longfellow, Lowell, Emerson, Hawthorne, Agassiz, Andrew, Dana, and Holmes; of distinguished achievement as the historian of the Dutch Republic, of ripe culture and great personal charm, of cosmopolitan experience, familiar with the universities and libraries of Europe, and of some diplomatic experience by reason of his service as Minister to Austria under the Lincoln and Johnson Administrations, which came to a distressing end through Seward's clumsy handling of an unknown critic's abusive letter and his own excessive sensitiveness. Sumner and his other friends pressed Grant to make him Minister to England partly as a balm for injured pride. But behind it also was Sumner's unexpressed assumption that through his position in the Senate he was to be responsible for the conduct of our foreign relations during the incumbency of an ignorant Executive and an inexperienced Secretary of State.

With our grievances against Great Britain pressing for a settlement, he wanted to have at London a representative in whom he could place perfect trust, and from his point of view Motley was the ideal man.

But in other ways the choice was not by any means

[1] The Saturday Club.

the best which could be made. With all his personal charm and social distinction, Motley was lacking in the tact and diplomatic skill which were required in an effective American representative in London at that time. In fact, he was not by nature adapted to diplomacy at all, although no finer type of American citizenship could have been chosen to stand as the enbodiment of our best ideals in other lands, and it is not surprising that shortly Grant and Fish should have found it necessary to take the negotiations with the British Government into their own hands, excluding him entirely from the ultimate adjustment.[1]

To understand all this and how the Administration's attitude toward Cuba and San Domingo helped to emphasize the split, one must first understand a clash of personalities, which came near to wrecking Grant's Administration at the beginning, and the effects of which were felt long after Sumner's death.

[1] E. L. Godkin, writing from London, on April 15, 1869, said: "Motley's appointment is a good one from the social point of view, bad, I think, in every other way. I do not think he has the necessary mental furniture for the discussion of the questions now pending between England and America; and he is a little too ardent. His lectures here have been very disappointing, commonplace rhetorics without any thought. . . ."

CHAPTER XXXII

ARBITRATION WITH GREAT BRITAIN

ON the very threshold of his Administration Grant found confronting him the problem of our grievances against Great Britain which had been accumulating ever since her recognition of Confederate belligerency in the first year of the Civil War. Upon the heels of recognition — a perfectly legitimate proceeding, although resented bitterly throughout the North — had come the devastating cruises of the Alabama, Florida, and Shenandoah, fitted out in British yards, under the eyes of British functionaries, and manned with Confederate naval officers with the express design of preying on our foreign commerce.

Charles Francis Adams, our Minister at London, had demanded reparation for damage caused by the British-built Confederate cruisers, but the British Government toward the end of 1865 had somewhat curtly declined consideration of our claims and nothing further was done about it until in August, 1868, Reverdy Johnson arrived in London as Minister by Johnson's appointment and undertook without delay negotiations looking toward a settlement. A noticeable change had come upon the spirit of English statesmen confronted with the probability of an embroilment in continental quarrels. They were now glad to reach an understanding with the United States so that the precedent established by the Alabama case might not be used to justify the fitting out of hostile cruisers in American ports to prey on English commerce in event of war.

Johnson was welcomed with effusiveness, and he was flattered by the marked attentions he received. He entered joyfully on a career of after-dinner oratory, gushed over those who had been most ostentatious in their sympathy for the Confederate cause, shook hands in public with Laird, who bragged about having built the Alabama, and went so far in his endeavor to ingratiate himself in his new post as to arouse distrust at home. When in January he concluded with the British Foreign Secretary the Johnson-Clarendon Convention, both he and Seward were dazed to find that terms which twelve months earlier would have been ratified with little opposition were now resented by the Senate and the people as the result of truckling to the English Government by a tuft-hunting diplomat. Besides, feeling against England had grown more bitter. The sympathy for Ireland in her struggle for home rule was gaining strength, and Fenian border raids against Canada had become a factor to be considered.

The convention was carried over into the new Administration, and when it came up for action in the Senate, it was almost literally without a friend. Ratification was defeated by a vote of 54 to 1, on April 13, 1869. The debate consisted chiefly in a speech by Sumner for which there was no need and which might much better never have been uttered. But Sumner, never discreet, insisted upon a spoken record of his attitude, and his impassioned attack upon Great Britain, from which the ban of secrecy was removed by formal vote, went into history to become a mischief-breeding influence on subsequent events.

It was close upon the heels of the rejection of the Johnson-Clarendon Convention, while Sumner's extraordinary demands still stirred public imagination, that Motley was named as Johnson's successor at the Court of St. James. Charles Francis Adams, the elder, recently returned from the British mission and watching at home the progress of affairs, wrote privately that the practical effect of Sumner's speech and the rejection of the treaty was "to raise the scale of our demands for reparation so very high that there is no chance of negotiation left, unless the English have lost all their spirit and character." Sumner with splendid efflorescence of mathematics had figured that our direct or individual losses "due to the foraging of the Alabama" were $15,000,000, but this modest sum left without recognition "the vaster damage to commerce driven from the ocean," which he reckoned at $110,000,000, and he added, "Of course this is only an item in our bill."

He traced the prolongation of the war directly to England. "The rebellion was originally encouraged by hope of support from England," he cried; "it was strengthened at once by the concession of belligerent rights on the ocean; it was fed to the end by British supplies . . . ; it was quickened into frantic life with every report from the British pirates, flaming anew with every burning ship; nor can it be doubted that without British intervention the rebellion would have soon succumbed under the well-directed efforts of the National Government. Not weeks nor months but years were added in this way to our war, so full of costly sacrifice."

Calculating that the rebellion was suppressed at a cost of more than $4,000,000,000 and that through British intervention the war was doubled in duration, he came easily to the conclusion that England was chargeable with half the total expenditure, or $2,000,000,000, making our entire bill against her $2,125,000,000, at a low estimate. This sounded large and bellicose, but the explanation seems to be that Sumner had no intention either of collecting such a claim or of risking war with England to enforce it. What Sumner had in mind was not the collection of an enormous indemnity in money, but rather the adjustment of all differences through annexation of British territory and the withdrawal of the British flag from North America.

The annexation of Canada, especially in view of the aggressive Irish sentiment at the time and the recurring Fenian demonstrations, was not a preposterous proposal, but there was a difference of opinion as to how best to go about it. Chandler in the Senate had suggested that it was an essential to continue peace: "We cannot afford to have our enemies' base so near us. It is a national necessity that we should have the British possessions. I hope that such a negotiation will be opened and that it will be a peaceful one; but if it should not be, and England insists on war, then let the war be short, sharp, and decisive." We have Grant's own authority for believing that he would not have been afraid of such an outcome. He thought at one time during the year that Sheridan could have taken Canada in thirty days. Moreover, British statesmen did not set such store on their American possessions fifty years ago as later, and they might have welcomed a separation effected in a creditable way. The real obstacle to annexation lay with the Canadians themselves, who have never seen the time when they did not prefer connection with the mother country to union with our own.

Grant was an expansionist as much as Sumner, but he looked upon expansion to the north more as a military problem than a question of sentiment. His mind dwelt much more readily on territorial extension to the south. Cuba, San Domingo, and Mexico, with their untold natural resources awaiting the inspira- tion of American development, appealed to him with greater force than the barren stretches of the Cana- dian Northwest, and here is where he differed radi- cally from Sumner, who, throughout a tempestuous career in studying his political compass, had been accustomed to associate the North with human lib- erty and the South with slaves.

It was in this divergence between Grant and Sumner that Fish, the conservative, unimaginative lawyer, elevated against his own inclination to be Secretary of State, found an opportunity for wise and courageous service. Sumner assumed that in his ca- pacity as chairman of the Committee on Foreign Re- lations and leader of the Senate, the shaping of the foreign policy would now devolve upon him. Motley, his lifelong friend, was unconsciously under his in- fluence, and might also be said in his new mission to regard himself as representing Sumner rather than the President or the Secretary of State.

Motley's first act after confirmation was to prepare a memorandum which he handed to Fish outlining the instructions which should be given him. The memorandum might as well have been dictated by Sumner, so accurately did it reflect his views. It questioned the advisability of trying to renew negotiations, dilated on the Queen's proclamation of May, 1861, recognizing Southern belligerency, as a wrong committed by Great Britain and deeply felt by the American people, — a sense of wrong declared gravely, solemnly, without passion, and not to be expunged by a mere money payment to reimburse a few captures and conflagrations at sea.

Grant was disposed to let Motley go ahead; but Fish, already sensible of his new responsibilities, had other things in view. In the first place, he had determined if possible to reopen negotiations and bring them to a successful conclusion. In the second place, events in Cuba were so shaping themselves as to affect the manner of our approach to the British problem. He took his own time in preparing Motley's instructions, and when completed, they bore little resemblance to the memorandum submitted. He declared that in spite of the failure of the Johnson-Clarendon Convention the Government of the United States did not abandon hope of "an early, satisfactory, and friendly settlement of the questions depending between the two Governments" and expressed the President's hope that the suspension of negotiations would be regarded by Her Majesty's Government, as it was by him, "as wholly in the interest of, and solely with a view to, an early and friendly settlement." Nothing here about "massive grievance," "indirect claims," "immense and infinite damages," or "ill-omened" and "fatal" proclamation which had "opened the flood-gates to infinite woes."

Fish always thought that negotiations could be conducted more satisfactorily in Washington than London; and within a week after the rejection of the Johnson-Clarendon Convention he had written to a friend: "Whenever negotiations are renewed, the atmosphere and the surroundings of this side of the water are more favorable to a proper solution of the question than the dinner tables and the public banquetings of England." This was before he had opportunity to appraise the diplomatic skill of Motley and before he had been regaled with a perusal of Motley's memorandum.

Motley reached England with his revised instructions early in May, 1869, still imbued with Sumner's conception of the measureless injury done the Union cause by the proclamation of belligerency. So complete was his misapprehension of the purpose of his mission that in his first interview with Lord Claren-

don he laid special stress upon the proclamation as
" the fountain head of the disasters which had been
caused to the American people, both individually and
collectively." With the submission to his superior
of the report of this interview, Motley's career as a
diplomat may fairly be said to have come to an end.

John Russell Young reports Grant as saying at
Edinburgh in 1877, " Mr. Motley had to be instructed. The instructions were prepared very carefully, and after Governor Fish and I had gone over'
them for the last time, I wrote an addendum charging him that above all things he should handle the
subject of the Alabama claims with the greatest delicacy. Mr. Motley, instead of obeying his implicit
instructions, deliberately fell in line with Sumner and
thus added insult to the previous injury. As soon
as I heard of it, I went over to the State Department
and told Governor Fish to dismiss Motley at once. I
was very angry indeed, and I have been sorry many
a time since. that I did not stick to my first determination. Mr. Fish advised delay, because of Sumner's position in the Senate and his attitude on the
treaty question. We did not want to stir him up
just then. We dispatched a severe note of censure to
Motley at once and asked him to abstain from any
further connection with these questions."

Motley's subsequent residence in England, however creditable and brilliant may have been its personal and social aspects, had little bearing upon results except as it may have retarded them. The negotiations leading to the Treaty of Washington and the settlement of the Alabama claims, through the Geneva Tribunal, were carried on to a successful conclusion in Washington without his participation. The final request for his resignation and his summary removal, though figuring dramatically in the history of the time, had no effect upon our diplomatic negotiations with the country to which he was accredited, though in part incidental to them.

It was through Caleb Cushing that the first steps were taken toward a renewal of negotiations. As counsel before the joint tribunal arbitrating the claims of the Hudson's Bay and Puget Sound Companies under the Treaty of 1863, he had made the acquaintance of John Rose, acting as British Commissioner, a man of prominence in Canadian public life described as "a natural diplomat of a high order." By suggestion of Rose, who may have spoken with authority, Cushing arranged an interview in Washington between Rose and Fish. On July 8, just four weeks after Motley's unhappy interview with Clarendon, they came together, and while Motley was discoursing despondently in London about "a path surrounded by peril" and "grave and disas-

trous misunderstandings and cruel war," Fish and
Rose were already well advanced on the road to a
renewal of negotiations.

These informal exchanges continued through the
summer and autumn. Sumner, not yet alienated
from Fish, was cognizant of them. He was even advised, although no names were given, of a letter now
historic, in which Rose, writing from London, asked:
" Is your representative here a gentleman of the most
conciliatory spirit? . . . I think I understood you to
say that you thought negotiations would be more
likely to be attended with satisfactory results, if they
were transferred to and were concluded at Washington; because you could from time to time communicate confidentially with leading Senators and know
how far you could carry that body with you. . . . But
again is your representative of that mind? And how
is it to be brought about? By a new or a special
envoy — as you spoke of — or quietly through Mr.
Thornton?" Sumner not only ignored the intended
hint for Motley's benefit, but treated it as an anon-
ymous attack entitled to contempt; while Oliver
Wendell Holmes, the loving and loyally biased bio
grapher of Motley, writing in 1879, two years after
Motley's death, refers to the then unnamed writer as
" a faithless friend, a disguised enemy, a secret emissary, or an injudicious alarmist."

After the earlier steps coincident with sending
Motley to London, Grant gave Fish a free hand with
the British Foreign Office. But Fish could never
have succeeded in his diplomacy if he had not felt
Grant behind him all the time, approving him in
every stand he made, and giving him unfaltering
support. It would be hard to say to which belongs
the greater credit for the final diplomatic triumph,
Grant or Fish; but the responsibility for success or
failure lay with Grant.

In his first annual message of December 6, 1869,
Grant commented with approval on the rejection of
the Johnson-Clarendon Convention. "The injuries
resulting to the United States by reason of the course
adopted by Great Britain during our late Civil War
. . . could not be adjusted and satisfied as ordinary
commercial claims, which continually arise between
commercial nations, and yet the convention treated
them as such ordinary claims, from which they differ
more widely in the gravity of their character than in
the magnitude of their amount, great even as is that
difference. Not a word was found in the treaty, and
not an inference could be drawn from it, to remove
the sense of unfriendliness of the course of Great
Britain in our struggle for existence which had so
deeply and universally impressed itself upon the people of this country." The rejection of the treaty,

"thus misconceived in its scope and inadequate in its provisions," he regarded as in the interest of peace. "A sensitive people, conscious of their power, are more at ease under a great wrong, wholly un-atoned, than under the restraint of a settlement which satisfies neither their ideas of justice nor their grave sense of the grievances they have sus-tained."

He expressed the hope that the time might soon arrive "when the two Governments may approach the solution of this momentous question with an ap-preciation of what is due the rights, dignity, and honor of each, and with the determination not only to remove the causes of complaint in the past, but to lay the foundation of a broad principle of public law which will prevent future differences and tend to firm and continued peace and friendship." How fully this hope was realized will appear in the result.

The Franco-Prussian War came in to help, for England, in the face of trouble on the Continent, was getting ready in the fall of 1870 to bring about a suit-able adjustment of all outstanding quarrels. Grant seized the opportunity in his second annual message, December 5, 1870, to stimulate the British Foreign Office to greater haste. He regretted to say "that no conclusion has been reached for the adjustment of the claims against Great Britain growing out of the course adopted by that Government during the rebellion. The Cabinet of London, so far as its views have been expressed, does not appear to be willing to concede that Her Majesty's Government was guilty of any negligence or did or permitted any act during the war by which the United States has just cause of complaint. Our firm and unalterable convictions are directly the reverse." He therefore recommended the appointment of a commission "to take proof of the amount and ownership of these several claims,". and that authority be given for settlement of these claims by the United States so that the Government would have ownership of the private claims as well as the responsible control of all the demands against Great Britain; and he added that whenever Her Majesty's Government should desire a "full and friendly adjustment," the United States would enter upon a consideration of the claims "with an earnest desire for a conclusion consistent with the honor and dignity of both nations."

The passage containing this hint appeared in the London newspapers on December 6, 1870. Exactly five weeks later, on January 9, 1871, Mr. Rose, having hurried from London, dined with Mr. Fish in Washington, and before the evening was over the two had agreed on a confidential memorandum which was to be the basis of negotiations. From that day until the signing of the Treaty of Washington on May 8, 1871, events moved in orderly progress under the firm guidance of the Secretary of State.

Sumner had broken completely with both Grant and Fish over the San Domingo affair during the negotiations, but he was still at the head of the "first committee of the Senate," a place which he regarded as "equal in position to anything in our Government under the President"; and Fish, with his eye fixed on the success of his undertaking, arranged through Patterson, another member of the Foreign Relations Committee, for an interview at Sumner's house. He left with Sumner on January 15 the written memorandum of his understanding with Rose. It was returned by Sumner two days later with a note admitting the propriety of Sir John Rose's idea that "all questions and causes of irritation between England and the United States should be removed absolutely and forever" and that "all points of difference should be considered together"; and concluding with this proposition: "The greatest trouble, if not peril, being a constant source of anxiety and disturbance, is from Fenianism, which is excited by the British flag in Canada. Therefore the withdrawal of the British flag cannot be abandoned as a condition or preliminary of such a settlement as is now proposed. To make the settlement complete, the withdrawal should be from this hemisphere including provinces and islands."

An astounding suggestion it seems, and coming from the chairman of the committee which would have to pass upon any treaty for which they might pave the way, not an encouragement to further parley along the lines which the negotiations had in view; but Fish and Rose, with Grant's fixed approval, took no account of Sumner's comment and went ahead with their arrangements without considering impossible demands.

The British Minister submitted a proposal for the appointment of a Joint High Commission, to be composed of members to be named by each Government, to hold its session at Washington, and to treat and discuss the mode of settling the different questions which had arisen out of the fisheries, as well as those affecting the relations of the United States toward the British possessions in North America. Fish, backed by Grant, insisted that the Alabama question should be within the scope of discussion and settlement by the commission, and the British Government assented.

Grant, on February 9, 1871, nominated as commissioners on the part of the United States: Hamilton Fish, Secretary of State; Robert C. Schenck, Minister to Great Britain; Samuel Nelson, Associate

Justice of the Supreme Court; Ebenezer R. Hoar, of Massachusetts; George H. Williams, of Oregon. If it had not been for Sumner's unreasonableness and Motley's petulance, the historian of the Dutch Republic might well have been a member of the commission, thus adding luster to his fine career.

The British members were: Earl de Grey and Ripon, a member of Gladstone's Cabinet; Sir Stafford Northcote, a conservative leader in Parliament; Sir Edward Thornton, British Minister in Washington; Professor Montague Bernard, of Oxford University; and Sir John A. Macdonald, the Premier of Canada.

Within six weeks the British and American Joint High Commission were at work in Washington upon the treaty. When it was laid before the Senate, on the 10th of May, Sumner was no longer at the head of the Committee upon the chairmanship of which he set such store. He had been deposed in March, for reasons not directly bearing on the negotiations with Great Britain, though, as it seems to-day, the ratification of a treaty was so vital to the maintenance of friendly relations with Great Britain, that the unprecedented action of the Senate might have been justified by that alone.

Shorn of his place Sumner accepted the treaty with reasonable grace. It was ratified in due course on May 24, 1871. The principle of arbitration in international disputes had won its first great triumph. Great Britain appointed as its arbitrator Chief Justice Alexander Cockburn; the United States, Charles Francis Adams. The King of Italy, the President of the Swiss Confederation, and the Emperor of Brazil named three neutral arbitrators. Lord Tenterden was the British agent and Sir Roundell Palmer the counsel. J. C. Bancroft Davis, Assistant Secretary of State, was agent for the United States. The American counsel were William M. Evarts, Caleb Cushing, and Morrison R. Waite.

The Board of Arbitration met at Geneva, on December 15, 1871, and in the following September it had done its work. But even to the very last the shadow of Sumner's "massive grievance" and "indirect claims" hung over it threatening in the crudeness of the manner of their presentation more than once to bring the arbitration to a futile end. Had it not been for the firmness, tact, and diplomatic comprehension of Charles Francis Adams the arbitration would have broken on those issues. On September 2, by a vote of four to one at the twenty-ninth conference, the tribunal decided to award in gross the sum of $15,500,000, to be paid in gold by Great Britain to the United States for the damage done by the Florida, Alabama, and Shenandoah. Cockburn alone dissented.

Thus Grant must have the credit for establishing the principle of arbitration in international disputes; for this was brought about by reason of the firmness with which he held to the validity of American demands. If anywhere along the line his conduct had been marked by vacillation, the result could not have been achieved. To him must also go the credit of being among the earliest to encourage the principle of a World's Congress, as afterwards embodied in the Hague Tribunal, when to the Arbitration Union in Birmingham he said: "Nothing would afford me greater happiness than to know that, as I believe will be the case, at some future day, the nations of the earth will agree upon some sort of congress, which will take cognizance of international questions of difficulty, and whose decisions will be as binding as the decisions of our Supreme Court are upon us. It is a dream of mine that some such solution may be."

CHAPTER XXXIII
THE SAN DOMINGO TRAGEDY

IN the geography of the Western Hemisphere Hayti and San Domingo are insignificant. Among the Latin American republics they cut no figure; yet they have had influence on the politics of the United States quite out of keeping with their own importance. It is a rare administration which passes without unhappy experience with one or the other of these misadventures in negro self-government. Grant found in San Domingo a tragedy of his career — his first unqualified defeat.

Although once nominally united, the two sections of the island had been independent revolutionary centers for twenty-five years. Hayti, originally under the control of France, occupied a third of the island and had four fifths of the population. San Domingo, which had been a colony of Spain, though sparsely settled, furnished frequent rotations in its crops of insurrection. For some years, two leaders, Baez and Cabral, had taken turns at being president, sometimes through violence tempered by a popular primary, sometimes through violence alone.

Baez at the time was called by enemies of Grant

a mercenary adventurer, but Andrew D. White, who talked with him in Domingo, describes him as a man of force and ability, a light mulatto with none of the characteristics generally attributed in the United States to men of mixed blood. "In all his conduct he showed quiet self-reliance, independence, and the tone of a high-spirited gentleman. His family was noted in the history of the island and held large estates near the capital city. . . . There was a quiet elegance in his manners and conversation which would have done credit to any statesman in any country. . . . I have never doubted that his overtures to General Grant were patriotic. As long as he could remember he had known nothing in his country but a succession of sterile revolutions which had destroyed all its prosperity and nearly all its population."

During Johnson's Administration, Baez, out of power for a while, had come to Washington seeking intervention. In 1868 he had another term as president; while Cabral hovered on the Haytian border, waiting to pounce on him again. Baez sent a confidential agent to Washington, and Johnson in his last annual message, at Seward's instigation, recommended the annexation of the entire island.

Baez repeated his overtures almost as soon as the new Administration was installed. He met with scant consideration at first except from Grant himself, who saw in San Domingo not only rich natural resources, but a refuge for the colored people of the South.

The project of annexation seems to have grown upon Grant before the Secretary of State or other members of the Cabinet were fully aware of it. There was talk about it in Cabinet meetings to which Grant listened without comment, and it was generally understood that the policy of the Administration was against intervention, until one day in May Grant casually remarked that as the navy seemed to want Samaná Bay for a coaling-station, he thought he would send General Babcock down to report upon it as an engineer.

Orville E. Babcock, who had been one of Grant's staff in the later years of the war, and was now detailed at the White House as an assistant private secretary, was a young man of great personal charm, energetic, intelligent, and a competent military engineer; but through his indiscreet activities and dubious associations he contrived in one way and another to get Grant into all kinds of trouble. Whatever merit there may have been in the proposed annexation, there was very little in Babcock's part in it, for which Grant with his customary loyalty accepted full responsibility. Babcock started for San Domingo in July, 1869, under instructions from the State department to make a complete inquiry into the pop-

ulation and resources of the island. A naval vessel
was placed at his disposal.

On September 4 Babcock executed with the Dominican authorities a protocol which stipulated for
the annexation of the Dominican Republic with the
payment of $1,500,000 by the United States for the
extinction of the Dominican debt. In the body of
the protocol he assumed the ambitious title of "Aide-
de-camp to His Excellency Ulysses S. Grant, President of the United States of America," and added
the extraordinary pledge that the President "promises privately to use all his influence in order that the
idea of annexing the Dominican Republic to the
United States may acquire such a degree of popularity among members of Congress as will be necessary
for its accomplishment."

Fish was astounded when he discovered what
Babcock had brought back with him. "What do you
think?" he exclaimed to Jacob D. Cox. "Babcock's
back and has actually brought a treaty for the cession of San Domingo; yet I pledge you my word he
had no more diplomatic authority than any other
casual visitor to that island!" Fish would have ended
the incident there and forgotten it. He did not
dream that Grant would father Babcock's queer
performance.

At the next Cabinet meeting Grant began by saying, "Babcock has returned, as you see, and has brought a treaty of annexation. I suppose it is not formal, as he had no diplomatic powers; but we can easily cure that. We can send back the treaty, and have Perry, the consular agent, sign it; and as he is an officer of the State Department it would make it all right."

There was an awkward silence, broken finally by Cox, who asked, "But, Mr. President, has it been settled, then, that we want to annex San Domingo?" Grant colored and smoked hard at his cigar. Fish was impassive, his eyes fixed on the portfolio before him. There was no response from any one. "As the silence became painful," writes Cox, "the President called for another item of business and left the question unanswered. The subject was never again brought up before the assembled Cabinet."

Fish was in an intolerable position. Not only had his department been compromised by Babcock's undertaking, but his own sincerity was called in question because in frequent conversations with Sumner he had always treated the talk of annexation as idle gossip. He tendered his resignation. Grant begged him to stay. He wanted San Domingo, but he needed Fish; and the Secretary, ambitious to bring the negotiations with Great Britain to a successful issue, yielded in San Domingo in order that

he might achieve the greater end. Babcock was sent
back to San Domingo, where he concluded two treaties, one for annexation, the other for the lease of the
Bay of Samaná, giving at the same time the President's guaranty to the Dominican Republic against
all foreign intervention until the treaties could be
submitted to the Dominican people, a guaranty
which was enforced for months by ships of our navy
under Secretary Robeson's explicit instructions.

Leaving our men-of-war in the neighborhood to
insure protection to Baez, Babcock came back to
Washington in December bringing his treaties with
him. Congress was in holiday recess and Grant undertook to assure himself of the support of Sumner who
was one of the few Senators remaining in town.

On the evening of the first Sunday in January the
President called at Sumner's house and found him
at dinner with two friends, Ben: Perley Poore, the
Washington correspondent, and Colonel John W.
Forney, the Secretary of the Senate. This interview
played a vital part in the subsequent history of the
Administration and marked the beginning of the
irreconcilable breach between Grant and Sumner.
Grant always contended that Sumner promised to
support the treaty. Sumner denied that he had done
anything of the kind. Of the two witnesses Forney
subsequently expressed the opinion that Grant was

justified in feeling he could count on Sumner's backing; while Poore declared that "the President and the Senator misunderstood each other."

According to Poore, Grant did not have the treaties or any memorandum of them with him. He dwelt especially upon the expenditure by General Babcock of a large sum taken from a secret service fund for promoting intercourse with the West Indies and impressed Sumner with the idea that he feared an attack in Congress over that expenditure. "While I know," wrote Poore in 1877, "that Mr. Sumner thought that the President had come to enlist his services in defending this expenditure by General Babcock, I have no doubt but that the President meant (as Colonel Forney thought and as I thought) the treaty for the acquisition of the Dominican Republic."

The President promised to send General Babcock to call on the Senator the next day, with copies of the papers, and left. As Mr. Sumner escorted him to the door he said, according to Forney: "Well, Mr. President, I am a Republican and an Administration man, and I will do all I can to make your Administration a success. I will give the subject my best thought and will do all I can rightly and considerately to aid you." Sumner gave his own version in the speech he made in the Senate December 21, 1870, as follows: "I have

heard it said that I assured the President that I
would support the Administration in this measure.
Never! He may have formed that opinion, but never
did I say anything to justify it; nor did I suppose he
could have failed to appreciate the reserve with
which I spoke. My language, I repeat, was precise,
well considered, and chosen in advance; 'I am an
Administration man, and whatever you do will always find in me the most careful and candid consideration.' In this statement I am positive. It was
early fixed in my mind and I know that I am right."

Upon such seemingly slight divergences of view
depended subsequent events. Upon a difference in
interpretation of a single sentence, Grant had no
right to charge Sumner later with a breach of faith,
but there was another feature seldom alluded to by
the historians of the time which contributed to the
bitterness. Sumner always maintained and declared
frequently in conversation that Grant was intoxicated that day, and the charge undoubtedly reached
Grant's ears. Poore says that Grant was "not in the
slightest degree under the influence of alcohol." He
thinks that Sumner drew his inference from the fact
that, before the subject of San Domingo came up for
consideration at all, the President became intem-
perately angry and "expressed himself with more
warmth than I ever saw him display either before or

since that evening," in discussing the case of ex-Representative Ashley, of Ohio, who had been deposed from his position as Governor of Montana, whom Sumner was anxious to see restored and whom Grant hotly denounced as a mischief-maker and a worthless fellow.

Babcock called on Sumner the next day with copies of the treaties, and Sumner plainly indicated his displeasure with the terms. He resented it that the President of the United States should be pledged to lobby the treaty through the Senate and this resentment intensified the prejudice he held against the annexation project as a whole, feeling as he did that the extinction of the Black Republic would be a wrong to the negro who had there an opportunity to work out a problem in self-government. On January 18 the treaties were laid before the Committee on Foreign Relations and a majority of the Committee expressed their disapproval.

Grant, quick to learn the Committee's attitude, became more set than ever in his purpose. He summoned Senators to the White House; he camped out in the President's room at the Capitol and begged one after another personally to support the treaties. But it was all in vain. The treaties lay with the Committee till March 15, when an adverse report was voted. Sumner, Schurz, Patterson, Cameron,

and Casserly in favor of rejection; Morton and
Harlan against. Grant still persisted in the face
of defeat apparently assured. Two days after the
adverse report he visited the Senate and sent for
fourteen Senators to meet him. He continued his
activities while the annexation treaty was under
consideration, and while it was laid aside for weeks
without action.[1] The day before the vote in Committee he had sent a brief message urging favorable
action and expressing the earnest wish that the Senate would not permit the treaty to expire by limitation. On May 31 he sent another message urging an

[1] Schurz tells how Grant, meeting him at a reception, asked
him to the White House where he plunged forthwith into the
subject he had at heart. "I hear you are a member of the Senate
Committee that has the San Domingo treaty under consideration,"
he said, "and I wish you would support that treaty. Won't you do
that?" Schurz said frankly he could not do so, and proceeded to
give his reasons at considerable length and with great earnestness.
"At first the President listened to me with evident interest, looking
at me as if the objections to the treaty which I expressed were
quite new to him, and made an impression on his mind. But after
a while I noticed that his eyes wandered about the room and I
became doubtful whether he listened to me at all. When I had
stopped he sat silent for a minute or two. I, of course, sat silent,
too, waiting for him to speak. At last he said in a perfectly calm
tone as if nothing had happened: 'Well, I hope you will at least
vote for the confirmation of Mr. Jones, whom I have selected for a
foreign mission.'" Schurz had never heard of Jones and when his
name came before the Foreign Relations Committee a few days
later, after his nomination to be Minister to Belgium, it appeared
that other members of the committee were equally in the dark.
He was interested in street-car lines in Chicago and was subsequently confirmed.

extension of time and pressing with fervor the advantages of annexation.

"I feel an unusual anxiety," he said, "for the ratification of this treaty, because I believe it will redound greatly to the glory of the two countries interested, to civilization and to the extirpation of the institution of slavery. The doctrine promulgated by President Monroe has been adhered to by all political parties, and I now deem it proper to assert the equally important principle that hereafter no territory on this continent shall be regarded as subject to transfer to a European power. The Government of San Domingo has voluntarily sought this annexation. It is a weak power numbering probably less than 120,000 souls, and yet possessing one of the richest territories under the sun, capable of supporting a population of 10,000,000 people in luxury. . . . The acquisition of San Domingo is an adherence to the 'Monroe Doctrine'; it is a measure of national protection; it is asserting our just claim to a controlling influence over the great commercial traffic soon to flow from east to west by the way of the Isthmus of Darien; it is to build up our merchant marine; it is to furnish new markets for the products of our farms, shops, and manufactories; it is to make slavery insupportable in Cuba and Porto Rico at once, and ultimately so in Brazil; it is to settle the unhappy condition of Cuba and end an exterminating conflict; it is to provide honest means of paying our honest debts, without overtaxing the people; it is to furnish our citizens with the necessaries of everyday life at cheaper rates than ever before; and it is in fine a rapid stride toward that greatness which the intelligence, industry, and enterprise of the citizens of the United States entitle this country to assume among nations."

Thus Grant's conception of the importance of annexation fattened on opposition, and when, on June 30, ratification was defeated by a tie vote in the Senate, 28 to 28, his anger was proportionately intense, especially against Sumner, who he believed had proved faithless after giving him assurance of support. In debate the Senator had denounced the manner of negotiations, and had bitterly assailed Babcock as Grant's personal emissary. Busybodies were quick to instill in Grant's mind the suspicion that charges of fraud and corruption which were widely spread really emanated from Sumner, so that Grant's resentment centered on the Massachusetts Senator. When, the day after the rejection of the treaty, Fish by Grant's direction asked Motley for his resignation the general conclusion was inevitable that this was an act of reprisal against Motley's friend and sponsor.

Grant never admitted this and Motley had been for months in bad favor with the Administration, owing partly to his early ineptness in the negotiations with Great Britain and partly to lack of tact in his dealings with the President, as when he refused to appoint young Nicholas Fish as one of his secretaries when Grant personally requested it. Adam Badeau declares that on May 15, six weeks before the vote on the treaty, Grant told him at the White House that he was going to remove Motley.

That a change in the English mission had been under advisement for some time before the rejection of the treaty, appears from Sumner's own statement in his subsequent recital of his grounds for grievance against the Administration. Fish, now loyally supporting the San Domingo project and at the time still friendly to Sumner, two weeks before the final vote, had a three hours' conference at the Senator's house one night, pressing his views, and in the course of conversation asked, "Why not go to London? I offer you the English mission. It is yours." Sumner coolly replied, "We have a minister there who cannot be bettered." He afterwards cited this suggestion as an attempt to influence him improperly. Fish said the suggestion was made impulsively through sympathy for Sumner, who had just referred to his domestic troubles. Whether it was fairly susceptible

to a sinister interpretation or not, it would certainly
indicate that even before the adverse vote upon the
treaty Motley's tenure was uncertain.

There came also then a sudden request for the
resignation of Attorney-General Hoar, Sumner's only
intimate friend in the Administration. Since Massachusetts had two cabinet members, Hoar early in
the Administration had placed his resignation in the
hands of the President, but nothing had been done
about it. Grant, who enjoyed Hoar's humor and
companionship in spite of their divergent tastes,
nominated him for a vacancy on the Supreme Bench
in December, 1869, but Southern Senators, whom
Hoar offended by refusing to honor their endorsement
of unfit men for federal judges and marshals in the
South, banded together in resentment and defeated
his confirmation. "What could you expect for a man
who had snubbed seventy Senators?" he remarked
philosophically to his friends of the Saturday Club
who were inclined to sympathize with him.

One afternoon in June, shortly before the San Domingo treaty was to be voted on, he was suddenly
asked for his resignation and was told frankly by
Grant that he had been obliged to take the step in
order to secure support in the Senate from Southern Republicans, who demanded the Cabinet place
for a Southern man. The President had no one in

particular in mind for the place, but sent in the name of Akerman, of Georgia, the next day on Hoar's own suggestion that quick action would save embarrassment through Southern pressure for the place.

Motley remained in London, touched to his sensitive soul, broken in spirit, awaiting the summary removal which finally came in December. The approaches to Great Britain proceeded deftly and continuously. San Domingo slumbered; but naval vessels hovered near her coasts. On the reconvening of Congress on December 5, 1870, Grant revived the issue in his annual message. He asked for authority to negotiate a new treaty, and suggested a resolution of annexation, as in the case of Texas. "So convinced am I of the advantages to flow from the acquisition of San Domingo and the great disadvantages — I might almost say calamities — to flow from the non-acquisition, that I believe the subject has only to be investigated to be approved." Morton, fearing the serious consequences of a defeat for the Administration, induced a compromise on a resolution to appoint a commission of investigation, which he forthwith offered in the Senate.

Sumner was in a rage. His wrath had been fed by tales of tattlers. His indignation and intolerance had grown through the summer. He "roared like the Bull

of Bashan" when he got to discussing the President
with his friends. Grant was equally bitter.

Sumner up to this time had not attacked the
President in open debate and now a better politician
and a wiser lawyer would have let the San Domingo
business alone, since it was plain that annexation
either by treaty or joint resolution was dead. He
could have consented gracefully to Morton's innocu-
ous commission of investigation and that would have
been the end of it; but his fateful propensity for putting himself right in the record followed him now as
at the time of the defeat of the Johnson-Clarendon
Convention. Morton urged him to let the resolution
pass without debate, but he refused; and though he
was warned that if he attacked the Administration
the President's friends would be forced to a defense,
and an open rupture would result, he was immovable.
He was obsessed with animosity, and even went so
far as to assure Morton that his life had been threatened at the White House by Grant and Babcock.
Morton could not laugh him out of his delusion.

He made the attack on December 21, 1870, in a
speech which he entitled "Naboth's Vineyard," beginning, "The resolution commits Congress to a
dance of blood," intimating that Grant was following
in the steps of Pierce, Buchanan, and Andrew Johnson, and speaking of the President in a manner

"bitter and excited," according to Morton, who adds, "his course is generally regretted by his best friends of whom I am one." Chandler and Conkling made bitter personal attacks on Sumner.

Morton's resolution was adopted in both House and Senate. A commission was appointed by the President consisting of Benjamin F. Wade, a radical Republican, Andrew D. White, an unbiased college president, and Samuel G. Howe, the abolitionist, a confidential friend of Sumner. This commission visited San Domingo accompanied by many newspaper correspondents and by other observers, and returned favorable to annexation. They made a report to Congress containing a statement of facts and indicating the resources of the country. "The mere rejection by the Senate of a treaty negotiated by the President," said Grant in a message of April 5, 1871, transmitting the report, "only indicates a difference of opinion between two coördinate departments of the Government, without touching the character or wounding the pride of either. But when such rejection takes place simultaneously with charges openly made of corruption on the part of the President or those employed by him, the case is different. Indeed, in such case the honor of the nation demands investigation. This has been accomplished by the report of the commissioners herewith

transmitted, and which fully indicates the purity of
the motives and action of those who represented the
United States in the negotiation. . . . And now my
task is finished and with it ends all personal solicitude upon the subject. My duty being done, yours
begins; and I gladly hand over the whole matter to
the judgment of the American people, and of their representatives in Congress assembled. The facts will
now be spread before the country, and a decision
rendered by that tribunal whose convictions so seldom err, and against whose will I have no policy to
enforce." Nothing further was ever done toward
annexation, though Grant returned to the subject
repeatedly in his messages to Congress expressing
regret that his recommendations had not been followed. He reiterated his arguments years later in his
book. Sumner's wrathful explosion had no effect
whatever upon the ultimate result. It simply served
to fan a feud, fateful alike to him and to the Administration he might have served.

Andrew D. White, who entered on the inquiry
with an open mind, sheds interesting light upon
the character of Grant, whom he interviewed at the
White House. "Instead of the taciturn man who, as
his enemies insisted, said nothing because he knew
nothing, had never cared for anything save military
matters, and was entirely absorbed in personal in-

terests, I found a quiet, dignified public officer, who presented the history of the Santo Domingo question, and his view regarding it, in a manner large, thoughtful, and statesmanlike. . . . As I took leave of him he gave me one charge for which I shall always revere his memory. He said: ' . . . You have doubtless noticed hints in Congress and charges in various newspapers that I am financially interested in the acquisition of Santo Domingo. Now, as a man, as your fellow citizen, I demand that on your arrival in the island you examine thoroughly into all American interests there; that you study land titles and contracts with the utmost care; and that if you find anything whatever which connects me or any of my family with any of them, you expose me to the American people.' The President uttered these words in a tone of deep earnestness."

However we may criticize the way Grant tried to force the San Domingo treaty through the Senate, he will be justified by history in his intent; for he foresaw far in advance of others that some time the island must be a part of the United States. If we had taken over San Domingo when we had the opportunity, we should have been spared unpleasant complications and sordid scandals running through many years. Annexation will come about in time, but never with so little friction or expense.

"In future while I hold my present office," Grant wrote in his second inaugural, "the subject of acquisition of territory must have the support of the people before I will recommend any proposition looking to such acquisition. I say here, however, that I do not share in the apprehension held by many as to the danger of governments becoming weakened and destroyed by reason of their extension of territory. Commerce, education, and rapid transit of thought and matter by telegraph and steam have changed all this. Rather do I believe that our Great Maker is preparing the world, in his own good time, to become one nation, speaking one language, and when armies and navies will be no longer required."

The big results of an episode futile in itself soon began to show. Motley, continuing in office months beyond the time set for his resignation, was finally, in December, 1871, subjected to the humiliation of a summary recall, and Robert C. Schenck, of Ohio, a person of entirely different type, was named for London in his place, Frelinghuysen and Morton having both previously declined the appointment. Motley's last official act was to write a controversial history of his mission, for the Secretary of State, an earnest defense of his conduct in office and a criticism of his official superiors. He referred in this to the rumor that his removal was due to Sumner's opposition to the San Domingo treaty. Fish in his reply, which bears internal evidence of having been written by another for his signature, asserted that this rumor had its origin in Washington "in a source bitterly, personally, and vindictively hostile to the President."

And then follows a passage which, when it came to Sumner's eyes on the publication of the correspondence, angered him beyond restraint as a gross and wanton insult. "Mr. Motley must know — or if he does not know it he stands alone in his ignorance of the fact — that many Senators opposed the San Domingo treaty openly, generously, and with as much efficiency as did the distinguished Senator to whom he refers and have nevertheless continued to enjoy the undiminished confidence and the friendship of the President, than whom no man living is more tolerant of honest and manly differences of opinion; is more single or sincere in his desire for the public welfare, or more disinterested or regardless of what concerns himself; is more frank and confiding in his own dealings; *is more sensitive to a betrayal of confidence or would look with more scorn and contempt upon one who uses the words and the assurances of friendship to cover a secret and determined purpose of hostility."*

On January 9 this correspondence was sent to the Senate. Sumner up to that time, in spite of his aliena-

tion from Grant, had continued in friendly personal
relations with Fish. Within a fortnight he had dined
at Fish's home. When he read this passage, which he
not unreasonably applied to himself, his wrath was
hot. He felt that he had been betrayed by a pre-
tended friend. From that time he had only formal
relations with Fish. It was on January 15, only a
week later, that Fish had to seek the interview with
regard to the mission of Sir John Rose through the
mediation of a common friend. Thereafter Sumner
was ignored by the Administration in handling questions of diplomacy. Grant had set his heart on being
rid of him.

A new Congress came into being on the 4th of
March. When the Senate entered on the task of
organizing its committees, the supporters of the
Administration served notice that Sumner should be
deposed from his position at the head of the Committee on Foreign Relations. The Massachusetts
Senator had few real friends among his associates.
His manner for years had been overbearing. Adams
says that, while not exacting deference, "habitual deference was essential to his good-will." Those who,
had he been of different temper, might have sustained him, now left him to his fate. Thenceforward,
he pursued Grant without mercy. His vehement denunciation inspired others to unsparing criticism,

and who can say how far the impressions of writers of history may have been due to him? Yet Grant said to Lowell years later at Madrid: "Sumner is the only man I was ever anything but my real self to; the only man I ever tried to conciliate by artificial means." A curious comment.

CHAPTER XXXIV

THE CUBAN PROBLEM — SOUND FINANCE —
"BLACK FRIDAY"

OVER half of Grant's inaugural was devoted to a discussion of the nation's financial credit. Four other
topics were treated. He pledged himself to enforce
all laws for the security of "person, property, and
free religion, and political opinion in every part of
our common country without regard to local prejudice," an unmistakable warning to the lawless element in the South. He declared that he would favor
any course toward the Indians which would tend to
their civilization and ultimate citizenship, the first of
our Presidents to take such advanced position. He
expressed a desire for the ratification of the Fifteenth
Amendment to the Constitution, giving to the negro
the right of suffrage, a wish fulfilled in the first year of
his Administration.

Grant in his inaugural enunciated his foreign
policy in a few robust and pregnant sentences, the
sturdy tone of which carried throughout his entire
Administration. "I would deal with nations as
equitable law requires individuals to deal with each
other, and I would protect the law-abiding citizen,
whether of native or foreign birth, wherever his

rights are jeopardized, or the flag of our country floats. I would respect the rights of all nations, demanding equal respect for our own. If others depart from this rule in their dealings with us, we may be compelled to follow their precedent."

The spirit of this declaration pervaded and galvanized our treatment of Great Britain and Canada in the Alabama claims and the fisheries and boundary disputes; of Spain in her relations with Cuba and in the Virginius affair; of Mexico and the South and Central American Republics in the maintenance of the Monroe Doctrine.

We have seen how delicately the British and San Domingan questions were interlaced. The Cuban problem was a third thread in the skein.

While Fish, with the aid of Rose, was trying to bring about a renewal of negotiations with Great Britain, Grant had turned his attention to the West Indies where Cuba and San Domingo filled for the moment the field of vision. Spectacularly the rapid developments in the Antilles counted for more than the deft and cautious diplomatic approaches between our State Department and the British Foreign Office, but Fish retained throughout a sense of international proportion. He did not personally approve Grant's course in San Domingo and felt it necessary to moderate his chief's desire to meddle in the Cuban insurrection, but so long as he had a clear path in what he deemed the greater problem, he was content in general to let Grant have his way without the risk of strained relations through offering unasked advice. There was much interest throughout the North, especially in New York financial circles, in the Cuban revolutionists, who had appealed to our Government for aid and had enlisted in their cause the sympathetic Rawlins, now Secretary of War.

Grant was strongly inclined to Rawlins's view, and as early as June 9, 1869, he asked Sumner about issuing a proclamation according belligerent rights to the insurgents, thus doing unto Spain as Spain had done to us at the beginning of the Civil War. Sumner advised against it, but Grant stuck to his idea, and having ordered a proclamation to be drawn up, he signed it on August 19 in the cabin of one of the Fall River boats and sent it to Washington by the hand of Bancroft Davis, the Assistant Secretary of State, with instructions to Fish to issue the proclamation after signing it and affixing the official seal. Fish, gingerly feeling his way toward reopening negotiations with Great Britain, was keenly alive to the difficulty involved in England's recognition of Confederate belligerency, too great emphasis upon the enormity of which by Sumner threatened to make his essay at negotiations abortive.

In his instructions to Motley he had sought to minimize the bearing upon our claims of the Queen's proclamation of May, 1861, but the proclamation still remained an ugly obstacle in his way, and he was conscious of the inconsistency of even a perfunctory assertion of our grievance while we ourselves might be upon the point of recognizing belligerent rights in a band of Cuban guerrillas who, as he afterwards wrote, "have no army, . . . no courts, do not occupy a single town or hamlet, to say nothing of a seaport." To his mind, "Great Britain or France might just as well have recognized belligerency for the Black Hawk War," and trusting to the efficacy of delay, he deposited the proclamation in a safe place after signing it, and left it there awaiting further instructions which never came.

Rawlins died September 6; "Black Friday" came; Grant's mind was fully occupied with pressing questions; and in the multiplicity of other things Fish had his way. In his annual message of December 6, 1869, the President contented himself with disclaiming any disposition on the part of the United States "to interfere with the existing relations of Spain with her colonial possessions on this continent." But public feeling was strong for recognition of belligerency, and when Congress met there was a growing pressure for the passage of resolutions to that end. Fish was the restraining influence at this time. Had it not been for him Grant would have doubtless aided those who called for recognition. Fish advised John Sherman, who had introduced the resolution in the Senate, "to prepare bills for the increase of the public debt, and to meet the increased appropriation which will be necessary for the army, navy, etc." As the time for a vote in the House approached, he impressed on Grant the necessity of sending in a message emphasizing the importance of refraining from recognition, and wrote a special message, which was sent to Congress on June 17, treating the whole subject comprehensively. Fish says in his diary that the President "was induced with great hesitation and with much reluctance to sign it, and after it was sent in he told me that he feared he had made a mistake. . . . It evoked a fierce debate, and much denunciation, but it evoked also much good sense in the speeches of those who sustained it; an expression of good sound international law, and of honesty of purpose, and it brought the gravity of the case to the consideration of Congress; and the Administration, after the severest debate on a question of foreign policy which has occurred for years, was triumphantly sustained."

Of impressive immediate effect was the clear declaration with regard to upholding the public credit. "A great debt has been contracted by us in securing to us and our posterity the Union," said Grant. "The payment of this principal and interest, as well as the return to a specie basis as soon as it can be accomplished without material detriment to the debtor class or to the country at large, must be provided for. To protect the national honor every dollar of government indebtedness should be paid in gold, unless otherwise expressly stipulated in the contract. Let it be understood that no repudiator of one farthing of our public debt will be trusted in public place and it will go far toward strengthening a credit which ought to be the best in the world, and will ultimately enable us to replace the debt with bonds bearing less interest than we now pay. To this should be added a faithful collection of the revenue, a strict accountability to the treasury for every dollar collected, and the greatest practical retrenchment in expenditure in every department of government."

It required some courage for the President and the Republican Party to take this attitude, for there was a strong sentiment in the country in favor of the payment of five-twenty bonds in greenbacks and a large issue of greenbacks for that purpose. A considerable party had come into being in support of this proposal, and the feeling had been accentuated by the rapid contraction of United States notes following the Civil War, $140,000,000 out of $737,000,000 having been withdrawn in the two years preceding 1868. Johnson, although he had at his elbow in Secretary McCulloch one of the soundest of financial ministers, had extraordinary ideas personally about the repudiation of interest on government bonds, which found expression in his last annual message; and the fact that, following the London panic of May, 1866, business had been in a bad way, with a decrease in the value of property and an increase in the face value of debts, was popularly attributed to the contraction of the currency. Yet there was no hesitancy on the part of the new Administration.

The Republicans in the platform upon which Grant was elected had denounced all forms of repudiation as a national crime and declared that the national honor required the payment of the public indebtedness "in the uttermost good faith to all creditors at home and abroad not only according to the letter but the spirit of the laws"; and the very first act of the Congress which came into existence on March 4, 1869, was a law "to strengthen the public credit," which, after passing both House and Senate overwhelmingly, was signed by Grant on March 18. The law solemnly pledged the faith of the United States to the payment, in gold or its equivalent, of the United States notes and all the United States bonds except in those cases where the law authorizing their issue provided expressly for their payment in "other currency than gold and silver." By the words of the law the United States also solemnly pledged its faith "to make provision at the earliest practicable period for the redemption of the United States notes in coin."

The episode which has come down in history as the "Gold Conspiracy," with "Black Friday" as its demoralizing climax, throws light not only upon Grant's ingenuousness, but also on the fashions of the hour. At the time of Grant's accession to the Presidency the two spectacular figures in New York financial circles were Jay Gould and James Fisk, Jr., — "Jim" Fisk as he was popularly known. Gould was the shrewdest, most subtle and ruthless trader and manipulator in the Street — a railroad wrecker after the manner of his day, with an extraordinary genius for getting money; slight in figure, reticent, keen of face, of a Semitic type. Fisk, his partner in many deals, was a speculator of another sort, big, coarse, florid in complexion, dress, and speech, a daring gambler for heavy stakes, a high liver, unscrupulous in his financial operations, immoral in his daily and nightly life.

These two, so strikingly contrasted in everything except their passion for speculation and financial power, had combined their diverse talents in 1868 to gain control of the Erie Railroad. They played with power as though it were a toy. They flaunted their control by putting on the board of directors "Boss" Tweed and Peter B. Sweeney, the chieftains of Tammany Hall.

Gould and Fisk also owned steamers, palatial for that day, plying between New York and Fall River, a fleet of which Fisk liked to be called Admiral, and in command of which he would float up Long Island Sound with bands playing and flags flying. Gould had a project to advance the price of gold till wheat should reach a price which would induce the farmers of the West to seek the English market with their breadstuffs, thus causing a movement of crops to the seaboard, which meant plenty of freight for the Erie road.

In the early summer of 1869 gold was heavy at $1.34. There had been little change for months. To manipulate the market Gould needed a free hand; but he had to reckon with the Treasury gold reserve, and Secretary Boutwell had his own ideas about the course gold ought to take. He had been selling gold ever since he took office, setting free $2,500,000 each month, thus bringing greenbacks nearer the gold level.

Gould's problem was to stop the sales of gold, and to this end he laid the wires to get in touch with Boutwell's superior. Abel Rathbone Corbin, aged sixty-seven, retired speculator, lobby agent, editor, and lawyer, recently married to Grant's sister, was living in New York. Gould used him to secure an introduction. On June 15, 1869, Grant visited New York on his way to the Peace Jubilee at Boston. He stayed at Corbin's house; Gould met him there.

Gould and Fisk invited Grant to continue his journey to Boston as their guest on one of the Fall River boats, and on the run up the Sound they led the conversation at dinner around to the subject of finance. "Some one," Gould testified in the investigation which followed the cataclysm, "asked the President what his view was," and to the consternation of the conspirators Grant replied bluntly that "there was a certain amount of fictitiousness about the prosperity of the country and that the bubble might as well be tapped in one way as another."

There was a vacancy in the position of Assistant Treasurer of the United States at New York, the custodian of the greatest deposit of gold in the country. The place was filled on July 1 by the appointment of General Daniel Butterfield, upon whose coöperation Gould felt he could rely. Gould did nothing to influence the market till the time for the movement of the crops approached. But in the last ten days of August, through a pool which he formed with two other large speculators, he bought from ten to fifteen millions of gold without, however, materially increasing the premium.

On September 2, Grant, quite oblivious to what was going on, passed through New York on his way to Saratoga, and stayed a few hours at Corbin's house, seeing no one else while there.[1] In the course of conversation Grant became convinced of the soundness of Gould's theory about marketing the crops, as expounded by Corbin. He stopped in the middle of a conversation in which he had expressed his views and wrote a letter to Secretary Boutwell. Before he had left the house the purport of this letter undoubtedly was communicated to Gould, who called privately upon Corbin without Grant's knowledge.

Before a Congressional investigating committee, Boutwell subsequently testified: "I think on the evening of the 4th of September I received a letter from the President dated at New York, as I recollect it. . . . In that letter he expressed an opinion that it was undesirable to force down the price of gold. He spoke of the importance to the West of being able to move their crops. . . . Upon the receipt of the President's letter on the evening of the 4th of September, I telegraphed to Judge Richardson (Assistant Secretary of the Treasury at Washington) this

[1] Henry Adams, *The Gold Conspiracy.*

dispatch: 'Send no order to Butterfield as to sales of gold until you hear from me.'"

Thus Gould had information that the policy of the Administration with regard to the sale of gold was to be reversed fully a day before the Secretary of the Treasury himself. He lost no time in taking advantage of his opportunity. Before leaving Corbin's house, he had agreed to carry a million and a half of gold as Corbin testified later "for the sake of a lady, my wife." That same afternoon his brokers began buying gold in large quantities. By the time Boutwell received his letter on September 4, 1869, the premium had risen from 32 to 37. Then the bears began to sell short. One of Gould's associates in the pool deserted him. The market broke. Corbin made Gould pay him twenty-five thousand dollars on account. Gold settled down to 35 and lingered there for a week. Then Fisk, at Gould's suggestion, went in to buy.

Gould placed a million and a half to Butterfield's account and half a million to the credit of General Horace Porter, the President's private secretary, sending word to them through Corbin. Porter repudiated the purchase promptly. Butterfield took no notice of the transaction. After the storm broke, though he denied that he was ever notified of the transaction, so great was the scandal that he was forced to resign.

From the 10th to the 13th of September, Grant was again in New York and Gould saw him at Corbin's house, though the President by that time had become suspicious of the motives of the financier; for according to Corbin he told the servant this should be the last time Gould should be admitted. "Gould was always trying to get something out of him." It is a pity he did not earlier shut the door in Gould's face.

Plainly he had given no definite assurance regarding his policy, for when he left on the 13th for a few days' stay in the little town of Washington among the mountains of western Pennsylvania, the conspirators in their anxiety, through the complaisant Corbin, chased him up. They had bought over fifty millions and had forced the market up to 40 in spite of the increased activity of the bears. They did not dare let go for fear of a collapse. It was vital to them that the President should not direct the Secretary of the Treasury to resume the sale of gold. Corbin wrote a letter advising him to maintain his present attitude regarding the sale of gold, which Fisk sent speedily by a special messenger to reach him before his return to the White House. In order to insure its immediate delivery the messenger carried also a letter of introduction to Horace Porter. It was not till after the messenger had gone that Grant discovered the elaborate precautions to insure the prompt delivery of an apparently unimportant communication. His suspicions were roused. At his request Mrs. Grant wrote that night to Mrs. Corbin that the President was distressed to hear that Corbin was speculating in Wall Street and hoped he would "instantly disconnect himself with anything of that sort."

Corbin wrote at once to Grant that he had not a dollar interest in gold — a letter which with the other he promptly showed to Gould who saw him daily, suggesting in order to make good the assurance to his brother-in-law that Gould should give him one hundred thousand dollars and take his gold off his hands. Gould, who had all the gold he could stagger under just then, declined the proposal, but offered him one hundred thousand dollars to stay in and not throw his million and a half on the market. Corbin refused, and then, realizing that an order to sell might come from the Treasury at any moment, Gould hurried down to Wall Street.

Fisk, still supposing that Grant was following the advice in Corbin's letter, was buying wildly. The market bounded to 162. The bears were dazed and at the mercy of the new Napoleon of the Street, when Gould without warning began to sell — the bubble burst. The Street was in a state of excitement without a precedent in all its checkered history. Within a few minutes gold had fallen to 135. The Treasury wired its order to sell, which Gould had been expecting, but which Fisk had not surmised. Gould had got rid of his gold and his brokers' firm were able to meet their contracts; but not so with Fisk. He repudiated all but one. Their victims turned on them in wrath. They escaped by back entrances to their uptown office, while armed guards beat back the ruined traders storming at their downtown doors. There have been no scenes to equal this in Wall Street before or since. It was Friday, September 24, 1869, "Black Friday."

The punishment of the conspirators did not fit the crime. Fisk and Gould continued in control of Erie, a little more discredited. Butterfield was permitted to resign. In addition to letting Gould carry his gold for him he had borrowed money from him and had speculated in government bonds. Brother-in-law Corbin, his dreams of fortune shattered, retired to Washington, where he was not made uproariously welcome in the President's house, though he was not cast adrift. He had accomplished nothing through his plunge in high finance, except to set malicious tongues wagging.

CHAPTER XXXV

THE LEGAL TENDER DECISION

WHEN Congress met in December, 1869, with the financial disturbances still unsettled, the President in his first annual message urged upon its attention the evil of an unredeemable currency, repeating the sentiments expressed in his inaugural. "It is the duty, and one of the highest duties of Government," he said, "to secure to the citizen a medium of fixed, unvarying value. This implies a return to a specie basis and no substitute for it can be devised. It should be commenced now and reached at the earliest practicable moment consistent with a fair regard to the interests of the debtor class." He earnestly recommended such legislation as would insure a gradual return to specie payments and put an immediate stop to fluctuations in the paper value of the measure of all values (gold) which "makes the man of business an involuntary gambler, for in all sales where future payment is to be made both parties speculate as to what will be the value of the currency to be paid and received."

At the time the national debt was $2,453,000,000. It had been decreased since March 1 by $71,903,000.

There had been set aside for the sinking fund $20,000,000 of bonds, to comply with the law of 1862, that one per cent of the entire debt should be set apart annually for this purpose. Boutwell, who, though endowed with little financial imagination, had economic common sense and thrift, concerned himself first of all throughout his administration of the Treasury in the reduction of the national debt, a policy which helped our credit at home and abroad, resulting in a total reduction during Grant's two Administrations of nearly a billion dollars.

Boutwell bought the five-twenty bonds carrying six per cent interest and sold four and one-half per cent bonds in a refunding plan elaborated by himself. He strove for the resumption of specie payments, and in his first report asked for authority to retire at his discretion two millions of greenbacks every month; but Congress failed to give him this power to contract the currency, a policy which had not been popular since McCulloch in Johnson's Administration had retired forty-four million dollars of greenbacks before further contraction was suspended by Congress in February, 1868. The contraction from McCulloch's retirement of greenbacks and from the withdrawal and funding of the compound interest legal tender notes had undoubtedly been too drastic treatment at a time when the country was none too prosperous,

Morton, of Indiana, called it the "Sangrado policy of bleeding the country nearly to death to cure it of a disease which demands tonics and building up."

Hardly had Grant's message of December, 1869, gone to the country before the whole currency question was brought vividly to the notice of the people, through the decision of the United States Supreme Court in the case of Hepburn *vs.* Griswold, that the Legal Tender Act, under which the greenbacks were authorized at the beginning of the war, was unconstitutional. The opinion of the court was handed down on February 7, 1870, by Chief Justice Chase, under whose administration as Secretary of the Treasury the law had been enacted. He now argued that the act impaired the obligation of contracts and was inconsistent with the spirit of the Constitution; that it deprived persons of property without due process of law, by forcing creditors to accept dollars of less value than those which were lent or which by the terms of the contract they had a right to expect in payment of claims. "We are obliged to conclude," said Chase as Chief Justice, "that an act [fathered by Chase as Secretary of the Treasury] making mere promises to pay dollars as legal tender in payment of debts previously contracted, is not a means appropriate, plainly adapted, really calculated, to carry into effect any express power vested in Congress; that such an act is inconsistent with the spirit of the Constitution; and that it is prohibited by the Constitution."

Justice Miller, one of the ablest jurists who ever sat on the Supreme Bench, delivered the opinion of the minority of the court. After quoting Chief Justice Marshall, he said: " With the credit of the Government nearly exhausted and the resources of taxation inadequate to pay even the interest on the public debt, Congress was called on to devise some new means of borrowing money on the credit of the nation; for the result of the war was conceded by all thoughtful men to depend on the capacity of the Government to raise money in amounts previously unknown. . . . The coin in the country . . . would not have made a circulation sufficient to answer army purchases. . . . A general collapse of credit, of payment, and of business seemed inevitable, in which faith in the ability of the Government would have been destroyed, the rebellion would have triumphed, the States would have been left divided, and the people impoverished. The National Government would have perished, and with it the Constitution which we are now called upon to construe with such nice and critical accuracy. . . ."

The court was divided in its decision as handed down, four to three: Nelson, Clifford, and Field

siding with Chase, while Swayne and Davis agreed
with Miller. Grier, who had sat with the court when
it first came to its decision on November 27, 1869,
and had then pronounced in favor of the constitutionality of the act, had resigned before the announcement of the decision on February 7, by unanimous
request of the other justices, his senile incompetency
having disclosed itself in the mean time through his
statement in another case of an opinion inconsistent
with his position on the Legal Tender case, and his
prompt reversal of his Legal Tender opinion when
the inconsistency was called to his attention. There
were two vacancies on the bench on the day the decision was handed down. Wayne had died and Grier
had resigned. E. R. Hoar, who had been nominated
for one of the places, had been rejected by the Senate
four days earlier. Edwin M. Stanton, who had been
nominated for the other vacancy and promptly confirmed on December 20, had died four days after his
confirmation.

It happened that on the very day the decision was
handed down Grant sent to the Senate the names
of William Strong, of Pennsylvania, and Joseph P.
Bradley, of New Jersey. Subsequently, two other
cases known as the Legal Tender cases were brought
before the court. A decision affirming the constitutionality of the acts and overruling the former

decision was reached and announced on May 1, 1871. The opinion of the court, as read by Justice Strong at the following term, on January 15, 1872, declared that "we hold the acts of Congress constitutional as applied to contracts made either before or after their passage. In so holding we overrule so much of what was decided in Hepburn *vs*. Griswold as ruled the acts unwarranted by the Constitution so far as they apply to contracts made before their enactment."

The coincidence of the appointment of these two justices, and the speedy reversal of the attitude of the court on the constitutionality of the Legal Tender Acts, led not unnaturally to the conclusion in many minds, that Strong and Bradley had been named for this specific purpose, and Chief Justice Chase, by indirection, gave color to the charge that the court had been packed in order to reverse the earlier decision in which he had participated. For many years this suspicion lurked in the public consciousness, and the motives of Grant and Attorney-General Hoar, on whose recommendation the appointments were made, have been frequently called in question.

There is no ground whatever for the charge. Senator George F. Hoar, loyally defending the memory of his brother, replied to it conclusively, with great detail of circumstance, in a letter which appeared

in the "Boston Herald" in 1896 and which afterwards was printed as a pamphlet, but it did not
require this marshaling of proof to clear the records
of the President and his Attorney-General. The vacancies were there; they had to be filled at that time;
and there was every reason why a Republican President should fill them with Republicans, as four of the
seven justices had Democratic affiliations, Chase
having been a candidate for the Democratic nomination for President less than two years before. It
would have been hard to find a Republican judge or
lawyer of prominence who was less likely than Strong
and Bradley to favor the constitutionality of the Legal Tender Acts, and there is not the slightest evidence that, when Strong and Bradley were decided
upon by the President and the Attorney-General
and approved by the Cabinet, any one of them had an
inkling of what the decision of the court was to be.
Grant did not "pack the court."

CHAPTER XXXVI

BITTER PROBLEMS — THE SOUTH — THE NEGRO — ENFORCEMENT ACTS

IT was Grant's misfortune to inherit the problem of the negro and the South in its most sordid and repulsive phase. The tragical blunders of Reconstruction, which under the pressure of political necessity he had half-heartedly consented to in their incipiency in Johnson's Administration, bloomed noxiously in his own. He had been sincerely the friend of the South at the close of the Civil War, and he was genuinely in favor of restoring promptly to the conquered Confederates the full rights of citizenship. He was brought by force of circumstances to accept the full measure of negro suffrage as an unwelcome reprisal for Johnson's stubbornness; but he did not regard it as inconsistent with his honest aspirations for a fully reunited country. "Let us have peace" as he penned it was not an empty phrase; yet it fell to him as President to secure what peace was feasible only through apprehension of the sword, to quell internal violence by show of force. Threats of turbulence and bloodshed in the South marked the entire period of Grant's occupancy of the White House; and with sanction of Congress he was driven more than once to measures not contemplated by the Constitution.

The black record of carpet-bag and scalawag political control of Southern States, through misuse of the negro vote, is an ugly picture to look back on. The work of the Ku-Klux Klans and the White Leagues was equally deplorable, unworthy of a proud-spirited race and inexcusable even in the distressing circumstances which inspired them. The former slaves who reveled ostentatiously in unsought opportunities were not the best representatives of their race, but they were victims in a measure of Northern zealots, who fatuously dreamed that the poor, unlettered, childlike creatures could be at once regenerated by the baptism of the franchise.

Neither were the Ku-Klux Klans and White League ruffians typical of the South. Those who at this day try to paint them so render poor service to a high-spirited, nobly nurtured people. The outrages, riots, and murders which figured so conspicuously in Grant's Administration were as a rule the work of the lower class of whites, and in justice to the South should be so credited, exactly as the political misrule of the carpet-baggers should not be attributed to those thrifty Northern settlers whose purpose in leaving their homes was to help restore a war-shattered territory and to participate in its renewed industrial prosperity.

The New Orleans riot of July, 1866, which Sheridan characterized as "an absolute massacre," was the first of the social disturbances which later became too prevalent. It was natural that they should begin in Louisiana; for this was the first of the Southern States to be "reconstructed," and the great negro population thus invited to participate in its government were largely plantation hands, the most ignorant and vicious of their race, many of whom had been "sold down the river" by their former masters for punishment as desperate characters. Northern adventurers were speedily on the ground at New Orleans, organizing the freedmen for political control. Corruption and legislative orgies on the one hand and violence on the other became the order of the day. A Republican majority of 26,000 in the spring elections of 1868 was transformed in November into a majority of 46,000 for Seymour and Blair.

From 1868 to 1872 misgovernment on the part of carpet-baggers and negroes, tempered by violence and intimidation on the part of the white minority, prevailed, not only in Louisiana, but in other States containing a large excess of negro population, although Virginia, thanks to the fact that Schofield had it long under military rule, escaped the invasion of carpet-baggers and was thus in Schofield's words "saved from the vile government and spoliation which cursed the other Southern States." Bribery, thievery, and extravagance were commonplaces in the legislatures and among state officials. There was corruption in the courts; property values fell; taxes were in arrears; the state debts soared to preposterous figures; industry was paralyzed.

In Tennessee, Georgia, North Carolina, and Virginia conservative forces gradually gained ascendancy during the early years of Grant's Administration; but this was not true of other States. In 1873, three fourths of the South Carolina Legislature were negroes, mulattoes, and octoroons, the most presentable of whom a few years earlier were gentlemen's servants, others of whom had been raising corn and cotton under the whip of the overseer. The State House had been lavishly refurnished; clocks and mirrors costing $600; chairs costing $60; cuspidors costing $14, had replaced the simple fittings of *antebellum* days. A free restaurant and bar was kept open day and night for the convenience of members of the Legislature and their friends. The public printing bills during the eight years of negro supremacy exceeded by $717,589 the total cost of printing during the seventy-eight years preceding. The total taxes paid by all the members of one Legislature were reported to be only $634; and 67 of the 98 negro members paid no tax at all.

Negroes and carpet-baggers were sent to Congress. Some of them were men of character; others not. Men like Blanche K. Bruce, H. R. Revels, John R. Lynch, Robert Elliott, negroes all, would do credit to any race.

There is testimony also to violence by negroes in reconstructed States, tales of burning barns, cotton gins, and dwellings; of rape committed upon white women; of outrages such as bestial beings exulting in unaccustomed license might be guilty of. There is no evidence that these things were as prevalent as has been represented; but they were sufficient in connection with the political orgies at the state capitols to rouse the whites to action. Hence the increased activity of the Ku-Klux Klans, the White Leagues, the terrifying night raids, the midnight whippings, the lynchings, and innumerable unspeakable offenses, some of them committed for private vengeance or as a method of political proscription. The record is one of infamy; and the late endeavor of a few Southern novelists, playwrights, and motion-picture producers to throw about it the halo of righteous retribution and romance will make it nothing else.[1]

[1] In spite of the notoriety attaching to the operations of the Ku-Klux Klans, it should be remembered that their operations

Thus Grant was called upon to meet conditions in the South for which there was no parallel or precedent and for the existence of which he was in no way

were by no means universal in the South. They were widely separated and their virulence was confined to the black counties of the afflicted States. The various secret organizations seem to have had little more than incidental relationship among themselves. The most authentic presentation of facts appears in the majority and minority reports of a joint committee created by resolution of Congress, April 7, 1871, consisting of seven Senators and fourteen Representatives — thirteen Republicans and eight Democrats — who were authorized " to inquire into the condition of affairs in the late insurrectionary States." The majority point out that the Ku-Klux Klan was in actual operation both in Tennessee and the adjoining States some time before there were any negro legislatures or any negro voters.

The report admits the sorry character of the governments imposed upon the reconstructed States. "The refusal of their former masters to participate in political reconstruction necessarily left the negroes to be influenced by others. Many of them were elected to office, and entered it with honest intentions to do their duty, but were unfitted for its discharge. Through their instrumentality, many unworthy white men, having obtained their confidence, also procured public positions."

In South Carolina, especially, corruption was flagrant. The testimony taken by the committee discloses the demoralization which prevailed among Radicals and Democrats, — black and white alike.

Dr. R. M. Smith, a Democratic member of the Legislature, when asked if he would impose a penalty upon a man who bribes a public official, replied: "No, sir; because when it is understood that a man is for sale like a sheep, or anything else, any man has a right to buy him."

General M. C. Butler, later a United States Senator, a Confederate who wore the United States uniform as a volunteer major-general in the war with Spain, had this to say concerning land commission frauds, by which native South Carolinians sold their to blame — conditions which would never have prevailed had the South been left a little longer under military control before being plunged into the experimental bath of Reconstruction. The steps he took to bring about a semblance of order were drastic and to some obnoxious; but at the moment they seemed obvious and necessary — and there was no lack of definiteness in his method of approach.

Virginia, Texas, and Mississippi having ratified the Fourteenth and Fifteenth Amendments, their Senators and Representatives were admitted to Congress under a resolution containing conditions calculated to prevent these States from slipping from Republican control. Hiram R. Revels, a quadroon, had the distinction of being the first colored man to hold a seat in the United States Senate, succeeding to the place last occupied by Jefferson Davis. All the Confederate States had now gone through the process of Reconstruction; but Georgia, which had been represented in the House of Representa tives since 1868 under Johnson's Reconstruction, was forced to go through the process again. After she

land at five dollars an acre to the State and allowed the commission to insert ten dollars an acre as the consideration in the deed: "It was human nature almost. I do not think a strictly honest man would do it. If I had ten thousand acres of land to sell and a Senator would come to me and say, 'I will buy that if you will give me five hundred dollars,' I would buy him up as I would buy a mule."

had once been admitted to the Union the conservatives in the Legislature had committed the offense of expelling all the negro members and seating in their place white men ineligible under the Fourteenth Amendment. Her Senators-elect had never been permitted to take their seats and her Representatives were now barred from the House on the organization of the Forty-first Congress in March, 1869.

There were comparatively few carpet-baggers in Georgia, but Bullock, the radical Governor, a man of force and not oppressed by scruples, had proved himself obnoxious. The finances of the State were involved in obscurity and confusion. The Western and Atlantic Railroad, which for years had been the pride of the State, was sacrificed to politics and loot. The superintendent of the road testified that he took charge "to manage its public and political policy." The auditor saved thirty thousand dollars a year on a three thousand dollar salary, as he said, "by practicing strict economy." Grant in his annual message, December 6, 1869, recommended the reorganization of the Legislature. A law was promptly enacted containing strict stipulations regarding membership in the Legislature, providing that before her Senators and Representatives should be admitted to Congress, Georgia must ratify the Fifteenth Amendment, and that upon the application of the Governor the President should employ what military force was necessary to enforce the act. Terry was assigned to command, the Legislature was summoned, and under his orders twenty-four Democrats were ousted. Their places were filled by Republicans, and the negroes who had been expelled were readmitted. Thus reconstructed, the Legislature ratified the Fourteenth and Fifteenth Amendments and elected two Senators.

In Congress there was a desperate attempt not only to prescribe for Georgia the "fundamental conditions" imposed on Virginia, Texas, and Mississippi, but to prolong for two years the life of the reorganized radical Bullock Legislature. Morton, Sumner, Wilson, and other radical leaders in the Senate carried on there a long and bitter but unsuccessful fight. The Bullock scheme for prolongation was beaten and the right of Georgia to have an election in 1870 as stipulated in its constitution was confirmed. Thus for the first time since the early days of Reconstruction the conservative element in the Republican Party showed itself in the ascendancy.

Beaten at Washington, Bullock got his hand-picked Georgia Senate to pass a resolution that the Legislature should not meet until January, 1872, that no election for members should be held until November, 1872, and that, until the election, all state officers should hold their place. There was a fierce fight in the House over the resolution which was finally defeated through the influence of Grant. Bullock then induced the Legislature to pass a law, setting December 22 as the beginning of an election which was to continue three days, the plan apparently being to give the negroes an opportunity to "repeat" from precinct to precinct. No votes were to be challenged; none refused. The poll tax levied for the past three years was declared illegal, so that no one need be disfranchised for non-payment of taxes.

The white Democrats, intent on clearing the negroes and carpet-baggers out of the State Capitol, took things into their own hands. There were no "outrages," no intimidation, no turbulence, but there was plenty of "persuasion." The negroes were unusually flush with spending-money for a few days after the election. Many of them voted the Democratic ticket. More of them stayed away from the polls. It was a test of the supremacy of intellect and cash over the passion of freemen for the ballot.

The Democrats elected two thirds of the Legislature and five out of seven Congressmen — a good beginning for a numerical minority. Thereafter Georgia had "home rule." A Democratic Governor was inaugurated two years later in 1872. The regenerated State has ever since cast its electoral vote for the Democratic candidate for President. A Southern woman, who late in the winter of 1869 wrote that "the negroes were almost in a state of anarchy," wrote two years later, "The negroes are behaving like angels." Such was the beneficent result of the new doctrine of "persuasion."

North Carolina was an old, substantial Whig State, uncursed by negro supremacy; and yet corruption ruled. Bribery in the Legislature was open and usual. All sorts of questionable enterprises were "put across." The debt of the State increased from $16,000,000 to $32,000,000. There were Ku-Klux outrages, though not so many as in other States. Holden, the Governor, declared two counties in a state of insurrection, and sent Colonel Kirk with a body of mountaineer militia to keep the peace. Kirk arrested a hundred citizens, many of good repute, and kept them in custody in daily dread of death under martial law.

"Kirk's Raid," as it was known, stirred Washington to wrath, and there was hot debate. The judge of the United States District Court issued a writ of habeas corpus commanding Kirk to bring his prisoners before him. Grant sent a regiment to the scene and the United States Marshal called upon the troops to execute the order of the court. Finally Grant turned the whole business over to Attorney-General Akerman, who sustained the federal judge;

whereupon the court discharged the prisoners from Kirk's "unlawful custody." While all this was going on, an election was held on August 4, which resulted in general Republican defeat. The Democrats carried the Legislature and elected five out of the seven Congressmen.

Holden, the Governor, made himself especially obnoxious by garrisoning Raleigh, the State Capital, with negro troops. He was impeached, found guilty, and removed from office.

In the midst of disturbances arising from the emancipation of the negro and his imposition upon the electorate of the South, the Fifteenth Amendment to the Constitution became valid through ratification by the Legislatures of three fourths of the States, among them North and South Carolina, Louisiana, Arkansas, Florida, Virginia, Alabama, Mississippi, Texas, and Georgia, reconstructed States of the Confederacy. The Secretary of State certified to this on March 30, 1870.

So impressed was Grant with the significance of the completion of the trilogy of changes in the organic law growing out of the Civil War that he made it the occasion of a special message to Congress, flaming with fervid rhetoric to a degree unusual for Grant. Although an editorial blue pencil would have helped the message, the recommendations it contained were sound: "Institutions like ours, in which all power is derived from the people, must depend mainly upon their intelligence, patriotism, and industry. I call the attention, therefore, of the newly enfranchised race to the importance of their striving in every honorable manner to make themselves worthy of their new privilege. To the race most favored heretofore by our laws I would say, withhold no legal privilege of advancement to the new citizen. The framers of our Constitution firmly believed that a republican government could not endure. without intelligence and education generally diffused among the people. . . . I would therefore call upon Congress to take all the means within their constitutional powers to promote and encourage popular education throughout the country and upon the people everywhere to see to it that all who possess and exercise political rights shall have the opportunity to acquire the knowledge which will make their share in the Government a blessing and not a danger."

But the first acts of Congress under the second section of the Amendment, giving that body power "to enforce this article by appropriate legislation," did not lie in the direction of popular education. On the contrary, they were intended to meet the turbulent conditions in Southern States which had resulted in so many instances in the intimidation of the negro and the suppression of his vote by an intelligent and ruthless minority bent upon restoring the political control of their state governments to those best qualified to administer them.

In quick succession Congress passed three "enforcement acts," the first of which was signed by Grant on May 31, 1870. "The scope and purpose of the bill," said Carl Schurz in its support, "is that no State shall enforce a law with regard to elections, or the processes preliminary to elections, in which in any way, either directly or indirectly, discrimination is made against any citizen on account of race, color, or previous condition; . . . neither a State nor an individual shall deprive any citizen of the United States on account of race and color, of the free exercise of his right to participate in the functions of self-government; and the National Government assumes the duty to prevent the commission of the crime and to correct the consequences when committed."

Thurman and other Democratic Senators denounced the act as "outrage and oppression" and Edmunds bitingly called attention to the irony of the circumstance that the machinery for the enforcement of the act should have been borrowed from the Fugitive Slave Law of 1850.

One section of the act was directed toward the suppression of the Ku-Klux Klan; another authorized the President to employ when necessary the military force of the United States " to aid in the execution of judicial process" under the act, and there were special provisions for the enforcement of the Fourteenth Amendment.

Having had its taste of blood Congress went to greater lengths. On February 28, 1871, a second Enforcement Act was approved by Grant, entitled "An Act to enforce the rights of citizens of the United States to vote in the several States of this Union." It placed the elections for members of Congress under federal control; provided for the appointment of supervisors by judges of the United States Courts to insure a fair vote and honest count; empowered United States Marshals to appoint deputies to prevent interference with the right of voting, any one of whom might summon the *posse comitatus* of his district to aid in the enforcement of the law.

The act, of course, applied to all the States; in fact, it was subsequently brought to bear upon the election frauds of Tammany in New York; but its immediate object was to protect the negroes in the exercise of suffrage in the South, where, by a strange perversion of the intention of the Emancipation Proclamation and the constitutional amendments,

the white population already were beginning to
realize that by counting the negro in the census and
failing to count his vote they could enjoy a greater
proportional representation in the House of Representatives even than before the war.

The third Enforcement Act had the like general
purpose in view of establishing order in the South.
The new Congress — the Forty-second — which began its sessions on March 4, according to the law
enacted to curb Johnson's activities, had before it
the report of a special committee appointed during
the preceding session to investigate affairs in the
South. On March 23, Grant called attention to the
report in a special message in which he said: "A
condition of affairs now exists in some of the States
of the Union rendering life and property insecure
and the carrying of the mails and the collection of
the revenue dangerous. The proof that such a condition of affairs exists in some localities is now before the Senate. That the power to correct these
evils is beyond the control of the state authorities I
do not doubt; that the power of the Executive of
the United States, acting within the limits of existing laws, is sufficient for present emergencies is not
clear. Therefore I urgently recommend such legislation as in the judgment of Congress shall effectu-
ally secure life, liberty, and property and the en-

forcement of the law in all parts of the United States."

Feeling was intense at the moment, and Congress quickly complied with the request of the President, by passing the law of April 20, 1871, "to enforce the provisions of the Fourteenth Amendment." This law conferred upon the President extraordinary powers. One section authorized him to suspend the privileges of the writ of habeas corpus, the authority to expire at the end of the succeeding session of Congress.

The election of 1872 was approaching and there were signs of division among Republican leaders, but with a few exceptions the party stood well together in support of the Ku-Klux Bill as it was called.

The Democrats of the Senate were vehement in opposition, even while admitting the existence of the outrages. Thurman declared the bill unconstitutional. But Morton, who led the Republican majority declared: "Shall Reconstruction be maintained; shall the constitutional amendments be upheld; shall the colored people be protected in their enjoyment of equal rights; shall the Republicans of the Southern States be protected in life, liberty, and property? —are the great issues to be settled in 1872."

Eleven years later the Supreme Court of the United States declared the act unconstitutional. The court already in 1875 had declared unconstitutional the principal sections of the first Enforcement Act of May 31, 1870, "as involving the exercise by the United States of powers in excess of those granted by the Fifteenth Amendment."

In only one instance did Grant make use of the extraordinary powers given him by the Ku-Klux Act; and that was in the case of South Carolina, which he had particularly in mind when he wrote his message. Scott, the carpet-bag Governor, had applied for troops, declaring that combinations of armed men, unauthorized by law, were committing acts of violence in the State. On the 3d day of May Grant issued a proclamation declaring: " I will not hesitate to exhaust the powers thus vested in the Executive whenever and wherever it shall become necessary to do so for the purpose of securing to all citizens of the United States the peaceful enjoyment of the rights guaranteed to them by the Constitution and laws."

On October 17, 1871, he issued a proclamation suspending the writ of habeas corpus in nine counties named. Under these proclamations many persons were arrested and some were prosecuted and punished.

The measures taken had a speedy effect. According to the report of the Ku-Klux Investigating Committee there was an "apparent cessation" of Ku-Klux operations by February 19, 1872. Grant in his annual message of December 2, 1872, declared that he could not question "the necessity and salutary effect" of the enforcement acts, and in his second inaugural, March 4, 1873, he felt justified in saying: "The States lately at war with the general Government are now happily rehabilitated and no executive control is exercised in any one of them that would not be exercised in any other State under like circumstances."

To Grant's firmness in using the instruments of enforcement placed in his hands by Congress must be attributed in great measure this result. A weaker Executive would have dallied with the disturbances until they passed beyond control. He regretted the necessity, but it was his nature to enforce obedience to the law — a part of his day's work. In Grant's second Administration there were racial and political conflicts in Louisiana, Mississippi, and South Carolina which necessitated the interposition of federal troops. That is an unhappy episode in American history, which in its proper place shall have a chapter to itself.

In bright contrast is the gradual extension of amnesty to former participants in rebellion. By special acts amnesty was extended to 3185 former Confederates during the Forty-first Congress, which came to an end March 4, 1871, but many Southerners were too proudly sensitive to petition for a removal of their disabilities. General legislation was needed to obviate these special acts.

A magnanimous and lucid paragraph illuminates Grant's annual message of December 4, 1871: " More than six years having elapsed since the last hostile gun was fired between the armies then arrayed against each other — one for the perpetuation, the other for the destruction, of the Union — it may well be considered whether it is not now time that the disabilities imposed by the Fourteenth Amendment should be removed. That amendment does not exclude the ballot, but only imposes the disability to hold offices upon certain classes. When the purity of the ballot is secure, majorities are sure to elect officers reflecting the views of the majority. I do not see the advantage or propriety of excluding men from office merely because they were before the rebellion of standing and character sufficient to be elected to positions requiring them to take oaths to support the Constitution, and admitting to eligibility those entertaining precisely the same views but of less standing in their communities. It may be said that the former violated an oath, while the latter did not; the latter did not have it in their power to do so. If they had taken this oath, it cannot be doubted they would have broken it as did the former class." But he added, with Jefferson Davis, Jacob Thompson, and perhaps others in mind: "If there are any great criminals, distinguished above all others for the part they took in opposition to the Government, they might, in the judgment of Congress, be excluded from such an amnesty."

A bill providing for general amnesty had passed the House. It would have passed the Senate had not Sumner insisted on his supplementary Civil Rights Bill as an amendment.

This Civil Rights Bill, which Sumner's biographer summarizes as prohibiting discriminations against colored people "by common carriers, by proprietors of theaters and inns, managers of schools, of cemeteries and of churches, or as to service as jurors in any courts, state or national," was peculiarly obnoxious to the Southern whites as an attempt to force upon them social equality with the negro, and it was equally offensive to Northern men who resented such an attempt by the National Government to interfere with perfectly natural social conditions within the States.

Its enactment would have done the negro a poor service; but this the devoted Sumner could not comprehend, and owing to his obduracy, in face of the appeals of some of the negroes' best friends in Congress, the Amnesty Bill failed of passage. Finally in May, 1872, a bill for general amnesty passed the House unanimously, and after Sumner's civil rights amendment had been voted down, passed the Senate with equal celerity. This bill did not go so far as the bill which Sumner killed in the Senate. It left between three hundred and five hundred former Confederates still subject to political disabilities.

Sumner, who cast one of two negatives, said he could not vote for it "while the colored race are shut out from their rights and the ban of color is recognized in this chamber. Sir, the time has not come for amnesty. You must be just to the colored race before you are generous to former rebels."

Grant signed the bill on May 22, 1872. It removed the disabilities of all except Senators and Representatives of the Thirty-sixth and Thirty-seventh Congresses, officers in the judicial, military, and naval service of the United States, heads of departments and foreign ministers of the United States. But the disabilities of men of this excepted class were removed later as occasion required, and many of them rendered their reunited country unselfish and patriotic service.

CHAPTER XXXVII

CAUSES FOR PARTY DISAFFECTION

"He has sat by and seen the country tolerably well governed," said Samuel Bowles in the "Springfield Republican" in November, 1871. Bowles was good at epigram. He was a journalist of rare attainments, of fine ideals in politics, of vivid personality, with a suggestion of the iconoclast. He never hesitated to differ with contemporaries, even his closest friends. With most of them he took issue at the very beginning of Grant's Administration, when, two days after the precedent-smashing appointments to the Cabinet were made public, he wrote to Henry L. Dawes: "I like the Cabinet — you ought to like it because it is a revolution, because it breaks up rings, and makes reform more easy and possible"; and he may have been less surprised than others because a month earlier he had written: "My opinion is that Grant's Cabinet and the way it is made up will prove a bomb-shell, in especial congressional and political circles."

Plainly a change had come upon the vision of the Springfield seer. The change was typical of many of his kind, and it foreshadowed happenings which, while they had but little influence on Grant's career, have had a share in fixing the repute of his Administration quite out of keeping with their bearing on the times. Though Bowles was not a bookish man, and gained his learning almost wholly from his daily contact with the world, absorbing information here and there as bees suck honey, he had the delicate sense of values with which all writers for the press should be endowed, combined with the fine fervor befitting one who had passed through the fires of a great moral conflict and a civil war, and thus had much in common with men like Adams, Godkin, Curtis, Schurz, and Sumner, who ranked him easily in scholarship, though not in high ideals. His taste was for the "literary fellers," whom Zachariah Chandler baptized with expletives when Lowell intruded on the patronage preserves by taking office as Minister to Spain. Men of his type idealized the finer qualities in Grant which marked heroic moments in his military career. Grant's quiet simplicity and reserve appealed to them, — his complete indifference to the fame which soldiers are supposed to crave.

"I am no great admirer of military heroes," wrote Motley to the Duchess of Argyle a few weeks after Appomattox, "but we needed one at this period, and we can never be too thankful that such a one was vouchsafed to us — one so vast and fertile in conception, so patient in waiting, so rapid in striking, had come, and withal so destitute of personal ambition, so modest, so averse to public notoriety. The man on whom the gaze of both hemispheres has been steadily concentrated for two years seems ever shrinking from observation. All *his* admiration warmly expressed is for Sherman and Sheridan. So long as we can produce such a man as Grant our Republic is safe. . . . There is something very sublime to my imagination in the fact that *Grant has never yet set his foot in Richmond*, and perhaps never will." A rare tribute and merited; but how strangely in contrast with the vituperative lashings by Motley's friend Sumner, six years later.

And this from Holmes to Motley is characteristic of exchanges between friends in the Boston group: "He is one of the simplest, stillest men I ever saw. . . . Of all the considerable personages I have seen, he appears to me to be the least capable of an emotion of vanity. . . . Did he enjoy the being followed as he was by the multitude? 'It was very painful.' This answer is singularly characteristic of the man. . . . I cannot get over the impression he made on me. I have got something like it from women sometimes, hardly ever from men — that of entire loss of selfhood in a great aim, which made all the common influences which stir up other people as nothing to him."

Such was the figure Grant cut in scholarly imag-

inations while the halo of successful generalship was
new upon him and before his garments had been
soiled by contact with the slime of politics. Had he
been endowed with a taste for things which men of
culture fancy, or been much inclined to their companionship, he might well have retained their liking
and support even though he had shattered their
ideals and their fine faith in his political impeccabil-
ity. They would have been more willing to charge to
the requirements of the time unhappy incidents
which offended them, and history would have been
spared the sorry spectacle of personal quarrels and
unjust attacks upon his motives and sincerity. The
times were doubtless ripe for punishment, but not
for such as that which men like Sumner, Godkin,
Bowles, and Schurz meted out to Grant, chiefly because he lacked the social atmosphere to comprehend
their point of view.

Even before he had been sworn in as President he
displeased many who would have been ready with
advice by quite neglecting to seek counsel or ask for
help in writing his inaugural and picking out a cabinet. He was ingenuous as a child in politics, and before he was thrown against the nation's consciousness by the rush of war had hardly shown even the
ordinary interest in public questions which is supposed to be the birthright of every true American.

His disagreeable encounter with the most unpleasant side of things in Johnson's Administration had emphasized his natural disinclination to fraternize with men trained in affairs. Before Appomattox he had known nothing of the ways of Washington except as he was made unpleasantly aware at times of bureaucratic interference with his military plans. He had never seen a legislative body in session, or visited a state capital, save to capture it, except when he was waiting at Springfield for a regiment.

His familiarity with literature hardly extended beyond his textbooks at West Point. He read novels sometimes for the story, never for the style. His library was limited to the books on the center table in the parlor and the what-not in the corner. He cared little about history, except as he helped to make it or learned it by attrition in the process.

He was indifferent to the literature even of his own trade. When he came home from the war Philadelphia and Washington presented him with houses; Boston thought to show its gratitude by giving him a library. Samuel Hooper undertook to find out quietly what military books he had so that duplicates might be avoided, and discovered to his astonishment that Grant had no military books whatever. His proficiency in war came to him through intuition, and his genius for adapting military principles to unforeseen emergencies and such capacity as he showed in public affairs came in the same way. " His statesmanship," says Boutwell, " had no other art or magic in it than what may be found in the relations of an honest country people."

The companions he liked and cultivated were not men who appealed to exquisite tastes. He had many more points of contact with the "generously good" George William Childs than with the scholarly George William Curtis, political essayist and reformer. He took advice from Zachariah Chandler, John A. Logan, and Roscoe Conkling more readily than from Charles Sumner, Carl Schurz, and Lyman Trumbull. He grouped Adam Badeau and John Lothrop Motley as historians of similar merit, and personally preferred Badeau, who says Grant once offered him Motley's place in London, a decoration which Badeau with commendable self-abnegation brushed aside.

Even with Fish, the ornament and pillar of his Administration, in whom he placed implicit confidence, and whom he favored as his own successor, there was so little intimacy that when years later the two were living near each other in New York, they hardly ever met.

Grant had not been in the White House a year before signs of party disaffection were discernible.

Sumner's break with the Administration over San Domingo was the first noticeable evidence of revolt against it, rendered all the more conspicuous because Grant took his defeat so much to heart, after displaying a pertinacity of method better fitted to the conduct of a desperate military campaign than to the delicate negotiation of a parliamentary controversy requiring strategy and compromise. Grant's personal visits to the Capitol, his pressure upon reluctant Senators, his persistent lobbying, his seeming lack of comprehension of the dignity of his high place, lowered him perceptibly in the estimation of men whose good opinion he should have been zealous to retain. The deposition of Sumner from his place at the head of the Senate Committee on Foreign Relations offended men of culture and literary attainments everywhere; for while they might not sympathize with Sumner in his various perversities, he had come to be regarded as an institution, one of the few public men in Washington at that day who could be safely matched against the statesmen of England, France, and Germany, trained in the universities.

It was bad enough to have Sumner humiliated, but to have his mantle fall upon Simon Cameron, seemed to those who were not familiar with the Senate tradition determining committee rank by seniority a brutal and wanton affront. The recall of Motley quickly followed, and that, too, was regarded by those who were not familiar with all the circumstances as a deliberate injustice to a diplomatist of learning and distinction. It was no salve to lacerated sensibilities when General Robert C. Schenck was named as his successor, an Ohio Congressman of moderate attainments, destined to earn some fame in London as promoter of the Emma Mine and author of a textbook on draw poker.

Grant's summary demand on June 15, 1870, for Judge Hoar's resignation as Attorney-General, and his appointment of the unknown Akerman to fill the vacancy, helped to intensify the feeling of distrust. It was not then generally known that Hoar was sacrificed because the Southern Senators whose votes Grant needed for his San Domingo Treaty insisted on his putting a Southerner at the head of the Department of Justice as the price of their support. It was known simply that one of the two members of the Cabinet whom the independents and reformers held in unreserved respect had been dismissed.

The other was Jacob D. Cox, of Ohio, who from their point of view had made a fine record as Secretary of the Interior, not only in honestly administering the affairs of his department, but in resisting the demands of patronage hunters in the Patent Office, the Census Bureau, and the Indian Office, in protecting his clerks against political assessments and in his unswerving devotion to civil service reform. Within four months after Hoar's resignation, Cox also resigned, making way for Columbus Delano, of Ohio, a politician of no special reputation whose service was characterized by acts of questionable propriety. Cox is the chronicler of the circumstances both of Hoar's withdrawal and of his own. He was in frequent friction with Cameron and Chandler, political managers who insisted that the clerks in the departments should contribute a portion of their salaries to the party funds. Grant had said at the time of Hoar's resignation that "there was no man whom he loved more than Governor Cox"; but Chandler, Cameron, and the rest were a political necessity to him in Congress; and as between them and Cox there was no choice, Cox had to go.

Cox's letter of resignation, written on October 3, 1870, tells the story frankly, and concisely: "When Congress adjourned in the summer I was credibly informed that a somewhat systematic effort would be made before their reassembling in the winter to force a change in the policy we have pursued in the Interior Department. The removal of the Indian Service from the sphere of ordinary political patronage has been peculiarly distasteful to many influential gentlemen in both houses; and in order to enable

you to carry out your purposes successfully, I am
satisfied that you ought not to be embarrassed by
any other causes of irritation in the same department. My views of the necessity of reform in the
civil service have brought me more or less into collision with the plans of our active political managers,
and my sense of duty has obliged me to oppose some
of their methods of action through the arrangement."

Hoar never had the satisfaction of thus recording
the reasons for his resignation, but Cox has saved the
story as Hoar told it at the time: "I was sitting in
my office yesterday morning attending to routine
business," Hoar said on the day the astonished Cox
saw the newspaper announcement of the Attorney-
General's resignation, "with no more thought of
what was to come than you had at that moment,
when a messenger entered with a letter from the
President. Opening it I was amazed to read a naked
statement that he found himself under the necessity
of asking for my resignation. No explanation of any
kind was given or reason assigned. The request was
as curt and as direct as possible. My first thought
was that the President had been imposed upon by
some grave charge against me. A thunderclap could
not have been more startling to me. I sat for a while
wondering about it, what it could mean — why there
had been no warning, no reference to the subject in

our almost daily conversations. The impulse was to go at once and ask the reasons for the demand; but self-respect would not permit this, and I said to myself that I must let the matter take its own course, and not even seem disturbed about it. I took up my pen to write the resignation and found myself naturally framing some of the conventional reasons for it, but I stopped and destroyed the sheet, saying to myself, ' Since no reasons are given or suggested for the demand it is hardly honest to invent them in reply'; so I made the resignation as simple and unvarnished as the request for it had been."

In spite of this unpleasant experience Hoar never wavered in his personal friendship for Grant and remained his stanch supporter to the end. Cox joined with Trumbull, Schurz, and Sumner in the Liberal Republican movement eighteen months later.

The substitution of Akerman and Delano for Hoar and Cox lowered still further in the estimation of the critics a Cabinet which had been generously denounced at its beginning. Robeson, the Secretary of the Navy, a man of brilliant qualities, was acquiring a newspaper reputation not altogether deserved for extravagance and favoritism in the administration of his department. W. W. Belknap, the Secretary of War, was laying the foundations for the scandals which later led to his resignation in the face of impeachment. The personnel of the Administration was held in light repute, especially with those who were far cleverer at writing history than at making it, though the ordinary citizen as shown in the election returns retained his confidence in Grant.

The White House was populous with military aides who performed the duties usually assigned to civilian secretaries, — General Horace Porter, an accomplished soldier with an aptitude for public service in which he afterwards gained high distinction; General Frederick Dent, the President's brother-in-law, companionable but useless; Babcock, likable, brilliant, and untrustworthy. Grant was fond of them all, and had faith in them, which in some cases was not wholly justified.

The moment Grant began to emerge from obscurity at the beginning of the war, he was beset by relatives for favors, and so long as he was President, he had his sisters, uncles, aunts, and cousins on his hands. His father was early at the game, as his correspondence shows. "Father also wrote about a Mr. Reed," Grant writes his sister from Cairo, in October, 1861. "He is now here, and will probably be able to secure a position. I do not want to be importuned for places. I have none to give and want to be placed under no obligation to any one. My influence, no doubt, would secure places with those under me, but I become directly responsible for the suitableness of the appointee, and then there is no telling at what moment I may have to put my hand upon the very person who has conferred the favor, or the one recommended by me." This was Grant's military instinct in time of war, but when it came to the Presidency, with innumerable places at his hand and no civil service regulations to interfere with their free distribution, it was not so easy to resist the appeals of relatives who wanted office for themselves and for their friends.

He found his father postmaster at Covington, Kentucky, and kept him there. He made his brother-in-law Minister to Denmark. Upon other relatives of himself and of his wife he good-naturedly bestowed more or less lucrative positions, not many in the aggregate, but numerous enough to give color to the cry of "nepotism." Sumner, in his ridiculous harangue against Grant in the Senate on May 31, 1872, devoted an amazing amount of space to showing " how the presidential office has been used to advance his own family on a scale of nepotism dwarfing everything of the kind in our history and hardly equaled in the corrupt governments where this abuse has most prevailed. . . . One list makes the number of beneficiaries as many as forty-two — being probably every known person allied to the President either by blood or marriage. Persons seeming to speak for the President, or at least after careful inquiries, have denied the accuracy of this list, reducing it to thirteen. It will not be questioned that there is at least a baker's dozen in this category — thirteen relations of the President billeted on the country, not one of whom but for this relationship would have been brought forward, the whole contributing a case of nepotism not unworthy of those worst governments where office is a family possession."

Truly an appalling picture of the peril to the republic embodied in consideration shown by a kindly disposed relative to old Jesse Grant, brother-in-law Cramer, and the other Grants and Dents.

Grant accepted without compunction gifts which were showered upon him by a grateful people after the close of the war. Houses in Philadelphia and Washington, articles of greater or less intrinsic value, for most of which he had no use, and many of which remained unopened in the White House basement so long as he remained in Washington. He saw no impropriety in taking presents even from those for whom he afterwards did favors, as sometimes happened. So straightforward was he in all his dealings that it never entered his own mind or the suspicions of those who knew him best that there was any improper connection between the favor and the gift, but traits of this kind offered rare ammunition to those who needed it in a political campaign.

Grant was not fastidious in his friends. He picked them as he chose without regard to others' liking. When Rawlins died he lost the only man whose judgment about others had a deciding influence on his own. No one could fill the place which Rawlins left in his affection and respect, and Grant's associates became more miscellaneous after death robbed him of Rawlins at the very threshold of his term.

"What Grant needs," Charles Eliot Norton wrote to Curtis, ". . . is independent, sympathetic, intelligent, and trustworthy counselors. . . . He is easily influenced by what one may call *second-class ideas* if skilfully put before him; and his magnanimity, which was conspicuous during the war, degenerates into something not far from a vice in the peaceful regions of politics." [1] Norton here deftly caught a phase of Grant which few have seen; and yet there is no patent on his remedy. It takes no prescience for a stranger to discern a ruler's need of suitable advice. The counselor whom Norton had in mind was Curtis or some one else agreeable to both. But Grant had his own tastes and ways; he could not be made over. It is just possible that in the long run it was quite as well.

[1] *Letters of Charles Eliot Norton*, vol. I, p. 413.

CHAPTER XXXVIII

REFORMS — THE TARIFF; THE CIVIL SERVICE; THE INDIAN

It was open season for reformers; they were trying their luck at all sorts of abuses, real and imaginary. The protective tariff was a favorite shot, and "revenue reform" a popular cry — a recrudescence of the "free trade" policy which had prevailed since the beginning whenever Democrats were in control. But now it was not limited by party lines, for there were good Republicans who strongly urged revision of the Morrill Tariff enacted just before the outbreak of the Civil War. This sentiment was strong especially among Republicans in the Middle West, who had come to look upon the tariff as a scheme to benefit New England and Pennsylvania manufacturers. Men like Allison and Garfield, just rising into prominence in the House, urged a reduction in duties. Garfield, a student, was almost a free trader, an honorary member of the Cobden Club of England, but he was "practical" in his conception of the application of reform. "Whatever may be the personal or political consequences to myself," he told the House, "I shall try to act, first for the good of all and within that limitation for the industrial interests of the district which I represent. . . . If I can prevent it I shall not submit to a considerable reduction of a few leading articles in which my constituents are deeply interested when many others of a similar character are left untouched or the rate on them increased."

The agitation resulted in the Tariff Act of 1870, in which after a hard struggle the friends of protection retained their advantage, the reduction in duties, counting both the free and dutiable list, averaging only about five per cent. The chief gain the reformers made was in reducing the duty on pig iron from $9 to $7 per ton. The battle raged around pig iron. Horace Greeley told Garfield that if he could he would make the duty one hundred dollars a ton, and all other duties in proportion. It was a time of general recrimination. The friends of protection then as now were charged with working for the "interests," while the attitude of the reformers was attributed to the malign influence of the Cobden Club and lavish expenditure of "British gold."

Grant made no boast of economic wisdom, but in his annual message of December, 1870, he said just enough to show that he had the tariff on his mind. It was the beginning of the short session of an expiring Congress and there could be no further legislation for at least a year. "Revenue reform has not been defined by any of its advocates to my knowledge," he wrote with pertinent irony, "but seems to be accepted as something which is to supply every man's wants without any cost or effort on his part." His own opinion was that "with the revenue stamp dispensed by postmasters in every community, a tax upon liquors of all sorts, and tobacco in all its forms, and by a wise adjustment of the tariff, which will put a duty only upon those articles which we could dispense with, known as luxuries, and on those which we use more of than we produce, revenue enough may be raised after a few years of peace and consequent reduction of indebtedness to fulfill all our obligations. . . . Revenue reform, if it means this, has my hearty support. If it implies a collection of all the revenue for the support of the Government, for the payment of principal and interest of the public debt, pensions, etc., by directly taxing the people, then I am against revenue reform, and confidently believe the people are with me. If it means failure to provide the necessary means to defray all the expenses of government and thereby repudiation of the public debt and pensions, then I am still more opposed to such kind of revenue reform."

A year later at the beginning of the new Congress he again took up the question urging that the surplus be reduced "in such a manner as to afford the greatest relief to the greatest number," and recommending the "free list" for many articles not produced at home "which enter largely into general consumption through articles which are manufactured at home from which little revenue is derived." Should a further reduction be advisable, he suggested "that it be made upon those articles which can best bear it without disturbing home production or reducing the wages of America's labor."

Two tariff bills were enacted by the new Congress; one which Grant signed on May 1, 1872, put tea and coffee on the free list, thus contributing to "the free breakfast table" extolled by Republican protectionists. The second, approved May 3, 1872, was a compromise. It lowered duties on a good many articles, among them salt, bituminous coal, tin, leather, manufactures of cotton, wool, iron, and steel, shaved the stamp taxes, and forgot to renew the friendless income tax. The act, like all tariff compromises, was a log-rolling affair. Samuel Bowles wrote one of his comforting letters to his dear friend Henry L. Dawes, who managed the bill in the House as chairman of the Ways and Means Committee: " You certainly have won a brilliant victory on the tariff. . . . It is not statesmanship and you know it. . . . There is a better way of making a tariff than by a combination or compromise of all the cotton mills and woolen mills and sheep farmers and pin factories and coal mines of all the congressional districts of the land."

The times were shaping for revolt. So virulent were the attacks on Grant by men like Sumner, Schurz, and Godkin, that it was easy to forget what he had done for causes they had much at heart. They were so busy throwing remorseless lights on faults which now, when we look back on them, seem trifling, that they neglected merits better worth their while, and left unpraised his high accomplishments.

Who now remembers that Grant was first among our Presidents to emphasize the need of change in federal appointments so that they should be made for merit, not for pull? Yet he went farther on the road to a clean civil service than all his predecessors in the preceding forty years. Lincoln, like every other President since Jackson, had accepted the spoils system as a commonplace of government. Political considerations decided almost every case of office-filling from clerkships to the Cabinet. All through the war the trail of spoils was visible in military things. Butler and McClernand were not the only politicians whose epaulettes bore stars. That Lincoln's final break with Chase should be upon a piece of petty patronage was taken as an incident in course. When Sumner introduced a bill in 1864 establishing the merit system it was treated lightly by his colleagues as one of Sumner's fads. Yet at the outset of his Administration Grant tackled this unprofitable question which others had ignored.

"Nor have we had from any President a single word of manly protest against this monstrous system," said George William Curtis, the accepted leader of the civil service reformers, before a group of men who thought with him in 1869, "until now President Grant says in words which in spirit are worthy to stand with those of Washington,' There has been no hesitation in changing officials in order to secure an efficient execution of the laws; sometimes, too, when in mere party view undesirable political results were likely to follow. Nor has there been any hesitation in sustaining efficient officials against remonstrances wholly political.' At last, thank God, we have got a President whom trading politicians did not elect, and who is no more afraid of them than he was of rebels, and these manly and simple words are as full of cheerful promise as the bulletins of his advance upon Vicksburg."

But such exuberance of eulogy was not to be maintained, though in his second annual message Grant denounced the spoils system as "an abuse of long standing" which he would like to see remedied at once. He would have the merit system cover not only the tenure but the manner of making all appointments. "There is no duty which so much embarrasses the Executive and heads of departments as that of appointments. Nor is there any such arduous and thankless labor imposed on Senators and Representatives as that of finding places for constituents. The present system does not secure the best men and often not even fit men for public place. The elevation and purification of the civil service of the Government will be hailed with approval by the whole people of the United States." Here was a new note in executive communications. A few weeks later he signed the first Civil Service Reform Bill ever passed by Congress, providing for a commission to establish regulations to ascertain the fitness of candidates for office; and he named Curtis as its chairman.

At the very beginning of the next session, in December, 1871, he urged on Congress in a special message appropriations to perpetuate the Commission. "If left to me without further congressional action the rules . . . will be faithfully executed; but they are not binding without further legislation upon my successor. . . . I ask for all the strength which Congress can give me to enable me to carry out the reforms in the civil service recommended by the Commission."

Congress, wedded to the spoils system, soon cut off the appropriation altogether. Ardent reformers blamed Grant for not doing more, but it would have taken all Grant's influence to force on Congress the merit system as a permanent policy at that time, and he had none to spare. Few Senators or Representatives had any use for it. The strongest of them, like Morton, Chandler, Conkling, Carpenter, and Cameron, held it in contempt; most people did not care. It was the favorite issue of a group of scholarly men, of high ideals, but neither numerous nor potential then or for years thereafter. It was greatly to Grant's credit that he went so far along the path they led, yet he was subject to attack because he did not force the unattainable. Had he urged a civil service propaganda in and out of season and made "reform" the cry of his Administration, he would no doubt have held the adoration of essayists and historians, and faults which they have emphasized might then have been excused. But the time was far from ripe for these new-fangled civil service methods and he had infinitely greater problems pressingly in hand — the maintenance of our prestige abroad, the safeguarding of American lives and property on foreign soil, the rigid execution of the law at home, the firm establishment of public credit. Reform might wait upon the growth of public sentiment and the dissemination of right ideas, but these fundamental things involving the perpetuity of gov-

ernment itself must be attended to at once or not
at all. All others must be made subordinate to
them.

Thus it came about that, after a few years of trial
with an unpaid board, he found it useless to keep
up the fight alone, and in his message of December,
1874, acknowledging the obvious, he frankly announced to Congress that, if adjournment came
without positive legislation in support of civil service reform, "I will regard such action as a disapproval of the system and will abandon it except so
far as to require examinations for certain appointees
to determine their fitness. Competitive examinations will be abandoned." He could not let the opportunity go by without a dig at a too common trait
of advocates of the merit system then and since:
"Generally," he said, "the support which this reform receives is from those who give it their support
only to find fault when the rules are apparently de-
parted from." On the whole he thought the rules
had been beneficial and had tended to the elevation
of the service. "The gentlemen who have given
their services without compensation as members of
the board to devise rules and regulations for the
government of the civil service of the country have
shown much zeal and earnestness in their work, and
to them as well as to myself it will be a source of

mortification if it is to be thrown away. But I repeat
that it is impossible to carry this system to a successful issue without general approval and assistance
and positive law to support it."

In all the circumstances this was common sense,
and Curtis recognized it later when he said: "A
President who should alone undertake to reform the
evil must feel it to be the vital and permanent issue
and must be willing to hazard everything for its success. He must have the absolute faith and the indomitable will of Luther, 'Here stand I; I can no
other.' . . . General Grant, elected by a spontane-
ous patriotic impulse, fresh from the regulated order
of military life, and new to politics and politicians,
saw the reason and the necessity of reform. . . . Congress, good-naturedly tolerating what it considered
his whim of inexperience, granted money to try an
experiment. The adverse pressure was tremendous.
'I am used to pressure,' smiled the soldier. So he
was, but not to this pressure. He was driven by unknown and incalculable currents. He was enveloped
in whirlwinds of sophistry, scorn, and incredulity.
He who upon his own line had fought it out all summer to victory, upon a line absolutely new and unknown was naturally bewildered and dismayed. . . .
It was indeed a surrender, but it was the surrender
of a champion who had honestly mistaken both the

nature and the strength of the adversary and his own power of endurance."

Grant did not then receive the credit as a pioneer which history must assign him. He had no gift for advertising his own wares, and he was so lacking in a politician's artifice that in the eyes of critics some of his very merits wore the guise of faults. In this as in too many other things he was the victim of his honesty.

Grant's interest in the Indians dates from his life in the Far West, when as a young army officer he saw with what injustice they were treated by the whites. George W. Childs says that he "then made up his mind if he ever had any influence or power it should be exercised to try to ameliorate their condition." He was as good as his word. Brief as was his first inaugural, it was long enough to contain a reference to "the proper treatment of the original occupants of this land," as deserving careful study. "I will favor any course toward them which tends to their civilization and ultimate citizenship." He appointed an Indian Commission headed by William Welsh, of Philadelphia, a strong, generous friend of the Indians, and composed largely of leading members of the Society of Friends, which he pointed out in his annual message of December, 1869, " is well known as having succeeded in living in peace with the Indians in the early settlement of Pennsylvania while their white neighbors of other sects in other sections were constantly embroiled." He adopted the novel policy of giving all the agencies to such religious denominations as had established missionaries among the Indians, the societies selecting their own agents subject to the approval of the Executive. In his second annual message, he wrote: "I entertain the confident hope that the policy now pursued will in a few years bring all the Indians upon reservations where they will live in houses and have schoolhouses and churches and will be pursuing peaceful and self-sustaining avocations and where they may be visited by the law-abiding white man with the same impunity that he now visits the civilized white settlements." Here we have the first serious attempt at a humanitarian treatment of the Indian by the Government — the germ of whatever benefit has come to him as the nation's ward. Yet Grant was duly censured because an Indian ring infested the Interior Department as had been the case before his day and has been ever since.

"The most troublesome men in public life," said Grant a few years later, "are those over-righteous people who see no motives in other people's actions but evil motives, who believe all public life is corrupt, and nothing is well done unless they do it themselves. They are narrow-headed men, their two eyes so close together that they can look out of the same gimlet-hole without winking." Fish in his "Diary" tells how during the San Domingo controversy Grant remarked: "It is strange that men cannot allow others to differ with them, without charging corruption as the cause of difference. . . . There is little inducement other than a sense of duty in holding public position in this country — but for that I do not know what there is to induce a man to take either the place I hold, or one in the Cabinet, and were it not for that I would resign immediately." Remarks which help us better to understand the loyalty with which he stood behind those men in his Administration who were most violently assailed.

CHAPTER XXXIX

THE GREELEY EPISODE

AMONG the public men of the Reconstruction period Carl Schurz had a place peculiarly his own. Never a force of much constructive influence he was for years a striking figure, an irrepressible critic, an apostle of unrest, who though not popular himself had popular repute. A Prussian by birth, a revolutionist and refugee of 1848, he came to comprehend the theory of American institutions as few Americans have comprehended it, yet in the very atmosphere of liberty he remained a revolutionist and dissenter to the end. He never became completely Americanized or localized. He lacked the "homing instinct." After leaving his native country, he lived successively in Switzerland, France, and England, and coming to the United States in 1852 he fluttered over Pennsylvania, Wisconsin, Michigan, and Missouri, before finally alighting in New York. He never remained long with any political group or respected party fealty.

Minister to Spain at the beginning of the war and afterwards a brigadier-general of volunteers, he was unsparing in censure of his military and civilian superiors. His admonitions at a trying moment in the

darkest days of the struggle elicited from the long-
suffering Lincoln a caustic rebuke which has become
an epistolary classic.[1]

As an editor in Missouri directly after the war,
Schurz supported radical Reconstruction measures.
As Johnson's messenger to the South in 1865, he
made a report which was used by radical leaders in
Congress against Johnson's policies. He was elected
a Republican Senator in 1869; yet he was hardly in
his seat before he broke with Grant, joining Sumner
in opposition to the San Domingo Treaty. He voted
for all except the last of the enforcement acts, which
he held to be unconstitutional, and had the satisfaction years later of seeing the Supreme Court declare

[1] "I have just received and read your letter of the 26th. The
purport of it is that we lost the last elections and the Administration is failing because the war is unsuccessful, and that I must not
flatter myself that I am not justly to blame for it. I certainly
know that if the war fails, the Administration fails, and that I will
be blamed for it, whether I deserve it or not. And I ought to be
blamed if I could do better. You think I could do better; therefore you blame me already. I think I could not do better, therefore I blame you for blaming me. I understand you now to be
willing to accept the help of men who are not Republicans, provided they have 'heart in it.' Agreed. I want no others. But who
is to be the judge of hearts or of 'heart in it'? If I must discard
my own judgment and take yours, I must also take that of others;
and by the time I should reject all I should be advised to reject,
I should have none left, Republicans or others — not even yourself. For be assured, my dear sir, there are men who 'have heart
in it' that think you are performing your part as poorly as you
think I am performing mine." (Letter to Carl Schurz, November
24, 1862. *Lincoln's Complete Works*, vol. II, p. 257.)

unconstitutional acts for which he voted as well as that to which he was opposed. He was a lucid and logical writer, a master of English style, a speaker of unusual ability when thoroughly prepared, a critic, a musician, a man of culture who in another country might have played a large part in Government, but whose talents were ineffective here because of his insatiate appetite for opposition amounting to a passion for minorities.

Schurz more than any other single individual was responsible for the Liberal Republican movement of 1872. It was at his instigation that the call was issued for the national convention which nominated Greeley in Cincinnati. Dissent in Missouri depended on conditions peculiar to the State, just as dissent in Illinois, New York, Massachusetts, and other places was determined largely by local conditions in every case. But it happened that Missouri furnished the earliest opportunity for organized protest against Administration tendencies. On a question of local interest — the reënfranchisement of Southern sympathizers — Republican dissenters nominated for Governor B. Gratz Brown, and he was elected by a combination with the Democrats, thus turning the State over to Democratic control. Frank P. Blair had already been chosen Senator.

There was nothing national in the issue of reën-

franchisement, for Grant had urged a general amnesty, and Congress was on the point of granting it,
but Schurz had become an advocate of tariff reform,
and that was made a plank in his new party platform. Greeley, in the "New York Tribune," characterized the Missouri Liberals as bolters. Schurz,
perceiving signs of discontent in other States as the
time for electing a new President approached, con-
vened his new party at Jefferson City on January 24,
1872. The name of "Liberal Republicans" was assumed and a call was issued to all Republicans opposing the Administration and favoring reform to
meet in Cincinnati on the first Wednesday in May.

There was plenty of material at hand for such a
gathering, although there was no common bond of
sympathy except dissatisfaction with Grant and his
Administration. In New York there was a factional
quarrel. The two United States Senators were in
fighting mood. Reuben E. Fenton, a crafty political
manipulator, had been the leader of the State while
Governor from 1865 to 1869, but Conkling had
gained ascendancy with the Administration in Washington. Greeley, always afflicted with the itch for
office, was Fenton's candidate for Governor in 1870,
but was beaten in convention. In the convention of
1871 there was a titanic struggle for supremacy, and
Conkling, taking command in person of his forces

on the floor, had driven the friends of Greeley and Fenton out, and assumed full control of the party organization.

Greeley had long been querulous about the National Administration. Both he and Fenton now attributed their defeat to Conkling's use of federal patronage and to Grant's support. They thus were ripe for the revolt which had been shaping in the West. It was hard for Greeley, the most vociferous advocate of high protection in the United States, to swallow the Missouri Liberals' declaration for "a genuine reform of the tariff," but let that question be laid aside, he intimated in the "Tribune," "and we will go to Cincinnati." In due season he signed the response of Eastern Republicans to the Missouri invitation, but outside their own State the New York men in the convention found few except free traders.

The Cincinnati gathering did not consist of delegates regularly chosen; but any person of Republican antecedents was permitted to participate. No such collection of curiously assorted men ever before or since has undertaken to organize a political party. The Liberal Republican movement, in so far as it embodied a real passion for reform, was peculiarly the product of writers for the press.

Schurz was an editor and pamphleteer by preference, and with him in the instigation of revolt were

Samuel Bowles, of the "Springfield Republican," Murat Halstead, of the "Cincinnati Commercial," Joseph Medill, Horace White, of the "Chicago Tribune," Alexander K. McClure, of the "Philadelphia Times," E. L. Godkin, of the "Nation," and William Cullen Bryant, of the "New York Evening Post." On some things they were agreed, on others they were wide apart. The movement at its inception was under the guidance of writers, theorists, dissenters, and doctrinaires, most of whom had done a vast amount of thinking about how the Government ought to be run, but few of whom had ever really tried their hand at helping run it. Almost without exception in the beginning they were men of fine ideals, but as the organization took shape, it drew in the customary quota of disappointed and discredited politicians.

There were a few men with both real political experience and high principles like John M. Palmer and Lyman Trumbull, of Illinois, Stanley Matthews, George Hoadley, and Jacob D. Cox, of Ohio, Austin Blair, the War Governor of Michigan. Finally there were men like David A. Wells, Theodore Tilton, Edward Atkinson, Frank W. Bird, and General William F. Bartlett, some of them faddists, none of them with experience in elective office. Sumner, David Davis, and Charles Francis Adams were among the later acquisitions. The germinating force was in the editorial rooms of the " Chicago Tribune," the " Springfield Republican," the " Cincinnati Commercial," the "Nation," the " New York Evening Post," the " New York Tribune," and the " Louisville Courier-Journal," this last a Democratic paper rich in the fulminations of Henry Watterson. Some of these were less intense in their allegiance at the beginning than others, but all in time joined in the cry against Grant, though most of them were sorely disappointed in the work of their convention.

Had they realized it they were doomed to failure from the start, for they were lacking, not only in the sagacity of the professional politician, but in the impulse of an absorbing moral issue. Perhaps their greatest lack was in a vivid personality to embody their conception of reform. It is strange that observant newspaper editors could have imagined a successful campaign against a party entrenched in power, under such leadership as that to which they were confined, — Charles Francis Adams, Lyman Trumbull, David Davis, Horace Greeley, — all men without organized political or personal following and none except Davis with practical political sense.

" The office-seeking fraternity," says Horace White, " were mostly supporters of Davis, whose appearance as a candidate for the Presidency was

extremely offensive to the original promoters of the
movement. As a judge of the Supreme Court his
incursion into the field of politics, unheralded, but
not unprecedented, was an indecorum. Moreover,
his supporters had not been early movers in the
ranks of reform. . . . Davis's chances were early
demolished by the editorial fraternity, who, at a dinner at Murat Halstead's house, resolved that they
would not support him if nominated, and caused
that fact to be made known. Greeley's candidacy
had not been taken seriously by the editors at Halstead's dinner-party. . . . Adams and Trumbull were
the only men supposed by us to be within the sphere
of nomination, and the chances of Adams were
deemed the better of the two. We had yet to learn
that there are occasions and crowds where personal
oddity and a flash of genius under an old white hat
are more potent than high ancestry or approved
statesmanship, or both those qualifications joined
together." [1]

The austere Adams at least was wise enough to
recognize his own defects as a candidate. "If I am to
be negotiated for and have assurances given that I
am honest, you will be so kind as to draw me out of
that crowd," he wrote to David A. Wells as he was
sailing for Europe to attend the Court of Geneva

[1] *Life of Lyman Trumbull*, pp. 380–81.

Arbitration, a fortnight before the convention. . . . "I never had a moment's belief that when it came to the point, any one so entirely isolated as I am from all political associations of any kind could be made acceptable as a candidate for public office; but I am so unlucky as to value that independence more highly than the elevation which is brought by a sacrifice of it. . . . If the good people who meet at Cincinnati really believe that they need such an anomalous being as I am (which I do not), they must express it in a manner to convince me of it, or all their labor will be thrown away."

Impossible material for a successful candidate for votes, yet such was the idealistic and impractical character of the disinterested devotees of the new cult that the optimistic Bowles made this deadly letter public in the innocent belief that it would bring about the writer's nomination and election.

Not only did Greeley capture the nomination, but he kept out of the platform any endorsement of tariff reform, the one live issue outside Grant's personality upon which the promoters of the convention came nearest to being united. He was the most irreconcilable protectionist in the United States; he was far less friendly than Grant to civil service reform, and had been profanely emphatic in expressing his contempt for the merit test. It was a cruel awakening for the protagonists of revolt, many of them scholars loyal to the universities, who with wry faces found themselves straggling behind the fantastic banner of the most trenchant opponent of the theories they had most at heart, and marveling at their complaisance as they recalled the pungent prayer with which tradition says he used to enliven the youthful meditations of aspiring writers for the "Tribune," "Of all horned cattle, God deliver me from the college graduate!"

Stanley Matthews, the temporary chairman, went back to Grant as soon as possible, writing to a friend: "I am greatly chagrined at the whole matter, my own participation in it included, and have concluded . . . that as a politician and a President-maker I am not a success." William Cullen Bryant wrote to Trumbull: "We who know Mr. Greeley know that his administration, should he be elected, cannot be otherwise than shamefully corrupt. . . . There is no abuse or extravagance into which that man through the infirmity of his judgment may not be betrayed. It is wonderful how little in some of his vagaries the scruples which would influence other men of no exemplary integrity restrain him." Trumbull could think of no better reason for supporting him than that he was "an honest but confiding man" who with proper surroundings "would be an improvement on what we have."

" The wiser heads in the convention were stunned,"
wrote Horace White. " Of all the things which could
possibly happen, this was the one thing which everybody supposed could not happen." Carl Schurz,
chagrined at the result, wrote Greeley inviting him
to withdraw, presenting all the discouraging features, " and now if the developments of the campaign
should be such as to disappoint your hopes, it shall
not be my fault if you are deceived about the real
state of things." Yet Schurz would support Greeley
" in a modified and guarded manner." So satisfied
was he of " the necessity of defeating Grant and dis-
solving party organization " that he was all ready to
use any instrument for the purpose, looking forward
" with a hopefulness bordering on enthusiasm to the
good things which will grow out of the confusion
following on Greeley's election " — an opportunist
view which Godkin could not accept, glad as he
should be to join Schurz in supporting Greeley,
" Schurz being the one man in American politics who
inspires Godkin with some hope concerning them."
Parke Godwin was even more bitter: " The man is a
charlatan from top to bottom, and the smallest kind
of a charlatan, from no other motive than a weak and
puerile vanity. His success in politics would be the
success of whoever is most wrong in theory and most
corrupt in practice. . . . Grant and his crew are bad

— but hardly so bad as Greeley and his would be."
The country surely was in sorry straits when those
who had constituted themselves its only hope were
limited to such alternatives.

The free traders in New York held a mass meeting
at Steinway Hall, invited to a conference those who
favored a less rigid protective policy than Greeley's,
and nominated William S. Groesbeck for President.
The invitation was signed by Carl Schurz, permanent chairman of the Cincinnati Convention, J. D.
Cox, W. C. Bryant, D. A. Wells, Oswald Ottendorfer,
and Jacob Brinkerhoff — dissenters from dissent, who
in due time came back to Greeley after the Democrats
at Baltimore had endorsed the Cincinnati ticket.

An "Address to the People of the United States"
was issued at Cincinnati to launch the platform of
principles. It was an undiluted denunciation of
Grant: "The President of the United States has
openly used the powers and opportunities of his high
office for the promotion of personal ends. He has
kept notoriously corrupt and unworthy men in
places of power and responsibilities to the detriment
of the public interest. He has used the public service
of the Government as machinery of corruption and
personal influence and has interfered with tyrannical
arrogance in the public affairs of States and munici-
palities. He has rewarded with influential and lucra-

tive offices men who had acquired his favor by valuable presents, thus stimulating the demoralization of
our political life by his conspicuous example. He has
shown himself deplorably unequal to the task imposed upon him by the necessities of the country and
culpably careless of the responsibilities of his high
office." His partisans were denounced for standing
" in the way of necessary investigations and indispensable reforms"; for keeping alive " the passions
and resentments of the late Civil War . . . instead
of appealing to the better instincts and latent patriotism of the Southern people"; for " base sycophancy
to the dispenser of executive power and patronage,
unworthy of republican freemen."

Following this denunciatory address the platform
reads tamely. It demanded the " immediate and absolute removal of all disabilities imposed on account
of the rebellion"; " local self-government with impartial suffrage"; " the supremacy of the civil over
the military authority"; the protection of the habeas
corpus; " a thorough reform of the civil service," to
which end " it is imperatively required that no President shall be a candidate for reëlection"; the maintenance of the public credit; a speedy return to specie
payments; and an end " to further grants of land to
railroads or other corporations."

The extraordinary plank in this reform platform

was the obvious straddle in regard to the tariff: "Recognizing that there are in our midst honest but irreconcilable differences of opinion with regard to the respective systems of protection and free trade, we remit the discussion of the subject to the people in their congressional districts and the decision of Congress thereon, wholly free from executive interference or dictation."

This was an admirable declaration of principles. It would have been more impressive had it not been that some of its most commendable paragraphs were duplicated in the Republican platform adopted at Philadelphia on June 5 and 6, when Grant was renominated with great enthusiasm, and by acclamation. The Republicans favored a reform of the civil service system "by laws which shall abolish the evils of patronage and make honesty, efficiency, and fidelity the essential qualifications for public positions without practically creating a life-tenure of office." They opposed "further grants of the public lands to corporations and monopolies"; declared that revenue, "except so much as may be derived from a tax upon tobacco and liquors, should be raised by duties upon importations, the details of which should be so adjusted as to aid in securing remunerative wages to labor and promote the industries, prosperity, and growth of the whole country."

His own party at Philadelphia was so thoroughly
united behind Grant that the only suggestion of division was in the nomination for Vice-President. Colfax would doubtless have been named again had he
not once withdrawn and then changed his mind after
Henry Wilson, of Massachusetts, had been brought
forward as a candidate. While Speaker of the House
in Johnson's time and for a while Vice-President
with Grant, he had stood well in general esteem, but
of late he had incurred the distrust of the representative newspaper correspondents at Washington, a
body as quick then as their successors now in detect-
ing false notes in our public men. Their efforts more
than any other one thing gave Wilson the nomination; a choice of special significance because Wilson's
colleague, Sumner, only a few days before, in the
speech of May 31, had portrayed Grant in riotous
violence of color as a military usurper debauching
his office with an unholy zest which any Roman
Emperor might have envied him. The Democrats at
Baltimore, on July 9, endorsed Greeley, thus completing an incongruous picture; for they could not
have picked another man so radically at odds with
every political theory which they held. His only
point of sympathy with either convention was discontent with Grant — no unusual attitude with him;
for he had been an unsparing critic of every Presi-

dent for thirty years, no matter whether his own party or the opposition happened to be in power.

Greeley really never had a chance of election from the day he was nominated, but so eager was the campaign against Grant that for a time some even of the most sagacious of the seasoned political observers were in doubt. Sumner's assault of May 31 furnished a text for hardened orators and writers of the opposition.

" Not only are Constitution and law disregarded," cried Sumner, " but the presidential office itself is treated as little more than a plaything and a perquisite — when not the former, then the latter. Here the details are ample; showing how from the beginning this exalted trust has dropped to be a personal indulgence, where palace cars, fast horses, and seaside loiterings figure more than duties; how personal aims and objects have been more prominent than the public interests; . . . how in the same spirit office has been conferred upon those from whom he had received gifts or benefits, thus making the country repay his personal obligations; how personal devotion to himself rather than public or party service has been made the standard of favor; how the vast appointing power conferred by the Constitution for the general welfare has been employed at his will to promote his schemes, to reward his friends, to punish his opponents, and to advance his election to a second term; how all these assumptions have matured in a personal government, semi-military in character and breathing the military spirit, being a species of Cæsarism or *personalism*, abhorrent to republican institutions, where subservience to the President is the supreme law.

" . . . I protest against him as radically unfit for the presidential office, being essentially military in nature, without experience in civil life, without aptitude for civil duties, and without knowledge of republican institutions."

Thus "Cæsarism" became the cry against the most diffident and unassuming soldier of his generation, one who signalized his first night at the White House by dispensing with the squad of soldiers detailed there as a night guard and ordering away from Washington all the troops on duty there at the time of his inauguration. "I was trying last night," said Matthew H. Carpenter replying to Sumner's tirade, "to recall a single instance if in conversation in regard to the late war I had heard General Grant allude to himself, and I could not. I have heard him speak in the most glowing terms of his comrades in arms. I have heard him speak of the exploits of Sherman. I have heard him allude to what was done by Logan, McPherson, and many other officers of

the Union army. I never heard him say, speaking
of a battle, 'at such a juncture I thought I would do
so and so,' or, 'I ordered a battalion this way or
that,' or, 'I turned the scale by such a maneuver.'
I never heard him allude to himself in connection
with the war. I believe you might go to the White
House and live with him and converse about the
war day after day, and you never would know from
anything he said that he was in the war at all."

Such is the uniform testimony of those who knew
him best. It is true that his companionships were
not all over-nice; that instead of spending his sum-
mers in Washington he spent them at the seashore,
as has been the habit of almost every President since
his day; that he liked to drive fast horses as when a
boy on his father's place; that he accepted presents
indiscriminately as a thing of course; that he had
relatives in the public service; but if these were faults
deserving censure, they were faults of judgment, not
of malign intent, and history will weigh them lightly.

Grant was keenly sensitive to the attacks upon
him, but he never had the slightest doubt of his success, though the most experienced political observers had their blue days. George W. Childs tells how
during the campaign Wilson, who had just made
a tour of the country, came to his house in Philadelphia greatly depressed. " I went to see General

Grant and I told him about this feeling particularly as coming from Senator Wilson. The General said nothing, but he sent for a map of the United States. He laid the map down on the table and went over it with a pencil and said, ' We will carry this State, that State, and that State ; until he nearly covered the whole United States. It occurred to me he might as well put them all in." He wrote to Washburne in August that even if Greeley remained in the field till November, he would not carry a single Northern State.

His foresight was justified. The only States Greeley carried were Maryland, Georgia, Missouri, and Kentucky. Grant received 286 electoral votes out of 349. His popular vote was 3,597,132, an increase over his vote in 1868 of 484,299.

It was a cruel thing for Greeley. He who had rioted all his life in searing Presidents and candidates cringed now when he felt his own soul pressed against the iron. The Scriptural admonition, that he who lives by the sword shall perish by the sword, was never more convincingly exemplified. "I was the worst beaten man who ever ran for high office," he wrote Colonel Tappan, " and I have been assailed so bitterly that I hardly knew whether I was running for President or the Penitentiary. In the darkest hour my suffering wife left me, none too soon, for she had suffered too deeply and too long. I laid her in the ground with hard, dry eyes. Well, I am used up; I cannot see before me. I have slept little for weeks, and my eyes are still hard to close, while they soon open again." Before the Electoral College met he died broken in heart and mind.

But Grant's great personal triumph had its taste of wormwood too; for he had been through slander and vituperation such as seldom comes to public men. How it had eaten into him became plain to his countrymen a few months later when they read the closing words of his second inaugural: —

" I did not ask for place or position, and was entirely without influence or the acquaintance of persons of influence, but was resolved to perform my part in a struggle threatening the very existence of the nation. I performed a conscientious duty, without asking promotion or command, and without a revengeful feeling toward any section or individual.

"Notwithstanding this, throughout the war, and from my candidacy for my present office in 1868 to the close of the last presidential campaign, I have been the subject of abuse and slander scarcely ever equaled in political history, which to-day I feel that I can afford to disregard in view of your verdict, which I gratefully accept as my vindication."

CHAPTER XL

CRÉDIT MOBILIER — THE BACK PAY GRAB — THE SANBORN CONTRACTS

As we look back upon Grant's early years as President, we see that he was criticized more for the manner than the matter of his deeds. The result in 1872 showed clearly that the conservative forces of the country retained their faith in him. While Greeley had great crowds to hear him speak, — so great as for a time to frighten old Republican campaigners, — the outcome demonstrated that they were drawn by curiosity to see and hear a man who had been writing to them many years. The "sober second thought" which he invoked brought voters to the polls for his opponent. He was himself submerged in the great "tidal wave" on which his visionary helpers set such store. Grant won because, however much his methods might be questioned, men felt that in the fundamental qualities then needed he was sound. He had sustained the country's credit in finance, had greatly added to America's prestige abroad, and had shown firmness in the execution of the laws both North and South, a trait which led strong men of all political complexions to believe in him. He had been guilty of two faults which fairly merited reproof. One was a weakness for unworthy friends, on whom he showered responsible positions without regard to their experience or capacity and who too often played on his good faith in furthering their aims; the other was the practice, which he carried to a greater length than any of his predecessors, of interfering with congressional affairs. Of these faults the first was personal to him and transitory; the other, in the hands of a more crafty President, might well become an evil packed with peril; for the growing ease with which our recent Presidents usurp the functions of the legislative branch threatens the very fundamentals of our Government. There could be no handier tool for one who had designs upon our liberties than a subservient Congress. With Grant the tendency was less alarming than it might be with others, more artful in the ways of politics; for Grant was not a demagogue; he never dreamed of such a thing as playing with his office for popular applause to hold himself in power. He acted always with a definite and patriotic aim, though often erring through his unfamiliarity with the machinery of civil government. He drove straight at his goal without regard to legal technicalities, and cut across lots with sublime indifference to signs forbidding trespass.

While he was gratefully accepting the verdict

of the country on his first Administration, freshly
gathered clouds were hanging over him. The Congress just then coming to an end was to be notable in
its disclosure of two scandals — the Crédit Mobilier
and the "Back Pay Steal," in one of which its only
office was to mete out justice, though both besmirched
the party in control, in spite of evidence that Democrats should share responsibility for whatever guilt
there was. Both were symbolic of the temper of the
hour, and symptomatic of conditions by no means
limited to Washington. "My own public life has
been a very brief and insignificant one," said George
F. Hoar about that time, "extending little beyond
the duration of a single term of senatorial office; but
in that brief period I have seen five judges of a high
court of the United States driven from office by
threats of impeachment for corruption or maladmin-
istration. I have heard the taunt, from friendliest
lips, that when the United States presented herself
in the East to take part with the civilized world in
generous competition in the arts of life, the only
product of her institutions in which she surpassed all
others without question was her corruption. I have
seen, . . . the political administration of her chief
city become a disgrace and a byword throughout the
world. . . . When the greatest railroad of the world,
binding together the continent and uniting the two

great seas, was finished, I have seen our national triumph and exultation turned to bitterness and shame. . . . I have heard in highest places the shameless doctrine avowed by men grown old in public office that the true way by which power should be gained in the Republic is to bribe the people with offices created for their service."

Thus marshaled, it presents a sorry record; but it would be absurd to charge it up to Grant or his Administration. The period just following the war was one of rude upheaval and of shattered standards. It cannot fairly be compared with more quiescent times. It was Grant's fortune to have fallen on it. Another in his place would hardly have done better; a weaker President might have been overwhelmed.

And in spite of Hoar it would be hard to name a country with equal opportunities where corruption was then less prevalent than in our own. The scandals of the day emblazoned by political assault were uncouth in comparison with finer faults in less distorted times, but they had precedents in earlier administrations and have been rivaled since. With all his classic phrase and fine ideals Hoar often was the victim of his own hyperbole. Like Sumner he was a dogmatic partisan even in a noble cause, and those who knew him best were well aware that in his eyes the things he greatly disapproved were monstrous, while "all his geese were swans."

In the midst of the campaign the "New York Sun" had sprung a charge of bribery in connection with the construction of the Union Pacific Railroad, for which Oakes Ames, a Congressman from Massachusetts, a forceful and far-seeing business man, had been responsible. It was asserted that Ames had distributed among influential Congressmen and Senators shares of stock in the Crédit Mobilier. This was a Pennsylvania company, the unused franchise of which had been acquired by the managers of the Union Pacific, that they might thus secure the contract for the building of the road. The device which Ames and his associates adopted was an ingenious adaptation of methods then prevailing in the construction of private lines.

It was not feasible at that time to secure subscriptions to the authorized capital stock in cash as was required by the statutes and as might have been done later. If Ames had not come forward with his credit, the enterprise would probably have fallen through; and the "spanning of the continent" would have been delayed for years. But through the aid of the Crédit Mobilier, the stockholders in which were almost identical with the stockholders in the Union Pacific, the road was opened in 1869. Whatever the benefits, this was an evasion of the law providing that the stock should be paid for in full in money, when as a fact it went to men "who paid for it at not more than thirty cents on the dollar in road-making." From the viewpoint of Ames the arrangement with the Crédit Mobilier was wise and necessary as well as profitable, for otherwise the work could not have been done. At the time when it was undertaken in 1865–66, he did not dare ask Congress to amend the charter, lest in the crush of Reconstruction legislation, permission would be indefinitely delayed.

Ames had been a member of the House since 1863, and from that vantage had watched the interests of the road. Washburne, of Illinois, "the watch-dog of the Treasury," had shown intermittent symptoms of demanding an investigation of the road's affairs. Ames wanted nothing further in the way of legislation, but he cannily conceived that friendliness among the leading men in Congress might be a handy asset. At his suggestion, in the fall of 1867, three hundred and forty-three shares of the Crédit Mobilier were transferred to him as trustee. "I shall put these," he wrote to an associate, "where they will do the most good to us. I am here on the spot and can better judge where they should go." Whereupon he entered into contracts with leading Senators and

Representatives to sell them stock at par with interest from the first day of the previous July. One hundred and sixty shares were thus contracted for. Large dividends were already due upon the stock and it was worth no less than double par. Some bought their shares outright, while Ames agreed to carry others.

This was the ground of charges exploited in the closing days of the campaign. The names of Senators and Representatives were given, based on a list made out by Ames before the distribution of the stock and disclosed that summer in a suit before a Pennsylvania court. They were a score of the most influential men in Congress, among them Colfax, Conkling, Garfield, Blaine, and Wilson. When Congress met a few weeks after the election, Blaine, then Speaker, took the floor and asked for an investigation. Two committees were appointed — one headed by Luke Poland, of Vermont, to investigate the charges against members of the House, the other headed by Wilson, of Indiana, and George F. Hoar to inquire into the management of the affairs of the Union Pacific and the Crédit Mobilier. The result was a complete exoneration of most of those whom Ames had on his list. Some, like Blaine, Conkling, and Boutwell, had refused the stock. Others had given it back when they discovered there were to be suspicious profits. Only those who, during the campaign or later, had prevaricated in wholesale denials, though guiltless of corrupt intent, were held in fault. Colfax, for his prevarication and for questionable transactions revealed in the inquiry, was driven out of public life. Patterson, of New Hampshire, was recommended by the Senate Committee for expulsion, but his term came to an end before the Senate was prepared to act.

Ames and James Brooks, a New York Democratic member, a government director of the road who was implicated with him, were recommended for expulsion from the House. Brooks died before his case was reached. The House censured Ames, and he too died within a month, the victim of a broken heart. Until the scandal broke, he had not thought of the transaction as anything except a public service in keeping with the habit of the times, for which he should be given praise, not blame: "The same thing," he explained to the committee, "as going into a business community and interesting the leading business men by giving them shares." He never dreamed of corrupting members of Congress in any way; "they were all friends of the road and my friends. If you want to bribe a man you want to bribe one who is opposed to you, not to bribe one who is your friend. . . . I never made a promise to or got one from any member of Congress in my life, and I would not dare to attempt it." His final statement, read in the House before the vote of censure, merits a record in the history of the time: "I have risked reputation, fortune, everything in an enterprise of incalculable benefit to the Government from which the capital of the world shrank. . . . I have had friends, some of them in official life, with whom I have been willing to share advantageous opportunities of investment. . . . I have kept to the truth through good and evil report; denying nothing, concealing nothing, reserving nothing. Who will say that I alone am to be offered up a sacrifice to appease a public clamor or expiate the sins of others?"

The revelations and the disrepute which followed them mark the beginning of a change in public conscience, which thenceforth was alive to wrong in methods hitherto unblamed. They had no rightful bearing on Grant's Administration, as the transactions were all before his time.

The Congress, which had done so well in handling the Crédit Mobilier affair, stirred public indignation in its dying hours by the enactment of the "Salary Grab," providing for an increase in salaries of Senators and Representatives and the higher officers of the Government. The salary of the President was raised from $25,000 to $50,000 a year, that of Senators and Representatives from $5000 to $7500. There was an increase in the pay of the Vice-President, of the members of the Cabinet, and of the Justices of the Supreme Court. These advances could not properly be criticized; for they were innocent and necessary, and should not have been delayed so long; but there was a provision that the increased salaries of Senators and Representatives should date from the beginning of the present Congress, so that each would be entitled to receive $5000 in addition to what he had been already paid — a retroactive arrangement which roused the people to a fierce storm of protest. It was depicted as a conspiracy to loot the Treasury, and those who voted for it were held up to public scorn.

Democrats and Republicans had joined in its support; one party was as guilty as the other, but as the Congress was Republican, that party had to bear the blame. The appropriation bill containing the obnoxious clause was not enacted till the day before adjournment, so that Grant could not refuse to sign the bill without compelling a special session of the newly chosen Congress, solely to make the necessary appropriations for the continuance of an essential governmental function. He afterwards urged Congress to give the Executive power to veto portions of appropriation bills without vetoing the whole — a reform which has been often advocated since without result.

So violent was the outcry against the "Back Pay Steal" that many Senators and Representatives turned back into the Treasury the back pay which had been voted them, and one of the first acts of the new Congress which met in December, 1873, was to repeal the law except as it applied to the President and Justices of the Supreme Court. The issue figured largely in the next congressional election and was in part responsible for the Republican defeat. Its shadow lay on Congress for over thirty years, and not until the Roosevelt Administration did any member dare propose the salary increase which all knew to be right, resorting rather to manipulation of their pay by petty subterfuge in separate allowances for mileage, clerk hire, and stationery, in timorous deference to a public feeling which did not exist.

No one has ever told why Grant as President took up with Butler, whom as Lieutenant-General he had sent home from City Point and who, in "Butler's Book" years later, smeared Grant's war record with a filthy brush. It may have been because of his dislike for Sumner, whose Massachusetts friends detested Butler's ways, or it may have been his inbred trait of standing in a fight by any one who seemed to him unfairly handled; but under all, we may surmise Butler's frank brutality of method, which perhaps appealed to him more strongly than the finer Brahmin touch. He always clung to those with whom he felt at home. The Massachusetts patronage he gave to Butler much to the general disgust. His choice of Simmons, "the young Christian Soldier," a Methodist class leader and Butler's henchman, for Collector of the Port of Boston, aroused resentment in the State and stirred to protest men like Sumner, Pierce, Whittier, and Holmes, all bitterly opposed to Butler's strong ambition to be Governor. Six New England Senators voted against Simmons, only one for confirmation. The Hoar brothers tried to induce Grant to withdraw the nomination; but Grant was obdurate.

"Butler says he has a hold on you," said Judge Hoar, as he sat beside the President; and Rhodes, to whom this story came direct, relates that "Grant set his teeth, then drew down his jaw, and without changing countenance looked Hoar straight in the eye, but said not a word. A long and painful silence ensued and Hoar went away." George F. Hoar in his "Autobiography" tells how he broached the Simmons topic while walking with the President by Lafayette Square. Grant quietly replied that to withdraw the nomination would do injustice to the young man. The conversation continued in a friendly vein until they turned the corner by Sumner's house, when Grant's whole manner changed, and shaking his closed fist he said, "I shall not withdraw the nomination. That man who lives up there has abused me in a way which I have never suffered from any other man living!" This was in the winter of 1873, only a few weeks before Sumner's sudden end.

The scandal of the Sanborn contracts grew out of Butler's influence with the Administration. William A. Richardson, who had been Assistant Secretary of the Treasury under Boutwell and who succeeded Boutwell when the latter became a Senator, came from Lowell, Butler's town. Richardson had no administrative service save in the Washington departments. It was of him that Judge Hoar remarked, when asked about his Massachusetts record, "His reputation is strictly national." In 1872 Congress had repealed the dangerous law by which informers received a moiety of the recoveries from delinquent payers of internal revenue taxes, but a clause had been smuggled into an appropriation bill empowering the Secretary of the Treasury "to employ not more than three persons to assist the proper officers of the Government in discovering and collecting any money belonging to the United States whenever the same shall be withheld." Under this clause, Richardson, first as Assistant Secretary, afterwards as Secretary of the Treasury, made contracts with John D. Sanborn, a Boston friend of Butler's, already in the Government's employ as special agent for the Treasury, to collect taxes which were said to have been evaded by distillers, railroad companies, legatees, and others. By successive amendments to his contract, Sanborn induced the Treasury officials to let him gather in his net several thousand individuals and almost every railroad company in the United States, and to wink at fraudulent swearing to delinquencies.

Under this contract $427,000 was collected, from which Sanborn received his moiety of $213,500. Of his share Sanborn testified that $156,000 was spent in hiring men to help him carry on the work, and most of this, it has been intimated, went to those who were engaged in the advancement of Butler's political designs. A congressional committee in 1874 found that a large percentage of the revenue collected was not a proper subject for contract under the law and would have been collected by the Internal Revenue Bureau in ordinary course; that many of the transactions were fraudulent, and that the Commissioner of Internal Revenue had been studiously ignored throughout. They agreed unanimously to report a resolution that the House had no confidence in Richardson and demanded his removal.

When Grant got word of this he sent for individual members of the committee and urged them to withhold the resolution, with the understanding that the Secretary should resign and be taken care of in some other branch of service. As no one intimated that

Richardson had profited by the arrangement and the real complaint against him was for negligence, the committee accepted Grant's proposal. Richardson was made a justice of the Court of Claims, and Benjamin H. Bristow, a Kentucky lawyer who had made a record for effectiveness as United States Attorney, was appointed Secretary in his place.[1]

[1] Henry L. Dawes, in a letter to Frank W. Hackett, on February 21, 1900, had this to say of President Grant's action: —

"It so happened that there was going on in the Committee of Ways and Means of the House a very earnest and vigorous investigation into the conduct of the affairs in the Treasury Department. Much feeling and criticism had been aroused, and there was something of a call for a change in its administration.

"One morning I, as Chairman of the Committee, received a note from President Grant requesting me to call at the White House. On my arrival he said that he desired some confidential information concerning the investigation into the conduct of affairs in the Treasury Department then going on in my committee. He said that he had come to the conclusion that a change had best be made in its administration. 'But,' he added, 'I am not in the habit of turning my back on a friend under fire. Therefore I would like to know from you whether anything has appeared in that investigation affecting the integrity of Mr. Richardson, for if there is not the way presents itself whereby I can make the desired change without striking down one in whom I have myself confidence, and highly esteem.'

"I replied that it gave me great pleasure to assure him that nothing had appeared in the least affecting the integrity of the Secretary, but that it was all decided against the laxity of conducting the affairs of the Department. I was glad also to add my conviction of the spotless character of Mr. Richardson. He said that he was exceedingly glad to hear it, and was entirely satisfied.

"The next day Mr. Richardson was nominated to a judgeship in the Court of Claims and Mr. Bristow to his place in the Treasury."

CHAPTER XLI

VETO OF THE INFLATION BILL — THE RESUMPTION ACT

FOR more than two years after the Supreme Court's reversal of its Legal Tender decision there was a period of seemingly unexampled prosperity. Business boomed; new railroads shot out through the Western country to gather up the grain for which Europe waited with outstretched hands; others pierced the coal and iron regions of Pennsylvania and the border States. In the four years from 1869 to 1872 the railroad mileage of the United States increased over twenty-four thousand miles — more than three times the average annual increase during the years from 1865 to 1868. All this meant a tremendous demand for iron and steel, a great expansion of shipping on the Great Lakes. Workshops and mills were run at full capacity; labor was in demand; wages were high; the tide of immigration was at flood. New issues of railway bonds were frequent, at high rates of interest; and they were widely distributed among people like clergymen, school teachers, and others of meager pay, who eagerly welcomed the unusual returns upon their small investments.

Many of these railway bonds, notably those of the Northern Pacific, were floated by Jay Cooke & Co., who, ever since their great success in handling the Government bond issues of the Civil War, had stood in the popular imagination as the house of Morgan later stood for so many years, the representative banking institution of the United States. Besides the legitimate business advancement, there were thousands of wildcat schemes.

Every one was busy about something; every one had money; the world was looking up; the Vanderbilts and other men, who for years had been doing the biggest things in the biggest way, were carrying on their constructive schemes with sublime confidence in the future. They saw no clouds ahead; why should the average citizen who had faith in their experience? Then in the late summer of 1873, a few months after Grant had entered on his second term, money began to tighten even more than usual for that season of the year, when it was needed for the movement of the crops. There were other indications which might well have been taken as warnings that the boom had gone too far. And finally on September 18, 1873, the country was stunned by the announcement that Jay Cooke & Co. had failed.

The props were knocked from under the flimsy structure of prosperity and it crumbled overnight.

Bank after bank went to the wall in all parts of the United States. The stock exchanges remained closed for eight days; greenbacks and national bank notes were hoarded; clearing-house certificates were issued for the first time in the history of panics; every conceivable device was resorted to for luring money back into circulation. The country was stricken with industrial paralysis. Grant did not see "good times" again while he was President.

At the height of the panic the frightened financiers of New York cried to Washington for help. Three days after the failure of Jay Cooke & Co., Grant came over to New York with Richardson, the Secretary of the Treasury, and was besieged at the Fifth Avenue Hotel by the business leaders of the city. "I happened in New York on that Sunday," said Morton, of Indiana, "and saw the crowds of bankers, brokers, capitalists, merchants, manufacturers, and railroad men, who throughout that day thronged the halls, corridors, and parlors of the Fifth Avenue Hotel, beseeching the President to increase the currency by every means in his power, and declaring that unless the Government came to the rescue nothing could save the country from bankruptcy and ruin."

Two measures of relief were at Grant's hand. Before McCulloch was stopped by Congress he had retired and canceled $44,000,000 out of $400,000,000 greenbacks authorized by law, leaving in circulation $356,000,000. Boutwell at times had reissued these notes in small amounts to meet the current expenses of the Government and had retired them again as the need passed. Grant now had it in his power to reissue these notes in the financial emergency. Some of the biggest men in the Street begged him to do it.

But he refused thus to inflate the currency in order to ease the money market. At best it would have been a temporary and fictitious relief and probably illegal, though that irregularity would doubtless have been overlooked in so great a crisis. There were other surplus greenbacks in the Treasury, however, and he directed the Secretary to use these to buy bonds, thus restoring to the savings banks $13,000,000 of currency, which, while it did not go directly into circulation for the benefit of Wall Street, was far-reaching in its moral effect.

Congress meeting in December, 1873, found the country in financial depths looking to Washington for relief. There were few Senators or Representatives without a remedy, fresh from home. The cry for inflation, which had been blatant many years, now gained in volume.

Grant called attention in his message to the falling-off of revenues " owing to the general panic now prevailing." It was the duty of Congress to provide "wise and well-considered legislation." "My own judgment is that however much individuals may have suffered, one long step has been taken toward specie payments, and we can never have permanent prosperity until a specie basis can be reached and maintained, until our exports, exclusive of gold, pay for our imports, interest due abroad, and other specie obligations, or so nearly so as to leave an appreciable accumulation of the precious metals in the country from the products of our mines. . . . To increase our exports sufficient currency is required to keep all the industries of the country employed. Without this, national as well as individual bankruptcy must ensue. Undue inflation, on the other hand, while it might give temporary relief, would only lead to inflation of prices, the impossibility of competing in our own markets for the products of home skill and labor, and repeated renewals of present experiences. Elasticity to our circulating medium, therefore, and just enough of it to transact the legitimate business of the country and to keep all industries employed, is what is most to be desired. The exact medium is specie, the recognized medium of exchange the world over. That obtained, we shall have a currency of an exact degree of elasticity. If there be too much of it for the legitimate purposes of trade and commerce, it will flow out of the country. If too little, the reverse will result.

To hold what we have and to appreciate our currency to that standard is the problem deserving of the most serious consideration of Congress."

John Sherman was chairman of the Finance Committee of the Senate; and under his sound guidance early in December the majority of the committee reported a resolution looking to the resumption of specie payments. Ferry, of Michigan, offered a resolution looking to inflation. Morton and Logan were eager advocates of cheaper money. Thurman called these three "the paper money trinity." Their demands ranged from the issue of $100,000,000 in greenbacks, which Ferry had in mind, to the reissue of the entire amount retired by McCulloch, which was Morton's plan. This latter would have brought the amount outstanding to $400,000,000, but it would have necessitated the actual issue of only $18,000,000; for without justification in law, Richardson had been busy ever since the panic in inflation on his own account to make up for falling revenues, and to provide for current disbursements. McCulloch had retired $44,000,000, and at the time of the September panic in 1873 the total amount of greenbacks outstanding was $356,000,000. Richardson at convenient intervals since that time had put out, by the middle of January, 1874, a total of $26,000,000 for the payment of current expenses.

There was a decided difference of opinion about the legality of Richardson's performance, but the immediate question before Congress was whether to authorize the issue of $18,000,000 more, while silently assenting to what he had done. It was a question of principle rather than of amount. "If now," said Sherman, "in this time of temporary panic, we yield one single inch to the desire for paper money in this country, we shall pass the Rubicon, and there will be no power in Congress to check the issue. If you want $40,000,000 now, how easy will it be to get $40,000,-000 again! . . . Will there not always be men in debt? Will not always men with bright hopes embark too far on the treacherous sea of credit? Will there not always be a demand made upon you for an increase?"

The debate covering a wide range lasted for four months. Sherman's committee reported a bill fixing the maximum amount of greenbacks at $382,000,000, where Richardson had left it. This was amended to provide for a maximum of $400,000,000, thus legalizing Richardson's issue and authorizing $18,000,000 more. In this form it passed the Senate and House by ample margins and on April 4, 1874, went to the President.

Now comes one of the most dramatic and creditable incidents in Grant's career. With the passage of the inflation bill the country settled down to the

expectation that it would become a law. There was
reason for this belief. While Grant's public and private utterances hitherto had been consistently on the
side of financial stability, there were passages both
in his private and public papers not inconsistent with
a moderate expansion of the circulating medium, and
he had tacitly assented to the irregularities of Boutwell and Richardson even though he may not have
approved them in advance. Morton and Logan were
his stanch political supporters. They had sustained
him when he had been most bitterly assailed. But
here was an occasion where he fully realized the
responsibility of his position of command.

It would have been easy to say nothing and sign
the bill; still easier to let the bill become a law without his signature. In either case he would have little
criticism. Whatever blame there was would fall on
Congress.

Grant never thought of shirking the responsibility.
He first expected to approve the bill and actually
wrote a message telling why: but when he came to
read his own production, he could not honestly endorse the arguments. He tore up his first message,
wrote another, and on the 22d of April astonished the
country with a veto.

"The only time I ever deliberately resolved to do
an expedient thing for party reasons, against my own

judgment," he later said, "was on the occasion of the expansion or inflation bill. I never was so pressed in my life to do anything as to sign that bill — never. It was represented to me that the veto would destroy the Republican Party in the West; that the West and South would combine and take the country, and agree upon some even worse plan of finance, some plan that would mean repudiation. Morton, Logan, and other men, friends whom I respected, were eloquent in presenting this view. I thought at last I would try and save the party, and at the same time the credit of the nation, from the evils of the bill. I resolved to write a message, embodying my own reasoning and some of the arguments that had been given me, to show that the bill, as passed, need not mean expansion or inflation and that it need not affect the country's credit. The message was intended to soothe the East and satisfy the foreign holders of the bonds. I wrote the message with great care and put in every argument I could call up to show that the bill was harmless and would not accomplish what its friends expected from it. When I finished my wonderful message which was to do so much good to the party and country, I read it over and said to myself: 'What is the good of all this? You do not believe it. You know it is not true.' Throwing it aside I resolved to do what I believed to be right, veto the bill! I could not stand my own arguments. While I was in this mood — and it was an anxious time with me, so anxious that I could not sleep at night, with me a most unusual circumstance — the ten days were passing in which the President must sign or veto a bill. On the ninth day I resolved inflexibly to veto the bill and let the storm come."[1]

Grant wrote his veto with his own hand, as was generally the case with his important messages. It was a sturdy and inspiring paper. He declared his unalterable opposition to any inflation of the currency as "a departure from true principles of finance, national interest, national obligations to creditors, congressional promises, party pledges (on the part of both political parties), and of personal views and promises made by me in every annual message sent to Congress and in each inaugural address." It was the turning-point in the financial policy of the United States. If Grant had done no other praiseworthy thing in his eight years of office, this in itself would have given him rank among our great executives. It fixed the place of the United States among the financial powers of the world.

But something still remained for him to do; for though inflation had been dealt a deadly blow, additional legislation was required to bring about a cur-

[1] Young, vol. ii, p. 153.

rency based unmistakably upon the monetary standards of the world. In 1874 the country was ready for a party change. Hard times, the record made by Congress, Crédit Mobilier, the "Back Pay Grab," and scandals like the Sanborn contracts, had culminated in a storm of disapproval which broke in the election of a Democratic House. The two-thirds Republican majority of the Forty-fourth Congress was almost reversed, and for the first time since 1861, Senate and House would be of differing political complexion. Whatever legislation looking to the resumption of specie payments the Administration had in mind must be enacted while a Congress in sympathy with this policy was still in power; for sound finance had no place in the Democratic creed.

When Congress met in December, 1874, for its last short session, Grant in his message brought resumption boldly to the front, pressing his argument with earnestness and with convincing force. He dwelt upon the national need which had devised a currency impossible to keep at par with the recognized currency of the civilized world, urged that a foreign indebtedness, contracted in good faith by borrower and lender, should be paid in coin, and according to the bond agreed upon when the debt was contracted — gold or its equivalent. "The good faith of the Government cannot be violated toward creditors without national disgrace." In his judgment the first step toward the encouragement of American commerce was "to secure a currency of fixed, stable value; a currency good wherever civilization reigns; one which, if it becomes superabundant with one people, will find a market with some other; a currency which has as its basis the labor necessary to produce it, which will give to it its value. Gold and silver are now the recognized medium of exchange the civilized world over, and to this we should return with the least practicable delay. . . . I believe firmly that there can be no prosperous and permanent revival of business and industries until a policy is adopted — with legislation to carry it out — looking to a return to a specie basis. . . . I believe it is in the power of Congress at this session to devise such legislation as will renew confidence, revive all the industries, start us on a career of prosperity to last for many years, and to save the credit of the nation and the people."

He suggested measures which seemed to him absolutely necessary to a return to specie payments. "The Legal Tender clause to the law authorizing the issue of currency by the National Government should be repealed, to take effect as to all contracts entered into after a day fixed in the repealing act. . . . Provision should be made by which the Secretary of the

Treasury can obtain gold as it may become necessary from time to time, from the date when specie resumption commences. To this should be added a revenue sufficiently in excess of expenses to insure an accumulation of gold in the Treasury to sustain permanent redemption. . . . With resumption, free banking may be authorized with safety, giving the same full protection to bill-holders which they have under existing laws. Indeed, I regard free banking as essential. It would give proper elasticity to the currency." And pressing home his plea he urged: "I commend this subject to your careful consideration, believing that a favorable solution is attainable, and if reached by this Congress that the present and future generations will ever gratefully remember it as their deliverer from a thralldom of evil and disgrace."

Congress was quick in its response. John Sherman, chairman of the Committee on Finance at the first party caucus, moved a committee to harmonize the various diverging views of the majority and formulate a bill. He was made chairman. By mutual concessions a bill was shaped, the vital section of which provided that on January 1, 1879, the Government should begin the redemption of greenbacks in coin; and, to make possible this resumption of specie payments, authorized the Secretary of the Treasury to use the surplus revenue and to sell bonds for the purpose of accumulating gold. The bill also provided for free banking, for the withdrawal of greenbacks as fast as national bank notes were issued in the proportion of $80 to $100 until the greenbacks were reduced to $300,000,000; for subsidiary silver coins to take the place of the paper fractional currency.

The bill promptly passed both Senate and House, and on January 14, 1875, Grant made it law, signalizing his approval in a message congratulating Congress, urging further steps to make the law effective through the increase of revenue, and suggesting other helpful legislation. It fell to Sherman as Secretary of the Treasury under Hayes to carry out the law with whose enactment he had so much to do, and thus complete a chapter in finance of which all good Americans may rightfully be proud.

CHAPTER XLII

A SOLID SOUTH IN THE MAKING

ONE cannot review the story of the South during these years without a feeling of deep melancholy. We have seen how in the flood of negro suffrage the States of the Black Belt had been misgoverned, and we have had a dark recital of the extravagance, dishonesty, and ignorance which laid a heavy hand upon a proud though conquered people. There are few instances in history of such complete misapprehension of a human problem by those entrusted with its settlement. The North, befooled by myths about the negro, failed utterly to comprehend the mental attitude of those who after exercising feudal power found themselves suddenly subordinate to former slaves, a race still looked upon by them as of a hopelessly inferior type. The hurried grant of universal suffrage was an offense for which both North and South have paid a grievous penalty. In throwing off a hateful burden, the people of the South, as if pursuant to a law of nature, have let all other problems wait upon the vital problem of local government. It would be hard to overestimate the injury done the nation as a whole by the existence of the "Solid South," where there is found the finest essence of the Anglo-Saxon race, yet where there is no adequate debate of timely themes because the negro question overshadows all. That it may now be a fantastic fear is quite beside the point. The dread of negro domination has become ingrained through memory of actual experience in Reconstruction times. The South itself must bear the cruel load of its solidity; but the North, which furnished the excuse unwittingly, must share the expiation because it shares the blame.

The part Grant had to play in his endeavor to do justice in the South is one he neither relished nor deserved. He did not favor negro suffrage at the start, and acquiesced in it as a necessity only when through others' folly it seemed unavoidable. But when corruption and malfeasance led to bloodshed his soldier's instinct led him to enforce the law. His use of federal troops, subject to hot denunciation at the time, has been thrown up against him ever since; as if it were the cause of violence and not intended as the cure. The opposition charged that he essayed to play the rôle of Cæsar, that he aimed to keep himself in office by military force, till men forgot that all the federal soldiers in the South could hardly have policed a single town. It took four years of fighting and two million men to put down insurrection in a territory which he was charged with trying to enslave with four thousand soldiers scattered through a dozen States. That was the highest number in the South under arms at any single time, embracing the garrisons of all the forts between the Delaware and the Gulf of Mexico.[1] It would have been a great thing for the South, in Grant's opinion, if some of the streams of emigration from New England and the Middle States had been diverted in that direction instead of toward Iowa and Kansas. In the light of history and his own experience we must examine with respect Grant's matured views upon the problem which pressed upon him heavily so long: —

"Looking back over the whole policy of Reconstruction, it seems to me that the wisest thing would have been to have continued for some time the military rule. Sensible Southern men see now that there was no government so frugal, so just, and fair as what they had under our generals. That would have enabled the Southern people to pull themselves together and repair material losses. . . . Military rule would have been just to all, to the negro who wanted freedom, the white man who wanted protection, the Northern man who wanted Union. As State after

[1] The whole number of troops in the States of Louisiana, Alabama, Georgia, Florida, South Carolina, North Carolina, Kentucky, Tennessee, Arkansas, Mississippi, Maryland, and Virginia at the time of the election was 4082. This embraces the garrisons of all the forts from the Delaware to the Gulf of Mexico! (Richardson, *Messages and Papers*, vol. VII, p. 298.)

State showed willingness to come into the Union, not on their own terms, but upon ours, I would have admitted them. This would have made universal suffrage unnecessary, and I think a mistake was made about suffrage. It was unjust to the negro to throw upon him the responsibilities of citizenship, and expect him to be on even terms with his white neighbor. It was unjust to the North.

"In giving the South negro suffrage, we have given the old slaveholders forty votes in the Electoral College. They keep those votes, but disfranchise the negroes. That is one of the gravest mistakes in the policy of Reconstruction. . . . I am clear now that it would have been better for the North to have postponed suffrage, Reconstruction, State Governments, for ten years, and held the South in a territorial condition. . . . It would have avoided the scandals of the State Governments, saved money, and enabled the Northern merchants, farmers, and laboring men to reorganize society in the South. But we made our scheme, and must do what we can with it. Suffrage once given can never be taken away and all that remains for us now is to make good that gift by protecting those who have received it." [1]

Such elections as were held in 1873 disclosed a Democratic trend, due partly to the panic, partly to

[1] Young, p. 362.

other things, and as election day approached in 1874, the Democratic trend throughout the North became intensified. In sympathy with the general tendency there was a recurrence in several Southern States of anti-negro demonstrations, which Grant described in his December message.[1]

In Alabama, "men of intelligence and property"

[1] "I regret to say that with preparations for the late election decided indications appeared in some localities in the Southern States of a determination, by acts of violence and intimidation, to deprive citizens of the freedom of the ballot because of their political opinions. Bands of men, masked and armed, made their appearance; White Leagues and other societies were formed; large quantities of arms and ammunition were imported and distributed to these organizations; military drills, with menacing demonstrations, were held, and with all these murders enough were committed to spread terror among those whose political action was to be suppressed, if possible, by these intolerant and criminal proceedings. I understand that the Fifteenth Amendment to the Constitution was made to prevent this and a like state of things, and the Act of May 31, 1870, with amendments, was passed to enforce its provisions, the object of both being to guarantee to all citizens the right to vote and to protect them in the free enjoyment of that right. Enjoined by the Constitution 'to take care that the laws be faithfully executed,' and convinced by undoubted evidence that violations of said act had been committed and that a widespread and flagrant disregard of it was contemplated, the proper officers were instructed to prosecute the offenders, and troops were stationed at convenient points to aid these officers, if necessary, in the performance of their official duties. Complaints are made of this interference by federal authority; but if said amendment and act do not provide for such interference under the circumstances as above stated, then they are without meaning, force, or effect, and the whole scheme of colored enfranchisement is worse than mockery and little better than a crime." (Richardson, *Messages and Papers*, vol. VII, p. 297.)

had determined to redeem the State. And there were reports which gained wide credence in the North of "riots, murderings, assassinations and torturings" more common than at any time since Lee's surrender. These stories were discredited by newspaper writers, but Grant under authority of the Enforcement Acts sent 679 soldiers to Alabama to insure a fair election. Yet in face of this display of force which emboldened the negroes to vote the Republican ticket, a Democratic Governor and Legislature were elected by comfortable majorities. A select committee of the House of Representatives investigated the election, and the Republican members reported that it was carried by "fraud, violence, proscription, intimidation, and murder." The Democrats admitted that there were riots in several places on election day, in which the negroes got the worst of it, but they maintained that in these riots the negroes were aggressors.

In Arkansas there had been in 1872 an armed dispute between the followers of Brooks and those of Baxter — rival Republican candidates for Governor. Grant recognized Baxter, the more conservative of the two, as the lawful executive. Baxter's Legislature passed a bill calling a constitutional convention. The people endorsed this action. The constitution framed by this convention was ratified on October

15, 1874, by popular vote and on the same day A. H. Garland, Democrat, afterward Attorney-General of the United States, was elected Governor with a Democratic Legislature and four Democratic Congressmen. The President took up the Arkansas problem from a new viewpoint. On February 8, 1875, he sent a special message to Congress, expressing the opinion that Brooks, instead of Baxter, had been legally elected Governor in 1872; that he had been illegally deprived of the possession of the office since that time; that "in 1874 the constitution of the State was by violence, intimidation, and revolutionary proceedings overthrown and a new constitution adopted and a new State Government established." He asserted that these proceedings, if permitted to stand, practically ignored all rights of minorities in all the States. ". . . I earnestly ask that Congress will take definite action in this matter to relieve the Executive from acting upon questions which should be decided by the legislative branch of the Government."

Grant's thought was that all proceedings under the illegal Baxter régime should be annulled, in which event Brooks would be restored to the office which was rightfully his under the old constitution till January, 1877.

A committee of the House, headed by Luke P. Poland, reported a resolution that "in the judgment of this House no interference with the existing government in Arkansas by any department of the Government of the United States is advisable," and the resolution was adopted by the overwhelming vote of 150 to 81, in a House overwhelmingly Republican. Poland in supporting his resolution asserted that the change from one constitution to another was as peaceful a change as ever took place in his own State of Vermont; that under the Garland Government everything was as peaceful and quiet as in Massachusetts.

In February, 1875, a Civil Rights Bill was enacted, not quite on Sumner's lines, aimed to secure to negroes equal rights in inns, public conveyances, theaters, and other places of amusement and to prevent their disqualification for services as jurors. It was a wanton irritant, futile in results; for eight years later, in 1883, the Supreme Court declared its chief provisions unconstitutional.

In Mississippi there was a condition different from either Arkansas or Alabama. The Legislature, in control of negroes and carpet-baggers, had laid heavy taxes for the support of an ambitious system of public schools which roused the indignation of the Ku-Klux Klan and led to persecution of the negroes and Northern women who came there to teach. Adelbert Ames, who had seen gallant service in the

Army of the James, was Governor. He was an earnest and consistent champion of the negro. In Vicksburg, where over half the population were negroes, the whites, exasperated by high taxes, forced Crosby, the Republican sheriff, to resign. Ames told the sheriff to hold his office, and Crosby called upon the negroes of the county to sustain him. There were riots in which twenty-nine negroes and two whites were killed. Sheridan, who was in command at New Orleans, sent soldiers to Vicksburg. Crosby was reinstated and peace restored.

In 1875 the "men of intelligence and property" organized to carry the election and control the Legislature. There were fifteen thousand more negro voters in the State than whites. The problem was to persuade the negroes to vote the Democratic ticket or stay away from the polls. "Peaceful persuasion" was the programme, but, unfortunately, Mississippi had the shotgun habits of other frontier communities; every one carried either a bowie knife or a pistol. Negro meetings were broken up by armed white bands. A few whites and many negroes were killed; negroes were shot down in cold blood by way of retribution for the killing of the whites. Ames telegraphed to Grant, asking him to proclaim martial law. But Grant refused. "The whole public," Grant telegraphed to Attorney-General Pierrepont

from Long Branch, "are tired out with these annual autumnal outbreaks in the South, and the great
majority are ready now to condemn any interference
on the part of the Government. I heartily wish that
peace and good order may be restored without issuing the proclamation, but if the proclamation must
be issued I shall instruct the commander of the
forces to have no child's play; the laws will be executed and the peace will be maintained in every
street and highway of the United States."

Ames, full of pugnacity, organized the state militia, mostly negroes, and armed them with Springfield
breech-loaders. The whites formed military companies of their own, and bloodshed would have been
general had it not been for a "peace agreement"
brought about through the conciliatory efforts of an
agent of the Department of Justice. Ames disbanded
his militia and the Democratic bands dispersed, but
while the menacing civil warfare was averted, intimidation proved equally effective.

The "Mississippi Plan," as it was called, consisted
in an organized conspiracy to frighten the negroes
away from the polls. Salutes with cannon were fired
on the public roads; "To let the niggers know that
there was going to be a fair election," Private John
Allen said. Horsemen with ropes tied to the pommels
of their saddles would ride up to a polling-place where

black voters were waiting to cast their ballots. "How soon will the polls be opened?" one asked another. "In about fifteen minutes," was the reply. "Then the *hanging* will not begin for about fifteen minutes," was the response. Not a word to the blacks, but before the fifteen minutes were up, they had all disappeared. The Democrats carried the election by nearly 31,000, had a majority of 93 in the Legislature, elected most of the county officers, and 4 out of 6 members of Congress.

Grant wrote on July 26, 1876: "Mississippi is governed to-day by officials chosen through fraud and violence such as would scarcely be accredited to savages, much less to a civilized and Christian people." Ames was impeached by the new Legislature, but the Legislature subsequently dismissed the charges and Ames resigned. "He bore himself," wrote Roger A. Pryor, "like a brave and honorable gentleman."

Of all cases that of Louisiana was the hardest. The struggle there was marked by differences between Republican factions as well as by Democratic resistance to carpet-bag rule. Henry C. Warmoth, heading one faction, disclosed conservative tendencies. Opposed to him were S. B. Packard, United States Marshal, and William Pitt Kellogg, who had been a lawyer in Illinois, Colonel of an Illinois regiment in the Civil War, and whom Lincoln had made

Collector of Customs at New Orleans in 1865. War-moth in 1872 had joined the conservative Democrats in supporting a fusion state ticket headed by John McEnery as candidate for Governor. Kellogg was the Republican candidate. Both sides claimed the election of Governor and Legislature. Under the Louisiana law a returning board composed of the Governor, the Lieutenant-Governor, the Secretary of State, and two others specifically named had the power of throwing out the returns from any voting-places which in their judgment had been carried by violence, intimidation, bribery, or corrupt influence. Warmoth, who had the returns in his own hands, reconstructed the returning board; the new board announced the election of McEnery and enough fusion members of the Legislature to make a major-ity. The Republicans got up a returning board of their own and declared Kellogg with a Republican Legislature elected. The United States Circuit Judge issued an order late at night directing the United States Marshal to take possession of the State House. Packard was not only sheriff, but chairman of the State Committee. By authority of the Attorney-General he had the United States troops at his dis-posal, and with them he seized and held the State House. Under his protection, Kellogg assumed the governorship.

Grant sent a special message, February 25, 1873, arguing in favor of the Kellogg Government. He said that if Congress took no action he should recognize and support it.

Turbulence followed in the trail of recognition. There was a massacre at Colfax on the Red River, three hundred and fifty miles from New Orleans, within two months, white men riding into the town and demanding that the negroes lay down their arms and surrender the court-house. The court-house in which sixty or seventy negroes had taken refuge was fired; as the negroes rushed out, some were killed and some were captured. Those captured were mercilessly shot down. In all, the negroes killed at Colfax were fifty-nine, whites only two. "This deed was without palliation or justification," wrote George F. Hoar, who as chairman of a congressional committee made a report. "It was deliberate, barbarous, cold-blooded murder. It will stand like the Massacre of Glencoe or St. Bartholomew, a foul blot on the page of history," — hyperbole again, perhaps, but the bloody deed was black enough to have a marked effect upon the feeling of the North, which was beginning at that time to turn against the men who were exploiting negro suffrage for their own political gain. A little over a year later, at Coushatta, a little farther up the river, there was another massacre, equally

foul. After an assault upon the blacks by members of the White League, with killing on both sides,
six white Republican office-holders, lately from the
North, gave themselves up to the White League, who
had demanded that they resign. While they were
being taken under guard to Shreveport, they were
set on by another band and murdered in cold blood.

Grant having withdrawn the federal troops, except
a few who were still garrisoned in New Orleans, the
white conservatives, on September 14, 1874, started
an insurrection in that city, barricaded the streets,
fought with the colored metropolitan police, and
seized the State House, where their leaders started
to reorganize the Government. Grant at once sent
troops, under whose protection the Kellogg Government was set up again. The armed force sustaining
the conservatives was broken up.

In the election for members of the Legislature in
1874, the conservatives on the face of the returns
elected a majority of 29. Kellogg's returning board,
after weeks of thought, threw out conservatives on
charges of intimidation and fraud till they found that
53 conservatives and 53 radicals had been elected.
With regard to five seats they rendered no decision.
When the Legislature met in January, 1875, there
were scenes of wild disorder. The conservatives
seized control, elected a speaker, and seated their

five contestants for the vacant seats. The Republicans withdrew in order to break a quorum.

General de Trobriand, armed with an order from Kellogg to clear the hall of all persons not returned as legal members by the returning board, appeared with a file of soldiers. With fixed bayonets the soldiers approached one by one each of the five members sitting in his place and forced him to leave the hall. The conservative Speaker and his party withdrew, the Republicans returned and organized as best they could.

Sheridan, whom Grant had ordered to New Orleans, now assumed command. "I think," he telegraphed, "that the terrorization now existing in Louisiana, Mississippi, and Arkansas could be entirely removed and confidence and fair dealing established by the arrest and trial of the ringleaders of the armed White League. If Congress would pass a bill declaring them banditti they could be tried by a military commission. . . . It is possible that if the President would issue a proclamation declaring them banditti, no further action need be taken, except that which would devolve upon me."

Belknap, the Secretary of War, telegraphed Sheridan: "The President and all of us have full confidence and thoroughly approve your course. . . . Be assured that the President and Cabinet confide in your wis-

dom and rest in the belief that all acts of yours have
been and will be judicious."

The opposition newspapers in the North and the
anti-Administration band in the Senate flamed out
against Sheridan, against de Trobriand, especially
against Grant. "If this can be done in Louisiana,"
cried Schurz, "and if such things be sustained by
Congress, how long will it be before it can be done in
Massachusetts and Ohio? . . . How long before a
general of the Army may sit in the chair you occupy,
sir, to decide contested election cases, for the purpose
of manufacturing a majority in the Senate? How
long before a soldier may stalk into the National
House of Representatives and, pointing to the
Speaker's mace, say, 'Take away that bauble!'"
Indignation meetings were held in Cooper Institute
and Faneuil Hall.

Charles Foster, William Walter Phelps, and Clark-
son N. Potter, a congressional committee who had
been in New Orleans to investigate the action of
Kellogg's returning board, and who were there during
the disturbances at the State House, united in a
report "that the action of the returning board on the
whole was arbitrary, unjust, and, in our opinion,
illegal," and that this alone prevented the return of
a conservative majority in the Legislature. They
asserted that "the conviction has been general among

the whites since 1872 that the Kellogg Government was an usurpation." Another committee, consisting of George F. Hoar, William A. Wheeler, and William P. Frye, reported that intimidation had prevented "a full, free, and fair election" in 1874 and that General de Trobriand's interference "alone prevented a scene of bloodshed." On their recommendation the "Wheeler Compromise" was accepted, giving a conservative majority in the House; the Senate was Republican; by resolution the Legislature agreed not to disturb the Kellogg Government.

South Carolina for a moment shot a ray of light across the gloom. Daniel H. Chamberlain, a Massachusetts soldier, a lawyer, a graduate of Yale, with high ideals, Attorney-General from 1868 to 1872, with fine courage set his face against misrule. He was elected Governor in 1874, succeeding the scoundrel Moses, who in his turn had followed the disreputable Scott. He vetoed numerous plunder bills, reformed the courts, and cut loose from the rogues. "My highest ambition," he said, "has been to make the ascendancy of the Republican party in South Carolina compatible with the attainment and maintenance of as high and pure a tone in the administration of public affairs as can be exhibited in the proudest State of the South." In his two years as Governor he partially succeeded. But he was not omnipotent.

CHAPTER XLIII

THE WHISKEY RING — THE BELKNAP CASE —
GRANT'S STEADFAST LOYALTY — THE CHIEF
JUSTICESHIP

"GRANT is honest as Old Jack Taylor," Sherman
wrote home from Vicksburg in reply to hints of deals
with traders who swarmed the Union camps bar-
tering their country for Mississippi cotton; and it is
history that attacks on Grant all through the war
originated with unscrupulous contractors whose crook-
edness he had exposed, forbidding them to ply their
wretched traffic in his jurisdiction. Yet he was fated
in the White House to be a ready target for the press
by reason of disclosures affecting men in whom he
placed his trust. Our Civil War, like every other war
in history, had left corruption in its trail, though differing from most others in the rapidity with which
men set themselves to cleaning out the thieves and
the contemporaneous publicity of the disclosures.
Many suspicious things which came to light while
Grant was President would have occasioned little
comment in other times or other countries. It is a
lasting tribute to the spirit of the day that evildoers
were so quickly brought to punishment, though at

the moment, the very triumph of reform cast on the period a cloud which history has not yet dispelled, for history, like politics, is ever true to form in over-emphasizing superficial faults at the expense of in-grained quality.

Grant did not seek the easy fame which comes to the crusader; he had no mission to reform the ways of other men; he was so wholly human that he could never quite divorce his public functions from his pri-vate life. As President he kept about him those he liked, and while we may regret his taste in choice of some of his companions, we cannot blame the faith with which he clung to them. "Grant was the only man I ever knew," says one who was for eight years at his side, "upon whose promise you could safely go to sleep. He never failed to keep his word even in the smallest things. If once he pledged himself you could dismiss it from your mind, and travel round the world. It would be done."[1] This trait of constancy contributed to his success, but in conjunction with his childlike trust it was a dangerous thing, which brought him bitterness of soul. Experience did not seem to profit him. He had the unsuspecting chivalry of friendship; throughout his life his sympathy went out to those he thought the victims of injustice; though they might be at fault, his instinct was to

[1] General C. C. Sniffen.

shield them from attack. In the grim chase of justice
his heart ran with the fox, not with the hounds.

Of all the men by whom he stood for good or bad,
Babcock, his aide and secretary, brought him the
greatest care, for Babcock had a genius for getting
into scrapes, some doubtless innocent for all their
ugliness. He was charged first with mercenary aims
in San Domingo; but there was never any evidence
that he was guilty there of anything but indifference
to proprieties. The fact that he was then exonerated
tied Grant more closely to him, as one who had been
persecuted in a cause Grant had at heart.

Babcock was charged with having had a hand in
paving contracts when Alexander Shepard was Governor of the District, but could be blamed apparently
for nothing worse than indiscretion. Shepard was
ruthless in his methods; undoubtedly his friends made
money out of real estate and contracts under his
régime; but nothing short of ruthlessness could have
wrought such miracles as he performed almost in a
night while changing Washington from a straggling,
ragged town of mud and huts into a Capital with spa-
cious avenues consistent with the splendid plans of
l'Enfant three quarters of a century before. The
country rang with cries against "Boss" Shepard at
the time, and Congress changed the form of government, creating a commission for the District in order

to get rid of him as Governor and eliminate the "District Ring." Grant aroused resentment when he sent Shepard's nomination to the Senate as one of the Commissioners. Shepard, discredited and poor, betook himself to Mexico, but when he came back, after twenty years of exile, he was the hero of a civic demonstration. His statue now embellishes the Avenue which he restored.

Babcock became the center of the scandal of the "Whiskey Ring," dragging the President himself into a compromising place. The story of the Whiskey Ring is an unhappy chapter of the time. Bristow, who succeeded Richardson as Secretary of the Treasury in June, 1874, had some experience as a prosecuting officer through having been a federal attorney, but he was little known outside Kentucky until he made his record in the Treasury as a minister of reform. There he found matters ready at his hand to test his quality and add to his repute.

For years there had been frauds upon the revenue through a conspiracy of distillers and rectifiers in the whiskey-making centers of the Middle West, — St. Louis, Chicago, and Milwaukee, — who, with the connivance of dishonest internal revenue officials, cheated the Treasury out of taxes due. The richest pickings were in Johnson's time, but it is said that during three years, under Grant, three times more whiskey was shipped from St. Louis alone than paid the tax, and that the Government in six years was defrauded out of revenue amounting to nearly $3,000,000. It had long been suspected that frauds were perpetrated on the revenue by the distillers; and with Grant's approval in the summer of 1874 steps had been taken to put a stop to them, but without success; the service was so honeycombed with clerks participating in illegal profits of the ring that any move to interfere with the conspirators was promptly known to every one involved. It was not till G. W. Fishback, editor of the "St. Louis Democrat," gave to Bristow secret information and with Bristow's sanction set unofficial agencies to work, that it was possible to ferret out the methods of the ring without some guilty partner in the Treasury divulging what was going on. This word was confidentially conveyed to Bristow in February, 1875, and on the 10th of May, after a train of evidence had been laid skillfully, he lit the fuse. Simultaneous raids were made all over the United States. In St. Louis, Milwaukee, and Chicago, sixteen distilleries and sixteen rectifying establishments were seized, and fraudulent packages were found in almost every other town of any size. The thing at once had public notoriety and for months thereafter newspapers spread the record of the revelations and the trials. Grant was well in touch with the inquiry and joined in the pursuit.

Before long it was found that Babcock had been corresponding with the leaders of the ring, and there were intimations, not only that he shared the profits, but that he used this means of raising funds for Grant's election in 1872 and was preparing to finance a third term by the same device. Helping Dyer, the Government Attorney, in the preparation of the case, was John B. Henderson, the former Senator, one of Grant's most malignant critics. McDonald, the supervisor at St. Louis, who was convicted and jailed, says that Henderson asked him to plead guilty and become a witness for the Government (promising him immunity from punishment). Because of his devotion, he says, he refused to testify against Grant and Babcock and went to the penitentiary willingly in order to preserve Grant and the Nation from scandal.[1] Barnard, a St. Louis banker, wrote to Grant, denouncing Henderson and Dyer, and urging that "the interest of the Government and your own past record should be protected by additional counsel . . . regardless of the prospective influence of press, party,

---

[1] Rhodes, vol. VII, p. 187. But McDonald's book, *Secrets of the Great Whiskey Ring*, which was issued as a campaign document in 1880, is a mass of falsehoods, and while some of the statements may have been correct by accident, it is not safe to accept a single one of them as true. McDonald could not have written the book himself. He was illiterate.

or self-aggrandizement." The letter gave the names of many who should be called as witnesses and told of revenue officials who had been quoted as saying Grant could not give them up or Babcock would be lost. This letter came to Grant at Long Branch on July 29, and he at once referred it to the Secretary of the Treasury with an endorsement in his own hand: ". . . I forward this for information and to the end that if it throws any light upon new parties to summon as witnesses they may be brought out. *Let no guilty man escape if it can be avoided.* Be specially vigilant — or instruct those engaged in the prosecution of fraud to be — against all who insinuate that they have high influence to protect — or to protect them. No personal consideration should stand in the way of performing a public duty."

The ink was hardly dry on this historic note before conspiracies began to multiply within conspiracies. Those implicated in the frauds upon the revenue, in wriggling to escape, were glad for a pretense to drag the scandal to the White House door, in hope that this might bring to them immunity. Bristow, an honest and courageous man himself, had in his train a stream of flatterers exciting his political ambition, and the press began to talk about him as a candidate for President. Around Grant there revolved a multitude of satellites, continually whispering a third term and poisoning his mind against the machinations of the friends of Bristow. Pervading the Administration was the venom of distrust. In August the investigators found a dispatch from Babcock addressed to an indicted officer, signed "Sylph," and reading, "I have succeeded. They will not go. I will write you." This was interpreted to mean that he had kept the ring informed about the Treasury's activities. Much was made of this dispatch till it was found to have no bearing on the frauds, though it suggested a companionship impure in other ways.

A little later Grant, with Babcock, visited several Western cities, St. Louis with the rest, and before he started Bluford Wilson, Solicitor of the Treasury, wrote to Henderson reminding him of the importance of neglecting no precaution "to reach the *bottom or top* of the conspiracy," and advising that the defendants be placed under strict surveillance "for the next ten days or two weeks"; and Wilson later said: "I wrote that letter intending that General Babcock should be looked after. If he was in the ring, I intended to catch him if it was in my power. If he was not, I intended to demonstrate his innocence beyond the shadow of a doubt if it were possible to do so."

The manner of this chase of Babcock angered Grant, who was convinced that a plot was hatching to besmirch himself. Two of the ring had been convicted, and in December, on evidence which these trials divulged, Babcock was indicted in St. Louis "for conspiracy to defraud the revenue," a special military court of inquiry having previously been called at Babcock's request. Critics of the Administration declared that this court, which never sat to hear the case, was granted to forestall the civil suit. Henderson in the course of one of the trials had cried: "What right had the President to interfere with the honest discharge of the duties of a Secretary of the Treasury? None whatever! Is it to continue in this country that because a man holds an office at the hands of another he is to become his slave?" — and much more to the same purport. When this was read by Grant, he promptly ordered Henderson's dismissal, a step which, coming the day after Babcock's indictment, caused a wild outcry in the press, though Henderson was replaced with James O. Brodhead, the Democratic head of the St. Louis bar, at least as good a man as Henderson had been. The change was first talked over in the Cabinet, and every member, including Bristow, voted for Henderson's removal, regarding his performance "as an outrage upon professional propriety."

Grant was viciously attacked because with his approval the Attorney-General sent a letter to all district attorneys to stop the wholesale granting of im-

munities, which had been instigated by the Treasury
to reach men "higher up." "Suggestions have been
made," he wrote, "that quite too many guilty men
are to go unpunished. . . . I am determined as far as
lies in my power to have these prosecutions so conducted that when they are over, the honest judgment
of the honest men of the country — which is sure in
the main to be just — will say that no one has been
prosecuted from malice, and that no guilty one has
been let off through favoritism, and that no guilty
one who has been proved guilty or confessed himself
guilty has been suffered to escape punishment."[1]

A copy of this letter fell into Babcock's hands and
he gave it to the press. "They were trying to destroy
me," he explained to the Attorney-General, "and I
had a right to anything I could get hold of"; and
Pierrepont testified before the House Committee,

[1] Out of all those indicted and as a result of several trials, only
three of the St. Louis ring served a jail sentence. One of these was
McDonald, who was sentenced to three years' imprisonment and
was pardoned after serving two. Former Paymaster-General Cul-
ver C. Sniffen, who was one of Grant's secretaries throughout both
Administrations, and who has made a careful study of the records,
says: "A surprising number of immunities from punishment were
granted to confessed criminals. Out of forty-seven persons indicted
in Chicago during October and November, 1875, *criminal* immunity
was granted in advance of the time for trial in almost every instance,
while up to August 4, 1876, but three of them had been given light
jail sentences and representatives of the distillers were then in
Washington claiming civil immunity. In St. Louis, out of fourteen
distillers, thirteen pleaded guilty in one day and none received
other than civil punishment, while the acknowledged organizer of

"I heard the President say five or six times in the progress of the case, 'If Babcock is guilty there is no man who wants him so much proven guilty as I do, for it is the greatest piece of traitorism to me that a man could possibly practice.'"

When Babcock's trial came off in February, Grant asked to be a witness, and at his request his deposition was taken at the White House by the Chief Justice of the United States, Bristow and Pierrepont present, with attorneys for Babcock and the Government. He swore that he had never seen anything in the conduct or talk of Babcock which indicated to his mind connection with the Whiskey Ring; that Babcock had evinced fidelity and integrity as regards the public interest, performed his duties as private secretary "to my entire satisfaction"; that "I have always had great confidence in his integrity and efficiency"; and that "I never had any information from Babcock or any one else indicating in any manner, directly or indirectly, that any funds for political purposes were being raised by any improper

the ring escaped punishment altogether. The court stated in advance that any one who pleaded guilty would not be sentenced until all the cases had been disposed of except those who had absconded, and most of the cases were later dismissed. According to a statement given out by the Attorney-General and printed in the *New York Herald*, February 29, 1876, there had been at that time 253 indictments. Of these 40 distillers, 6 distillery employees, and 21 others had pleaded guilty. There had been 17 trials, resulting in 13 convictions, 3 acquittals and 1 disagreement."

methods." He swore that Babcock never spoke to
him about the charges against the Whiskey Ring,
and had not sought to influence him in any way.
He went with full detail into his own relation to the
investigation; said that if Babcock had been guilty
of misconduct he would have known it. The unprecedented spectacle of the President proffering his
testimony in a case like this, his boldness in coming
forward to defend his secretary, his accepted honesty, had a far-reaching influence, and silenced all
but the most raucous critics. Not through Grant's
testimony, but through the absence of convincing
evidence, Babcock was speedily acquitted.

The "New York Tribune," which up to that moment had been vitriolic in its comments, declaring
that a President with such a complete misconception
of the nature and limitations of his authority "is
better fitted to rule an Asiatic kingdom than a free
American republic," now had to congratulate the
country heartily on the result: "The indictment has
been submitted to the severest legal tests. No one
can complain that the court was biased in General
Babcock's favor, or that the prosecution was inefficient, or that the jury were prepossessed. . . . At the
entrance of the White House, the scandal has been
met and turned back."[1]

---

[1] *New York Tribune*, February 25, 1876.

Babcock was acquitted on February 24. When he returned to Washington he went as usual to his desk. Grant followed him, and the two were closeted for a long time. When Grant came out, his face was set in silence. A little later Babcock locked his desk and left the room. He never came back to the White House as a secretary, and thereafter occupied his other office blocks away as Superintendent of Public Buildings and Grounds. It has been said that Babcock for a time was restored to his old place. That is not true. His intimate relations with the President were not renewed.[1]

Nor did Grant forgive the men whom he believed had tried to bring the White House into the affair. Bristow to his mind was one of these. He had not liked the manner of Bristow's handling of the case, and in the progress of the investigation they had many differences.[2] Bristow was beset with enemies

[1] E. Rockwood Hoar, a hard-headed man and an acute judge of his fellows, knew Grant through and through and believed him strictly and thoroughly honest. "But, do you feel sure," he was asked, "that in all these suspicious transactions no money stuck to his fingers?" With a purposed anachronism to give emphasis to his quaint remark, he replied: "I would as soon think St. Paul had got some of the thirty pieces of silver." (Rhodes, vol. VII, p. 188.)

[2] "As for the President, those who know the most of the secret history of this move are freest to declare that in no instance did he do anything designed by him to protect the guilty or impede the course of justice. That his acts and his delays often accomplished both is now painfully apparent.

"At the same time it is true that whenever the ring, by false

who carried tales to Grant and Grant had critics who
encouraged Bristow. The Secretary more than once
resigned, but was induced by Grant to stay. And
Grant once had made up his mind to ask for Bristow's
resignation. After Babcock's acquittal Bristow was
summoned before the investigating committee of the
Democratic House, looking for material to use in the
political campaign, but he declined to testify, claiming that proceedings of the Cabinet were privileged.
Grant released him promptly: "I beg to relieve you
from all obligations of secrecy on this subject, and
desire not only that you may answer all questions
relating to it, but that all members of my Cabinet
and ex-members of my Cabinet may also be called
upon to testify in regard to the same matter." Grant

representations, had developed serious Executive opposition to
some feature of the prosecutions, or excited suspicion against the
Secretary, the latter, until a late day, was always able to remove
both, and disconcert the ring by a plain and courageous talk with
the President. On these occasions General Grant always inclined
to the right. But the constant recurrence of such explanations,
and the infamous character of the plottings which made them
necessary, continually impeded the prosecutions and discouraged
the Secretary. It is also true that on several occasions when he
had decided to resign, the President insisted upon his remaining,
and for a time thereafter the contingency of a resignation for such
causes seemed to render the President alive to the situation.

" Considering the nature and influence of the forces arrayed
against the Secretary, and the facilities they enjoyed for constant
access to the President, it is scarcely a matter of wonder that at
times his eyes were blinded and his deepest prejudices aroused."
(Henry V. Boynton in *North American Review*, October, 1876.)

was angry, too, because the Treasury sought to indict Logan, against whom there was no evidence, and to discredit others of his friends who were supposed to be in favor of a third term. Four days after the Cincinnati Convention, Bristow walked over to the White House, met the President at the foot of the stairs leading to the Executive offices, took from his pocket an envelope and handed it to Grant, who went his way without a word, entered his buggy at the door and took his usual drive. It was Bristow's resignation. A few days later Grant asked Postmaster-General Jewell to resign. He had sided strongly with Bristow all the time, and had had other differences with his official chief. The next day James N. Tyner, the Assistant Postmaster-General, was summoned to the White House. "Mr. Tyner," said the President, "I have decided to ask you for your resignation,"— and paused. Tyner reddened to the neck and bowed submissively. "And appoint you Postmaster-General," continued Grant.

The Democratic House elected in 1874 had set itself to work as soon as possible to get political material for the campaign then near at hand, which promised to be closely fought. Almost at once, when Congress met, the House began to poke around for scandal. Committees were soon raking every bureau of administration for evidence of those Republican misdeeds concerning which the press had been so clamorous.[1] They had comparatively little time for ordinary legislation. After weeks of unrequited labor, one of the committees investigating expenditures in the War Department fell on the Belknap case. The Belknaps had been socially ambitious and the women of the family were extravagant. The Secretary had no money and his salary was small. His wife in trying to devise new means of income was told of the post traderships, which had for years been let by contract to favored bidders, and offered generous rewards to thrift. Belknap, who became Secretary after Rawlins, had not been in office long when Mrs. Belknap, visiting the New York house of Caleb P. Marsh, suggested that Marsh apply for a post tradership and give to her a share of the emoluments. Marsh made application for a rich post at Fort Sill, in Indian Territory, and was told to see the incumbent Evans,

[1] " Members of both parties have been represented in every great fraud yet discovered in Washington. The old Indian Ring of the days when Democracy ruled eclipsed all later efforts of Republican thieves. The palmy days of the Whiskey Ring were in Andrew Johnson's time; for then the spirit tax was higher. Crédit Mobilier had its Democratic participators; so of Black Friday and Pacific Mail; so of the District Ring; so of land jobs; and so of the Memphis and El Paso swindle. It was even impossible for Republican rascals to shake off Democrats when they came to rob the black man's savings-bank." (Henry V. Boynton in *North American Review*, October, 1876.)

who was then in Washington looking to keep the place. The two agreed that Marsh should not press for the position, but should receive from Evans as the price of his withdrawal $12,000 annually, to be paid him quarterly in advance. Payments began in 1870, and as each arrived one half was sent to Mrs. Belknap. There was no certain evidence that Belknap knew about the deal. It was said in his defense that he supposed the money to be income on investments, as his wife was understood to have some property before she married him. Mrs. Belknap died, and payments were continued as before, although they were reduced by half as Marsh's dividends from Evans were cut in two. In all, the Belknaps received $20,000. Heister Clymer, as chairman of the Committee on Expenditures in the War Department, reported on March 2, 1876, that at "the very threshold of their investigation" the committee had found uncontradicted evidence of Belknap's malfeasance, and recommended that he be impeached of high crimes and misdemeanors while in office. The House at once adopted a resolution of impeachment by a unanimous vote.

Clymer's report was not presented until three o'clock that afternoon, but by ten o'clock that morning Belknap, anticipating what would happen, had resigned his place, and Grant immediately accepted

the resignation "with great regret." Proceedings in
the Senate hung on till August, and conviction failed
for lack of a two-thirds majority. Most of those who
voted against conviction were said to have believed
in Belknap's guilt, but as he was already separated
from his office, doubted the Senate's jurisdiction in
the case. Belknap took up his residence in Washington, and though in disgrace and poverty, he retained
his personal popularity until his death. There still
lurks around the Capital a tale of knightly sacrifice
to save a woman's name.

When Cox resigned as Secretary of the Interior,
because he thought the President did not sustain
him in his fight against the politicians bent on spoils,
Grant said the trouble was that Cox had made himself impossible, because he thought himself of too
great consequence.[1] Columbus Delano, who took the
place, was an Ohio lawyer of good repute at home, but
lacking in the quality to circumvent the schemers
who from the establishment of the department have
sought its exploitation for pecuniary gain. Indian
rings and land rings reveled in his administration,
much to the public scandal, and at last, discouraged

[1] "The trouble was that General Cox thought the Interior
Department was the whole government, and that Cox was the
Interior Department. I had to point out to him in very plain
language that there were three controlling branches of the Government, and that I was the head of one of these and would like so to
be considered by the Secretary of the Interior." (Garland, p. 427.)

by his inability to handle his accumulating evils, he resigned. Chandler, of Michigan, had just been beaten for the Senate, and Grant gave him the place. Chandler did not stand well with the professional reformers, and they received the tidings with alarm. Some thought it meant the triumph of corruption, for Chandler, always forceful and direct, had bitterly denounced "reform" and treated its apostles with contempt. He was a Stalwart to the marrow, and a Republican of the unbending type, a sturdy Western pioneer, who had had a striking business success. He believed in spoils and patronage and all the ways of politics which men like Schurz and Godkin specially abhorred, but his administration stands as an example of effectiveness which none of his successors has surpassed. He drove the money-changers out of the department, squelched the rings, and cleaned the place where public plunder had intrenched itself for many years. He gave a new exemplification of practical reform.[1]

Grant was one of the few Presidents to whom has fallen the impressive responsibility of selecting a Chief Justice of the Supreme Court of the United

[1] Schurz in succeeding him was impelled to write: " I think I am expressing the general opinion of the country when I say you have succeeded in placing the Interior Department in far better condition than it has been in for years, and that the public is indebted to you for the very energetic and successful work you have performed." (*Life of Chandler*, p. 355.)

States. When the chance came to him upon the death of Chase in 1873, he went at it as if he were called upon to pick a chief of staff. It must be said that in this temper he did not differ much from other Presidents whose antecedents should have given them respect for the great functions of the court, but who for personal or party reasons have chosen justices without considering first of all preëminence on the bench or at the bar. The highest service done their country by Taft and Harrison was in the way of their upholding the noblest standards of the court. No poorer service can be done by any President than to lower that court's prestige; one who would consciously force on the bench a lawyer who, whether justly or unjustly had been charged with unprofessional practices, would thus prove his own unfitness for his place.

Grant was a layman with no pretensions in the law, and so might be excused some lack of sympathy with its traditions. Yet his selections for the bench were on the whole of a high order. Stanton, Hoar, Bradley, Strong, and Hunt were thoroughly equipped in legal knowledge for the court, and all but Stanton had a fine judicial temper. Stanton was named because the Senate asked for his appointment when he was at the point of death. Hoar, though an ideal judge at every point, was turned

]own by the Senate in a pet. In each case, though
in different ways, the Senate made of lawyers had
treated lightly the traditions of the court. Why then
should Grant hold it in greater sanctity?

His first choice fell on Conkling, his closest friend
in politics, who had ability commensurate with the
place and might have taken rank among the noted
jurists of the time, not only as a lawyer, but in the
dignity of bearing which marked him as a leader in his
State and on the Senate floor. Conkling was lordly
in his ways, and supercilious, which told against his
popularity, a lover of good books who packed the
classics in a capacious memory, an orator tremen-
dously imposing in his way, whose speeches, carefully
elaborated and rehearsed, have not survived the fame
of their occasion. He was a Stalwart politician with
no illusions or fine dreams, a firm believer in the doctrine of the spoils, and a past master in its practice.

He had, by his frank detestation of reformers and
reform, roused the hostility of the independent press,
and when word passed that Grant would like to have
him as Chief Justice, a storm of censure fell upon
Grant's head. Conkling refused the place because he
much preferred the fray of politics. He was still
young and had no wish to shrine himself upon the
bench. Then Grant, for lack of something better
close at hand, offered the place to George H. Wil-

liams, his Attorney-General. Williams, who hailed
from Oregon, had little reputation as a lawyer, and
had acquired the sobriquet of "Landaulet" because
his family made social calls in a department carriage
at the Government's expense. The Bar Association
of New York remonstrated against his confirmation,
as he was "wanting in those qualifications of intellect, experience, and reputation which are indispensable to uphold the dignity of the highest national
court." The Senate dallied with the nomination,
which was withdrawn at Williams's request.

Then Grant sent in the name of Caleb Cushing, a
learned lawyer who had fame at the bar and in diplomacy and who had been the leading counsel of the
United States in the Geneva Arbitration. But with
all his intellectual astuteness, wide culture, and plaus-
ibility, Cushing's political and professional record
was at fault. He had been listed as a Copperhead at
the beginning of the war, and his professional probity
was seriously in question, though Grant did not know
this when he sent in his name. Among right-thinking
men he was condemned, as Howe and Hamlin wrote,
"because he lacked principle." For this reason, the
nomination would have been rejected if it had been
kept before the Senate, but Grant's supporters spared
him this rebuff by offering in evidence a letter which
Cushing wrote in March, 1861, to his "dear friend"

Jefferson Davis to recommend another friend for an appointment in the Confederate Civil Service. Giving this letter as an excuse, the Senate Republicans in caucus asked that the nomination be withdrawn, and this was done. Cushing's is almost the only case in the entire history of the court where the professional integrity of a nominee to that tribunal has been in question. Even to have the question raised should be sufficient reason to disqualify; for confirmation by a partisan majority cannot remove the stain; and one who takes his place upon the bench in face of charges not disproved shows himself by that act alone to be unworthy of the gown. Grant tried again for Conkling, but without success, and then named Morrison R. Waite, a little-known Ohio lawyer, whose only national repute had come from service among the counsel before the Geneva Tribunal. Waite was a modest man who stood well at the Ohio bar. He was not open to objection. His fourteen years of service as Chief Justice reflected credit on the court and fully justified his choice.

CHAPTER XLIV

THE DISPUTED ELECTION OF 1876

As the time drew near for choosing a new President, parties began to take account of stock. Grant, though the target for sustained abuse by the Democratic and the independent press, still stood high in the estimation of the people, and there was talk about another term. The faults of his Administration had been overemphasized, but the public was not fooled, though in the way of politics men looked for change. They had not been enamored of the Democratic House with which they had been saddled as the price of discontent. Its muck-raking propensities, its petty scramble for cheap spoils, its parade of party spawn like Doorkeeper Fitzhugh, boasting that he was "biger than old Grant," had made it something of a stench and failed to whet the country's appetite for more. But industry was paralyzed and times were out of joint.

Stalwart Republicans like Conkling, Cameron, and Logan felt that, while the party had lost ground, talk of a third term for Grant would keep the ranks intact. But Grant was tired of controversy and wanted to retire. Early in 1875 the Pennsylvania

Republicans were ready to endorse him for another term, and the President of their convention wrote him so. He made up his mind at once, called a meeting of the Cabinet to tell them what he was going to do, and mailed personally a letter in reply declaring:

"The idea that any man could elect himself President, or even renominate himself, is preposterous. Any man can destroy his chances for an office, but none can force an election or even a nomination. I am not nor have I ever been a candidate for renomination. I would not accept a nomination if it were tendered, unless it should come under such circumstances as to make it an imperative duty — circumstances not likely to arise."

The censorious said there was a string to this refusal, but it did the work.[1] Before the meeting of the National Republican Convention in June, 1876, the third-term talk had died away.

Blaine, the most fascinating figure of the day, out of touch with the Administration group, was mar-

[1] So persistent did the pressure become as time went on that, when Congress came together in December, a resolution in the House, presented by the Democrats and supported by 77 out of 88 Republicans, was passed as follows: " That, in the opinion of this House, the precedent established by Washington and other Presidents of the United States, in retiring from the presidential office after their second term, has become, by universal occurrence, a part of our republican system of government, and that any departure from this time-honored custom would be unwise, unpatriotic, and fraught with peril to our free institutions."

velously popular, but there were whispers that as
Speaker he had been involved in questionable deals,
and in spite of all he and his friends could say this
led to his undoing. Conkling and Morton had their
followers and each hoped for Grant's support, but
he kept his hands off the convention. He had a secret
notion that in case of a close struggle Fish was a likely
compromise, and he wrote a letter to be used if Fish
should have a chance.[1] Bristow was a strong favorite
with the reformers. They could not stand with any
one who stood with Grant, but they were equally at
odds with Blaine. Hayes was the Ohio candidate —
a man of unassuming merit with a record in the Civil

[1] "I took no part in the discussions antecedent to the Cincinnati
Convention, because the candidates were friends, and any one,
except Mr. Bristow, would have been satisfactory to me, would
have had my heartiest support. Bristow I never would have supported for reasons that I may give at some other time in a more
formal manner than mere conversation. Mr. Blaine would have
made a good President. . . . I did not see any nomination for
Blaine, Morton, or Conkling. Bristow was never a serious candidate, never even a probability. Looking around for a dark horse,
in my own mind I fixed on Fish. Bayard Taylor said to me in
Berlin that the three greatest statesmen of this age were Cavour,
Gortchakoff, and Bismarck. I told him I thought there were four,
that the fourth was Fish, and that he was worthy to rank with the
others. This was the estimate I formed of Fish after eight years of
Cabinet service, in which every year increased him in my esteem.
So I wrote a letter to be used at the proper time — after the
chances of Blaine, Morton, and Conkling were exhausted — expressing my belief that the nomination of Governor Fish would be
a wise thing for the party. The time never came to use it. Fish
never knew anything about this letter until after the whole convention was over." (Young, vol. II, pp. 273–75.)

War, who in 1874 had led the fight against inflation. in his State, defeating "Fog Horn" Allen, Democratic candidate for Governor, thus for the time eliminating that financial heresy from the Democratic creed. There were other "favorite sons."

There is little doubt that Blaine would have been chosen but for a chain of circumstances which need not be detailed. The deadly enmity of Conkling and the dramatic series of disclosures skillfully staged to catch the public notice as the convention was about to meet make a rare chapter in the history of the time. Not even Conkling's hatred or the work of the machine could have defeated him had it not been for the pervasive dread that he might prove a vulnerable candidate. The elements opposed to Blaine at last combined on Hayes, and on the seventh ballot Hayes was nominated. No other name could have been found to cause so little disappointment among the friends of rival candidates, and when the Democrats a few days later named Tilden, who had been elected Governor of New York in 1874, there was a feeling that the lines were drawn for a respectable campaign. "There is very little to choose between the candidates," wrote Lowell, and many Liberal Republicans came back into the fold.[1]

[1] Henry Watterson has given us a charming picture of the Democratic candidate, who was his personal friend: —

"To his familiars, Mr. Tilden was a dear old bachelor, who lived

But the contest developed virulence. The Democrats were voluble against Republican misrule. "Reform is necessary!" was their cry, and ."Turn the
Rascals out!" Their platform called for the repeal of
the Resumption Act, but Tilden was regarded as a
friend of sound finance. The Republicans, deprived
of the inflation issue on which they counted, began to
"wave the bloody shirt" and to point the finger at
the "Rebel Brigadiers" who, through "bull-dozing"
and intimidation, they said, were conspiring to return
to national control by joining to a "Solid South" the
slums of the great cities of the North. Tilden had
made false income tax returns during the Civil War;
he was the first of presidential candidates to "tap
a bar'l" or employ a "literary bureau." Zachariah

in a fine old mansion in Gramercy Park. Though sixty years of age
he seemed in the prime of his manhood; a genial and overflowing
scholar; a trained and earnest doctrinaire; a public-spirited, patriotic citizen, well known and highly esteemed, who had made
fame and fortune at the bar, and had always been interested in
public affairs.

"He was a dreamer with a genius for business, a philosopher yet
an organizer. He pursued the tenor of his life with measured tread.
. . . His home life was a model of order and decorum, his house
as unchallenged as a bishopric, its hospitality, though select, profuse
and untiring. . . . He was a lover of books rather than music and
art, but also of horses and dogs and out-of-door activity. His
tastes were frugal, and their indulgence was sparing. He took his
wine not plenteously, though he enjoyed it . . . and sipped his
whiskey and water on occasion with a pleased composure, redolent
of discursive talk. . . . His judgment was believed to be infalli-
ble." (*Century*, May, 1913.)

Chandler was chairman of the committee in charge of the Republican campaign and William E. Chandler, who had been secretary in the two preceding campaigns, was now, as a member of the Committee from New Hampshire, specially assisting him — two brainy and courageous managers, who knew no sentiment in politics except success, and who, while representative of different Republican schools, were both intensely loyal in the party faith. Abram S. Hewitt was the Democratic chairman, but Tilden was himself a deft political manipulator and really handled the campaign.

It looked on Election night as though the Democrats had won, and with two conspicuous exceptions, every newspaper in the United States made that announcement, basing this judgment on the fact that Tilden had carried New York, New Jersey, Connecticut, and Indiana, and the assumption that he had the "Solid South," which would have given him a safe majority. And now there comes a passage in our history hardly surpassed in fiction.

William E. Chandler, who had gone home to vote, arrived at headquarters in the Fifth Avenue Hotel just before daylight to find the place deserted, the other officers of the committee having gone to bed convinced that Hayes had lost. He met there John C. Reid, news editor of the "New York Times," with information that the late returns bore indications of possible Republican success, and by a process of swift calculation perceived that the result depended on the votes of Florida, Louisiana, South Carolina, Oregon, and California. He sent at once to party leaders in each State dispatches of which the following is typical: "Hayes is elected if we have carried South Carolina, Florida and Louisiana. Can you hold your State? Answer immediately."

Here began a controversy which put our form of government to a crucial test. Zachariah Chandler later in the morning endorsed the action of the younger Chandler, announcing that "if the dispatches are correct, and he has no reason to doubt them, Governor Hayes is elected beyond a doubt," and a dispatch was sent broadcast which has become historic: "Hayes has 185 electoral votes and is elected." [1]

[1] "On election day in the afternoon I went from Concord to Boston and on to New York by night train, reaching the Fifth Avenue Hotel a little before complete daylight. Mr. Vilas at the clerk's desk told me that Tilden was elected. I said I could not believe it and went around to the committee room No. 1. There was no one there. In the hallway I met John C. Reid, of the *New York Times*, just arriving. He told me that if we had carried South Carolina and Florida, also one or two small far Western States, we had saved the election. We went into the committee room, I examined the various dispatches on the deserted desks and then went up to Senator Chandler's room and with difficulty aroused him from sleep and told him what we hoped, and asked him if he knew to whom he had been telegraphing in several

There were days of great excitement, claims and counter-claims. Hayes must have all the votes of the disputed States to win. It was known almost at once that Oregon and California were safe, and that South Carolina was Republican on the face of the returns. As Chamberlain, the Governor, was candidate for reëlection, it was assumed that in that State there would be no change. Chamberlain, remembering the "Hamburg Massacre" and fearing election riots, had asked for troops. Grant had sent them, and they were now at the state capital.[1]

States the night before. He was very weary and gave me little information and told me to do what I thought best. Returning to the committee room I wrote various dispatches, signing to some Mr. Chandler's name and to others my own, and Mr. Reid took them downtown to send by telegraph. Then I went to breakfast and came back to the committee room about the time that various callers began to arrive and shortly Mr. Chandler came down. We discussed the situation and he sent out his famous telegram, 'Hayes has 185 votes and is elected.' Our spirits arose during the day, and in the afternoon there was a consultation as to what should be done. Among other plans adopted it was decided that I must go south." (Statement by William E. Chandler, hitherto unpublished.)

[1] "In no case, except that of South Carolina, was the number of soldiers in any State increased in anticipation of the election, saving that twenty-four men and an officer were sent from Fort Foote to Petersburg, Virginia, where disturbances were threatened prior to the election.

"No troops were stationed at the voting-places. In Florida and in Louisiana, respectively, the small number of soldiers already in the said States were stationed at such points in each State as were most threatened with violence, where they might be available as a posse for the officer whose duty it was to preserve the

On the face of the returns, Tilden had a majority in Louisiana and Hayes in Florida, but "the face of the returns" was an uncertain problem at that juncture, and party leaders on both sides sped South, while those at home awaited the result with tense solicitude.

On Grant rested the responsibility for keeping peace. He did not wait for violence to develop. On November 10, three days after the election, he sent to Sherman, the General of the Army, this dispatch: "Instruct General Augur in Louisiana, and General Ruger in Florida, to be vigilant with the force at their command to preserve peace and good order, and to see that the proper and legal boards of canvassers are unmolested in the performance of their duties. Should there be any grounds of suspicion of a fraudulent count on either side, it should be reported and denounced at once. No man worthy of the office of President should be willing to hold it if counted in or placed there by fraud. Either party can afford to be disappointed in the result. The country cannot afford to have the result tainted by the suspicion of illegal or false returns."

peace and prevent intimidation of voters. Such a disposition of the troops seemed to me reasonable and justified by law and precedent, while its omission would have been inconsistent with the constitutional duty of the President of the United States ' to take care that the laws be faithfully executed.'" (Richardson, *Messages and Papers*, vol. VII, pp. 419–20.)

On the face of the returns it appeared that Florida had gone for Hayes by a plurality of 48 votes, a narrow margin, which the Board of State Canvassers increased into a plurality of 925 on the ground of frauds and irregularities. Only by leaning backward could the Republican board have given the State to Tilden. The real contention was in Louisiana, where on the face of the returns, the Democratic electors had majorities ranging from 6300 to 8957, and where the returning board, having the final word, was the same board which made the trouble in 1874 and had been condemned by two congressional committees.

The chairman was J. Madison Wells, the former Governor, whom Sheridan had characterized ten years before as a political trickster and a dishonest man. The three other members of the board were of his moral stripe; and two of them were negroes. All were Republicans, the only Democrat having resigned two years before, leaving a vacancy which had not been filled. With such material, almost any result might be expected, and the country centered its attention on New Orleans. "Visiting Statesmen" were quickly on the ground, Grant having invited prominent Republicans like Sherman, Garfield, Kasson, Stanley Matthews, and Lew Wallace, while Hewitt asked as many Democrats, among them Palmer, Trumbull, Randall, Curtis, Julian, and

Watterson. Committees of these "Visiting Statesmen" attended the meetings of the returning board
and on December 6, the board announced that Hayes
electors had been chosen by majorities varying from
4626 to 4712, securing this result by throwing out
13,250 Democratic votes and 2042 Republican. The
final sessions of the board were held in secret and it
was claimed by Hewitt that Wells and his associates
tried to sell out to the Democrats for cash. No evidence was ever offered. A number of the Republican "Visiting Statesmen" on the day of the return
signed a statement which was sent to Grant giving
the names of parishes along the Mississippi and
Arkansas border where outrages had been per-
petrated and where, "when violence and intimidation were inefficient, murder, maiming, and mutila-
tion were resorted to." The Democratic statesmen
signed a letter to Hewitt, in which they said, "The
fact that there was no riot or bloodshed in any local-
ity, no force, intimidation, or violence in any parish
in Louisiana where both parties voted, gives strong
presumption that there was no valid excuse for the
Republican voters in absenting themselves from the
polls, but they were purposely kept away to subserve
partisan ends." Of the Democratic "Visiting Statesmen" Palmer, Trumbull, and Julian were formerly
Republicans. "New converts are proverbially bitter

·and unfair towards those they have recently left," remarks John Sherman.

In a letter to Hayes just prior to the determination by the returning board, Sherman had written of the bull-dozed parishes: "It seems more like the history of hell than of civilized and Christian communities. . . . That you would have received at a fair election a large majority in Louisiana, no honest man can question."[1]

When the electors came to ballot in the several States on December 6, two days after Congress met, Hayes had 185 duly authenticated votes, Tilden 184. The Democrats protested that the four votes from Florida and the eight from Louisiana rightfully belonged to Tilden. They also claimed one from Oregon, where a Republican elector, Watts, was held to be ineligible under the Constitution, being a deputy postmaster. If this claim were granted, Tilden would still have 185 votes even though the two Southern States were credited to Hayes.

Had both branches of Congress been Republican the contest would have ended here, and Hayes would have been declared elected in due course, perhaps with oratorical objection on the part of the minority. But the Senate, Republican by a majority of 17, was offset by a Democratic House with a majority of 74.

[1] *Recollections*, p. 558.

The Constitution and the statutes were inadequate to meet this situation. Republicans, among them Hayes himself, contended that when the Constitution said, "The President of the Senate shall, in the presence of the Senate and the House of Representatives, open all the certificates and the votes shall then be counted," it implied that when there were two certificates from a State, the President of the Senate must decide which one was valid, count the votes and declare the result; that it was a mere ministerial duty; and that Congress had no right to interfere.

But there had been adopted in 1865 a joint rule providing that "No vote objected to shall be counted except by the concurrent votes of the two Houses." The rule had been rescinded by the Senate almost unanimously, and it was not now regarded by the Senate as in force. Should the House, insisting on the rule, reject the votes of Florida and Louisiana, Tilden would have a majority. The Senate could not retaliate by rejecting votes of other Southern States, because, in that event, there would be no election and the Democratic House would then proceed under the Constitution to elect Tilden in a vote by States.

There seemed to be no common ground. Republicans throughout the country, with few exceptions, believed that whatever might be the technicalities about returning boards, Hayes was entitled to the office, because if there had been a fair election he would undoubtedly have carried all the disputed States with others in the South. The Democrats were even more vehement in contending that they had chosen the electors in Florida and Louisiana and made much also of the undisputed but irrelevant circumstance that throughout the country Tilden electors had received a majority of 300,000 in the popular vote.

There was wild talk by frenzied partisans; all sorts of tales had currency; it was said that Grant aspired to dictatorial power. There were reports of Southern rifle clubs to march on Washington to help seat Tilden; and Tilden "minute men" were said to be enrolling through the North — an Army of Democratic veterans of the Civil War. Any mad story, no matter how impossible, was sure to have its dupes, and there was need of a firm hand in Washington. Grant was self-contained and imperturbable. He used all his influence to bring the embittered factions into line, and so insure a peaceful settlement of the dispute.

McCrary, of Iowa, who afterwards was made by Hayes a member of the Cabinet, introduced a resolution in the House for a committee to act in conjunction with any similar committee appointed by the Senate to report without delay a measure through which might be removed "all doubts and uncertainty" as to the manner of determining questions as to the legality and validity of returns, "to the end that the votes may be counted and the result declared by a tribunal whose authority none can question and whose decision all will accept as final."[1]

Grant knew about this resolution in advance and summoning Hewitt to the White House secured his acquiescence in the compromise, which promptly passed both House and Senate without debate. Edmunds was chairman for the Senate, Henry B. Payne, of Ohio, for the House.

The committees unanimously reported a bill for an Electoral Commission, to be composed of five Senators, five members of the House, and four Justices of the Supreme Court, who were to choose another Justice of the Court, thus making a commission of fifteen. The bill provided that "No electoral vote or votes from any State from which but one return has been received shall be rejected except by the affirmative vote of the two Houses." In the case of States from which there was more than one return "all such returns and papers should be submitted to the judgment and decision, as to which is the true and lawful electoral vote of such State," of the Electoral Commission. The decision of the Commission

[1] Haworth, *The Hayes-Tilden Disputed Election*, p. 190.

could be overthrown only by the concurrence of both Houses acting separately.

Edmunds, Conkling, and Thurman delivered arguments for the bill which take high rank. Morton, Blaine, and Sherman antagonized it. They said it was unconstitutional, but their real reason was the fear that it would work unfavorably to Hayes. The bill was carried in both branches by Democratic votes; 26 Democrats and 21 Republicans voted for it in the Senate, 16 Republicans and one Democrat against. In the House the ayes were 159 Democrats and 32 Republicans; the noes were 18 Democrats and 68 Republicans. It was expected by both parties that the Commission would be more likely to favor Tilden than Hayes.

On January 29, Grant signed the bill and at the same time sent a virile message announcing his approval. "It is the highest duty of the lawmaking power," he said, "to provide in advance a constitutional, orderly, and just method of executing the Constitution in this most interesting and critical of its provisions. . . . It must be that one of the two candidates has been elected; and it would be deplorable to witness an irregular controversy as to which of the two should receive or which should continue to hold the office. . . . The country is agitated. It needs and it desires peace and quiet and harmony between all parties' and all sections. Its industries are arrested, labor unemployed, capital idle, and enterprise paralyzed by reason of the doubt and anxiety attending the uncertainty of a double claim to the Chief Magistracy of the Nation. It wants to be assured that the result of the election will be accepted without resistance from the supporters of the disappointed candidate, and that its highest officer shall not hold his place with a questioned title of right."

During these strenuous days, when history was in the making and his own future with his country's was at stake, Tilden withdrew himself into his cloistered sanctuary in Gramercy Park, feebly and stealthily whispering now and then a futile scheme. While others struggled with the tremendous problem, he "devoted more than a month to the preparation of a complete history of the electoral counts from the foundation of the Government, to show it to have been the unbroken usage of Congress, not of the President of the Senate, to count the electoral votes," a work which could have been prepared almost as well by a skilled lawyer's clerk.[1] He was inadequate to a great opportunity, and had he been made President would have been a weak executive, of the Buchanan type.

[1] Bigelow, *Life of Tilden.*

The Democrats in Congress were fated to a cruel disappointment. The Justices of the Supreme Court indicated in the bill were Clifford, Strong, Miller, and Field, representing four great geographical divisions, and equally divided in their political beliefs. It was agreed that they would choose as the fifth Justice, David Davis, who had once been a Republican, but who had wavered in the faith; but at the last minute, just before the bill was laid before the House, word came from Illinois, where the Legislature had been for weeks in deadlock over a second term for Logan in the Senate, that the Democrats had joined the independents and elected Davis. Thus he was barred. The four Justices selected Bradley in his stead, a jurist with a delicate sense of honor, and of singularly fine grain.

The Senate chose as members of the Commission Edmunds, Morton, Frelinghuysen, Thurman, and Bayard; the House, Payne, Hunton, Abbott, Hoar, and Garfield. When the joint session met on February 1, all went smoothly till Florida was reached, with three certificates, and on objection that case went to the Electoral Commission which held its sessions in the room of the Supreme Court. Here was to be a precedent for all the other cases. Could the Commission go back of the returns? After a week of arguments and secret sessions, the Commission held

that it could not. The interest in Bradley's opinion
was intense. Later he wrote that it "expressed the
honest conclusion to which I had arrived, and which,
after a full consideration of the whole matter, seemed
to me the only satisfactory conclusion of the question." "It seems to me," he said, "that the two
Houses of Congress, in proceeding with the count,
are bound to recognize the determination of the State
Board of Canvassers as the act of the State and as
the most authentic evidence of the appointment
made by the State; and that while they may go behind the Governor's certificate, if necessary, they can
only do so for the purpose of ascertaining whether
he has truly certified the results to which the board
arrived. They cannot sit as a court of appeals on
the action of that board."

The decision of the Commission was reported to
the joint session. The Senate retired to its chamber
and ratified the decision; the House refused ratification, and by the terms of the act creating the Commission, the two Houses not having concurred in
overthrowing its decision, the decision stood. There
were similar proceedings with regard to Louisiana,
Oregon, and South Carolina. The Democrats became more angry, as the count progressed from
day to day. They were convinced that they were
being swindled out of what was fairly theirs, and

blindly reaching for a victim of their wrath, they hit
on Justice Bradley and rained denunciation on his
head. For a time he was the most detested man in
the United States. One would have thought that he
had sought this opportunity to perpetrate a fraud,
instead of shrinking from the lot that fell to him. No
graver instance of injustice could have been conceived. The cabalistic number 8 to 7 was bandied
back and forth and Bradley's name became a byword
and reproach.

Yet Bradley was merely one of a tribunal. There
was no better reason for upbraiding him than for
denouncing Strong and Miller, his associates. He
was not chosen as the umpire; he was an individual
member of the Commission clothed with the same
responsibility as the rest — a responsibility which he
had looked forward to with dread. Besides, there is
good ground for the belief that Davis would have
done as he did in his place.[1]

Sixty Democratic Representatives, most of them
from the North and West, tried by a filibuster to delay

[1] " The day after the inauguration of Hayes, my kinsman Stanley Matthews said to me, ' You people wanted Judge Davis. So
did we. I will tell you what I know, that Judge Davis was safe for
us as Judge Bradley. We preferred him because he carried more
weight.' The subsequent career of Judge Davis in the Senate
gives conclusive proof that this was true." (Henry Watterson,
" The Hayes-Tilden Contest for the Presidency," in the *Century*
for May, 1913.)

the count until March 4, when Congress would expire
by limitation, leaving the Presidency hanging in the
air. But as soon as the Florida decision foreshadowed
the result, 42 Southern Democrats "solemnly pledged
themselves to each other upon their sacred honor to
oppose all attempts to frustrate the counting of the
votes for President." Speaker Randall, with patriotic
firmness, held the House in hand till, at the close of
an all-night session, at four o'clock in the morning of
March 2, the count was finished and the President
pro tempore declared Hayes elected.

The 4th of March was Sunday, and to save further
complications Hayes was quietly sworn in that day
by Chief Justice Waite, with Grant and Fish as witnesses. On Monday he was formally inaugurated as
peacefully as though there had been no controversy.
Grant rode to the Capitol by his side.

There is no doubt the country as a whole believed
that Tilden should have been declared elected; the
question will always be open to dispute. The North
had tired of talk about intimidation in the South and
were beginning to lose all interest in the negro now
that it was found that he could not exercise without
support the right of suffrage which had been imposed
upon him. The violence and fraud in the back parishes of Louisiana were only vaguely pictured in the
public consciousness, while the fact of throwing out

13,000 Democratic votes by the returning board was obvious to all. There is no reasonable doubt that, with a fair election, more Southern States than those finally accorded him would have been carried for Hayes, and it is not forgotten that the South, by reason of increased representation due to the suppressed negro vote, had 35 votes in the Electoral College with which to overcome Republican majorities in Northern States. There was great clamor at the time and for years after about a "stolen Presidency," and Hayes is thought by many fair-minded men to-day to have been a fraudulent incumbent; but with strict accuracy it must be said that he was legally elected. If there was "stealing," it was not in Washington. If the Electoral Commission, for which the Democrats were willing at the time of its creation to accept responsibility, by its decision made it possible for Congress to count the contesting Democratic electors, there would have been no talk of fraud. Yet there is no fair ground for saying that the minority of the Commission were right, and the majority wrong. It happened that all voted along party lines. If there was "stealing," it must have been in Florida and Louisiana, and in the multitude of testimony it will always remain a question there as to who committed the first theft.

Before the count of electoral votes had been completed, Ohio friends of Hayes, perhaps without his knowledge, had told Southern Democrats that after his nomination he would not continue military intervention in the South, but this assurance had no bearing on the ultimate result.[1] Hayes had hardly taken his seat before he sent for Chamberlain and Wade Hampton, who had set up rival governments in South Carolina, and with the consent of both withdrew the federal troops from the state capital, leaving the Hampton Government in control.

In Louisiana, where Packard and Nicholls were still contesting the governorship and where Packard had made a better showing in the returns than Hayes, the troops were also withdrawn, and the Nicholls Government, representing white supremacy, assumed control of state affairs. Grant, just before he went out of office, had been appealed to by the Packard Government, but had replied that public opinion in the North would no longer tolerate military interference.[2]

[1] The Wormley Conference.

[2]   EXECUTIVE MANSION,
                          WASHINGTON, D.C., March 1, 1877.

To Gov. S. B. Packard,
       New Orleans, La.: —

In answer to your dispatch of this date, the President directs me to say that he feels it his duty to state frankly that he does not believe public opinion will longer support the maintenance of the State Government in Louisiana by the use of the military, and that he must concur in this manifest feeling. The troops will hereafter, as in the past, protect life and property from mob vio-

The time had manifestly come for the new order in the South, which has ever since prevailed.

Grant's attitude throughout this time of general upheaval had been a powerful factor in preserving peace, and helping a harmonious solution. To him is due a great share of credit for creating the Electoral Commission and assuring acquiescence in the result.[1]

lence when the State authorities fail, but during the remaining days of his official life they will not be used to establish or to pull down either claimant for control of the State. It is not his purpose to recognize either claimant.

C. C. SNIFFEN, *Secretary*.

[1] George W. Childs tells in his recollections how Grant sent for him in Washington and said: "I have spoken of an Electoral Commission, and the leaders of the party are opposed to it, which I am sorry to see. They say that if an Electoral Commission is appointed you might as well count in Mr. Tilden. I would sooner have Mr. Tilden than that the Republicans should have a President who could be stigmatized as a fraud. If I were Mr. Hayes I would not have it unless it was settled in some way outside the Senate. This matter is opposed by the leading Republicans in the House and Senate and throughout the country." . . . I named a leading Democrat in the House, . . . whom it would be well for General Grant to see in the matter, and the suggestion was acted on. I sent for this gentleman to come to the White House, and put the dilemma to him in President Grant's name. . . .

The answer at once was that the Democrats would favor it; and it was through that gentleman and General Grant that the matter was carried through. He sent for Mr. Conkling and said, with deep earnestness: "This matter is a serious one, and the people feel it very deeply. I think this Electoral Commission ought to be appointed." Conkling answered: "Mr. President, Senator Morton (who was then the acknowledged leader of the Senate) is opposed to it and opposed to your efforts: but if you wish the Commission carried I can do it." He said: "I wish it done." Mr. Conkling took hold of the matter and put it through. The

"Nothing could have been wiser than the Electoral Commission," he said a little later, "and nothing could be more unpatriotic than the attempt to impair the title of Mr. Hayes as fraudulent. There was a good deal of cowardice and knavery in that effort. Mr. Hayes is just as much President as any of his predecessors. . . . I never believed there would be a blow, but I had so many warnings that I made all my preparations. . . . I was quite prepared for any contingency. Any outbreak would have been suddenly and summarily stopped. . . . If Tilden was declared elected, I intended to hand him over the reins, and see him peacefully installed. . . . I would not have raised my finger to have put Hayes in, if in so doing I did Tilden the slightest injustice. All I wanted was for the legal powers to declare a President, to keep the machine running, allay the passions of the canvass, and allow the country peace. . . . I felt, personally, that I had been vouchsafed a special deliverance. It was a great blessing to the country. . . . We had peace, and order, and observance of the law, and the world had a new illustration of the dignity and efficiency of the Republic. This we owe to the wisdom and foresight of the men who formed the Electoral Commission, Democrats as well as Republicans."

leading Democrat I have spoken of took the initiative in the House and Mr. Conkling in the Senate.

CHAPTER XLV

THE ADMINISTRATION IN REVIEW

DIVESTED of his rank and office, Grant found himself once more the looming figure of the time, as he had been directly after Appomattox. The venom of attack was dissipated with the disappearance of official power. There was a quick rebound in public sentiment as often happens with a people jealous of those on whom they have conferred supreme authority. There was no more talk of Cæsarism, nepotism, or corruption. The folly of the first was obvious now that the "Cæsar" pictured by the party press was a plain citizen seemingly thankful to return to private life; the silliness of the attacks on nepotism was manifest now that the little flock of office-holding relatives found their petty titles and emoluments at the disposal of a President on whom they had no claim; as for corruption and gift-taking, here was Grant at the close of sixteen years of service in such financial straits that he was puzzled how to get along.

True, he had houses presented by the people, but they were not endowed, and in them he could not afford to live; he had a farm at Gravois, near St. Louis, the site of the Dent homestead, on which he had spent borrowed money and which had never paid; he had used up his salary while President, and though he had a little income from investments, he would have been far better off if he had spent the sixteen years in trade. Those who had been most virulent in their attacks upon him for eight years now felt that they had done him wrong. He was again the idol of his countrymen, who at last could comprehend the merits of an administration, thrown in the shadow for a time by superficial faults. They realized how they had leaned on him during the months when the succession was in doubt, and it began to dawn upon them that the United States during his term as President had held high rank, that there had never been a period in our history when an American citizen could count so surely on worldwide respect, and that we now stood higher in the world's regard than at any other moment since the Government began.

No President ever had a firmer or more consistent foreign policy than Grant. Fish is entitled to all the credit which belongs to him and which Grant himself was always generous to bestow, but Fish alone could not have carried through the diplomatic triumphs which shed on Grant's Administration their resplendency. Fish was far-seeing, firm, and sensible, but he would have been quite futile without Grant. It was the steady backing of the White House that made it possible for Fish to carry through his foreign policy, and in most instances the programme was as truly Grant's as his.

A case in point is the Virginius incident early in the second term, which might have brought on war with Spain if badly managed, but which was handled with such firmness and discretion that without war we won in our contention and held our national respect. The Virginius was an American-built steamer which for some years had been employed at intervals in landing military expeditions to aid the Cuban insurrection. On October 31, 1873, while bound from Kingston in Jamaica to a Cuban port, flying our flag but carrying war material, it was captured by a Spanish man-of-war and taken into Santiago. She had on board one hundred and fifty-five passengers and crew, most of them Cubans planning to join the insurrection, but some of them citizens of the United States. Early in November fifty-three of the passengers and crew were sentenced by court martial and shot, among them eight of our citizens. "If it prove that an American citizen has been wrongfully executed, this Government will require most ample reparation," Fish promptly cabled Sickles, our Minister to Spain. Castelar, the Spanish President, at once and no doubt with sincerity expressed regret.

The country was ablaze with wrath. The press demanded swift revenge. Mass meetings heard hot
speeches. Fish was too slow. The people east of the
Missouri were for immediate hostilities. War seemed
at hand.

But Fish, sustained by Grant, proceeded cautiously. He was not swept off his feet by clamor, but
he had lost no time in stating our position and he did
not now dally with well-phrased diplomatic notes.
"Unless abundant reparation shall have been voluntarily tendered," he cabled Sickles on November
14, "you will demand the restoration of the Virginius
and the release and delivery to the United States of
the persons captured on her who have not yet been
massacred, and that the flag of the United States
be saluted in the port of Santiago and the signal punishment of the officials who were concerned in the
capture of the vessel and the execution of the passengers and crew. In case of refusal of satisfactory
reparation, written twelve days from this date, you
will . . . close your legation and leave Madrid."

Feeling ran high in Madrid as well as in the United
States, and Sickles was at times hysterical, but Grant
and Fish retained their poise. Fish took the business
up in Washington with Polo, the Spanish Minister,
and these two reached a satisfactory agreement.
The Virginius and her survivors were to be restored

immediately. Spain was to have an opportunity to prove that the Virginius at the time of capture was not entitled to fly our colors, and if unable to prove this before December 25, she must salute our flag. Officials guilty of illegal acts of violence toward citizens of the United States were to be punished.

On December 18, the Virginius, flying our flag, was delivered to our navy at Bahia Honda in Cuba, but while on her way to New York sank in a storm. Two days later the surviving prisoners were surrendered and reached New York in safety. Investigation showed that the Virginius when captured was improperly carrying the American flag and consequently there was no salute. In the hands of Grant and Fish the whole affair was handled with dignity and self-respect. Pending negotiations, Grant put the navy on a war footing, "trusting to Congress and the public opinion of the American people to justify my action."[1]

"I would sum up the policy of the Administration," Grant had said in his second annual message, "to be a thorough enforcement of every law; a faithful collection of every tax provided for; economy in the disbursement of the same; a prompt payment of every debt of the nation; a reduction of taxes as rapidly as the requirements of the country will admit;

[1] Richardson, *Messages and Papers*, vol. VII, p. 242.

reductions of taxation and tariff to be so arranged as to afford the greatest relief to the greatest number; honest and fair dealings with all other peoples, to the end that war with all its blighting consequences may be avoided, but without surrendering any right or obligation due to us; a reform in the treatment of Indians and in the whole civil service of the country; and finally, in securing a pure, untrammeled ballot, where every man entitled to cast a vote may do so just once at each election, without fear of molestation or proscription on account of his political faith, nationality, or color."

And at the beginning of his second term he thus outlined his purposes in his inaugural: "My efforts in the future will be directed to the restoration of good feeling between the different sections of our common country; to the restoration of our currency to a fixed value as compared with the world's standard of value — gold — and, if possible to a par with it; to the construction of cheap routes of transit throughout the land; to the end that the products of all may find a market and leave a living remuneration to the producer; to the maintenance of friendly relations with all our neighbors, and with distant nations; to the reëstablishment of our commerce and share in the carrying trade upon the ocean; to the encouragement of such manufacturing industries as can be economically pursued in this country to the end that the exports of home products and industries may pay for our imports — the only sure method of returning to and maintaining a specie basis; to the elevation of labor; and by a humane course to bring the aborigines of the country under the benign influences of education and civilization."

No programme was ever more faithfully carried out by any President. We have seen how firmly he upheld American rights abroad; how he was first in history to establish arbitration in the settlement of international disputes; how he stood for the Monroe Doctrine in all his dealings with other American Republics. He was equally firm with Mexico, with Spain, with France, with England, respecting no distinction between weak and powerful governments when national dignity was involved. He demanded the recall of Catacazy, the Russian Minister, who had abused American officials and had interfered obnoxiously in the relations · between the United States and other powers. "It was impossible," he said to Congress, "with self-respect or with a just regard to the dignity of the country, to permit Mr. Catacazy to continue to hold intercourse with this Government." He settled boundary disputes with Great Britain, and claims with the American Republics, took up with Spain and England questions of extradition, securing from Spain the extradition of "Boss" Tweed who had escaped to Cuba; would have taken over San Domingo while the time was ripe; maintained peace with all the world amid grave international problems, yet never thought to make a sanctimonious merit of having kept the country out of war.

Congress interfered with his ambition to establish firmly a reformed civil service, but he gave reform an impetus which has continued to this day. He enforced the laws, maintained economy in government expenditures, lowered taxes, and reduced the national debt. That he could not secure a pure, untrammeled ballot was not his fault. He tried; but here he ran against impossible conditions which no Executive could hope to overcome.

He urged in every way the building-up of an American merchant marine. "It is a national humiliation," he said, "that we are now compelled to pay from twenty to thirty million dollars annually . . . to foreigners for doing the work which should be done by American vessels, American-built, American-owned, and American-manned."[1]

"A revival of shipbuilding, and particularly of iron steamship building," he said again, — for he kept returning to this theme, — "is of vast impor-

[1] Richardson, *Messages and Papers*, vol. VII, p. 53.

tance to our national prosperity. . . . I would be willing to see a great departure from the usual course of Government in supporting what might usually be termed private enterprise. I would not suggest as a remedy direct subsidy to American steamship lines, but would suggest the direct offer of ample compensation for carrying the mails between Atlantic seaboard cities and would extend this liberality to vessels carrying the mails to South American States and to Central America and Mexico, and would pursue the same policy from our Pacific seaports to foreign seaports on the Pacific. . . ."[1]

He was the first President to call emphatic attention to the peril of an ignorant foreign-born electorate, lacking in knowledge of the significance of our institutions. "The compulsory support of the free school and the disfranchisement of all who cannot read and write the English language, after a fixed probation, would meet my hearty approval. . . . Foreigners coming to this country to become citizens, who are educated in their own language, should acquire the requisite knowledge of ours during the necessary residence to obtain naturalization. If they did not take interest enough in our language to acquire sufficient knowledge of it to enable them to study the institutions and laws of the country intelligently, I

[1] Richardson, *Messages and Papers*, vol. VII, pp. 301–02.

would not confer upon them the right to make such laws or to select those who do." [1]

He suggested a readjustment of the tariff "so as to increase the revenue, and at the same time decrease the number of articles upon which duties are levied. Those articles which enter into our manufactures and are not produced at home, it seems to me, should be entered free. Those articles of manufacture which we produce a constituent part of, but do not produce the whole, that part which we do not produce should enter free also." [2]

When Grant entered on the Presidency, to use his own words "the country was laboring under an enormous debt contracted in the suppression of the rebellion; and taxation was so oppressive as to discourage production." There was danger of a foreign war. Not only was the war averted by the Treaty of Washington, establishing the principle of arbitration, but in the first seven years of his Administration taxes were reduced by nearly $300,000,000, and the national debt by $435,000,000. By refunding operations the annual interest on the debt was reduced from $130,000,000 to $100,000,000, an adverse balance of trade amounting to $130,000,000 was transferred to a balance of $120,000,000 in our favor.

[1] Richardson, *Messages and Papers*, vol. VII, p. 411.
[2] *Ibid.*, pp. 293–94.

Provision had been made for the resumption of specie payments and inflation, which was rampant, had been dealt a deadly blow.

For one who entered on his service with no political experience whatever, who was a stranger to the ways of statecraft and diplomacy, Grant's Presidency presents a record of success almost as striking though less dramatic than his career in war. His messages, from which citations have been made, were mostly written with his own hand, and he was always in close touch with the innumerable important questions in which the various members of his Cabinet were immediately concerned.

Considering all these things there is a needless note of pathos in the personal reference which he incorporated in his last message in December, 1876: —

"It was my fortune, or misfortune, to be called to the office of Chief Executive without any previous political training. From the age of seventeen I had never even witnessed the excitement attending a presidential campaign but twice antecedent to my own candidacy, and at but one of them was I eligible as a voter.

"Under such circumstances it is but reasonable to suppose that errors of judgment must have occurred. Even had they not, differences of opinion between the Executive, bound by an oath to the strict performance of his duties, and writers and debaters, must have arisen. It is not necessarily evidence of blunder on the part of the Executive because there are these differences of views. Mistakes have been made, as all can see, and I admit, but it seems to me oftener in the selections made in the assistants appointed to aid in carrying out the various duties of administering the government — in nearly every case selected without a personal acquaintance with the appointee, but upon recommendation of the representatives chosen directly by the people. It is impossible, where so many trusts are to be allotted, that the right parties should be chosen in every instance. History shows that no Administration from the time of Washington to the present has been free from these mistakes. But I leave comparisons to history, claiming only that I have acted in every instance from a conscientious desire to do what was right, constitutional, within the law, and for the very best interests of the whole people. Failures have been errors of judgment, not of intent." [1]

In constructive achievements, coming as it did directly after the demoralization of the war and the upset of traditions due to Lincoln's military measures in that imperative emergency, Grant's Administration ranks second only to that of Washington, who

[1] Richardson, *Messages and Papers*, vol. VII, pp. 399–400.

had to set the Government in motion under the Constitution. He might safely "leave comparisons to history." If we except the baneful Southern problem which was bequeathed to him, and where his fault, if fault there was, lay in the rigid execution of the law, it would be hard to place the finger now on an executive policy approved by him which subsequent experience has condemned.

CHAPTER XLVI

THE TRIP AROUND THE WORLD — THE THIRD TERM

A FEW weeks of adulation and then Grant went abroad. He sailed from Philadelphia in middle May. His daughter Nellie, who had married Algernon Sartoris in the White House, was living in her husband's home in England. Beyond seeing her he had few plans.

Great crowds bade him good-bye in Philadelphia, thronging the wharves from which he sailed with Mrs. Grant and Jesse, his youngest boy. To his amazement even greater crowds were at the wharves in Liverpool. Ten thousand Englishmen pushed through the custom house to welcome him. He was presented with the freedom of the city, both at Liverpool and Manchester, and his run toward London was like a triumph. In London the experience was repeated. English tradespeople and workingmen held him in higher honor than he thought. To them he was the world's most famous living general, personifying in their eyes the marvel of democracy.

Shortly, the scions of nobility took him in hand.

When Fillmore and Van Buren were visitors in England they had little more attention than any other private citizen and trudged along complacently at the tail end of the line, but Grant, through some diplomacy by our Minister in London, was treated as a former sovereign — not that he cared for it especially, but Pierrepont felt that as a former President of the United States he must not be slighted. Whatever those at home might think about it, the Englishman familiar with court etiquette would size it up as an indignity, not alone to Grant, but to the country whence he hailed.

Aside from minor incidents the pleasure of the English visit was undimmed and the example of the London court followed Grant around the world. He visited every capital of Europe and almost every important town. He talked with Bismarck and Von Moltke in Germany, with Gambetta and MacMahon in France, with Gortchakoff in Russia, with Castelar in Spain, with kings and queens and emperors, the Czar, the Pope. In almost every capital he was asked to witness a review of troops and he invariably declined. To the Crown Prince of Germany he said: "The truth is I am more of a farmer than a soldier. I take little or no interest in military affairs. I never went into the army without regret and I never retired without pleasure." He wandered dumbly through the galleries and museums, was bored by paintings, sculptures, and cathedrals, but was impressed by the imposing grandeur of the Alps, great engineering works, and by the Pyramids. He loved especially to stroll the streets and see the common people. James Russell Lowell, our Minister to Spain, who entertained him at Madrid, has left a picture which may apply to all his wanderings: —

"As he speaks nothing but English, he was as incommunicable as an iceberg and I think is rather bored by peregrination. What he likes best is to escape and wander about the streets with his Achates Young. After being here two days I think he knew Madrid better than I. He seemed to be very single-minded, honest, and sensible — very easy to be led by anybody he likes. He is perfectly unconscious and natural, naïvely puzzled, I fancied, to find himself a personage, and going through the ceremonies to which he is condemned with a dogged imperturbability that annotated to me his career in general." [1]

From Europe Grant went to Egypt and the Pyramids, and then to Asia, visiting the Holy Land, and later India, Siam, China, and Japan. He was greatly taken with the Orient. Japan he marveled at. China appealed to him. Li Hung Chang, with whom he

[1] To Charles Eliot Norton, *Letters of James Russell Lowell*, p. 233.

talked, he rated among the world's four master minds in statecraft and diplomacy.

While Grant was lingering abroad, finding new scenes to lure him on and pleased by the attention showered upon him, politics was shaping up at home. Hayes had pledged himself against a second term, and in no event could he have been elected if he had tried to run, so general was the feeling that his title had a taint. His course as President had alienated the men who had done most to put him in the place. The group which had been influential under Grant now found themselves of little consequence with the Administration. Conkling, Cameron, Logan, and others of the Stalwart wing were out of favor and out of sorts, while Sherman, Evarts, Hoar, and Schurz had Hayes's ear, and Southern Democrats were called in council when it came to naming office-holders in the South. The new Administration knew not Joseph. It was completely out of sympathy with "the machine" and recognized few party obligations of the old-fashioned kind. Blaine, who was pressing forward as the candidate for President, had not much in common either with Hayes or with the Stalwart group. The Stalwarts turned instinctively toward Grant.

Word kept coming back about his European progress, and the tidings stirred the people's pride, no matter what their politics; for in Grant's person they could see the Old World paying honor to the New. It was soon clear that his return would be a sequel for great popular acclaim. The thing to do was to prevent his coming back too soon so that the impetus of his reception might carry on to the Republican Convention. He had not been gone a year when the Stalwarts began to send him messages asking him not to hurry home and hinting at political developments. He was human and took pleasure in the flattering hints. "Most every letter I get from the States, like Porter's to you, asks me to remain abroad," he wrote from Rome to Badeau in March, 1878. "They have designs on me which I do not contemplate for myself. It is probable that I shall return to the United States early in the fall or early next spring." But he did not return that fall. It was September, 1879, when he sailed up the Golden Gate, and found still greater crowds awaiting him than he had seen at Philadelphia or Liverpool. He wandered up and down the coast, visited old haunts at Humboldt and Vancouver, which his experience there, if what it has been sometimes pictured, might have made him shun; then started east across the continent, arriving at Galena the day following election, after a sweeping progress through the cities of the West. There he was greeted by his old neighbors, and

after loafing with them for a week, he started east
again through demonstrations all along the line from
crowds in cities numbered by the hundred thousands,
at last in Philadelphia completing his circuit of the
world.

To Grant the country must have seemed unanimous, but from the politician's point of view his
coming back was premature — six months too early
for their calculations. Besides, neither Grant nor the
"Old Guard" seems to have been fully conscious of
the deep-seated feeling against a third term in the
Presidency. The people's adoration could not have
been transmuted into votes. He did nothing to encourage or discourage what was going on. He was
quite ready to await results.

He went to Mexico and Cuba continuing in this
way his world itinerary — the most widely traveled
citizen of the United States.

Those who engineered the Third Term plan were
daring and resourceful leaders. In the whole history of our politics there has never been another
group to rival them in intellectual force, in discipline,
in ruthlessness, in organizing skill. We have since
often had "Old Guards" on paper and in frenzied
campaign cries; for "Old Guards" are easy buga-
boos, but most of them have been the creatures of
disordered fancies or demagogical appeal. The ele-

ments of which they are assumed to be composed have seldom stood consistently together or wielded their imaginary power. But here was an "Old Guard" in truth whose members had no squeamishness about the name, whose faults at least were manly faults, and who were strangers to hypocrisy. Conkling in New York, Don Cameron in Pennsylvania, Logan in Illinois, each at the head of his battalions, formed a "Triumvirate" which derived its fitting title from Roman history, and like its Roman prototype was entitled to respect. They had their disciplined allies in other States, and, reaching into every corner of the country, they had their pickets placed.

In February, while in Cuba, Washburne had written Grant about the prospects for another nomination. The tone of his reply showed that he then expected it, though he betrayed no great concern. "All that I want is that the Government rule should remain in the hands of those who saved the Union until all the questions growing out of the war are forever settled. I would much rather any one of many I could mention should be President rather than that I should have it. . . . I shall not gratify my enemies by declining what has not been offered. I am not a candidate for anything, and if the Chicago Convention nominates a candidate who can be elected, it will gratify me, and the gratification will be greater if it should be some one other than myself. . . . Blaine I would like to see elected, but I fear the party could not elect him." [1]

Later, from Galveston, on March 25, he wrote again to Washburne, who had suggested that he should authorize some one to say that in no event would he consent even to be a candidate after 1880: "I think any statement from me would be misconstrued, and would only serve as a handle for my enemies. Such a statement might well be made after the nomination, if I am nominated in such a way as to accept. It is a matter of supreme indifference to me whether I am or not. There are many persons I would prefer should have the office to myself. I owe so much to the Union men of the country that if they think my chances are better for election than for other probable candidates in case I should decline, I cannot decline if the nomination is tendered without seeking on my part."

From these expressions there could be little question about his expectation that he would be called to serve or about his readiness to heed the call. Coming back from Mexico he followed up the Mississippi from New Orleans to Cairo, by way of Vicksburg and Memphis, tracing back the militant journey

[1] *Letters to a Friend*, Havana, Cuba, February 2, 1880.

he had taken nearly twenty years before — and at last was at Galena, where he awaited the convention, seemingly indifferent himself about the outcome, but acquiescent in the wishes of his family and friends.

Meantime the "Old Guard" had been diligent. They were not too fastidious in their ways. They rushed resolutions through the New York and Pennsylvania Conventions in February, imposing the unit rule upon the delegations from those States. In Illinois the State Convention elected Grant delegates from every district, ignoring protests from districts whose representatives did not approve. Similar tactics prevailed in other States.

When the National Republican Convention met in June, they had three hundred delegates for Grant including a clear majority from New York, Illinois, and Pennsylvania, and almost all the Southern and border States. Blaine had fewer votes than Grant, but they were well distributed throughout the North, while Sherman had, besides his own State of Ohio nearly solid, a scattering support, including some negro delegates in the South. Edmunds, Windom, and Washburne each had his friends, although no one of these was ever really in the running.

As June approached, and it was evident that Grant could not be named without a bitter contest, some of his intimates, who feared for the result in case the nomination came that way, earnestly begged him to withdraw, but by that time he had gone too far and could not quit without embarrassing his friends. His family were smitten with a longing to get back to Washington, and he acceded to their importunities. John Russell Young went to Galena and with much difficulty, in opposition to their wishes, induced Grant to write a letter addressed to Cameron, once in his Cabinet and now chairman of the Republican National Committee, authorizing his supporters if at any time so minded to withdraw his name. No copy of the letter was preserved and it was never used.

In all the history of conventions there has never been another such as this. No gathering of any party has been so rich in stirring incident, so fertile in dramatic scenes, so pregnant in the tragedy of personal and party feuds. It wrecked ambitions, opened new careers, and brought about strange combinations in the field of politics. The Triumvirate were beaten in trying to impose the unit rule, which would have given Grant the solid vote of New York, Illinois, and Pennsylvania, and with the impetus thus gained have carried him at once across the line. They failed in other arbitrary schemes which gave rise to many hours of strategy and hot debate.

Conkling led their forces on the floor, showing superb contempt for opposition, stirring resentment among friends of Blaine and other candidates, repelling by his domineering ways those whom another would have tried with tact to win, questioning their party loyalty, sneering at their political consistency, exulting in their hate. No one at all familiar with convention records is unfamiliar with the speech in which he introduced Grant's name, the opening lines of doggerel transmuted into eloquence by his audacious, dominating personality: —

> "And when asked what State he hails from,
> Our sole reply shall be,
> He hails from Appomattox
> And its famous apple tree."

Convention oratory in its extravagance and swift impressions is a thing apart, and Conkling's ranks among its great examples, but there were sentences in this speech of his which were to be remembered beyond the moment: "His services attest his greatness." "His fame was earned, not alone by things written and said, but by the arduous greatness of things done." "To him immeasurably more than to any other man is due the fact that every paper dollar is at last as good as gold." "When he refused to receive Denis Kearney of California, he meant that communism, lawlessness, and disorder, although it might stalk high-headed and dictate law to a whole city, would always find a foe in him." [1]

[1] "From his first utterance in the convention to the last, Mr. Conkling's manner was one studied taunt to his opponents. Nothing approaching it in arrogance and insolence has been witnessed in a political convention, either before or since. If there had been any chance of a compromise of one faction in favor of the other, he destroyed it utterly in the first half-hour.

"His first act was to move a resolution binding the members of the convention to support the nominee, whoever he might be. In doing this he took pains to intimate with unmistakable plainness his belief that the Blaine men would bolt in case Grant was nominated, unless they were pledged in advance not to do so. This resolution was adopted, but the debate upon it made him the most unpopular man in the convention with the supporters of all other candidates than Grant, and thus debarred the latter from hope of recruits. His next important effort was to have the unit rule enforced upon all delegations in order that a majority in each should be able to cast the solid vote of the State for the candidate of their choice. In this effort he was as offensive as he had been in his previous one. A long chapter might be filled with Mr. Conkling's astounding arrogance. . . .

"In his speech nominating Grant he went out of his way to give mortal offense to the Blaine forces and to all other elements of the convention that were opposing Grant. In his written copy of the speech, which was given out in advance to the press, he had this simple sentence at the beginning: 'When asked whence comes our candidate, we say from Appomattox.' There is dignity, simplicity, and dramatic force in that sentence, which is certainly not to be found in the 'improved' version which seems to have been an inspiration of the moment.

"When the balloting began and it was his duty as chairman of the New York delegation to announce its vote, he did so with studied insolence toward the anti-Grant members. His favorite formula was: 'Two of the New York delegates, Mr. Chairman, are said to be for Mr. Sherman, seventeen for Mr. Blaine, fifty-one are for Grant.' He repeated this with slight variations till the chairman of the West Virginia delegation mimicked his manner and

For thirty-six ballots, and for two days, the "Old Guard" battled, holding their lines with a stern discipline never rivaled before or since. Others weakened here and there as the maneuvering went on — not they. On the first ballot they threw to Grant 304 votes. In the two days they did not fall below 302, and even on the thirty-fifth ballot, after the tide began to set toward Garfield, they were 313. On the last ballot, when the stampede was on, their line remained unbroken, and the 306 who voted at the very end for Grant have won their place in history.

Garfield, who had entered the convention pledged to Sherman, who had led the forces against Conkling on the floor, and who from the beginning had received a single vote in almost every ballot, was nominated by the friends of Blaine in a resistless rush which some said had long been prearranged, although the evidence of this was never clear. To mollify the "Old Guard," Arthur, whom Grant had made Collector of the Port of New York and who had been removed by Hayes, was nominated for Vice-President. Conkling would have spurned the sop when the New York delegation was requested to select a man,

method so perfectly that the whole convention roared. After that he did not venture on further repetition, but resorted to such sayings as that a member who was absent was possibly 'meditating some new form of treachery.'" (Bishop, *Presidential Nominations and Elections*, pp. 80–84.)

but Arthur, who was a delegate-at-large, whispered to Conkling that he would like the place — a hint which had far-reaching consequences.

Through it all Grant went about his business at Galena. Conkling, in nominating him, with a covert sneer at Blaine had said: "He has no place; and official influence has not been used for *him*. Without patronage, without emissaries, without committees, without bureaux, without telegraph wires running from his house or from the seats of influence to this convention, without appliances, without electioneering contrivances, without effort on his part, Grant's name is on his country's lips."

This was all true. During the convention, while bulletins were coming in, he spent his time with two or three at Rowley's office. When word arrived that Conkling's lines on Appomattox had been greeted by a storm of cheers which lasted half an hour, he went home saying to his son with something like a sigh: "I am afraid I am going to be nominated." Throughout the hours of balloting he gave no sign. When he was told about the final vote, he brushed the ashes from his cigar, said, "Garfield is a good man. I am glad of it. Good-night, gentlemen," and walked home without another word. But he was not impervious to defeat. He was hurt to think that with the Cameron letter in their hands the "Old Guard" let him go so far. "My friends have not been honest with me," he said. "I could not afford to be defeated. They should not have placed me in nomination unless they felt perfectly sure of my success." And some whom he thought had not played him fair he never quite forgave — among them Washburne, who let his own name be used to divide Logan's strength in Illinois.

CHAPTER XLVII

THE END

WHEN Grant left the White House he should have said good-bye to politics. That was a game in which he was not qualified to play; he would have been happier if he had frankly recognized the truth. But he had friends to whom he felt under obligation and for their sake he bared his dignity to his successors in the Presidency, laying it open to rebuff. During most of Hayes's term Grant watched the Administration from abroad. He did not sympathize with Hayes's course in Louisiana and South Carolina, abandoning the local governments while profiting himself by practically the same returns as those on which both Chamberlain and Packard based their claims.

Not only did Hayes reverse Grant's Southern policy, but he alienated Conkling by the summary removal of Cornell and Arthur from the New York Custom House. During his Administration there was a general softening of party fiber.

After Garfield's nomination Grant went to Colorado. He sent no message of congratulation. Many thought that he would sulk; some even that he would support Hancock, his former comrade in arms.

But in September, when things looked blue for
Garfield, he publicly declared his purpose to support
the ticket, and brought Conkling into line, with
others of the Stalwart group. Grant and Conkling
both went on the stump — for Grant had learned to
speak in public while abroad. After the election, for
the result of which he felt himself in large part responsible, he was not asked for his advice and did not
tender it. He was displeased and mortified when told
that Blaine was booked to head the Cabinet, yet went
to Washington after the 4th of March and pledged
Garfield his support. But quickly came the Robertson appointment in New York, the resignation of
Platt and Conkling from the Senate by way of protest, and the ill-fated struggle for their reëlection.

Robertson, who had led the fight against Grant in
the New York delegation at Chicago, was especially
obnoxious, and Grant strongly sympathized with
Conkling in the feud. He was angered, too, because
without consulting him Garfield had made a place for
Merritt, the deposed New York collector, by arbitrarily transferring his own particular appointees
abroad.[1]

[1] " In their letter of resignation, addressed to Governor Cornell
on May 14, 1881, Senators Conkling and Platt say: — 'Some
weeks ago the President sent to the Senate in a group the nominations of several persons for public offices already filled. One of
these offices is the collectorship of the port of New York, now held
by General Merritt; another is the consul-generalship at London,

Grant was in Mexico that spring, whence he wrote in May: "I am completely disgusted with Garfield's course. It is too late now for him to do anything to restore him to my confidence. I will never again lend my active aid to the support of a presidential candidate who has not strength enough to appear before a convention as a candidate. . . . Garfield has shown that he is not possessed of the backbone of an angleworm. I hope his nominations may be defeated." His feeling against Garfield was generally known through personal letters which slipped into print. When Garfield was shot, Grant for a time, like Conkling, was a target for the people's wrath, which had hardly died away when in September he followed Garfield's coffin, as he had followed those of Sumner, Motley, and Greeley — each in turn.

now held by General Badeau; another is chargé d'affaires to Denmark, held by Mr. Cramer; another is the mission to Switzerland, held by Mr. Fish, a son of the former distinguished Secretary of State. . . . All these officers save only Mr. Cramer are citizens of New York. It was proposed to displace them all, not for any alleged fault of theirs, or for any alleged need or advantage of the public service, but in order to give the great office of Collector of the Port of New York to Mr. William H. Robertson as a "reward" for certain acts of his said to have "aided in making the nomination of General Garfield possible." The chain of removals thus proposed was broken by General Badeau's promptly declining to accept the new place to which he was sent.' A protest against the change in collectorship signed by Arthur, Conkling, Platt, Postmaster-General James, and Governor Cornell, had been addressed to the President and ignored." (A. R. Conkling, *Life and Letters of R. Conkling*, pp. 639–40.)

With Arthur he was at first on cordial terms and
Arthur freely asked him for advice. At his suggestion
Frelinghuysen was appointed Secretary of State, and
Governor Morgan of New York was asked to take the
Treasury. Morgan declined, and Grant proposed
John Jacob Astor, first for the Treasury and then
for Minister to England, but neither suggestion was
adopted. Before long Arthur came to shun his Stalwart friends, perhaps because he felt that they pre-
sumed on old association. He wanted to be President
in his own right, and to accomplish this, saw the necessity for different ties. That was a trait entirely
foreign to Grant's nature, the sort of thing he could
not understand. Through all his life he had been
loyal to his friends even to the peril of his own good
name.

Invited to the White House for a visit, he was beset by satellites and relatives begging him to urge
upon the President their claims for office or for favor,
and he good-naturedly yielded to their importunities
till Arthur plainly showed displeasure and at times
evaded him. He wanted his friend General Beale
made Secretary of the Navy. Arthur appointed in
his stead William E. Chandler, who as the friend of
Blaine had been a leading factor in the defeat of
Grant for a third term. After that the coolness
between Grant and Arthur grew. "He seems more

afraid of his enemies and through this fear more influenced by them than guided either by his judgment, personal feelings, or friendly influences," Grant wrote in February, 1883, and a year later, on the eve of the National Convention, he wrote: "Arthur will probably go into the convention second in the number of supporters, when he would not probably have a single vote if it was not for his army of officials and the vacancies he has to fill."

He had a grievance, not due to patronage, but to Arthur's failure to right what Grant had come to look on as a wrong — his own refusal while President to allow Fitz John Porter a second trial. Since then, through a more thorough study of the evidence, he had become convinced that Porter was innocent of the charge of which he had been convicted by court-martial during the war. The sentence having been reversed at last by the board of which Schofield was the head, Grant worked hard to put the bill through Congress authorizing the President to restore Porter to his former rank, and when Arthur vetoed the bill on the ground that Congress had infringed upon the executive prerogative in designating a person by name whom the President was to appoint, Grant did not hesitate publicly to criticize the motive behind the veto. As between Blaine and Arthur in 1884, Grant preferred the nomination of Blaine, but owing to his illness he did not vote for him. A year before the election he had written: "The Republican Party, to be saved, must have a decisive, declared policy. It has now no observable policy except to peddle out patronage to soreheads, in order to bring them back into the fold, and avoid any positive declarations upon all leading questions." [1] In his political convictions Grant was a Stalwart to the end.

Grant had no sooner come back from his trip abroad than he began to think about a livelihood. He was obliged to turn his hand to making money, a trick in which he never had shown skill. Just before coming East from Colorado he had written: "One thing is certain; I must do something to supplement my income, or continue to live in Galena or on a farm. I have not got the means to live in a city."

He always had a lively interest in Mexico, and now, after the third term episode, his friend Romero, for years the Mexican Minister in Washington, joined with him in organizing a company, of which Grant became president, the purpose of which was to build a railroad south to the Guatemalan border. The enterprise was not successful, but in 1882, at Frelinghuysen's hint, Arthur made him a commissioner to negotiate a commercial treaty with Mexico,

[1] *Grant in Peace.* Badeau, p. 345.

an appointment which he accepted solely because of his ambition to establish closer business and political relations between the two Republics.

The treaty was concluded. Grant would have had quick action by our Senate; for delay he knew would give to foreign interests an opportunity to influence adversely the Mexican authorities, but the Administration did nothing further. The treaty was not ratified, and no more was heard of it.

Here ends the record of Grant's public service. Had this been all, it would have been a tame and futile termination of a great career which had its crown in the tumultuous welcome home after his triumphal march around the world. In three years he had fallen in the popular esteem. His fatal acquiescence in the third term move; his meddling with the patronage; his good-natured readiness to place his influence at the disposal of his friends, had all contributed to blur his fame. He had gone into Wall Street and the people knew it. He thought that he was making money. So did they. Prosperity alarms idolatry; incense burns grudgingly on the Stock Exchange; and Grant in this followed the way of other heroes. But his life, already packed with contrasts, was to undergo one more swift transformation. The few months left him were to bring both tragedy and triumph,

misfortune in the end restoring him to his own rightful province in the people's love.

When Grant went abroad he entrusted to Ulysses
S. Grant, Jr., what property he had, and the son, who
was supposed to have a business head, enlarged the
trust. He had married the daughter of Senator
Chaffee, a Colorado millionaire, and had settled in
New York, where in 1879 he became acquainted
with young Ferdinand Ward, just blossoming as a
Napoleon of the Street. Through some of Ward's
ventures he made money for the General, which
enabled Grant to complete his trip around the world.
In the fall of 1880, Ward proposed a private banking
firm to do a Wall Street business under the style of
Grant & Ward, he to be financial agent, young
Grant to be an active partner, with the General and
James F. Fish, Ward's father-in-law, the President of
the Marine Bank of Brooklyn, as silent partners.
The new firm ranked high; Ward was the marvel of
the Street; he had unbounded credit; the market
boomed; the firm's investors received amazing divi-
dends. From operations in stocks, bonds, and railway
contracts, the firm of Grant & Ward, beginning with
a paid-in-capital of $400,000, mostly contributed by
Chaffee, and other connections of the Grants, — both
Fred and Jesse had married well and settled in New
York, — had in three years acquired a rating of

$15,000,000 and a deposit of nearly a million in Fish's bank. Grant having put in all his money paid no attention to the business details, nor did his son. They simply saw their income pouring in and trusted Ward implicitly. But while Ward talked to them of railway contracts and huge rates of interest for emergency loans to subcontractors, he talked to customers about Grant's influence in getting contracts from the Government — a form of business which Grant expressly stipulated the firm should never undertake. He knew that this would be an impropriety.

"I had been President of the United States," he later testified, "and I did not think it was suitable for me to have my name connected with Government contracts, and I knew that there was no large profit in them except by dishonest measures. There are some men who get Government contracts year in and year out, and whether they manage their affairs dishonestly to make a profit or not, they are sometimes supposed to, and I did not think it was any place for me."

Grant, all unconscious of impending fate, was looking forward to prosperity in his remaining years. Some of his nearest friends were men of wealth, and now he felt that he could associate with them on even terms. He had a handsome house in Sixty-sixth Street, near Fifth Avenue, and there, surrounded by his family and trophies, he planned to end his days in profitable ease. Besides his generous dividends from Grant & Ward, he had a $15,000 income from a fund subscribed for him by New York financiers. He had no public cares or aspirations, no lingering restlessness for power; his skies were clear of clouds; he was content.

The day before Christmas in December, 1883, he slipped on the icy sidewalk before his house, crushing the muscles of his leg. He did not leave his bed for weeks. Then for months he hobbled about on crutches, recovering his strength somewhat in Washington and Fort Monroe, but never quite regaining his health. At home again in April, still lame but prosperous, he drove about and went downtown on business, free from financial worry.

One Sunday evening, May 4, 1884, Ward came to see him, told him the Marine Bank was in trouble, that the City Chamberlain had drawn heavily late the afternoon before, imperiling the bank's reserve, and unless $400,000 could be raised at once the bank must close its doors on Monday morning, tying up the firm's deposit of $660,000 and threatening ruin. He had himself raised $250,000, but could go no farther and Grant must raise the rest. This was new business for the General. He did not know where to turn, but Ward suggested W. H. Vanderbilt, and

Grant saw Vanderbilt that night, told him the story, and obtained from him $150,000—not for the sake of the Marine Bank or of the firm of Grant & Ward, as Vanderbilt assured him, but as a personal loan. The next day the loan was paid, so Grant supposed, through the firm's check drawn on the bank. On Tuesday morning, when Grant limped into the firm's office, he was stunned by his son's greeting: "Grant & Ward have failed and Ward has fled!" He turned away without a word, ascended slowly to his own private room, and late that afternoon the cashier found him sitting there, close to his desk, clasping the arms of his chair convulsively, head bowed.

Before night it was known that every dollar he possessed was swept away. The firm had no deposits in the bank. The securities Ward talked about were worthless. All the Grants were pauperized; their entire fortunes were tied up with the firm. Tradesmen's bills came pouring in, and had it not been for prompt and generous action by a stranger,[1] who forced Grant to accept a loan "on account of my share for services ending April, 1865," he could not have bought provisions for a meal. He was too proud and silent to appeal for credit then.

In order to save something from the vultures, Vanderbilt insisted on security for his personal loan,

[1] Charles Wood, of Lansingburg, New York.

and to him Grant assigned his farm, his wife's real estate in Philadelphia and Chicago, and all his personal property — including the trophies of the war, his medals, swords, and uniforms. The debt to Vanderbilt was one of honor. With him it had precedence over obligations of the firm of Grant & Ward.

Vanderbilt afterwards tried to transfer the property to Mrs. Grant, but she refused his offer, except as to the trophies, which she accepted in trust, to be placed at the disposal of the Government. For their conspiracy to defraud, Fish was sentenced to seven years in prison, Ward to ten.

Stripped of his livelihood, harassed by obligations, chagrined by failure, smarting under unjust stings, feeble in body, with age creeping on, Grant had again to face the world. He could no longer justify his simple faith in human nature. "I have made it the rule of my life," he said, "to trust a man long after other people gave him up; but I don't see how I can ever trust any human being again." Yet his bitterness of soul was sanctified. Without it history could not record the last fine chapter of his contradictory career, shedding a halo over all that went before. His bearing in adversity beatified him in the world's regard.

Before his failure the "Century Magazine," which had begun its series on the battles of the Civil War, had urged him to write the story of Shiloh or of the Wilderness. But he was not inclined to do it. Writing was not his trade. Now they came back with their proposal. It would divert his mind; he could earn money in this way; his need decided him. He wrote an article on Shiloh and was astonished at himself to find that he could make a story full of human interest as easily as he had once indited orders and reports. He had the faculty of narrative in an unusual degree, as he had often shown among his intimates; for all his life he was an entertaining talker, at times monopolizing conversation in choice groups of friends. His stillness fell upon him only in public or with those he slightly knew.

After Shiloh came Vicksburg, Chattanooga, and the Wilderness for the "Century," and from these grew the "Memoirs." He was absorbed in his new work, and urged on by the demand for more. Thus he occupied the summer at Long Branch, writing daily with the help of Badeau and his oldest son, who verified his records and combined his notes; but he was daily growing feebler, till in October on his return to town he became conscious of pains shooting through his throat. The physicians told him it was cancer. Soon he could not swallow without torture. He had no wish to live if he could not recover. For a time he did not care to write or talk. He "often sat for hours propped up in his chair, with his hands clasped, looking at the blank wall before him, silent, contemplating the future; not alarmed, but solemn, at the prospect of pain and disease; and only death at the end. It was like a man gazing into his open grave. He was in no way discouraged," writes Badeau, "but the sight was to me the most appalling I have ever witnessed."

Then there came a change. He grimly turned once more to his new work. He would complete his task for his own sake, his family, and those to whom he was in debt. The first money he received he sent the stranger who had given him the loan in May. But he could hardly hope to wipe out all his obligations, and when in January came the doctor's final verdict that he could not recover, he was in mental agony; not that he had to die, but that he might not live till he had fully cleared his name.

A bill had passed the Senate the preceding winter to restore his rank and place him on the retired list of the Army, but Arthur had hinted that he would veto it, as in the Fitz John Porter case, if Grant were to be restored by name. He felt this keenly and it contributed to his distress.

Soon the world knew that he was dying and sympathy came pouring in from everywhere. The bill for his retirement, modified to meet the President's

objections, was revised, but was held up for party
reasons in the House, the Democrats attempting to
embarrass Arthur by forcing through the earlier bill,
and thus compelling him to reverse himself or veto it.
Congress was near its end, and Grant, who looked
upon the measure as in some way a vindication, felt
the rebuff. The bill was beaten in the House on
February 16, the anniversary of Donelson. It was
felt then that any day might be his last. The country
was aroused and public sentiment prevailed. On the
4th of March, in the closing hours of Congress, the
bill, amended as Arthur wished, was rushed through
House and Senate by unanimous consent, and Arthur sent in Grant's name just in time. Cleveland
signed the new commission — the second act of his
Administration.

Grant's life thenceforward was a desperate fight
with death. More than once the end seemed right at
hand, and once the doctors thought that it had come.
For months he could not lie in bed, but sat propped
up in chairs, suffering excruciating pain. Even those
with whom he had long been in feud now shared the
universal sympathy. On the anniversary of the day
that Richmond fell he dictated this message: "I
am very much touched and grateful for the sympathy and interest manifested in me by my friends —
and by those who have not hitherto been regarded as

friends. I desire the good-will of all, whether hitherto friends or not."

It is not necessary to prolong the story. Its plain recital cuts one like a knife. He kept at work upon his book, dictating when he could not speak above a whisper, more often penciling his sentences on pads. The passages he wrote in the last weeks were just and lucid. They read so simply that we can hardly realize how every paragraph was drenched in pain. In June they carried him to Mount McGregor, and there on July 23 he died. He did not drop his pencil till his work was done. Three weeks before his death, on July 2, he wrote to his physician, Dr. Douglass, a letter with which this record of his life may fittingly conclude: —

"I ask you not to show this to any one, unless the physicians you consult with, until the end. Particularly, I want it kept from my family. . . . I know that I gain strength some days, but when I do go back it is beyond where I started to improve. I think the chances are very decidedly in favor of your being able to keep me alive until the change of weather towards winter. Of course there are contingencies that might arise at any time that would carry me off suddenly. . . . I would say, therefore, to you and your colleagues, to make me as comfortable as you can. If it is within God's providence that I should go now, I am ready to obey His call without a murmur. I should prefer going now to enduring my present suffering for a single day without hope of recovery. As I have stated, I am thankful for the providential extension of my time to enable me to continue my work. I am further thankful, and in a much greater degree thankful, because it has enabled me to see for myself the happy harmony which has so suddenly sprung up between those engaged but a few short years ago in deadly conflict. It has been an inestimable blessing to me to hear the kind expression towards me in person from all parts of our country, from people of all nationalities, of all religions and of no religion, of Confederates and of National troops alike, of soldiers' organizations, of mechanical, scientific, religious, and other societies, embracing almost every citizen in the land. They have brought joy to my heart, if they have not effected a cure. So to you and your colleagues I acknowledge my indebtedness for having brought me through the valley of the shadow of death to enable me to witness these things."

THE END

INDEX

G. displeased with his handling of the cases, 485, 486; resigns, 487; as candidate for presidential nomination in 1876, 498 and *n.*

Brodhead, James O., 481.

Brooks, James, 434.

Brooks, Mr. (Arkansas), 461, 462.

Brown, B. Gratz, nominated for Governor of Missouri, by Republican dissenters in 1872, 409.

Brown, John, of Ossawatomie, 8.

Brown, Owen, father of John, 8.

Bruce, Blanche K., 361.

Bryant, William Cullen, quoted, on nomination of Greeley, 416; 412, 418.

Buchanan, James, 38, 72, 270, 327.

Buchanan, R. C., forces G.'s retirement from the army in 1854, 35.

Buckner, Simon B., at West Point with G., 21; in Mexican War, 30; helps G. in time of need, 37; in command at Bowling Green, 69; takes command at Donelson, and surrenders to G., 73, 74.

Buell, Don Carlos, at West Point with G., 21; at Shiloh, 90–92; 57, 69, 70, 77, 78, 84, 85, 86, 93, 94, 95, 133, 150.

Bullock, Rufus B., Governor of Georgia, 364, 365, 366.

Burnside, Ambrose E., 130, 131, 136, 137, 139, 150.

Butler, Benjamin F., at New Orleans, 104; his blunders in command of Army of the James upset G.'s plans, 170, 171; his quarrels with "Baldy" Smith, 174, 175; alleged by Smith to have blackmailed G., 175; sent home "for the good of the service," 175, 176; G.'s friendship for, during his presidency, a mystery, 437; *Butler's Book*, 437; controls patronage in Mass., 437, 438; selects Simmons for Boston collectorship, 438; had he a "hold" on G.? 438; and the Sanborn contracts, 439 *ff.*; 59, 159, 161, 215, 272, 398.

Butler, Matthew C., 361 *n.*

Butterfield, Daniel, Assistant Treasurer at N.Y., and the "Gold Conspiracy," 344 *ff.*; forced to resign, 346.

Cabinet of Pres. Johnson, and the quarrel with G., 264, 265, 266.

Cabinet, G's first, 275–78.

Cabral, José M. (San Domingo), 312, 313.

"Cæsarism," 423, 457, 521.

Cameron, J. Donald, 496, 537, 540, 543, 547.

Cameron, Simon, 145, 320, 385, 387, 401.

Campaign of 1876, the, 500, 501.

Campbell, John A., 188.

Campbell, Mr., Minister to Mexico, 245, 247.

Canada, annexation of, suggested, 297; real obstacle to annexation, 297, 298; Sumner demands Great Britain's withdrawal from, 307, 308.

Carpenter, Francis B., 168.

Carpenter, Matthew H., defends G. against Sumner, 423, 424; 401.

Carpet-baggers, 272, 358, 359.

Casserly, Eugene, 321.

Castelar, Emilio, 524.

Catacazy, M., 527.

Cavour, Count, 498 *n.*

Cedar Creek, battle of, 180.

Century Magazine, G. writes stories of his battles for, 560, 561; 499 *n.*, 515 *n.*